from the mid-century decades has occasioned both amicable interaction as well as ethnic tension, in contradictory but concurrent trends that are the subject of much discussion by academics and others. Regrettably, ethnic friction has been exacerbated by the formation of political parties along racial lines in all three countries. Antagonisms have been the most acute in Guyana, where the racist dictatorship of People's National Congress of Forbes Burnham, installed by the CIA in 1964 and outlasting his death (in 1985) until 1992, bankrupted the country and left a legacy of racial bitterness. Indians in Suriname (independent since 1975) have had less sense of discrimination and subjugation, with political power being shared, however contentiously, among parties largely representing the three main ethnic constituencies of blacks, Indians, and Javanese. In Trinidad, the Indian- and Creole-based political parties have for decades been traditional antagonists, albeit with shifting stances and alliances. Well endowed with oil and other natural resources, Trinidad since the 1970s has enjoyed a relative prosperity that, together with its well-established democratic tradition, has made for a more moderate racial climate wherein differences are negotiated more in parliamentary and journalistic debates than in violent confrontation. In Guyana and especially Trinidad the dynamics of cultural relations have often been played out in the realm of culture, and especially music, given its importance in national ethos (Manuel 2000c). In both countries, former conceptions of national identity based on the notions of a hegemonic Creole mainstream have perforce given way to a pluralism that recognizes the legitimacy of Indian culture. As of 2014 both countries have East Indian prime ministers, representing primarily Indian-oriented parties, and Indo-Caribbeans have become leaders in commerce as well as agriculture.

The Indo-Fijian experience, to which this book shall refer in several contexts, has exhibited marked parallels with that of Indo-Caribbeans. The migrants to Fiji were essentially the same stock of people—primarily young peasants from the Bhojpuri region, with the same cultural legacy. The Indo-Fijian indentureship program, with its somewhat tardy commencement, was essentially contemporaneous with that of Suriname. Most Indo-Fijians, like Surinamese Hindustanis, have retained fluency in a form of Bhojpuri Hindi, which has facilitated continuity in the realm of folk culture and has afforded potential access to North Indian Hindi-based religious and commercial pop culture. The Indo-Fijians, like their Caribbean counterparts, found themselves sharing their new homeland with darker-skinned prior inhabitants—in this case, indigenous Fijians—who saw them as foreign intruders foisted on them by British overlords. As in the Caribbean (and perhaps especially Guyana), ethnic and political discrimination, with eruptions of violence, impelled a substantial percentage to emigrate in recent decades.

Perhaps the most significant and conspicuous differences between the legacies of Indian indentureship and Afro-Caribbean slavery involved the ability of Indo-Caribbeans to retain much more of their traditional culture than was possible for blacks. To be sure, many factors inhibited the smooth transference of Indian culture to the Caribbean. Most of the immigrants came as young men, typically in their early twenties, rather than as mature elders steeped in Indian culture, whether local folkways or panregional traditions. Further, the vast majority were lower-class peasants, who would have had scarce exposure to urban culture, whether in its traditional or increasingly modernizing forms. Under the leveling proletarianization of plantation life, caste—that most basic feature of Hindu society—gradually lost its significance, and many lesser regional traditions, from folksongs to the worship of local godlings, were destined to disappear. Moreover, as discussed below, after the last ships of immigrants arrived in 1917, contact with the Bhojpuri region whence most immigrants had come ceased altogether, never to resume. Most important, the inexorable decline of spoken Bhojpuri and Hindi in Trinidad and Guyana undermined many aspects of the Indian cultural legacy.

At the same time, however, conditions favored a considerable degree of cultural continuity. Unlike most New World Africans, East Indians came essentially of their own volition, arrived relatively late in the colonial period, and were not subjected to the deculturating milieu of the slave plantations. Many aspects of traditional religious practices, family structures, and expressive culture forms could be re-created and maintained, however idiosyncratically, in the insular Indian communities that came to proliferate in the countryside (see, for example, Klass 1961). Also unlike the ethnically and linguistically more diverse African slaves, Indians were able until recent generations to maintain a single language, Bhojpuri, as a spoken lingua franca. Bhojpuri is not a written language in the Caribbean, and unlike English and standard Hindi it has never enjoyed prestige, being typically referred to as *ṭūṭi Hindi* or "broken Hindi." Nevertheless, it has served as a rich repository of traditional oral culture, and it is close enough to standard Hindi to provide access to that language's greater corpus of literature, learning, mythology, and poetry, as transmitted by literate pandits, interested laypersons, and even musicians. Although literacy in Hindi has never been widespread in the Caribbean, it has always been common enough to contribute to the maintenance of tradition and ties to India. Cultural continuity was further facilitated by the relatively elaborated and formalized nature of the panregional Indian "great traditions" of learning, religion, and fine arts, which lack any counterpart in Africa. For British missionaries and teachers in the Caribbean, the contrasts between Indians and Africans were overt; as one chronicler wrote, "If Africans were regarded as clay that could easily

be moulded into a Christian and Western shape, the Hindus (and Muslims) of India were more like stone that could only be worked painfully and with much toil" (Wood 1968, 110). Hence, for example, the frustration of missionaries, who never managed to convert more than ten percent of Indians.

The cohesiveness and resilience of Indian culture were further enhanced by the arrival of Hindu and Muslim religious activists from India and by the importation of Hindi films and records from the 1930s on. Hindi films played a particularly important role in reviving a sense of Indian pride and of being reconnected with the ancestral homeland. Film songs came to be widely enjoyed and performed in the Caribbean, at once enriching the local music scene while undermining the popularity of the transplanted Bhojpuri folk music and the newly emerging local-classical styles. India-goods stores also imported inexpensive booklets containing verses of bhajans, folksongs, and genres like chowtal (primarily in Braj-bhasha), which were widely used by literate singers as reliable sources of old and new song texts. With the advent of video and audio cassettes in the 1980s, the availability and popularity of Bollywood culture increased dramatically, intensifying its dual nature as being both enriching and stultifying. Most important, all these imports served to strengthen Indian consciousness and the maintenance of Indian culture, whether deriving from traditional folkways or Bollywood. The ongoing inflow and eager consumption of goods from the Old World had no counterpart in Afro-West Indian society.

Diaspora Cultures and Their Ancestral Homeland Cultures: The Indo-Caribbean Experience in Comparative Perspective

Recent decades have seen exponential growth in the field of diaspora studies, which can be seen both as a response to the increased movements of populations in the modern era as well an enhanced appreciation of the cultural distinctiveness and vitality of new as well as old diasporas. Academics have failed to agree on a precise definition of diaspora. However, there may be a general consensus that the term should connote something more specific than any displaced community but at the same time be less restrictive than the criteria proposed by Safran (1991), who would insist on, among other things, an ongoing desire to return to the ancestral homeland (see, for example, Clifford 1994, Cohen 1997). For the purposes of a work such as this one, a diasporic group may be thought of as a demographically substantial emigrant community that does retain some sort of distinctive ethnic sense of identity animated by an affective link to the ancestral homeland. (This criterion would thus exclude, for example, ethnic Turks in Turkey, who maintain no particular sentimental attachment to the Central Asian steppes whence their forebears came a millennium ago.) As

is occasionally noted, diasporic groups range widely in character, variously comprising descendants of refugees, exiles, slaves, trading communities, and, last, the proletarian labor migrations of the colonial period, in which category would fall the Indo-Caribbean diaspora.

It could be said that a disproportionate amount of diaspora studies literature has focused on the relationship of migrant communities to their new homelands rather than to their ancestral homelands. Such has certainly been the case with the Indo-Caribbean diaspora, as reflected, for example, in the vast and ongoing scholarly and journalistic discourse regarding the political, cultural, and economic relations between Creoles and Indians in the West Indies, especially Trinidad. Such relations are certainly relevant to the present study, but my special attention to neotraditional musics calls for at least as much attention to the relations between Indo-Caribbean cultural forms and their Old World counterparts and sources, without which the dynamics of the diasporic context itself cannot be understood.

Just as diasporas vary in character, so do their relationships to ancestral homelands. While there is no need here for a lengthy typology of diasporas, the distinctive features of the Indo-Caribbean case do stand out in clearer relief when compared with those of other typical categories of diasporas, in terms of their cultural links, or absence thereof, to former homelands. One category of diasporas would comprise those ancient or "classical" scatterings whose expatriate communities, while perhaps celebrating historical links to the ancestral homeland, cease to have any cultural interaction with it. The quintessential example would be the Jews, who since the Babylonian conquest may have "wept for Zion," but whose far-flung communities over the millennia maintained no cultural, or especially musical, relationship with whatever remnants of Jewish society remained in Palestine.

A related type would be the "amnesiac" pattern in which a diasporic group, despite being of more recent origin and retaining some ancestral cultural features, ceases to have any particular interaction with or substantial retentions of Old World expressive cultural forms. Here the archetypical example could be the black populations of the United States. Scholars in music and other fields, from Melville Herskovits to Robert Farris Thompson and Gerhard Kubik, have rightly noted the presence and significance of continuities with African traditions, ranging from the Sahelian roots of the blues to a general emphasis on rhythm in Afro-American music. At the same time there is no doubt that the sociohistorical experience of black people in the United States, and in most of the British West Indies as well, has been marked by a dramatic rupture of links to African heritage and an inability (or unwillingness) to maintain direct cultural continuities. Distasteful as the notion may be to many, it is clear that

a massive process of deculturation, loss, and assimilation to Euro-American norms took place in the slave plantations and post-slave society, and that the forms of extant Old World continuities, important as they may be, are incomparably less than counterparts in other diasporas, including the Indo-Caribbeans (or, for that matter, Yoruba culture in Cuba). In many cases, of course, the amnesia or assimilation occurs in a benign fashion over the generations, such that, for example, a fourth-generation Polish-American might regard her Polish ancestry with indifference and fail to take the slightest interest in European Polish culture.

Perhaps a more typical and, one might even say, "standard" pattern for diasporas in the modern era has been one in which enhanced transportation and communication networks have enabled expatriate communities to maintain (whether motivated to do so or not) substantial and ongoing cultural contact and continuities with their former homelands. Hence, to choose an example from the Indian subcontinent, many people of Punjabi descent in the United Kingdom and United States may opt to assimilate to Euro-American mainstream society. However, many others have chosen retain a strong sense of Punjabi identity; they may maintain some linguistic competence, dance bhangra at Punjabi weddings and clubs, keep one ear tuned to new recordings from the Punjab, and perhaps even visit relatives there. Often their links are enhanced by chain migrations, with a steady, ongoing stream of immigrants, including relatives, from one particular locale to another. Punjabi communities in one area, such as the United Kingdom, may be linked rhizomatically to those in another site such as the United States via their direct ties to the Punjab.

From the late twentieth century, as flows of goods, money, people, and media content have become even more intensive, many diasporas have assumed a transnational nature, characterized by regular contact and often travel between old and new homelands, dual senses of loyalty, and ways in which the geographically dispersed population may be seen to constitute a single entity. The secondary diasporas of Indo-Caribbeans to North America constitute exemplars of this model. The Indo-Guyanese immigrant to Queens, New York, can read Guyanese newspapers on the internet, buy fresh fish from Guyana in the neighborhood market, call her relatives at home inexpensively, visit them occasionally, and, if she chooses, live in an overwhelmingly Indo-Guyanese social milieu. (Contacts with the ancestral Bhojpuri region, however, are likely to remain nil.)

A final diasporic category, of which the Indo-Caribbean case may constitute an idiosyncratic member, comprises what could be called "isolated transplant" diasporas. In this model, a diasporic population, arriving before the era of telecommunications and modern globalized networks, largely loses contact with

its ancestral homeland but is nevertheless able and determined to maintain a prodigious amount of traditional culture, perhaps even in spite of language loss. While assimilation, creolization, and a degree of cultural rupture occur, many aspects of traditional culture flourish like transplants in the new homeland's fertile soil; in some cases, they change or evolve significantly, but less through acculturation or external influence than through orthogenetic development or consolidation and streamlining of related Old World traditions. Such developments, in linguistic terms, are best likened to a koine, that is, a mixture of related languages from the same family, rather than a creole, involving languages from different families.

West African Yoruba culture in Cuba may be taken as one example of such a transplant diaspora. Descendants of enslaved Yorubas brought to Cuba in the mid-1800s have long since lost contact with West Africa and competence in spoken Yoruba, and they have in many ways and in differing degrees assimilated to a mainstream Cuban creole culture. However, a version of Yoruba culture—especially forms of traditional religion and music—can be said to be thriving in Cuba. In particular, the religion of Santería may be regarded as a somewhat streamlined consolidation of diverse but related and mutually compatible Yoruba beliefs and practices, with a thin veneer of Roman Catholicism. For its part, Santería music—especially batá drumming and associated songs—represents a similar sort of koine, in the form of a set of transplanted seeds that have evolved into a cohesive entity, differing in some ways from Nigerian counterparts but remaining overwhelmingly West African in form. (Indeed, the music includes many marginal survivals, especially in the form of songs forgotten in modern-day Nigeria.)

The Indo-Caribbean diaspora—and especially the Bhojpuri experience—can be seen as a variant of the "isolated transplant" diaspora, albeit with some distinctive features. The migration occurred prior to the era of (post)modern globalization, such that once immigration ceased, contact and interaction with the ancestral homeland—in this case, the Bhojpuri region—ceased almost entirely. Accordingly, after a few generations Indo-Caribbeans had invariably lost touch with their relatives on the subcontinent, and Bhojpuri Hindi declined as a spoken language in Trinidad and Guyana. Nevertheless, many aspects of Bhojpuri culture, from religion to music, flourished vigorously in the Caribbean. In some cases (such as chowtal singing) they persisted in traditional forms, but in others (such as tassa drumming) they continued to evolve, although primarily along Indian aesthetic and structural lines as neotraditional genres, without creolization or acculturation in their forms. However, a distinguishing feature of the diaspora is that while contact with the Bhojpuri region ended, Indo-Caribbeans did continue to receive a significant amount of influence from

greater India itself, whether in the form of visiting godmen or, from the late 1930s, commercial films and their music. In this sense their experience differed from that of the Yoruba and what might be considered a quintessential isolated-transplant model.

Cultural Trajectories, from Retention to Invention

If the distinctive features of the Indo-Caribbean diaspora may be highlighted by comparison with other diasporas, so may the trajectories of its various cultural components be better understood when contextualized in a broader typology of scenarios of cultural contact. The anthropological literature on culture contact is, of course, substantial, and explores such particularly relevant themes as the notion of acculturation (as employed by Franz Boas, Melville Herskovits, and others), criticized (justly or not) for its implicitly unidirectional focus. In the realm of music studies, one useful article is Bruno Nettl's "Some Aspects of the History of World Music in the Twentieth Century" (1978), which enumerates possible trajectories of world music cultures and genres when they come into contact with the West. Indo-Caribbean culture history, of course, involves less contact with "the West" per se than with a West Indian Creole culture, but in other respects his taxonomy may constitute a useful analytical starting point. Nettl lists the following possible responses of a non-Western music culture to Western music:

1. Abandonment, in other words, of a given traditional music culture, or aspects thereof
2. Impoverishment, which might comprise abandonment or decline of certain entities
3. Preservation of entities in a fossilized form, as folkloric "heritage"
4. Diversification, in which Western elements or genres may be accommodated alongside traditional ones
5. Consolidation, in which a complex and heterogeneous music tradition is streamlined into a newly standardized idiom
6. Reintroduction, "the return of musical styles to their place of origin after a sojourn elsewhere"
7. Exaggeration of certain non-Western features in response to a Western taste for exoticism
8. Satire
9. Syncretism (a process that, as subsequent writers have noted, must not be used in such a way as to imply that the cultures in contact are previously pure and unalloyed entities)
10. Westernization
11. Modernization (which is not identical with Westernization but is often integrally related to it)

Kartomi followed this article with a quite similar exercise (1981), in which she offered a few refinements, including recommending the term "transculturation" over the by-then-unfashionable "acculturation." She also proposed a few additions to Nettl's list, including *rejection* (of elements of an impinging culture), *transfer of discrete traits* (without inducing major musical change), *pluralistic coexistence, compartmentalization*, and *nativistic revival* (see also Nettl 1985, 23–29, adumbrating these and other earlier publications).

Several of these responses can be easily observed in Indo-Caribbean music history, as discussed in subsequent chapters. As for replacing the disparaged "acculturation" with "transculturation," in the West Indian context the customary and preferable term would in fact be "creolization." Since "creole" culture connotes the syncretic local hybrid of Afro-Caribbean and European-derived constructs, in Trinidadian and Guyanese discourse "creole" is thus conventionally, but not unproblematically, contrasted with East Indian; hence, as discussed below, the "creolization" of some aspect of Indo-Caribbean culture would connote acculturation or assimilation to the Afro-Saxon culture that was until recently propounded as a mainstream.

Constituents of Indo-Caribbean music culture could also be categorized by more general criteria than those Nettl sets forth, in terms of their respective relations to the ancestral homeland or, alternately, to Afro-creole culture. One category would comprise the set of genres and practices, derived from Bhojpuri tradition, that have been perpetuated in more or less intact forms. These may resemble present-day counterparts in India's Bhojpuri region, or they might constitute marginal survivals of entities that have declined there. Another category would consist of neotraditional genres that have evolved and changed dramatically in orthogenetic fashion, without any substantial adoption of Afro-creole elements. Local-classical music represents one such genre; tassa drumming would constitute another. A third category would include overtly creolized genres like chutney-soca.

In this study I shall rather extensively use and explore the notion of retention, a term which, fairly or not, has been as much maligned as "acculturation" and "syncretism." Certainly the term, if employed, should be defined closely, and could be contrasted with the notion of "persistence." Morton Klass, in his 1961 study of an Indo-Trinidadian village, writes: "*Retention*, as the term is traditionally used, refers to the continued presence of *traits*—discrete items of some particular cultural inventory (mother-in-law avoidance, say, the design on a pot, or the practice of clitorodectomy) . . . *Persistence*, at least in my view, is a much more fluid concept, reflecting a deep structural continuation, whether or not surface features (language, clothing, foodstuffs, and sometimes even elements of religion) are replaced" (1961, xxx; original emphasis). There

is no doubt that Indo-Caribbean music, like Indo-Caribbean culture in general, contains instances of both retention as well as persistence, and indeed, the difference between the two may often be unclear and subject to interpretation. If we find in tassa drumming a specific rhythmic feature that can be plausibly traced to North Indian practice, do we consider that a "mere" retention, that is, a superficial "trait," or might it reflect a "deep structural continuation," in other words, of a rhythmic aesthetic that might "persist" even as new elements are incorporated? The ultimate goal, obviously, is not merely to point out retentions, but to understand them, as well as persistences, in context and thereby gain a more profound appreciation of the dynamics of Indo-Caribbean cultural history.

The notion of retention might also be criticized on the grounds that its focus on a particular formal trait can distract from the new social meanings that entity may have likely acquired in the new diasporic context. Discovering retentions, such as finding the Bhojpuri-region source of a Guyanese folk song, may of course afford a certain giddy excitement to a researcher such as myself, but the goal of a scholarly study is naturally to seek the broader significance of such a continuity. Quite possibly the retained trait has been rearticulated and resignified in the new context. For example, as shall be discussed below, the North Indian custom of erecting a *jhanḍi* flag in a Hanuman temple may acquire a markedly new meaning in the diaspora, where the jhanḍi became a standard domestic ornament serving to proclaim ethnic pride in a multicultural society. Some scholars have concluded that such transformations render the study of retentions fruitless and misleading; Kartomi, for example, wrote: "It serves no purpose to try and disentangle the musical elements from their new cultural matrix and trace them backwards, because they are intermeshed and reorganized on entirely new and specific lines" (1981:233).[1] I am quite in disagreement with this sort of assertion, which is perhaps reflective of an academic trend to celebrate syncretism and resignification to the exclusion of other cultural dynamics. One could in fact easily enumerate several purposes that could be served by disentangling musical elements and tracing them backward. First, the origins of a musical entity are sometimes the subject of contention and sociopolitical import, as has certainly been the case in Trinidad. In some cases, as mentioned earlier, Indo-Trinidadians have claimed a North Indian origin for an entity, perhaps in order to give it legitimacy; in other cases, as with the dantāl and even tassa drums, some Indo-Trinidadians have argued for a local origin, perhaps to emphasize how their community, rather than merely perpetuating Old World traditions, has been actively creative, like the Afro-creole inventors of calypso and the steel drum. Obviously, a dispassionate and scholarly archeology of the origins of such entities might be of considerable interest and value, whether or not its findings please all those concerned. Further, while some

entities might well be traced back to India, a rigorous inquiry might serve to highlight what elements actually *were* created locally. In the process, such an investigation could illuminate the deeper cultural dynamics that condition the various trajectories Nettl and Kartomi enumerate; ideally, indeed, the goal of the ethnomusicologist is not merely to document such processes (for example, "consolidation," or syncretism) but to understand why they occur in some contexts and in certain ways and not others.

As well, the notion that musical elements in a new "cultural matrix" are "intermeshed and reorganized on entirely new and specific lines" might well be true in some cases, but in others it might be false. Even in the diasporic contexts it remains possible that the function and meaning of a formal retention may in fact closely cohere to traditional models. It has often been asserted, for example, that Indo-Caribbeans in many respects reconstituted their traditional Indian villages and folkways, especially in the decades preceding the 1930s and the spread of mass media and urbanization. Hence Klass, whether correctly or not, described the village where he resided as being in its basic structure "an 'Indian' community and not a 'West Indian' one" (1961, 239). Insofar as such a description was correct, it could imply that evident retentions were not necessarily rearticulated or resignified but reflected persistences in meaning as well as form.

Clearly a formal retention—that is, an entity (such as a rhythm, tune, or a kind of drum) that corresponds in form to its Old World ancestor—may have varying sorts of significances, which analysts might interpret either positively or negatively. A retention may reflect a kind of xenophobic inertia and ossification, and the impending extinction of a given genre. It may come to constitute a kind of resistance to a hegemonic dominating culture. It may have acquired a new value as "heritage," to be deliberately preserved as an emblem of traditional culture. It may be rearticulated or resignified, as in, for example, the fitting of a Christian devotional text to a folk tune. Or it may be dynamically combined with innovative or creole features as part of a vital neotraditional or modernized genre. None of these phenomena can be properly and holistically understood without, in Kartomi's words, "disentangling" their origins.

I offer one further instance of the potential value of tracing musical elements back to their origins. While many aspects of Indian folk music have been studied in the late twentieth century, pathetically little is known about the history of such oral traditions. However, as I show in chapter 3, the existence of nearly identical chowtal styles in the Caribbean and Fiji—whose communities have had essentially no contact since 1917—enables us to posit with absolute certainty their origin in the Bhojpuri region during the indentureship period. Tracing these features back thus affords a kind of historical

insight that has no counterpart in any other realm of Indian folk music, un-documented as its evolution is.

If the notion of retention may be potentially problematic, the concept of "creolization" is at once equally indispensable and equally in need of careful definition. As mentioned above, in the West Indian context, "creolization" has traditionally been understood as the historical process that animated the interaction between Afro-Caribbeans and Europeans and the evolution of a distinctive local culture. By extension, the term has also described the process by which another group, such as Indo-Caribbeans, have assimilated to "creole" Afro-West Indian values and practices. From the conservative Indo-Caribbean perspective, the pejorative equivalent term to the latter meaning is "douglarization," a dougla being a person of mixed black and Indian descent. In the complex West Indian sociopolitical climate, one man's dynamic syncretism may be another's degenerate impurity and dilution. Analytical problems emerge when "creole" is understood not in purely racial terms, as "syncretic Afro-Caribbean," but as a general cultural disposition characteristic of mainstream Caribbean society over the centuries. Mintz (1996), for example, persuasively identifies Caribbean creolism not merely with racial and cultural hybridity but with a spirit of dynamism, creativity, and an expectation of and openness to change. Accordingly, others, including Gilroy (1993), have characterized the Caribbean creole disposition as quintessentially modern, rather than only tangentially so.

The interpretive challenge emerges when this broader, attitudinal sense of the "creole" is applied to multiracial Trinidad and Guyana, where local discourse identifies the term specifically with the erstwhile "mainstream" culture of a specific race, namely, Afro-West Indians. Thus, on one discursive level, the celebrated Trinidadian trinity of calypso, carnival, and steelband is creole because of its overwhelming association, especially in terms of historical origins, with Afro-Trinidadians rather than East Indians. (In this sense, creole Trinidadian culture would also be contrasted with a neo-African entity like the Yoruba-derived Orisha worship.) Meanwhile, in the broader, more conceptual terms of Mintz, calypso, carnival, and steelband are creole less by racial affinity than because of their embodiment of the values of dynamic openness and innovative creativity. Much of Indo-Caribbean culture, it could well be argued, is fundamentally conservative and traditional, and is thereby comfortably contrasted with "creole" culture, both in terms of racial affiliation and attitudinal disposition. However, insofar as other aspects of Indo-Caribbean culture, or other Indo-Caribbean individuals, reflect a sense of dynamism, creativity, and openness to change, must these features be automatically interpreted as deriving from Afro-creole culture? Is it not possible for East Indians to be dynamic and innovative without necessarily being douglarized?

Inspired by these concerns, Sri Lankan anthropologist Viranjani Munasinghe (2001, 135–140) argues that the concept of creolization be dislodged from its racial moorings and identified, à la Mintz, with general cultural orientations so that it can be detected in East Indians without necessarily involving assimilation to any Afro-Trinidadian mainstream. On a mundane level, the distinction is terminological: if, following Munasinghe, we use "creole" to connote a general sensibility rather than a socioracial feature, then we are not only at odds with established Trinidadian discourse but are also obliged to use a different term from that standard "creolization" to denote "Afro-West Indian syncretism" (aside from the value-laden "douglarization"). However, the contradiction involves an interpretive level aside from the lexicographical one. In chapter 5 I discuss tassa drumming, which could be seen as a concrete musical embodiment of these analytical issues. Tassa drummers of recent generations have certainly been animated by a spirit of creativity and openness. Must this sensibility be interpreted as deriving from "creole"—that is, Afro-West Indian—influence, or should it be seen as reflecting, *pace* Mintz, a general disposition characteristic of Caribbean culture as a whole (whose mainstream, in most of the region, happens to be primarily black or mulatto)? Or, finally, should it not be ascribed either to any particular Caribbean or Afro-Trinidadian inspiration but instead be seen as something that could have comfortably emerged from East Indian society itself, which has never been as inherently and unequivocally static and conservative as some may have argued? Is it not insulting, and perhaps even racist, to presuppose that any sort of creativity in Indo-Caribbean culture must be attributed to Afro-Trinidadian influence? What, then, is the best way to interpret the dynamism of tassa drumming? As Afro-Trinidadian-inspired, or as essentially *Caribbean*, or as orthogenetically East Indian? Should tassa be regarded as "creole" in any sense at all? Is it not possible that an art form like tassa can be dynamic, innovative, and distinctively local without being "creole" in any sense? And if so, should we not acknowledge that creolization, while justly celebrated, should not be regarded as the only form of dynamic creativity, and the only criterion of being truly Trinidadian? While I shall explore these questions more deeply in chapters 5 and 6, at this point I will suggest that it may be a mistake to attempt to shoehorn Indo-Caribbeans even into an expanded notion of creole identity, when some of the most vital aspects of their expressive culture—such as tassa—are at once dynamic, rich, and wholly Trinidadian without being significantly creolized. Accordingly, if cultivation of new cultural entities on Trinidadian soil is to be hailed as an insignia of national belonging, then it should be understood that such entities should comprise not only creole creations like steelband and calypso but also neotraditional genres like tassa that owe little to Afro-West Indian contributions.

Colonial-Era Music Culture in North India's Bhojpuri Region

The Bhojpuri region of North India, whose musical legacy in the Caribbean is the subject of this book, is a linguistic rather than geopolitical entity, being defined by the ambitus of the Bhojpuri dialect of the Hindi group of languages.[2] Today straddling eastern Uttar Pradesh and western Bihar, the *pūrab* or "eastern" region, as it is often called, is roughly delimited by the Nepal border on the north, Patna on the east, the state lines of Jharkhand and Madhya Pradesh on the south, and the axis of Jaunpur and Mirzapur to the west. Today it is home to some sixty million souls, most of whom are agriculturalists.

As a center for Indian high culture, the region's heyday eclipsed more than two millennia ago. In the sixth century B.C.E., it was the site of the Magadha kingdom, which, with its capital in Pataliputra (modern Patna), was the pre-eminent center of civilization in the subcontinent. In that period it was home to the Buddha, whose followers made Bodhgaya, in modern Bihar, an important pilgrimage site. It was also the legendary birthplace of Rama—perhaps a small tribal chieftain—who became immortalized in the Ramayan epic and identified, millennia later, in the eighteenth century C.E., with the town of Ayodhya (formerly Saket). The Magadha kingdom was succeeded by the dynasty of the Mauryans, whose scion Ashoka in the third century B.C.E. conquered most of the subcontinent and has been revered as one of the most enlightened rulers in Indian history. With the subsequent collapse of the Mauryan Empire and its replacement by a loose, decentralized Indian feudalism, the region's cultural and political preeminence ended for good. In the nineteenth century Banaras emerged as a bustling commercial and pilgrimage center, and in the twentieth century the region filled up with far more people than it could sustain, but nothing remains of its bygone centrality except for the miscellaneous ruins and stupas that dot the otherwise flat and monotonous landscape. As V. S. Naipaul wrote, with his characteristic disdain, "It is a dismal, dusty land, made sadder by the ruins and place names that speak of an ancient glory. For here was the land of the Buddha; here are cities mentioned in the Hindu epics of three thousand years ago—like Ayodhya, from which my father's family came, today a ramshackle town of wholly contemporary squalor" (1976, 39).

Bhojpuri is a member of the Hindi group of languages whose constituents would also include such tongues as Braj-bhasha, Haryanvi, Marwari, the *khari-boli* of the Delhi-Meerut axis, and the closely related border dialects Avadhi (on the west) and Maithili (on the east). Khaṛi-bolī, enriched with Perso-Arabic vocabulary, formed the basis for Urdu and, with a more or less Sanskritized lexicon, became during the colonial period the "standard" Hindi that serves as a written and spoken lingua franca throughout most of North India, including the

Bhojpuri region. Despite the abundance of its speakers, the Bhojpuri language, like such regional Indian idioms as Haryanvi, has never enjoyed the status of a literary language. In this sense it can be contrasted, for example, with Braj-bhasha, which, because of its association with worship of Krishna, became a favored medium for poetry throughout North India, including in classical song genres like *khyāl* and *thumri*. It also contrasts with Avadhi, which was the language of the *Rāmcharitmānas*, a version of the Ramayan epic penned by Tulsidas (d. 1623). The *Rāmcharitmānas* (or simply "*Mānas*") inspired many imitators and effectively established Avadhi (formerly known as Baiswari) as a legitimate literary medium. On the eastern side of the Bhojpuri region the Maithili dialect was the idiom of the late-fourteenth-century poet Vidyapati, but his work did not spark a substantial literary tradition.

Bhojpuri and (standard) Hindi are closely similar in grammar, phonemes, and lexicons, roughly comparable to Castilian Spanish and Catalan in degree of differentiation. Today, Bhojpuri, in its subregional dialects, is the informal colloquial idiom of villagers in the *pūrab* region. Standard Hindi, by contrast, is the language of schools, newspapers, radio, and television, pulp fiction, urban discourse in general, and especially Bollywood cinema, which is as popular in the Bhojpuri region as anywhere else in the north. Although the population of the region has expanded dramatically, the spread of standard Hindi has in some respects marginalized Bhojpuri as a set of pocket dialects. However, the recent vogue of Bhojpuri cinema and folk-pop music has lent a new vigor and prestige to a standardized form of the dialect. Today, unlike a century ago, even the illiterate villager is likely to understand Hindi, though he might have difficulty speaking it properly, whereas the urbanite reared on lingua-franca Hindi might be hard pressed to follow the rustic rural dialect spoken by the day laborers repairing his house.

If Bhojpuri is not itself a literary medium, its speakers have not been foreign to written verse. The Bhojpuri region has always hosted its share of poets, who, today as earlier, would generally compose in Braj (in other words, Braj-bhasha) or, if urban Muslims, in Urdu. Thus, for example, the lyrics of chowtal—a Bhojpuri-region and eastern Uttar Pradesh folksong genre—are predominantly in Braj, even if penned by locals. Further, Tulsidas's *Rāmcharitmānas* has long been fervently cherished by all social classes in the region and is so frequently narrated and sung in diverse contexts as to minimize whatever linguistic difficulties might be posed by its archaic Avadhi. In general, although the vast majority of Bhojpuri dwellers—and Indo-Caribbean immigrants—would have been illiterate, literacy was widely venerated, and many villagers would have been not only intimately familiar with a text like the *Mānas* but would have

been able to recite long passages of it from memory. The popularity of the *Mānas* also contributed to a generally strong presence of Avadhi elements in the folksongs of the Bhojpuri region.

Scholars of Indian culture have often used and adapted the categories of "great tradition" and "little tradition," first proposed by Robert Redfield in the 1950s as a general categorization of religious beliefs and practices. In the Indian context, as elaborated by Milton Singer (1972), the great tradition would connote the panregional Brahminical Hinduism grounded in Sanskritic texts like the Mahabharat and Ramayan, while little traditions would comprise the myriad regional forms of folk religion, with their village godlings and local superstitions. The taxonomy has been problematized on various grounds, as will be discussed in chapter 4, but has nevertheless been productively extended to other aspects of culture, including music (see Powers 1980). Thus, with certain appropriate caveats, one could speak of the "great traditions" of North Indian and South Indian classical music, constituting, as they do, panregional art musics grounded in elite patronage and a music theory expounded variously in Sanskrit, Persian, and vernacular-language treatises over the millennia. With some liberty one might even liken Bollywood Hindi film culture to a kitsch form of great tradition insofar as it constitutes a panregional entity using a lingua franca, in contrast to the variety of regional-language entertainment forms, from traditional bardic recitations to contemporary commercial videos accompanying Bhojpuri folk-pop songs. The great traditions have always coexisted in a complex dialectic—at once competitive and mutually nourishing—with regional little traditions, in a manner well evident in the Indic Caribbean, as we shall explore in chapter 4.

During the indentureship period, the great tradition of North Indian classical music, or Hindustani music, was sustained in several Bhojpuri-region courts, such as that at Darbhanga, and the emerging light-classical genres of thumri and ghazal were fairly widely performed by courtesans in Banaras, Gaya, and other towns. As I discussed in my book *East Indian Music in the West Indies*, a handful of musicians with some knowledge, whether complete or fragmentary, of this music presumably immigrated to the Caribbean and planted the seeds of what would develop into the idiosyncratic genre of "local-classical music." However, the vast majority of indentured immigrants from the Bhojpuri region would have been low-caste peasants with little or no exposure to—nor use for—the rarefied urban culture of the court and courtesan salon. Rather, their musical heritage would have consisted of the little tradition—indeed, the plural little traditions—of Bhojpuri folk music, in all its subregional linguistic and stylistic diversity.

The little-tradition folk music of the Bhojpuri region, like that of India in general, is poorly documented prior to the 1970s. The remarkable scholar-administrator George Grierson published a few articles on Bhojpuri folk music in the 1880s, which, though consisting mostly of songtexts and their translations, offer several pithy observations. As this book discusses, much can be learned about the region's music during the indentureship period—including the form of actual melodies—from the study of continuities in the Caribbean and Fiji. Moreover, from these and other sources, and from modern studies of Bhojpuri folk music (especially Henry 1988), we can construct a plausible image of the region's musical practices and repertoire, as well as its prevailing cultural ambience, that were transplanted to the Caribbean between 1845 and 1917.

The Bhojpuri villager of the indentureship period would have known nothing of the Buddhist and Jain religions that emerged from his region millennia before, nor would he have had any particular exposure to the esoteric traditions of literary Sanskritic Hinduism. Rather, his socioreligious worldview would have been shaped by the folkways of his particular village, the simplified form of great-tradition Hinduism practiced and perhaps expounded by the local pandits, and above all, promoted by the *bhakti* movement, which since the eleventh century had supplemented Brahminical orthodoxy with a more personal devotionalism, often expressed through verse and group singing. From the 1880s, moreover, a different sort of reformist challenge to Brahminism began reaching some villages in the form of the Arya Samaj movement, which would subsequently take root in the Caribbean.

Islam had also established its presence in the Bhojpuri region, spread on the upper social level by military conquests, and on the vernacular level by pacifist Sufi missionaries. Accordingly, most Muslims consisted either of urban hereditary nobility or else, in the villages, descendants of low-caste Hindu converts. Centuries of Hindu-Muslim cohabitation in the countryside had led to shared beliefs, practices, and patterns of village life that far overshadowed the incompatibilities between orthodox forms of the two religions. Finally, the colonial presence would also have made some mark on village worldviews, whether in the form of respect for British technology or, for many, spite for the foreigners who had committed such atrocities in repressing the 1857 revolt and whose onerous taxation policies were engendering recurrent famines. In general, the villagers, however provincial their attitudes and narrow their experiences may have been, were heirs to a strong cultural legacy that would enable them to resist the proselytizing pressures of the indentureship experience.

The folk music of the Bhojpuri region, during the indentureship period as now, was heterogeneous and rich. The main categories of the region's folk music would include the following:

- Women's songs, including work songs, and songs associated with life-cycle events, especially childbirth songs (*sohar*), funeral songs, and wedding songs; the latter are particularly numerous and include lewd and humorous abuse ditties (*gālī*) directed at the groom, and bawdy songs and dances, performed out of sight of men, at the (*maṭkor*) dirt-digging ceremony
- Seasonal songs, sung primarily but not exclusively by men, including rainy-season *sāvan*, and especially songs enlivening the vernal Holi or Phagwa festival, such as chowtal
- Songs by unpaid specialists and medicants, including *birha*, originally a field holler, which developed into a vehicle for topical verse; *Ālhā*, a martial epic sung by bards; the devotional songs of itinerant *jogi* mendicants; and *qawwāli*, a Muslim devotional song heard in Sufi shrines;
- Instrumental music, especially that played on the *nagāra* drum pair, and by the tassa ensemble
- Religious songs, especially Hindu devotional *bhajans*, sung either solo or collectively, and renditions of Tulsidas's *Rāmcharitmānas*, again in a variety of either solo or group antiphonal styles

Since the indentureship period the Bhojpuri folk music scene has been enriched by various modern specialist entertainment genres, especially contemporary birha, consisting of narrative texts sung to a medley of tunes by a troupe of professionals, and *Mirzapuri kajri*, in which, most typically, two teams of poet-singers stage a duel in verse and song. Since these genres emerged after the end of the indentureship program, they have had no presence in the diaspora.

The most common instrumental accompaniment for Bhojpuri-region folk-song is the familiar double-headed *dholak* barrel drum, and since the mid-twentieth century, the harmonium, both of which are also standard in the Caribbean. These are often supplemented by some sort of metallophone, such as *manjira* chimes, the somewhat larger *jhāl* or *jhānjh*, or a metal rod struck by a U-shaped clapper, which might variously be called *sīk*, *gaj*, or—especially in the Caribbean—*ḍanḍtāl* (dantāl). Melodies are typically strophic, often in a two-part verse-refrain (*sthāi-antara*) form. Texts to women's songs tend to be repetitive, often consisting of reiterative lines in which only one or two words are altered. Rhythms typically consist of variants of the syncopated quadratic meter that classical musicians might call *kaharva*, though that term is not used in the same way by folk performers. A fast seven-beat meter (which might segue to quadratic meter) is common in several genres; stylized forms of this *tāl* in light-classical music would be called *dīpchandī, chānchar*, or *jat*.

Many Bhojpuri folk music genres, such as women's wedding songs, group and solo bhajans, and panregional genres like *qawwāli* can be said to resemble counterparts elsewhere in North India. In Bhojpuri folksong one also finds

some of the same stock tunes as in the Braj region and elsewhere. A few further observations, however subjective and impressionistic, might also add some perspective to the region's musical profile. At the risk of crudely generalizing, I would opine that melodic richness and variety are not pronounced features of the region's folk repertoire, to the extent that they are, for example, in Rajasthan. A great portion of tunes, such as those that predominate in chowtal, Ālhā, and birha, adhere to the simplest of melodies, typically centering in the lower tetrachord of a major scale (do-re-mi-fa, or *sa-re-ga-ma* in Indian solfege). In Ālhā the crude stock tune, endlessly repeated, is little more than a mnemonic scaffold on which to hang the narrative verses. The scales corresponding to the ("Phrygian") rāg Bhairavi, or the ("thirdless") Sārang, such as abound in Punjabi music, are atypical of the Bhojpuri region, and even "minor"-sounding scales with flat third degrees are less common. The timbral sweetness that the *kamāicha* and *sārangi* fiddles add to Rajasthani Manganhar and Langa music finds little counterpart in Bhojpuri music, whose Ur-format consists of a singer doubling his melody on a harmonium, typically with serviceable but unremarkable dholak accompaniment. Meanwhile, however, one lively stylistic format that is prominent in the region, and quite atypical of other regions, is the antiphonal or responsorial format of chowtal, *chaitā*, *chahkā*, *baiswāra*, Ramayan singing, and a few other genres, in which two sets of men, or a leader and a male chorus, reiterate singing text lines at full voice while segueing through a set of rhythmic modulations, accelerations, and decelerations, including alternating between seven-beat and quadratic meter. These genres—meant to be actively sung rather than listened to—generate great excitement and exhilaration for the singers, especially when a well-rehearsed group skillfully negotiates the dizzyingly fast line renditions and segues.

With the cassette revolution of the 1980s, an essentially new genre of commercial hybrid folk-pop emerged, which has continued to expand in the era of cheap VCDs (video compact discs), DVDs, and mp3 discs. This new Bhojpuri pop music, through the sheer size of its linguistic market as well as its inherent merits, has become a substantial presence on the North Indian musical landscape, especially as heard via the bland tenor of Manoj Tewari or the sublime mezzo of the Assamese-born Kalpana Patowary.

The Bhojpuri Musical Legacy in the Caribbean: An Overview

During the extended indentureship period, the Caribbean—together with faraway Fiji and to a lesser extent, Mauritius and South Africa—established itself as a small but vigorous outpost of Bhojpuri culture. This diasporic version of Bhojpuri culture, however, differed somewhat from its Old World ancestor,

including in ways that had nothing to do with "creolization," in any of the meanings of that term. In terms of social structure, the most salient change was the drastic weakening of caste, due to the leveling and proletarianizing effect of plantation life. Meanwhile, since most immigrants arrived as individuals rather than families, kinship networks required a few generations to be reestablished. Moreover, as carriers of Bhojpuri culture, the ranks of indentured did not constitute a representative cross-section of Bhojpuri society but instead contained a disproportionately large amount of lower-caste peasants. Literate Brahmans and city-dwellers in general would have been less motivated to apply and in any case were likely to have been weeded out and rejected by the British recruiters, who sought sturdy young farmers rather than pandits and tailors unaccustomed to fieldwork. For the same reason, members of musician castes—whether urban *ḍhāḍhis* or itinerant village *jogis*—would have been underrepresented in the diaspora, as the British sought workers adept with the scythe rather than the sitar.

A second difference involved the processes of streamlining and consolidation that transpired in language and, undoubtedly, in music culture as well. British colonists were known to remark that many of the indentureds were unable to communicate with each other, hailing as they did from different parts of the subcontinent, or even different ends of the Bhojpuri region. Bhojpuri itself, far from being a unified, standardized tongue, comprised a set of subdialects of varying degrees of mutual intelligibility. In the Caribbean, however, except for the subculture of "Madrasis" who could constitute a critical mass able to remain linguistically distinct, Bhojpuri emerged as a lingua franca, in the form of an immigrant koine, that is, a new dialect that forms in a community settled by immigrants speaking two or more mutually intelligible dialects of the same language. The dialects in this case were the myriad regional variants of the Bhojpuri region and also elements of Avadhi. (Indeed, throughout this volume my use of the term "Bhojpuri" should be taken to imply incorporation of Avadhi aspects as well.) Thus, both the worker from an obscure corner of the Bhojpuri region as well as the odd immigrant from another North Indian state such as the Punjab would find themselves obliged to master this newly consolidated form of Bhojpuri in order to converse. The preeminence of this Bhojpuri as a koine naturally increased over the generations, and even a Madrasi descendant like local-classical vocalist Isaac Yankaran (d. 1969), though not of a Bhojpuri/Hindi-speaking family, was obliged to learn a certain amount of Hindi in order to sing properly. Despite this stage of consolidation and expansion, however, Caribbean Bhojpuri, like its subcontinental counterpart, never developed the status of a written idiom, or even of a legitimate language in its own right. Accordingly, the word "Bhojpuri" itself is essentially an unfamiliar

neologism among Indo-Caribbeans, who would instead traditionally refer to their tongue as *ṭūṭi Hindi* or "broken Hindi" (or occasionally as *theth*, "slang").[3] Even today the term is not widely used in Indo-Caribbean discourse, though convenience occasions my extensive use of it in this text. (During the colonial period in India, the term "Bihari" was also used interchangeably with "Bhojpuri.") In Suriname, the Bhojpuri-Avadhi koine became known as Sarnami, which also includes a sprinkling of common Dutch words (for example, as in "*Snell karo*"—Do it fast!).

There can be no doubt that a similar process of consolidation occurred in the realm of folk music. The Bhojpuri folksong culture brought to the Caribbean would have included not only some genres and styles familiar throughout the region, but also innumerable songs and perhaps entire subgenres that were peculiar to a particular North Indian district. Many of these would survive in the Caribbean, as evident, for example, in the different forms of chowtal that can be found, not only in Trinidad, Guyana, and Suriname, but also even within Guyana itself. However, there would have been a natural tendency toward the coalescence of a standardized Bhojpuri music culture, at least within each colony, that would either actively incorporate a given obscure musical element or else marginalize and effectively obliterate it.

One initial obstacle to transplanting Bhojpuri culture in the diaspora was the aforementioned fact that the vast majority of immigrants were young men, typically in their early twenties, who were thus unlikely to have been well versed even in the more subtle and rich aspects of their own village folkways. It is obvious, however, that the immigrants were not content to live crude and brutish lives of cultural deprivation in hopeless and insuperable isolation from their rich homeland culture. Nor, for that matter, were they inclined to forsake their own heritage to adopt the ways of the white *bakra* or the black "kirwāl." Further, even if illiterate, they, like their village kin at home, held a deep veneration for literacy and learning, whether in the form of the pandit's incantations or the mellifluous narrative of the *Mānas*. Thus, they avidly sought to reconstruct and reestablish in their new homeland their ancestral culture, in as much wholeness and richness as possible. Hence, many accounts attest to the zeal with which the immigrants welcomed and sought the company of those who had some cultural expertise, whether in the form of Hindi literacy, Ramayan recitation, or folksong. Accordingly, Indo-Caribbeans were even able to cultivate some genres that, in North India, had been the domain of professional specialists; a prime example would be the forms of "intermediate" theater—especially "Harichand" (Raja Harishchandra), a series of songs, dances, and action scenes woven into a loose narrative that in India would later be subsumed into the category of *nautanki* theater (see Manuel 2000a, 28–31).

Given such a commitment to nurture traditional culture, it is clear that within a few decades after the commencement of the indentureship program, Bhojpuri culture, in its various forms, was well established in the Caribbean, which hosted its own ranks of pandits, poets, and songsters. One octogenarian related to me how his grandfather, though born in British Guiana, was a fluent reader and speaker of Hindi and an expert in the arcane forms of chowtal, which he taught to young and old enthusiasts, including recent immigrants. Thus, it is easy to image a young immigrant in the 1890s, illiterate and largely ignorant of song forms like chowtal, arriving in British Guiana and, with proper motivation and opportunity, proceeding to learn at least as much about Bhojpuri folklore, the Ramayan, and chowtal singing as he could ever hope to do back in his provincial village in Bihar.

Much of Indo-Caribbean Bhojpuri folk-music culture has corresponded, at least until the last generation, to the categories of North Indian Bhojpuri music outlined above. Arya's study of Suriname in the 1960s documented a wide range of flourishing folksong traditions, including *sohars*, wedding songs, birha, Phagwa songs like chowtal, and miscellaneous devotional and work songs. Researching in a Trinidadian village in the 1970s and 1980s, Myers found that women still sang traditional songs at weddings and other events, despite the drastic decline of Hindi/Bhojpuri. However, aspects of change and decline were evident even in Arya's period of research. As he noted, due to the relative homogeneity of seasons in Suriname, songs like *bārahmāsa*, narrating the twelve months of the year, had disappeared. Caste-specific songs of, for example, *kahār* water carriers and *kumhār* potters were also dying out, along with work songs whose associated activities, such as grinding, were extinguished by mechanization. Further, as he noted, the increasing presence of standard Hindi through Bollywood films, Arya Samaj proselytizing, and other sources was generating "a feeling of inferiority and often an apologetic attitude among those who speak or sing in the dialect forms," notably Sarnami Bhojpuri (1968, 4).

By the time I commenced my own fieldwork in the early 1990s, the changes—especially in the form of decline—were dramatically more evident. Folksong traditions have been most resilient in Suriname, where Sarnami remains widely spoken. Women still sing wedding songs, and chowtal and Ramayan-singing flourish as elsewhere in the region, along with a unique set of more specialized song forms such as antiphonal Ramayan bhajan singing with *khanjri* hand-drum. Even in Suriname, however, the relative absence of a concerted movement to promote Indo-Surinamese ("Hindustani") culture has exacerbated the general indifference to folkways Arya commented on decades earlier. Birha singing and nagāra playing are known only to handfuls of elders or folkloric special-

ists, and predictably, premodern entertainment genres like Ālhā recitation and Harichand theater are essentially defunct.

In Trinidad and Guyana, Bhojpuri is fluently spoken and understood only by a fast-dwindling handful of octogenarians and nontogenarians, and text-driven genres like women's songs have attenuated accordingly. However, in the course of my fieldwork I occasionally encountered men, especially amateur singers, who had acquired a certain sort of command of Hindi, including in its Bhojpuri and Braj variants, through a variety of sources. These latter typically included regular experiences in one's youth of hearing elders speak Bhojpuri, watching unsubtitled Hindi films, absorbing the prayers and incantations of pandits at religious events, and attentively listening to all kinds of Indian music, from film songs to temple bhajans. Some such enthusiasts had greatly increased their comprehension by learning to read the Devnagari script, enabling them to read the cheap bhajan songbooks marketed in India-goods stores. While these individuals might not be able to converse fluently, they often had a vast knowledge of songs, from chowtals to local-classical pieces, and were well able not only to understand them but also to expound their meaning. (Indeed, the nature of their command of Hindi contrasted markedly with my own, as I am relatively comfortable in conversing, and more schooled in Urdu, while being sorely challenged by Braj and Sanskritized Hindi vocabulary.)

Sustained especially by the zeal of such knowledgeable amateurs, chowtal flourishes in both Trinidad and Guyana (as well as in Suriname), and traditional antiphonal Ramayan singing survives in pockets. Genres like wedding songs, insofar as they are still performed, are less likely to be sung by amateurs than by a hired duo or troupe of semiprofessional singers, who may themselves rely on songbooks with romanized renderings of lyrics. Due to the legacy of the Burnham/PNC dictatorship (1964–1992), which bankrupted the country and embittered race relations, cultural patronage and activity in Guyana have been disastrously low for decades, such that Indo-Guyanese culture may be surviving more in the secondary diaspora sites of New York and Toronto than in Guyana itself. Due to unchecked piracy, production of music recordings and any form of literature in Guyana is essentially nil. In Trinidad, Hindi language attrition is as dramatic as in Guyana, and the influence of creole culture even stronger, but other factors have made the island a fertile site for Indo-Caribbean music, whether in traditional or modern hybrid forms. Political stability and openness, and, since the 1970s, material affluence have contributed substantially to cultural vitality, but such factors can only partially explain the preternatural level of musical activity on the island, both in creole and Indian domains. While Afro-Trinidadians are largely responsible for the island's renown as the cradle of calypso, steelband, and Carnival, East Indians have both taken inspi-

ration from such creole activities as well as drawn from their own traditions to cultivate a music scene of prodigious vigor, both on amateur and professional levels. Of particular importance is the lively renaissance of Indo-Trinidadian culture that has taken place since the 1970s. This renaissance has animated all manner of music competitions, public and private performances and song sessions, religious events, mass media projects, academic conferences, scholarly publications and journals, classes in everything from Hindustani art music to wedding songs, and a general sense of healthy cultural assertiveness and pride (see Vertovec 1992, chapter 4). Indian music and culture are also the subjects of ongoing lively debate, with continual polemics about the relation of Indian music to creole culture, the dialectics of continuity and change, the controversial chutney phenomenon, and other topics (see Manuel 2000c).

For my own purposes as a researcher, I found Guyana itself, with due respect, to be a somewhat dangerous and depressing site, much of whose cultural vitality is better accessed in the secondary diaspora site of New York; Suriname, with its Bhojpuri/Hindi-speaking population and its resilient folk culture, is an ethnomusicological gold mine in some ways, but its music scene is limited by its sheer smallness and the very finite numbers of its active performers in any given genre. For its part, Trinidad is not only the most accessible but in most senses the richest in terms of numbers and variety of artists, cultural activists, and events. Hence, it is not out of pure convenience that I have spent the most research time there, following the footsteps of Myers, Tewari, and others.

Concluding Thoughts

The subsequent chapters of this book can be seen, from one perspective, as a set of case studies illuminating different sorts of musical responses to the changing objective circumstances faced by Indo-Caribbeans over the generations. It may be useful to conclude this section by supplementing or reframing some of the considerations presented above with mention of four basic conditions underlying the Indo-Caribbean experience, each of which could potentially constitute a challenge to the persistence and vitality of Bhojpuri music traditions in the new milieu.

The first of these basic conditions is the fact of geographical isolation from India, the ancestral homeland. Even when records, films, booklets, and godmen started arriving from the subcontinent in India, these constituted a unidirectional flow rather than an interaction, and contact with the Bhojpuri region remained essentially nil. However, this isolation in itself did not necessarily doom Bhojpuri folkways to extinction. By the 1880s the Indo-Caribbean population in Trinidad, Guyana, and Suriname constituted a critical mass demographically

able to sustain its own traditional culture, especially due to its concentration in rural enclaves (as opposed to dispersion, as was the case in Jamaica). As the population grew exponentially from increased immigration and high birth rates, so did the potential resilience of its culture. (Particularly fecund was Suriname's East Indian population, which grew from some 34,000 in the indentureship period to 125,000 in 1980 [Vertovec 1992, 4]).

A second basic condition was the presence of—and to some extent the obligatory engagement with—the Afro-creole community and the British (or in Suriname, Dutch) administrators. There is no doubt that this sociocultural context engendered a substantial amount of assimilation to creole Western practices and values, often at the expense of Indian ones. This sociomusical acculturation could take many forms, from the Christian convert singing hymns instead of bhajans, to the teenager who prefers ragga to raga, that is, who favors dancehall reggae over any form of Indian music. However, the creole presence, like the geographical isolation, did not necessarily in itself entail acculturation to Western or creole music at the expense of Indian music. Most Indo-Caribbeans have resided in communities that, whether isolated or not, have been predominantly East Indian; even those in mixed neighborhoods have enjoyed easy access to nearby Indian religious centers and sociocultural events, such that they have been well able, if so inclined, to remain immersed in Indo-Caribbean culture, with only casual interactions with others. Further, creole practices and institutions could even be used to strengthen and celebrate Indian culture itself. An obvious example is the proliferation of Indo-Trinidadian music competitions, whether involving renditions of filmsongs, tassa drumming, or local-classical music. Moean Mohammed, founder of the island-wide Mastana Bahar competitions, assured me that the institution, which became the largest amateur Indian music network, was originally inspired by and patterned after the creole calypso competitions. With commercial sponsorship now surpassing state support, such competitions, despite their original Afro-creole inspiration, have become dynamic aspects of the Indo-Trinidadian music scene.

A third and related core phenomenon has been the decline of the Bhojpuri language in Trinidad and Guyana, which has obviously constituted a more serious blow to the vitality of various aspects of Indo-Caribbean music culture. Many, if not most, genres of Bhojpuri folk music, like other North Indian counterparts, are essentially text driven, consisting of strophes set to simple repeated melodies. Both in narrative genres like Ālhā and in women's group songs, the aesthetic interest may lie more in the text than in the purely musical parameters, which may be monotonous on their own. Even local-classical music, with its prodigious musical richness, was deeply enjoyed by earlier generations of enthusiasts for its lyric content (as remains the case in Suriname). Hence, there is no doubt that language loss has been a primary factor

undermining the vitality of Ālhā, birha, women's songs, and other genres. For its part, while Trinidadian local-classical music retains much vigor, the inability of audiences to appreciate its poetry has eliminated a significant dimension of its depth and appeal (see Manuel 2000a, 72–74, 88–91).[4]

However, the erosion of linguistic basis need not in itself vitiate a music genre, even in the case of a text-driven one. Many music genres worldwide have, in one form or another, survived such circumstances, and Trinidad itself hosts some notable examples. One is the devotional song repertoire of the Shango or Orisha religion, derived from the practices of Yoruba indentured workers immigrating in the 1850s. Yoruba is no longer a living language in Trinidad, and the songs themselves, with their garbled, archaic, regional-Nigerian dialect, are only partially understood by those who sing them. However, like the Yoruba-derived Santería in Cuba and Candomblé in Brazil, Orisha worship and its music are flourishing, with the appeal of the religion and, it might be said, the beauty and power of the music overcoming the language barrier represented in its song texts. Meanwhile, the same phenomenon is also illustrated by a quite different kind of music, the Christmas-season song genre called parang. Parang consists of Venezuelan-derived Spanish-language songs, sung to the accompaniment of the ukulele-like *cuatro* and other instruments. Like the Puerto Rican *aguinaldo*, it is traditionally sung by roving groups (in Spanish, *parrandas*) of creole revelers who stroll from house to house, singing and partying. Despite the fact that hardly any Trinidadians speak Spanish today, parang, far from declining, is thriving, both in its informal ambulatory context and as performed at public dances, competitions, and other events.

Like parang and Orisha songs, several kinds of Indian music have managed to survive and even flourish in spite of linguistic barriers. First, as mentioned earlier, several Trinidadian and Guyanese enthusiasts do cultivate a certain idiosyncratic familiarity with Hindi, enabling them to understand most songs they sing even if they are unable to converse. I have found that most members of chowtal groups are more or less aware of the general meaning of most lyrics, perhaps as explained by the group leader or a pandit. Indeed, a kind of didacticism has become a typical feature at many Trinidadian and Guyanese functions (as in other South Asian diasporic events), in which, for example, the pandit explains the meaning of the bhajan he is about to lead, or the leader of a hired troupe of female wedding singers provides a spoken introduction, into a microphone, to each song the group sings. Some Trinidadian troupes use locally published anthologies of song texts, in roman, with English translations. Even if most listeners cannot follow the lyrics, they appreciate the songs as dynamic and even familiar components of a proper Hindu wedding.

Further, a genre like chowtal, with its considerable rhythmic and melodic interest, is well able to sustain aesthetic interest by virtue of its formal musical

qualities, aside from its poetic content. In the case of local-classical music, it is safe to say that performers over the past few generations have compensated for the language barrier by cultivating the purely musical aspects of the genre, perhaps especially in the form of virtuoso drum accompaniment. On a broader level, such a process may also promote the popularity of instrumental music in general, such as tassa drumming, which enthusiasts can appreciate as an icon of Indianness without having to confront any language barrier.

If isolation from India, the creole presence, and the decline of Hindi constitute three basic, though not insuperable, challenges to the viability of Indo-Caribbean music, a broader and perhaps ultimately more formidable set of challenges is presented by the general condition of modernity in all its ramifications. The destructive effects of modernity on traditional musics, and especially oral traditions, are familiar and well documented. Mechanization of tasks like grinding dooms the associated work songs. Narrative ballads, with their monotonous tunes and meandering texts, are unable to compete with mass-mediated entertainment genres and the entire aesthetic they promote. Commercial popular musics can undermine the performance and popularity of all manner of traditional folksongs, whose underlying social values may be themselves increasingly incompatible with modern sensibilities.

The impact of modernity on Indo-Caribbean traditional music constitutes, of course, a sprawling topic and is accordingly an underlying theme of this volume. At this point, it will suffice to make a few preliminary observations without dilating on the various phenomena constituting modernity. First, the influence of modernity on Bhojpuri music, far from being a purely diasporic phenomenon, is conspicuous in India itself. While some forms of traditional music have fared reasonably well in the modern era, many have not, and several of my elderly Bhojpuri-region informants lamented the decline of genres like chowtal due to the inexorable and diverse effects of modernity. At the same time, however, the impact of modernity on traditional music need not always be negative. While it may be that the overall effect of the commercial mass media on folk culture may be destructive, the mass media can also serve to disseminate traditional culture and, in some cases, to give it new legitimacy and vitality. Further, modernity can also generate not only affluence but also a heightened sense of ethnic pride, both of which can contribute to a revival of traditional musics, albeit often in rearticulated forms. As has been noted, precisely such a process occurred in Trinidad from the 1970s and has precipitated a lively renaissance of Indo-Trinidadian culture that has in several ways offset the otherwise deleterious effects of modernity on traditional folkways. Such developments, however, are better appreciated through focused studies of individual genres, to which we may now turn.

The Trajectories of Transplants

Singing Ālhā, Birha, and the Ramayan in the Indic Caribbean

Most of the North Indian music heritage brought to the Caribbean consisted of folk styles and genres that were predominantly text-driven, in that their expressive interest lay primarily in lyric content rather than purely musical dimensions. The vitality of such genres in the Caribbean has been gravely undermined by the decline of the Bhojpuri language. And yet, the fate of these music idioms has not been one of uniform decadence, especially in the case of chowtal, the subject of chapter 3. The present chapter discusses three genres of Bhojpuri-region narrative song, exploring how diverse factors—including their presence as written rather than purely oral idioms, and the degree of their nontextual "musicality"—have conditioned their trajectories in the diaspora.

As mentioned in the preceding chapter, the predominantly text-driven nature of Bhojpuri music culture in the Caribbean was a characteristic of Bhojpuri folk music as a whole. Bhojpuri-region vernacular music, both at present and during the indentureship period, has indeed included purely instrumental forms, such as tassa and nagāra drumming, but these have been musics performed by professionals, less rooted in collective amateur music-making than vocal genres. This dominance of text-driven song contrasts, for example, with a music culture like that of West Java, where instrumental music, in the form of gamelan ensembles, has long enjoyed special prominence. In most Bhojpuri folksong, the primary aesthetic interest lies not in purely musical aspects like melody, but in the text, as musically rendered. Hence, for example, the preponderance of melody-specific genres, each of which relies on a simple stock tune to which diverse lyrics are set.[1]

In the Caribbean diaspora a variety of factors conspired against the vitality

of these Bhojpuri folksong genres. New technologies undermined work songs, and caste-specific songs either entered the generalized repertoire or else, like the boatmen's *mallah gīt*, disappeared along with the caste identities that had sustained them. In the tropical latitudes of the Caribbean, the relative absence of distinct winter and summer vitiated seasonal genres like *ghāṭo* and *kajri* (although vernal *phagwa* songs, associated with the still-popular Holi festival, survived vigorously). Commercial popular musics—whether Bollywood hits, chutney, or reggae—have further marginalized folksongs, literally drowning out women's songs at weddings and other events. In Suriname, the sheer smallness of the population and its ongoing dispersal to the Netherlands and elsewhere have weakened traditions that require a certain demographic critical mass for sustenance.

The Decline of Bhojpuri Hindi

In Trinidad and Guyana, by far the gravest challenge to the vitality of Bhojpuri folksong has been the inexorable decline of Bhojpuri as a spoken tongue and its wholesale replacement by English. As mentioned above, in the late nineteenth century, a version of Bhojpuri mixed with Avadhi had become a standardized colloquial koine in Trinidad, Suriname, and British Guiana. The predominance of this lingua franca—which even Madrasi immigrants felt obliged to learn— was reinforced by the insular nature of Indo-Caribbean society, as the first generations of indentureds and their children tended to cluster in ethnically homogeneous villages, avoiding contact with sometimes hostile blacks, arrogant whites, and proselytizing missionary schools.

As in India's pūrab regions, many Indo-Caribbeans for whom Bhojpuri served as a mother tongue, would also acquire some familiarity with related forms of Hindi, especially since Bhojpuri itself lacked the status of a written language. Most of the lyrics in the songbooks circulating in the Indic Caribbean—such as chowtal chapbooks and the *Brahmanand Bhajan Māla* (1901)— were in Braj-bhasha (or simply "Braj"), the Mathura-region dialect that, through its association with Krishna worship, had become a literary lingua franca for poetry in North India. Similarly, many Indo-Caribbeans, like their cousins in the Bhojpuri heartland, would also acquire a certain passive familiarity with medieval literary Avadhi through hearing and, in many cases, singing Tulsidas's *Rāmcharitmānas*. Meanwhile, pandits visiting from India and locals who managed to receive some sort of formal training in Hinduism would use a form of Sanskritized standard Hindi in their dilations on scriptures. From the late 1940s a more colloquial standard Hindi would be promoted by the popularity of Bollywood films and their songs. Collectively, these sources provided for

many a mutually reinforcing set of resources for Hindi competence extending beyond the Bhojpuri dialect itself.

In Suriname, the relatively late commencement of Indian indentureship in 1879, together with the polyglot, multiethnic milieu of Javanese, blacks, whites, and East Indians, generated a situation in which Sarnami—the local Bhojpuri/Avadhi dialect sprinkled with Dutch—has continued to be widely used among the Indian population. Most Indo-Surinamese ("Hindustanis") are also competent in standard Hindi, which is used in broadcast media, imported Bollywood films, and local language schools. However, many young Indo-Surinamese nowadays eschew Sarnami, which they see as a relic of their grandparents' rustic "coolie" culture. (My own fieldwork in Suriname was inevitably conducted in standard Hindi; when an elderly informant with less command of that idiom would lapse into Sarnami, my comprehension would drop precipitously.)

In Trinidad and Guyana, the decline of Bhojpuri was more inexorable, as Indians were increasingly obliged to interact with the English-speaking world of schools, politics, trade, the media, and their creole neighbors. The effective demise of Bhojpuri followed the conventional pattern of a language unsupported by family transmission not extending to the third generation. While many elders were competent in Bhojpuri through the 1950s and 1960s, since that period very few young people have learned the language. Most Indo-Trinidadians and Guyanese of the current generations know only a limited lexicon of miscellaneous terms pertaining to cuisine, religion, Hindu festivities, and kinship. Since the revival of Indian ethnic pride in the 1970s, classes in elementary standard Hindi have come to be offered at various schools (especially those of the Sanatan Dharm Mahasabha), and many people of different generations can cheerfully sing along with Bollywood filmsongs, if only half understanding the lyrics. Similarly, Trinidadians and Guyanese sing Hindi bhajans at temples (perhaps reading from notebooks), where they also listen to pandits expound on verses from the *Rāmcharitmānas* and other texts, explaining Hindi passages and promoting familiarity with religious terms and concepts. Such varied sources of exposure to Hindi dialects can afford interested individuals opportunities to cultivate a certain familiarity with Hindi, even if it falls far short of conversational fluency.

It bears mention that although Hindi/Bhojpuri usage has dwindled, Hinduism remains vigorously resilient in Indo-Caribbean culture. Hindu temples continue to function as community centers, and neighborhood life features a steady stream of public Hindu events, including nine-evening *bhāgvats* and *pūjas*, with bhajan singing and discourses by pandits, and weddings with a full panoply of Hindu prayers, rituals, and women's songs—all of which promote, at the least, a certain passive familiarity with forms of Hindi. It is not difficult

to meet young people who have been inspired to cultivate a deeper knowledge of Hinduism, studying basic Hindi, immersing themselves in the *Mānas*, and perhaps becoming disciples of some local pandit. Several seek to become professional pandits, as practitioners of that trade are widely venerated; on diverse occasions, when I have attended religious functions, I have been impressed by the extent to which people—including the young—not only tolerate but seem to enjoy listening to pandits deliver perorations lasting several hours, far longer than could sustain my own interest.

In my own experience in Trinidad and Guyana, only on a few occasions in the 1990s did I hear some elderly "aunties" conversing in Bhojpuri, and those matrons are probably no longer of this world. However, I did have occasion to meet several elders who had formally studied Hindi as youths. One Trinidadian pandit, Boodram Jattan (b. 1933), related to me how he learned:

> When I was eight years old [in the early 1940s], I'd go to school, and in the evening help my parents, but from about 7:00 to 9:00, there was an old man in the village, and he'd spread a bag, the *pāl*, and he'd teach the village children Hindi, and he never took a cent. And I tell you something more important: he was not a Brahmin or pandit. He was a [low-caste] *sūdra*. He was born in India, and could read and write Hindi, didn't know too much English. Same as in school, you learn the alphabet, the mantras, then start reading the first books. (p.c.)

The decline of Hindi/Bhojpuri comprehension, as mentioned, has gravely eroded the vitality of much of Indo-Caribbean Bhojpuri song, especially since so much of that repertoire is text-driven. However, in chapter 3 I discuss one genre, chowtal, which has thrived in spite of the decline of Hindi; in chapter 4 I show how wedding songs have managed to retain a presence, albeit diminished, in Hindu nuptials. In the present chapter, I examine how three different neotraditional song genres—the Ālhā epic, narrative birha, and antiphonal Ramayan-singing—have fared in their changing linguistic milieus. My research into these genres has been undermined by my having missed their heyday by two or three generations. Nevertheless, my findings may offer some insight into the dynamics of the Indo-Caribbean diaspora, while also providing some basic documentation of these understudied genres even as they exist in India's Bhojpuri region as well.

Birha

In 1886 the erudite folklorist, linguist, and civil servant George Grierson published an article, "Some Bhojpuri Folk-Songs," much of which was devoted to

an unpretentious North Indian rural genre called birha (birhā, birahā).[2] Given the evident popularity of this form in the Bhojpuri region during the heyday of the indentureship period, it is not surprising that it was transplanted to the Caribbean, where it flourished as a vehicle both for traditional lore as well as contemporary expression. Meanwhile, in India birha evolved into an entirely different musical genre after the indentureship period. As with twins separated in childhood and reared in remote milieus, the disparate trajectories of the two genres reflect how sociocultural surroundings—especially those of the Caribbean diaspora—can condition the style, lyric content, and relative vigor of a musical form.

The presumably primordial form of Bhojpuri birha is essentially what Henry characterizes as a field holler, called *khari birhā* ("standing-up birha"), consisting of one or more couplets sung *fortissimo* to a simple "tumbling strain," quintessentially by an Ahir peasant seeking to commune with brethren some distance away (see Henry 1988, 150–53; Henry 2001–02). (Ahirs, who nowadays in India prefer to be called Yādavs, are a traditional cowherding caste, low in rank but proud of their traditional image as virile and martial.) The term *khari birha* can also comprise a somewhat more ample form, in which a solo amateur singer, perhaps aided by one or more accompanists who shout out the final verse words, sings a narrative text of indeterminate length for entertainment at various social events (see, for example, Prasad 1987, 95–96). While Grierson does not use the term *khari birha*, the genre he describes seems to correspond to this narrative form of the genre. Prefacing his presentation of forty-two songtexts, he remarks:

> I cannot say that they possess much literary excellence; on the contrary, some of them are the merest doggerel; but they are valuable as being one of the few trustworthy exponents which we have of the inner thoughts and desires of the people. The Bir'hā is essentially a wild flower. To use the language of one of them, "it is not cultivated in the field, nor is it borne upon the branches of the fruit-tree. It dwells in the heart, and when a man's heart overflows, he sings it." (1886, 210–11)

Lest such a description be misunderstood as to suggest a straightforward sentimentality, it should be noted that the birha texts he presents cohere to the most conventional and even hackneyed themes of North Indian vernacular verse, whether the mythical exploits of Rama or the young woman's stylized pining for her absent husband (voiced, of course, by a male singer and composer). Nevertheless, their colloquial character is manifest in their unpretentious style, their use of rustic Bhojpuri, and their freedom from the clichés of the literary *rīti* verse that dominated Hindi poetry for the past few centuries, with its

standardized similes, its emphasis on rhetoric rather than expression, and its limited subject matter (especially regarding Krishna, the playboy cowherd). As to birha's musical form, Grierson merely relates that it is a typical Bhojpuri folksong genre in having a single stock tune, to which all texts are set. As we shall see, familiarity with the Caribbean transplant enables us to identify this tune.

In the first half of the twentieth century, after the indentureship period, when modernity began to vitiate various folk genres, Indian birha, rather than declining, underwent a dramatic metamorphosis. Under the leadership of a few energetic innovators, birha assumed the form of an extended narrative song accompanied by percussion and, eventually, the ubiquitous harmonium. As performed by professional or semiprofessional singers organized in formal *akhāras* (clubs), it became a vehicle for competitive poetic-musical duels (*dangals*) performed on stages at weddings and other events both in the countryside and in cities like Banaras, while retaining its use of colloquial Bhojpuri. Most strikingly, from the 1940s its melodic resources were exponentially expanded by the practice of omnivorously borrowing tunes from all manner of sources, whether *dhobi gīt* (washermen's songs) or the latest Bollywood hits (see Marcus 1989). The cassette boom of the 1980s afforded birha a medium for wide and unprecedented mass media dissemination (Manuel 1993), which has continued to the present day as cassettes gave way to MP3 discs and VCDs (video compact discs). The birha described by Grierson and sung in the Caribbean represents a sort of intermediate subgenre, more extended than the field holler but shorter, less elaborate, and melodically far more limited than the modern professional birha.

In the Bhojpuri region, short birha fragments—akin to the more musical version of khari birha—may also be sung to accompany Ahir dance (*Ahīrva kā nāch*) or, or more properly, during interludes between dancing. However, more essential in accompanying this genre is the venerable nagāra (*nakāra*, *naqāra*) drum pair, consisting of a large rounded bass kettledrum and a smaller partner, played with a pair of wooden sticks. The nagāra is found throughout North India; in the Bhojpuri region it is also played at temples (especially those dedicated to Devi, the mother goddess), funeral processions, and other events. It is particularly beloved by the Ahirs (and *kurmis*), although they themselves generally do not play it but reserve that task for Chamārs, the untouchable caste traditionally associated with leather working. A typical nagāra ensemble might comprise two nagāra pairs, a large *dafla* frame drum, and a metallophone such as a small gong. Depending on context, the ensemble could play a variety of composite rhythms, generically referred to as *lakrī* (wood), *hāth* (hand), or some other term.

At rural weddings and other festivities, Ahir men may dance energetically, invigorated by the thunderous drumming, by the consumption of spirituous liquors, and, it may be said, by their own self-image as a physically vigorous race. The Ahir dance can include pneumatic pelvic pumping, athletic leaps, and even cartwheels, with some of the movements being associated with particular drum patterns, such as *khari kilaiya*.[3] During breaks in the dancing, someone might informally shout out a short *birha*, typically with one hand cupped over his ear and the other arm raised theatrically.

Birha in the Caribbean

Prior to the emergence of professional narrative birha in India, the many Ahirs (perhaps more than thirty thousand[4]) who immigrated to the Caribbean brought their cherished birha with them. Living in their insular village and plantation communities, and striving to maintain their culture in the unfamiliar surroundings, the Ahirs cultivated birha both as a link to tradition and as a vehicle for merrymaking and original lyric creation. Moreover, just as Bhojpuri became a lingua franca for Indians from various parts of the subcontinent, so did birha extend its popularity beyond the caste boundaries that were, in any case, steadily eroding. As Arya noted in 1968, "The *Ahīrs* seem to have created the Indian *birahā*, which was for long particularly their form of song but has now become the vehicle of creative poetry for all the Hindus of Surinam" (28).

As a musical form, Indo-Caribbean birha is the epitome of simplicity, consisting essentially of a simple stock tune to which verses are set. As Grierson (1886, 212–23; 1884, 199) noted, each pair of lines should ideally follow a prosodic meter of 6+4+4+2, 4+4+3 (or 4), but this convention is perhaps more honored in the breach than in the observance. Elderly singers stressed to me that many different texts could be twisted to fit in the birha form, as long as the rhythm and the setting flowed smoothly. Rupnarayan Gayadeen (b. 1932), one of the few birha "stalwarts" surviving in Trinidad in 2009, told me, "You could take anything and put it in a birha tune, as long as it fits."

A proper birha rendition commences with a *dohā*, or Hindi couplet in a standardized meter, which is sung free-rhythmically, essentially to the same tune as the birha proper. Then, upon the entrance of the drum (ideally a nagāra, but often a dholak, tassa, or, in Suriname, occasionally a dafla frame drum) follows the birha itself, invariably in its simple air, which descends from the fourth degree to the tonic, rising again to the third and then subsiding; subsequent lines center around the tonic, starting with the sixth scalar degree below and continuing indefinitely. Elderly Surinamese vocalist Mangre Siewnarine,

that country's most knowledgeable and respected birha exponent, designated these subsequent lines as *lāchāri*, in a manner evidently corresponding to that suggested by Arya (1968, 30), who, however, did not provide any transcriptions. Example 1 illustrates this form, which is standard—indeed, strikingly so—among Indian exponents throughout Suriname, Guyana, and Trinidad.

Indo-Caribbean birha is ideally accompanied by the nagāra drum pair, which, as mentioned, is traditionally associated, like birha itself, with Ahirs. A Surinamese informant (Ramdeo Rughoebir) related to me that until recent decades, nagāras were common in Ahir homes and were indispensable at festive functions. While accompanying birha singing, the nagāra typically plays a pattern like // x-xxx-x-/x-xxx-x- ://; between verses it plays more varied patterns. In some situations, as in a solo that might precede the singing, a knowledgeable nagāra drummer may play in a distinctively capricious manner, flitting from one tempo and pattern to another. During these breaks, the singer, or one or more men, could dance in the athletic "bare-back" *Ahirvā kā nāch* style, ideally wearing the characteristic three-quarters pants and a sash the dancer might twirl in one hand.

Indo-Trinidadian music savant Narsaloo Ramaya described birha in its heyday:

> On such a night large crowds of people from the village would gather to witness the entertainment. The Ahir dance seemed to have been the most popular. This style of dance was forceful and virile with well-coordinated steps and movements. The participants were only men and the combination of drummers, singers and dancers, presented a fascinating scene in which the dancers with naked backs and willows on their feet made rhythmical movements of the body to the beating of the Nagāra drums while the singer, with fingers in his ears sang his Biraha songs with great gusto, the total effect of the performance giving much pleasure to the spectators. The Ahir dance has always been one of the main attractions on wedding nights and its performance survived until quite recently. (1965, in Myers 1998, 119)

On other occasions, birha could serve as a vehicle for two individuals, perhaps with assistants, to engage in a lyric duel, typically testing each other's knowledge of Krishnaite (*Krishna-autāric*) or Ramayan (*Ram-autāric*) mythology, as related by Arya in reference to Suriname:

> [Birha] is a topical song, sung by both sexes, like the calypso of Trinidad. It may be composed instantaneously by any person on any subject. It may break all bounds of propriety and social rules. It may protest against any practice, custom or person, or may praise these. The author has heard long *birahās*, composed on the spot to celebrate an occasion, for example, the presence

Example 1. Indo-Caribbean birha tune.

of an honoured guest. . . . It may be sung on a *dholak* or without any instrument at all. There are, now fewer and fewer, all-night competitions of *birahā* composition and singing in which two parties may compete with questions and answers . . . or discussions on any topic, in a challenging manner . . . until one party accepts defeat. . . . The fame of a good *birahā* singer travels far and wide. (1968, 29)

Trinidadian folk singer Sagar Sookhraj also recalled such events:

Yes, birha is simple, but sometimes the two people clash, without stopping, and if they singing on Rām-autaric you have to stay on that til you finish up and then you know who has won, like if you ask me a question and I can't remember. They makin' up the wordin's. And if you the winner, then you can change to Krishna-autaric or whatever. (p.c.)

Boodram Jattan also recalled birha in its midcentury heyday:

In a wedding, on Sunday, after the tassa groups had their jassle [duel], the birha will start, the dulhan's side competing with the girl's side. Is anyone can sing, not professionals. Question and answer, and you have to know Hindi, you have to respond, and if you can't, you lose. And everyone knew Hindi. But it was all in good humor, though the competition would be fierce. Also in every village, on farewell night they'd play the nagāra and sing birha. The elders knew it, my father and all, they were great singers. (p.c.)

Indo-Caribbean Birha and Its South Asian Counterpart

A comparison and contrast between birha as it has evolved in India and the Caribbean can afford insights into both incarnations, as well as into the dynamics that have conditioned the genre's course in the Americas. The most obvious difference, of course, is that Indo-Caribbean birha bears no structural

resemblance whatsoever to modern Bhojpuri birha, with its precomposed narratives set to medleys of miscellaneous film and folk tunes sung in night-long
stage performances by professional troupes. In effect, Bhojpuri-region birha,
as a popular secular song form not limited by association with any season,
sect, or ritual, became a suitable vehicle for elaboration by professionals, with
both its narrative and melodic content exponentially expanded. In Bhojpuri-
speaking Suriname (and Fiji), insofar as conditions favored the cultivation of
a narrative topical song form, the more suitable genre for such purposes was
qawwāli, which was never constrained by being associated with a particular
stock tune. By contrast, Caribbean birha, while remaining a vehicle for amateur
versification, never abandoned its traditional stock tune. It thus remained, in
Grierson's terms, a "wild flower," unlike the hybrid rose that has been cultivated by Bhojpuri-region singers since the 1940s; in that sense, and especially
in its reliance on a sole traditional stock tune, it constitutes a striking example
of a marginal survival.

The fact that the same stock tune is used with only minimal variation[5]
throughout the three Caribbean countries strongly suggests that this was the
standard tune used in the Bhojpuri region during the indentureship period, and
it is precisely the fixed tune mentioned, but not notated, by Grierson in 1886.

In 2009 I interviewed a few elderly folk music performers in Banaras, the
stronghold of modern professional birha. One informant, upon hearing my sung
version of "Ramaji ki bagiya," opined that it was a tune more characteristic
of *lāchāri*, a term that designates a variety of genres, but most typically in the
Banaras region denotes a women's folksong genre. His statement was of interest
insofar as it cohered with Surinamese usage of that term to denote the melody
used in birha verses. Laxmi Prasad Yadav, a retired birha singer with a keen
interest in birha history and other genres, offered more specific perspectives
on the Caribbean tune, which I sang for him. First, he plausibly noted that it
roughly corresponds to the archaic birha melody called *jorni*: "First came the
original birha tune [presumably, the khari birha field holler]; then came jorni;
what you sang is jorni." He then sang some examples of jorni, which were
similar to (though not identical with) the Caribbean melody. He went on to
demonstrate how the same tune can be found in other genres, including renderings of Tulsidas's Ramayan.[6]

In fact, the "standard" tune of Caribbean birha, in slight variants, is not uncommon in the Bhojpuri region. Although the modern professional birha has
adopted other melodies, what may be regarded as old-fashioned birha renditions still employ versions of it, perhaps sung responsorially.[7] The tune is also
nearly identical to a standard Bhojpuri *dhobi gīt* melody (which is also often
sung responsorially, with the chorus sustaining the final tonic note of a line);

the melody also forms the basis of the *āchāri* (or, perhaps, *lāchāri?*) recorded by Laxmi Tewari in Uttar Pradesh,[8] and it appears, with variants, in genres like the *phaguā* documented by Henry (1988, 298–99). In general, it is clear that the melody has been common in Bhojpuri folksong and was the stock tune for birha during the indentureship period. Certainly there is no reason to believe that the Caribbean birha tune originated in that region; Siewnarine, for example, assured me that the same birha tune was sung by his father, an Ahir who emigrated from Bihar.

Grierson does not mention the use of birha in formal competitive duels, and some evidence suggests that it was not until the early twentieth century that such events (called *dangal* or *muqābila*) became popular in North India. Such was the case with birha, chowtal (see chapter 3), Mirzapuri *kajri* (*kajli*), and Hathrasi (Braj-region) *rasiya*, all of which came to be sung in competitive formats by semiprofessional teams called *akhāras* (see Marcus 1989, Manuel 1993, 207–12). In the Caribbean, the terms *akhāra*, *dangal*, and *muqābila* did not enter popular usage, but the duel format became common in birha and Surinamese qawwāli (see Manuel 2000a, 47), suggesting that it was in fact present in India prior to the end of indentured emigration in 1917. The diverse subgenres of Indian birha described by Prasad (1987, 94–109) and Hiralal Tiwari (1980, 142–50) are found neither in Grierson's account nor in the Caribbean, suggesting that they developed in India only after the indentureship period.[9]

While as we have seen, Ahirs in India dance to the nagāra but do not play it, in the Caribbean context this caste distinction evaporated, presumably in accordance with both demographic necessity and the general relaxation of caste boundaries. Hence, in the 1960s in Suriname Arya found nagāra masters who were Ahirs (1968, 9),[10] and by the 1970s most Indo-Caribbeans had ceased to identify with any particular caste. As Trinidad's Rupnarine Gayadeen (b. 1932), an Ahir, told me when I asked about his caste's identification with birha, "Plenty Brahmin sing birha."

Birha as Vox Populi

Both Grierson and Arya, writing of India and Suriname, respectively, emphasized how birha served as a vehicle for a wide variety of lyric themes, ranging from the pious to the prurient, from traditional to contemporaneous, and from the precomposed to the spontaneously improvised (see also Henry 1988, 150–54). The most popular single category in Caribbean birha has consisted of *Rām-autaric* verses, narrating events and scenes from the exploits of Ram, especially as derived from the *Mānas*. One of these texts (as presented in example 1) is the most popular text throughout the Caribbean:

Doha: *Rām nām ki dor meṅ baṅdhe raho din rain*
    Kripa kareṅ Sri Ram ji sadā karoge chain
Birha: *Rama-ji ki bagiya Sita ke phulavāri*
    Lachimana devara baitha rakhavāri
    Chori chori nebulā pathāveṅ sasurāri
    Ohi nebulā ke banāveṅ tarakari
    Jeṅvan baithe Kuṅjbihāri bhajale man Sitārām

Doha: Remain attached to the name of Ram day and night
    With Ram's mercy you will always be at peace.
Birha: In the garden of Ram and the flower garden of Sita
    Her *devar* [husband's younger brother] Lakshman is keeping watch
    He steals lemons and sends them to his in-laws' home
    A curry is made from the same lemons
    Krishna sat to enjoy that meal; O mind, recite 'Sitaram.'
    (adapted from Tewari 1994, 71)

The popularity of this text is remarkable, and curious. Aside from Tewari's 1994 citation, a slight variant of it is also presented in Arya (1968, 146), and I have encountered it on several occasions from different Surinamese, Guyanese, and Trinidadian singers (including Suriname's erudite Mangre Siewnarine, who identified it as the most popular text he knew). Indeed, it constitutes a sort of default lyric, employed to accompany Ahir dance, or constituting the only text that an aficionado might know. Remarkably, it is also one of the few birha texts presented in Hiralal Tiwari's study of Bhojpuri-region folk music in India, attesting to its contemporary popularity there as well (1980, 149)—in addition to its evident popularity during the indentureship period.[11] The ubiquity of this bit of doggerel is enigmatic, as there is nothing particularly extraordinary, memorable, or excellent about it. (Its jumbled insertion of Krishna into Ram's story is not atypical of folk versification.) It is difficult to imagine what circumstance may have accounted for its ubiquity; in general, its appeal may serve to remind us that the travels of cultural entities may sometimes have their own inscrutable logic, which may confound the scholar's attempts at explanation.

Arya provides a few other examples of Surinamese birhas on traditional topics, including portrayals of a young bride fearing leaving her parents' home for her husband's house, and a woman praying to Kali for her elderly husband's death. One text he cites—in which a woman relates how she reported her husband's gambling to the police in Gorakhpur, India—illustrates how verse written about a specific situation may take on its own life and travel afar (Arya 1968, 29–31, 140–58).

While many birhas adhere to traditional stock themes, and others describe incidents that occurred in the ancestral homeland, the convention of singing

birhas about contemporary life inspired much verse dealing with the quotidian reality of life in the Caribbean. Arya (1968, 30–31) portrays Surinamese birhas as documenting a series of attitudinal stages toward the new homeland:

> In the earlier period the singers were more concerned with their migration, for example, song 97A gives caste oppression as the reason for it. Then came the question of whether or not to return to India. . . . Later the singers were concerned with the need for social reform both in India and, inspired by its success there, in Suriname, together with the Indian struggle for independence. . . . But slowly *Bhārat*, that is India, was replaced by Surinam and the singers sang of the problems of the Surinam Indian community. . . . The conflict of loyalties divided between India and Surinam has been resolved by the modern singer by paying homage to the Indian deities in religious terms and to the land of Surinam in patriotic terms . . ., and by adapting Hindu ideas to a Surinam geo-political context, for example "*mukti* (spiritual salvation) by bathing in Cola Creek."

Arya (1968, 157) cites a typical birha that hyperbolically praises the size and grandeur of Surinamese towns and the Marienburg estate, which was the only one to persist until the 1960s. Mangre Siewnarine, a first-generation immigrant, also sang for me a birha he composed about the travails of hacking brush on the swamps of the same estate, with caimans snorting angrily nearby. Ramdeen Chotoo (1917–2006), a revered exponent of Indo-Trinidadian chowtal and other folk genres, recorded a similar birha about clearing land for the train being built by the "firangiyas" (Hindustani for "Europeans"—in other words, the British).[12]

Other birhas comment sardonically on the decline of Hindu traditions, perpetuating a tradition dating back at least to Kabir's sixteenth-century laments about the "topsy-turvy" world of his time. The prolific Siewnarine sang a few such birhas for me:

Dekho sir se odhani le utār
Aur lahanga pahire gher ke koto misi ho
Okar edia na karkar ghisarāye
Aur hamāro sirimati devi ji ke deb
Okar theu na theu par dekhe
Main kyā karu . . .

See how they remove their headscarfs
While the [black] "missies" wear skirts down to the floor,
So that you can't even see their ankles
See how our own "srimati devis" [Indian women]
Wear skirts above their knees
What can I do? . . .

In a similar vein is the following, also by Siewnarine:

Are pītā ke nām suno Dharam Singh bābu
Aur māta ke Dharam Dei hai nām
Aur putra ke nām suno "Honey Johnny Wimpy"
Aur putri ke Maricha Luisa nām
Dharāvat bate putri ke Maricha Luisa nām

Aur bara umang hai aur tarang se bābu
Dekho rādio me yau dele badhāi
Jai ke bhai rādio men yau dele badhāi
Aur sunne wāle mitrajan sunāte
Hañsat hai thathāi aur thathāi
Aur jab tak bāte heni joni milti ke badhāi

The father's name is Dharam Singh Babu
And the mother is Dharam Dei
Listen brother, mother's name is Dharam Dei
And the son's name is "Honey Johnny Wimpy" [?]
And the daughter is Maricha Luisa
With much pleasure they are sending their good wishes on the radio
And their friends are listening and laughing
On hearing the greeting sent by "Honey Johnny Wimpy"[13]

Other birhas comment with satisfaction on the diasporic experience and Indian achievement therein, as in this songtext composed and recorded by Sadho Boodram Ramgoolam, one of the few professional birha singers still active in Trinidad in 2009[14]:

Aja āji tāta tāti Bhārat desh se āi hai
kāli pāni pār karke Trinidad men āi hai
Trinidād men āke dekho kārik bharke [?] basāya hai
mehnat karke āji āja larke ko padhāya hai
koi teacher-lawyer koi business chalāya hai
koi doctor judge koi magistrate banāya hai

My parents and grandparents crossed the *kāla pāni* (black waters)
To come from India to Trinidad
They settled in Trinidad, worked hard, and educated their children
Some have become teachers, lawyers, and businessmen . . .

In formal contexts, the opening birha fragment would consist of an introductory invocation called a *sumiran* (such as also commences sessions of chowtal and Ramayan singing.)

Caribbean Birha in the New Millennium

Birha continued to enjoy considerable vigor in the Indic Caribbean through the 1960s, sustained by a critical mass of Bhojpuri speakers and its own resilience as a simple but catchy musical vehicle for traditional and newly composed verse. Since that period, however, its attenuation has been severe, although reports of its complete demise (see, for example, Myers 1998, 413) have been premature. In Suriname, the persistence of Bhojpuri as a spoken language has served to sustain birha in a limited capacity, such that it can be occasionally encountered in weddings, temples, and stage shows[15]; Sarnami poet Amarsingh Raman has also penned several literary verses in that idiom (some of which he sang for me in a 1990s meeting). However, the Surinamese birha tradition has been crippled by the dispersal of musicians and the general lack of a local Indian cultural revival such as has enlivened the Indo-Trinidadian scene. Even Arya, writing of the 1960s, noted the rarity of once-common all-night birha sessions (1968, 29). In Guyana, the problems found in Suriname have been compounded by the decline of Bhojpuri, the emigration of half the population, and a generally dismal economic and cultural milieu; however, the odd birha fragment might occasionally be intoned on various occasions, whether in Guyana or in the secondary Guyanese diaspora in New York or elsewhere.

In Trinidad, as in Guyana, Bhojpuri has ceased to be a living language, but the general vigor of the local Indian cultural scene has sustained a certain afterlife for birha, in diverse contexts. By the 1990s Ahir dance no longer flourished as an amateur pastime, but a handful of troupes have continued to perform it, with birha and nagāra or dholak accompaniment, as invited entertainment at weddings and other events.

Elder birha vocalist Ramlal Jaggernath told me in 2008: "Occasionally we do perform. I have three dancers, and I sing, and for two hours we takin' $1200 TT [about US$200]. At weddings, prayers, anything you want it for. Ahirwa ka nāch is the dance; we call it naked-back dance. People like the way birha goes, even if they don't understand the wordin.'"

In 2000 and beyond, Sadho Boodram Ramgoolam, another elderly Trinidadian performer, was still leading a troupe that incorporated birha, Ahir dance, and comedy into a "Sarvan Kumar" show, based on an episode from the Tulsi Ramayan. This obscure theatrical tradition, also formerly perpetuated in Guyana, is presumably of Old World Indian derivation, though in my finite experience I have not encountered it in the Bhojpuri region.[16]

Rupnarine Gayadeen (b. 1932), whose father came on the last ship from India to Trinidad in 1917, also performed in a birha and Ahir dance group, as

he related to me in 2008: "Our group was the Aranguez Agriculture Chowtal and Nagāra Group. And we sang Ramayan too. We were the only group of that kind, that did everything, but there were twenty-four of us and twenty-two have died. My father was mostly a dancer but he knew plenty birha and could play nagāra." The elderly Gayadeen, raised in a Bhojpuri-speaking home, expressed little respect for the handful of younger birha singers on the scene. "You have fellas singing for years and they can't do the timing right even if they know a hundred birhas. They can't put the tune in it. There are some people who still do birha and dance, they charge two to three thousand TT, but they're no good, nothing for nothing. They call them for a wedding, birthday, Ramayan, and so on. But they can't sing, and the dancers don't know the music." Despite such disparagement, I was impressed to occasionally encounter younger amateur and semiprofessional singers who included a few birhas in their repertoire, whether or not they might satisfy the standards of a veteran like Gayadeen. One such vocalist, Rawatie Ali, who leads a women's troupe that sings traditional songs at Trinidadian weddings and other events, told me:

> Yes, I do some birha, I have a few in my head. At a wedding, after we do the folksinging, while the haldi [application of turmeric to the bride's hands] goin' on, for entertainment I might sing it. You'd laugh, but I sang it at a wake on Sunday night. This lady died, and she had taught me a lot of songs, so after the bhajan and thing, I sang it and said now we gonna get up and dance a little bit, because when she was teaching us she used to get up and dance. Something was inside me to please her, that she was not around but her soul was around, to hear.

Semiprofessional singers like Rawatie Ali may have memorized a few birhas, but more typically, they have a notebook in which they have written a few that they have acquired from one source or another.

Birha has also been perpetuated, in diverse forms, by Ajeet Praimsingh, who has been Trinidad's most energetic and inventive patron of Indo-Trinidadian neotraditional music and culture. Praimsingh owns a store in Chaguanas, one half of which—the profitable half, he tells me—is devoted to miscellaneous Indian goods; the other half proffers musical paraphernalia, including Indian and local CDs, song books, and other items. His store serves as a meeting place for the island's Indian musicians. Through his organization "Mera Desh" (Our Country), he has with remarkable entrepreneurial energy organized a steady stream of stage shows and competitions promoting all manner of traditional Indian cultural practices, from tassa to the making of local culinary staples of "doubles" and roti. He has also produced several recordings, whether of relatively remunerative genres like chutney or of traditional styles with less com-

mercial viability. Aware of the need to preserve, or possibly even revive, the formerly vigorous arts of birha and Ahir dance, in 1991 he staged a competition for these genres; almost all of those participants have since passed away. He has also showcased these arts in other cultural festivities and released a few CDs of local birha performers singing in both traditional and modernized styles. Prominent among the latter are items—including the warhorse "Ramaji ki bagiya"—sung by veteran local-classical vocalist Sam Boodram[17] and younger singer Rasika Dindial, enlivened by soca-style accompaniment. These enjoyed some ephemeral popularity around 2004, with birha serving in this case essentially as a simple, catchy melody suitable for soca/chutney-style dance. In Suriname, versatile singer Kries Ramkhelawan recorded a similar soca-style rendition of the "Ramaji ki bagiya" chestnut.[18] Meanwhile, if knowledgeable nagāra players no longer exist in Trinidad, the "nagāra" hand—based on birha accompaniment patterns—has become one of the three or four most popular and familiar tassa rhythms, especially for accompanying dancing at weddings and other festivities.

Thus, even if birha's heyday passed a century ago and its linguistic basis is thoroughly eroded, in Trinidad, and to a lesser extent elsewhere, the genre continues to survive, albeit in a reduced and transformed capacity. No longer does it serve as a vehicle for erudite lyric duels or for versified commentary on quotidian experience. Rather, insofar as it survives, it has been demoted to the status of a nursery-rhyme-like ditty, which is at once catchy and redolent of a certain venerable rusticity, and with a largely unintelligible text. Instead of being a featured item, it functions more typically as an accompaniment to dance (whether by a stage performer or "wining" revelers). Further, it has gone from being a quintessentially oral idiom to one preserved, for singers' purposes, in handwritten notebooks.

Tulsidas Travels to the Tropics:
Singing the Ramayan in the Caribbean

Around 1580 c.e. a Brahmin poet named Tulsidas, evidently residing in Banaras, completed a lengthy reworking of the Ramayan, the tale of Rama. A shorter partner to India's other great epic, the Mahabharata, the Ramayan narrates the travails of the righteous prince Rama (colloquially, Ram), who, unjustly exiled to the forest, was obliged to wage war against the demon-king Ravan, who had abducted Ram's wife, Sita. Upon eventually killing Ravan, Ram returned to his rightful throne in Ayodhya (and banished Sita to the forest). The story of Ram had circulated in various forms in the subcontinent for centuries, with its canonic written recension being the Sanskrit version attributed to the

sage Valmiki. What was unprecedented about Tulsidas's version, aside from its literary merit, was that it was penned not in Sanskrit, but in a regional ver-nacular—literary Avadhi, the idiom spoken to the west of the Bhojpuri area.

Tulsidas's epic—called the *Rāmcharitmānas*, or more concisely, the *Mānas*—came to permeate Hindu culture in the Avadhi- and Bhojpuri-speaking regions in the subsequent centuries. The epic could in some ways be seen, like Greek or Norse myths, or like the Mahabharat, as an essentially secular tale, with the gods comprising enlarged human beings. However, as theistic worship of Ram spread and intensified during the period of Muslim rule, the *Mānas*, in addi-tion to constituting an action-packed epic, came to serve as a core devotional text and a sort of regional Bible, celebrated as a source for moral and spiritual guidance.[19] If a work such as Homer's *Odyssey* was a written version of a fun-damentally oral-tradition narrative, the *Mānas*, by contrast, is an essentially literary work, penned by a poet well versed in the (primarily Sanskrit) poetic and religious literature of India. At the same time, the *Mānas* soon came to be widely—and perhaps even primarily—disseminated via various forms of oral tradition; these latter have included *Rāmlīla* theater, *kathā* (discourses by specialists), and diverse forms of rendering as song.[20] Written in rhymed and metered verse (primarily *dohā* and *chaupāī* couplets, totaling 12,800 lines), the *Mānas* lends itself well to being chanted or sung, and accordingly, various styles of musical rendering emerged in the Bhojpuri region and elsewhere. The spread of printed versions of the *Mānas* from the mid-1800s further promoted amateur singing of the text.

Philip Lutgendorf's study *The Life of a Text* (1991) provides a thorough and insightful ethnography of *Mānas* performance traditions in Banaras, includ-ing *Rāmlīla* theater, *Mānas-kathā*, and a few of the prominent chant and song forms. Some of these styles took root in the Caribbean, where popular fondness for the *Mānas* has continued unabated since the indentureship period. In my own fieldwork I have had occasion to meet several individuals with an ency-clopedic knowledge of the *Mānas*, which they regard as a fount of wisdom, entertainment, and ethical precepts, aside from providing a connection to Indian tradition. Contemporary sources attest to the popularity of the Ramayan in the Caribbean by the 1880s,[21] and the tale of Ram's exile may have had particular poignancy for the early generations of indentureds, in their own state of self-exile from India, including, in the case of many immigrants, from Ayodhya itself. In Trinidad, the economic boom dating from the 1970s has promoted a prodigious revitalization of Hinduism, much of whose activity has been centered around the Ramayan (see Vertovec 1992, chapter 4). Particularly noteworthy are the nine-day events called *yagna* (*yajna*, *yaj*, *jag*), and the one-day *Ramayan puja* (or *kathā*), both of which feature discourses and rituals by a hired pandit,

communal meals, and songs—whether devotional bhajans or renderings of the *Mānas*—by invited neighborhood ensembles, local-classical singers, or the pandit himself. Families expend considerable resources and energy hosting such events, which are attended by neighbors and friends who enjoy the collective socializing and eating, and to various degrees, the singing and the pandit's leisurely speechifying. Bhajans based on Ramayan themes, preceded by a pandit's discourse, may also be sung in temples at weekly *satsangs*, which often acquire the character of neighborhood amateur music soirees. Most of the songs at these events are in a somewhat generic North Indian mainstream bhajan style, with simple, familiar tunes accompanied by the standard format of harmonium, dholak, and dantāl. Stylistically, they can be said to derive from contemporary North Indian models, as disseminated via cassettes from the 1980s and via conventions introduced by pandits who have visited North India, as well as the visits to the Caribbean of subcontinental pandits, godmen, and bhajan-singers. On the whole, such bhajans and Ramayan styles cohere more to a quasi-pop mainstream North Indian style than to any distinctively Bhojpuri-region counterpart.

The Bhojpuri region, however, was the direct source for some of the forms of rendering the *Mānas*. Of particular interest, in terms of relating Caribbean genres to Bhojpuri counterparts, is a format called "jhāl Ramayan" in Trinidad and "Ramayan bānī" in Guyana. This subgenre derives directly from a format popular in the Banaras area (and presumably elsewhere in the Bhojpuri region), insightfully described (albeit without musical analysis or notation) by Lutgendorf (1991, 97–110). The genre in question has no particular name, such that he aptly refers to it simply as "*Mānas* singing," a practice I shall follow in these pages. *Mānas* singing is an antiphonal style, involving either two singers, or, more typically, two sets of singers, who may repeat a given line several times before moving to the next. (A third format, which I witnessed in the Banaras region, is responsorial—in other words, involving a skilled leader and a chorus, which may only approximate the flourishes sung by the leader.) Lutgendorf estimated that there may be at least a hundred such groups in Banaras alone. Like the Banaras *kirtan-mandali* clubs studied by Slawek (1986), the groups typically pride themselves on being democratic (at least while singing), in that participants are welcomed regardless of caste. Aside from being devout Hindus, they also tend to hail from the less Westernized and secularized social strata, who seek entertainment in personal participation in localized groups rather than in Bollywood cinema (Lutgendorf 1991, 103). Typically, they might meet one evening every week, taking great pleasure in the vigorous collective singing, the devotional fervor, and the atmosphere of camaraderie and shared enthusiasm.

Lutgendorf highlighted two distinctive features of this form of *Mānas* sing-ing. One involves the rhythmic modulations, in the "progression from medi-tative opening to frenzied climax, lapsing back into quiescence" (89). As he noted, this sequence is typical of other local folksong styles; it is especially similar to that of chowtal, which is discussed in chapter 3. The other and more conspicuous feature of *Mānas* singing is the practice of weaving a nonscriptural refrain into the *Mānas* verses. Lutgendorf described this practice:

> With the completion of the couplet [the opening *dohā*], drum [dholak] and cymbals came in and accompanied the singing of succeeding *caupāis*, which gradually increased in tempo. An individual line might be sung only once in fairly straightforward fashion, with its two halves divided between the two singers, or it might be elaborated on, with certain words or phrases repeated or combined with phrases not found in the written text. These might be rela-tively simple, such as the exclamation "He Rāmā!" added at the end of each line. More often, however, they would consist of full lines of an entirely independent Kajli [rainy-season folksong] song interwoven with the lines of the stanza and including a periodic refrain. The ever-increasing pace and emotional intensity climaxed in the final lines of the stanza—terminating in a sudden silence broken by sighs and exclamation of delight. (1991, 106–7)

Lutgendorf proceeded to show how the extraneous text—in this case, from a rainy-season folksong genre called *kajli*—is interspersed with *Mānas* verses. On other occasions, the nonscriptural verses might come from other folksongs, their text ideally relating at least tangentially to the *Mānas* passage being sung.

This form of *Mānas* singing, brought by the indentured immigrants, flour-ished in the tightly knit Indo-Caribbean communities, sustained by the persis-tent fondness for the *Mānas* and for communal singing, and by the desire to maintain tradition in spite of isolation from India. In accordance with its lack of a specific name in India, the genre acquired different designations in the New World; Trinidadians came to call it "jhāl Ramayan," after the small cymbals played by the singers,[22] while Guyanese labeled it "Ramayan bānī"—"bānī" being the term for the inserted verse fragment. Whatever its designation, its musical form and social practice are essentially the same as those witnessed by Lutgendorf in Banaras in the 1980s, with a few minor differences. Veterans like Boodram Jattan related to me that in their childhood, groups in which they sang included elders raised in India, who sang in the same style. It is also safe to assume that most of the melodies used also derive from Bhojpuri tradition, especially since innovation is not prized for its own sake in the genre. One common Trinidadian tune is roughly identical to the *līlā vānī*, the single most common tune in Banaras *Mānas* singing.[23]

The typical Caribbean *Mānas*-singing group is called a Ramayan *gol* or Ramayan *mandali* (both meaning group, party, circle). The participants are often associated with a Hindu temple (of the Sanatanist mainstream, as opposed to Kali worship or Arya Samaj), though they might meet either at the temple or at an individual's house. An active group might convene regularly on a weekday evening, and also perform at various other occasions. The session might to some extent have the character of a rehearsal or practice, although participants should generally both enjoy the singing as well as feel that they are perfecting their rendition. In such quasi-practice sessions, the group might work its way slowly through two or three pages of the *Mānas,* resuming the next session where they had left off, and perhaps completing the entire work over the course of several months. At other occasions, the group would sing a passage appropriate to the event in question. Thus, a group might be invited to sing at a Ramayan *satsang, kathā,* or *yajna,* in which the pandit, after dilating on some *Mānas* passage, would invite the music group—a bhajan ensemble, a local-classical group, or a Ramayan gol—to sing an appropriate song, dealing with the same passage. (Knowledgeable local-classical singers disparage how incompetent youngsters with small repertoires and poor command of Hindi often sing songs unrelated to or even thematically incongruent with the *kathā* being discussed.) A group might also be invited to a private home to commemorate some family or religious event. As discussed below, formal competitions were also formerly a lively part of the Trinidadian scene.

A *Mānas*-singing ensemble consists of two rows of at least four singers each (who also play jhāl), and a dholak player. Trinidadian and Bhojpuri-region groups freely add a harmonium, but the Guyanese prefer an austere traditional format with no melodic instruments. In both India and the Caribbean many temples nowadays have simple amplification systems with a few microphones, which might on occasion be deployed, but usually the sound of the raised voices, jhāls, and dholak is ample, if not deafening, such that amplification is superfluous. At a satsang I attended in Suchit Trace, south Trinidad, the session commenced with a solo lead vocalist (with microphone) and a responding chorus; later, another singer joined the leader, such that the format became properly antiphonal rather than responsorial; in any case, as with Lutgendorf's descriptions of Banaras groups, the style is the same.

In subsequent pages I describe a typical song session, including its musical form, in some detail; at this point a brief description may suffice. At a gol meeting, the participants sit facing each other in two lines, with the dholak player at one end. They usually commence with an invocatory *ārtī* prayer, chanted antiphonally. Then, with their copies of the *Mānas* in front of them, they locate

the appropriate passage, as instructed by the group "captain." That person, or another singer, commences with a two- or three-line bānī, which may or may not be familiar to the other singers. The group, after hearing the bānī a few times and perhaps recognizing it, then joins in, playing their handheld jhāls and being accompanied by the dholak player. After the bānī is repeated several times, the *Mānas* verse is finally intoned, in the same primary tune and rhythm that have been established. The group proceeds through the stanza, with a conventional set of repetitions and bānī reiterations. Generally, near the end of the penultimate couplet, the meter shifts—in the case of *chaupāīs*, from medium-tempo seven-beat pattern to a faster quadratic meter (which some drummers might call "chaubola," I term I shall henceforth use). From this point, the singing and drumming intensify dramatically, enlivened by excited shouts as the group races through text lines, trying to render the verses in proper rhythm; then the end is abruptly reached with a shouted cadential tag.

As in Banaras, participants sing with great zest and relish, especially when the singing goes well. While an unambitious group might satisfy itself with merely getting through the *Mānas* passage, most groups strive for a cleaner rendition and for the pleasure that it affords. There are several factors that make for collectively skilled singing. Ideally, the participants have strong voices and can sing in tune, while playing the jhāls in time. A talented drummer can add a great deal of excitement and vigor. If singers must be looking down at the text in front of them, they will be unable to project their voices; hence the best singers are able to recall a verse merely by glancing at it, and can sing with their heads up, facing each other. The true "stalwarts" have memorized practically the entire *Mānas*. Meanwhile, the group must be able to negotiate the rhythmic and textual transitions smoothly, instantly following the leader's cues even at fast tempos. Hindi pronunciation must be uniformly correct and must follow conventions of oral-tradition articulation that may differ from the printed version. Some of these variations are familiar and standard, such as the rendering of "*brahmā*" as "*bramhā*," and "*mo so*" as "*mo se*," and the separation of consonant clusters (*dharm* and *Lakshman* becoming *dharam* and *Lachiman*, respectively, as is typical of colloquial speech). Other alterations are more recondite and might vary regionally. What is perhaps most important is the proper setting of the verse to the rhythm of the melody, a task that is particularly challenging for the row of vocalists that sings a verse for the first time. Essentially, they must be able to glance at the line and instantaneously sense exactly how it is to be set. Especially at fast tempo, there is a clear difference between a ragged and disjointed group rendering of a line, and one that is crisp and tight; for singers, when done properly the effect is a bit like a group collectively steering a bus at high speed through sharp turns and corners.

In general, it might be said that there are two distinct approaches to *Mānas* singing, with groups or sessions occupying points on a continuum between these antipodes. In many cases, a group may sing for the simple pleasures of making music collectively, of perpetuating a hoary (and in some cases family-based or neighborhood) tradition, and of expressing religious devotion. The singing in such groups may be cheerfully ragged, with jumbled renditions of phrases and a parallel-organum effect created by melodically challenged singers chanting a given contour at different pitch levels. Meanwhile, other groups, while sharing these motivations, may also take a special pleasure in trying to hone their singing so that it sounds clean and skillful, with tight and synchronized text renderings and modulations. In the process, a competitive spirit may emerge, providing a new dimension of zest for singers and arguably reinforcing its primarily secular rather than devotional nature.

Elderly informants describe how *Mānas*-singing flourished vigorously in Trinidad and British Guiana until around the 1960s.[24] Tej Singh (b. ca. 1920), a venerable expert on Ramayan and chowtal singing, talked of his early years in Guyana, before mass media had become commonplace in the countryside: "I was taught by an India man how to read Hindi. Then I became leader of a Ramayan group in 1959. Back then we learned the Ramayan from the book and put it in the head [in other words, memorized the verses]. There were two, three, four groups in every village, and every two hundred yards there's a village." As Singh and other Guyanese informants related, while there were no formal competitions in their homeland, there was a strong but friendly spirit of rivalry between groups. British Guiana in this period was a stronghold of *Mānas*-singing and chowtal (and of the regional variety of local-classical singing). Meanwhile, however, Trinidad's lively cultural ambience seems to have lent a special vigor to *Mānas*-singing, along with other genres. In particular, the fondness for organized competitions—inspired at least indirectly by the calypso competitions—extended to *Mānas*-singing by the 1930s. Boodram Jattan, leader of the Sumati Sabha Ramayan Gol in the genre's heyday, spoke nostalgically about the excitement and rivalry surrounding the competitions:

> The competitions were so intense. One thing is that the wording has to be concrete, with no error; any error and points will be deducted. The jhāl and everything has to coincide, and there is a panel that's judging the language, the rhythm, the timing. In the north, those groups were no match for us in quality. There was one group who had a little bit of flair—the group of Ramdeen Chotoo of Aranguez [mentioned above by Roopnarine Gayadeen]. But the others were just marking time; they did it for love, knowing they probably wouldn't win. But in the south, Tulsa Trace and Suchit Trace were always in stiff competition. Tulsa Trace had won the jhāl Ramayan singing for twenty-

four years in succession; they had some stalwarts. When my group would lose, I used to cry. These Tulsa Trace fellas were real champions, especially because they had one of the best drummers, Kalool Ramsamooj. That made a big difference. I was a little younger than them, I'd always lose to them, but I was learning from them, and from the mistakes we made.

The climax of Jattan's *Mānas*-singing career was the competition held in Arouca in 1962 at "the last big jhāl Ramayan competition":

There must have been sixty or seventy groups then. Now there are just two or three. In Arouca, the judges were a group of pandits. These guys were my main target. When this competition was announced, I got the group together. I took it so seriously, it was make or break. I made very strict rules for the group, for success. For one month, I told them, we have to practice every day. . . . So we sang in an order; there's a basket, and every group pulls a number and sings according to the number. Tulsa Trace was the first group to sing. Kalool was the drummer. They had a strong side, they were well prepared. But this day, I don't know—they started the first chaupai and made a mistake in the wordin.' . . . The competition was so fierce, and by the end, people became so agitated that the judges couldn't give a decision, they held off. So they announced the decision over the radio three days later. And we got first. That was a big victory.

Jattan recalled the trials he experienced in learning the art:

The people who taught me—I used to read Ramayan, before an audience, and if I'm reading, if I slip, the slightest error, they'd never spare me. They'd say *"Chup raho, chaupāi phir se kaho!"* [Quiet! Now read the *chaupāi* again!] I would get so embarrassed in front of the audience, I'd swear I'd never read it again. And those elders weren't even looking at the book, they knew it so well, they'd read it so many times. But if they'd correct me, and I walk away, they could see that I'm dejected, and they knew that I might drift away from it, so they will get me and talk to me, yes, to encourage me. And I remember the sacrifice I'd make, the rain would be fallin,' but I have to go to practice, I'd wrap up the Ramayan, sometime I'd go home with wet pants, but I'd have to go to the practice.

Mānas Singing in Decline

As Jattan noted, the 1962 Arouca event was one of the last large jhāl Ramayan competitions in Trinidad, and in subsequent years the art as a whole declined precipitously. While sixty or seventy groups competed in that event, at present there are only two jhāl Ramayan groups in Trinidad, those of Tulsa Trace and Suchit Trace; in the north, the daughter of veteran Ramdeen Chotoo also

attempts to lead a group. In Guyana, a handful of groups remain, and two or three Guyanese groups are active in the New York area. The decline is especially conspicuous when compared with the remarkable popularity of chowtal groups, whose style, antiphonal format, use of Hindi texts, and social function are so similar to those of *Mānas* singing. Chowtal also involves the same sort of tight group coordination in negotiating Hindi texts through rhythmic modulations at fast tempos. Indeed, traditionally, chowtal and Ramayan were often performed by the same groups, who simply switched to chowtal during Phagwa season. In that sense, the existence of chowtal groups has facilitated the perpetuation, however limited, of *Mānas* singing, by constituting a certain infrastructure of groups and a familiarity with antiphonal singing. (The two genres are distinguished primarily by their texts, and by the typical melodies used in each.)

Certain factors contributed to the decline of *Mānas* singing without undermining the ongoing vitality of chowtal. Most important, the attenuated literacy in Hindi weakened *Mānas* singing more severely than it did chowtal. As discussed in chapter 3, chowtal lyrics are indeed in Hindi, but the smaller repertoire, together with the use of handouts or pamphlets with romanized texts, allows singers to render a dozen or so familiar songs in spite of illiteracy in Hindi; through repeated rendering of individual songs, group members can well learn how to fit the words to the intricate rhythms. However, *Mānas* singing involves proceeding slowly through the entire lengthy text, rather than simply perfecting a few stanzas; vocalists not skilled in Hindi would have considerable difficulty in properly rendering the lines, many of which are sung only once before segueing to the next. Further, while both chowtal and *Mānas* singing require skilled leaders and drummers, a Ramayan group also requires at least one particularly knowledgeable individual who commands a repertoire of nontextual bānīs that are appropriate to each given *Mānas* passage. The decline in numbers of groups itself further reduces the emergence of such trained leaders. The survival of the genre thus depends on the presence of erudite elders and younger enthusiasts motivated to perpetuate the tradition. In the Guyanese *Mānas*-singing realm, the most dynamic, erudite, and energetic such individual was Rudy Sasenarine, whose untimely death in 2012 constituted what may turn out to be a mortal blow to this tradition.

Mānas Singing: Style and Structure

Most of the *Rāmcharitmānas* consists of stanzas comprising one or two dohās (couplets) and around four or five chaupāis (quatrains), set in their respective standard prosodic meters. The individual line is called a *pad* (rhyming with

English "bud"), two of which constitute an *ardhālī*. Stanzas in a few other poetic meters, such as *sorath* and *chhand,* also occur. Since the musical form of *Mānas* singing, as it flourishes in the Caribbean and the Bhojpuri region, has never been described (except in Lutgendorf's presentation [107–9] of a typical text and bānī), a basic formal analysis at this point may be of use to interested readers.

In *Mānas* singing, a given "item" (the term "song" being inappropriate) usually consists either of a given set of chaupāis or else one or two dohās. The sung *Mānas* passage is preceded by a bānī, which subsequently punctuates the chaupāis or dohas. In effect, the bānī can be said to serve a number of purposes. It embellishes the text; it is often a more familiar verse, perhaps being in simpler Hindi, or deriving from a familiar source like the *Hanumān Chalīsa*, thus rendering the textual passage more "listener-friendly" than the *Mānas* alone, with its dauntingly archaic dialect. Further, the bānī personalizes the rendering, since it often consists of an adaptation by a group member, or a relative thereof.[25] Finally, it serves as a textual and melodic refrain that punctuates the *Mānas* verses.

The typical bānī is of two to four lines and can derive from one of various sources. Some are composed by elder Caribbeans competent in Hindi. Lutgendorf noted that groups in Banaras often used lines from seasonal folksongs like *kajri*. In the Caribbean the declining folksong repertoire has occasioned a greater reliance on songbooks, for bānīs as well as other practices. Hence the bānīs might be adapted from a chapbook like the *Bhajan Rāmāyan* (a nineteenth-century adumbration of the epic in simple Hindi), from the *Hanumān Chalīsa* (a prayer to Hanuman, attributed to Tulsidas and memorized by many millions of Indians), or other books. As mentioned, in the context of a *kathā* or *yajna* the theme of the bānī and subsequent passage should cohere with the passage being discussed by the pandit. Knowledgeable singers have a repertoire of bānīs that may be used for different *Mānas* passages. Many bānīs are of a generic devotional nature and could preface almost any *Mānas* verses.

The tunes used for the bānī and subsequent *Mānas* verses, as suggested above, are generally unremarkable, being plain, syllabic, and easy, with stepwise movement in familiar diatonic "major-" or "minor"-type modes. In general, however, the musical interest for performers lies less in the tunes per se than in the tightly coordinated setting of sequential text lines to the proper rhythm and negotiating the metrical and textual segues.

A number of melodies occur in bānīs. In theory, a bānī verse could be set to any tune, but a given vocalist will generally be accustomed to singing the bānīs he knows to certain melodies. The bānī melody then becomes the tune of the subsequent *Mānas* verses. That is, the chorus hears the leader sing

the bānī a few times; whether they have heard the bānī and its tune before, both are simple enough that the singers can join in (with their jhāls) after a few renderings; a bit of floundering may occasionally occur until everyone has settled on the right pitches. The group then proceeds to sing the doha or chaupāīs to that tune.

Example 2 below schematizes a typical Guyanese-style rendering of a chaupāi with its bānī (sung by Sasenarine's New York Youth Chowtal and Ramayan Gol). This bānī consists of three *pads* of text; after the first *pad* is sung, the second half of it ("umiri rahe tori") is sung twice as an additional *pad*, and the second text *pad* is treated in the same way. Its simple *svar* (tune) consists of a line centering around the tonic, and another ascending to the fourth and above, and thence down to the tonic. For convenience, I refer to these two melodies using the Hindustani terms *sthāī* and *antara*, respectively, although Caribbean musicians do not use or know these designations, and the terms do not adequately describe their function.[26] Every line is sung at least twice, that is, by the first and second rows of singers; subsequent repetitions are at the discretion of the leader, who may shout instructions to his neighbors—for example, "chaupāī" to proceed from the initial bānī to the *Mānas* verse, or "bānī!" to return from the chaupāī to the first line of that insertion, or "ādhā!" (half) to repeat the second half of the chaupāi's third *pad* (although that repetition should be automatic). The chaupāīs themselves generally proceed in a standard fashion, so there may be no need for such instructions.

In Guyanese singing, the bānī-chaupāī set commences in a medium-tempo meter that could be counted in seven or fourteen beats. Sasenarine designated this meter by the Hindustani term *dīpchandi*; although that term is not known to other Caribbean musicians, I use it here for convenience, with the caveat that it is not identical to the dīpchandi of North Indian light-classical music (especially thumri).[27] At a certain point—usually the last pad of the second- or third-to-last chaupāī—the leader gives a signal for a modulation to the *daur*, that is, an accelerated section in quadratic meter. (As Sasenarine commented, "You don't want to start the daur too early, because people will get a heart attack, and also some of them maybe can't read that fast.") North Indian classical musicians might call the daur's meter kaharva, but that term is not known in the Caribbean, where instead, it would be called chaubola.[28] In the daur, the same melodies are simply adapted to quadratic meter. The singing and drumming intensify, especially as the tempo further increases. After the last chaupāī, the entire bānī is sung, and the passage concludes with a shouted "RAM-a-CHAND-ar KI JAY!" (Long live Ram!). The entire set of chaupāīs might span about ten or twelve minutes.

A typical bānī would be sung roughly as indicated below, with "ādhā" (half) indicating a verse line consisting of a twofold repetition of the concluding words (the second half) of the preceding line.

text	tune	
1st *pad*	sthāī	(Ab Shiva sumiri umri rahe tori)
ādhā	antara	(umri rahe tori, umri rahe tori)
2nd *pad*	sthai	(bin Shiva gyān dhyān nahin hoi)
ādhā	sthai	(dhyān nahin hoi, dhyān nahin hoi)
3rd *pad*	antara	(yatan karo man lākh karori)
1st *pad*	sthai	(Ab Shiva sumiri umri rahe tori)

(Now let everyone sing Shiva's praise
Without Shiva there is no wisdom,
Let a trillion hearts try.)

After several renditions of the bānī, the group proceeds without pause or marker to the *Mānas* chaupāī (if need be, after hearing the leader shout "chaupāī"). As mentioned, each chaupāī comprises two lines, each of which consists of two *pads*. The passage in this example consists of six and a half chaupāīs (bracketed in the text by dohās), near the beginning of the introductory *Bālkhānd* chapter.[29] The first chaupāī is sung essentially as follows, closely resembling the manner of singing the bānī:

text	tune	
1st *pad*	sthai	(daras paras majjan aru pānā)
2nd *pad*	sthai	(hare pāp kah bed purānā)
3rd *pad*	sthai	(nadi punīt amit mahimā ati)
ādhā	sthai	(amit mahimā ati, amit mahimā ati)
4th *pad*	antara	(kahi na sake sārdā bimal mati)
bānī	sthai	(Ab Shiva sumiri umri rahe tori)

The very sight and touch of the river, a dip in its stream or a draught from it cleanses one's sins—so declare the Vedas and the Puranas. Even Saraswati, the goddess of learning, with all her cloudless intelligence, cannot describe the infinite glory of this very holy river. *Now let everyone sing Shiv's praise.*

The subsequent five chaupāīs are all sung in the same manner, except that, as mentioned, in the last *pad* of the penultimate chaupāi, the daur commences and the tunes are adapted to fast quadratic meter (chaubola). Finally, the full bānī is sung, with further acceleration, and the shouted cadence brings the passage to a rousing and abrupt halt.

Example 2. Setting of three-line bānī.

The typical Trinidadian style of singing chaupāīs differs in a few respects. In some cases, the passage proceeds, as in Guyana, from dīpchandi to a daur in quadratic meter, but often there is no use of dīpchandi, such that the entire set is in chaubola. The most distinctive "Trini" feature occurs during the final bānī rendition, where the singers shout an exuberant phrase on the upper tonic, descending to the fifth. Possibly this signature phrase derived from India, or it may have been the innovation of a local group which was subsequently imitated and became a norm.[30]

The Ālhā-Khānd: A Medieval Epic in the Land of Calypso

Thus far in this chapter we have looked at two distinct sorts of traditional narrative genres and their similar, though not identical, downward trajectories in the Caribbean. If birha is still encountered in a few contexts, and *Mānas* singing thrives in a few isolated pockets, the epic of Ālhā represents a narrative tradition whose definitive demise is clearly imminent and not likely to be postponed by some trendy fusion with soca. Hence our discussion of Ālhā in the Caribbean need not be lengthy and may serve primarily as a point of comparison and contrast with birha and *Mānas* singing.

The Ālhā-khānd, or tale of Ālhā, is a quintessential oral-tradition narrative ballad. As disseminated by amateur and professional bards, it has been the most popular heroic epic of the Hindi-speaking Gangetic plains, its domain encom-

passing the Bhojpuri region on the east and Kannauj, Avadh, Bundelkhand, and Haryana in the western and southwestern Doab. Although the history of the ballad per se is undocumented, it narrates, with much fanciful embellishment, the heroic exploits of the brothers Ālhā and Udal (Udan, Rudal) in the conflicts of three Rajput kingdoms on the eve of Muslim conquest in the late twelfth century.

The Ālhā-khānd is sung throughout these regions in a variety of styles, contexts, narrative variants, and local Hindi dialects. Singers might be professional or semi-professional bards, able to perform the entire saga, or they might be amateurs who can only negotiate one or two favorite battle episodes. Some singers rely on inexpensive chapbooks containing episodes of the written recension (see, for example, Henry 1988, 159). Narrative content in their renditions might vary considerably while remaining faithful to the core events of the "lay." An Ālhā-singer, or *alhet*, might perform in a histrionic style, waving a sword about, or in a straightforward, unpretentious manner. Performance contexts also vary, encompassing stage competitions, formal renderings at weddings or festivals, or informal sessions by a villager for his friends and neighbors.[31] In recent years, video picturizations of the ballad have been marketed by regional VCD and DVD producers, some of whose output can be seen in YouTube postings.

Generally, Ālhā is performed by a solo singer, accompanied by dholak and some sort of metallophone—typically manjira chimes or a metal rod variously called *gaj*, *sariya*, or dandtāl (about which more will be said later).[32] The dholak maintains a straightforward quadratic meter (like "kaharva"), while the metallophone plays a steady *ching chickaching chickaching* pattern (which is also the basic Indo-Caribbean dantāl pattern). Some performers acquiesce to modernity by incorporating a harmonium in their accompaniment. Since the aesthetic interest lies in the narrative rather than in the purely musical aspects, the verses are set to a simple, repetitive stock tune, which varies according to region, discipular tradition, and individual preference. Example 3 presents the tune used by Trinidadian singer Lalram Jaggernath, which presumably derives from South Asian practice.[33]

The Ālhā-khānd is a secular tale of battles, treachery, and heroism; although traditionally enjoyed by members of all castes, it embodies the martial valor that Ahirs and Rajputs in particular consider to be part of their clan character. In modern times, performances have been arranged for Indian Army units to stimulate their fighting spirit. The epic, with its vivid descriptions of quasi-historical battles and other events in specific towns in the Doab, has special resonance for residents of those areas, who enjoy picturing the thundering of cavalry over the plains they now till, centuries later. Traditionally, Ālhā is sung only during the monsoon season (July through August).

Example 3. Ālhā tune.

In typical oral-tradition fashion, Ālhā singers over the generations have freely elaborated, forgotten, reinvented, compressed, and expanded various episodes in accordance with their abilities, local traditions, and the tastes of their particular patrons. However, like many oral epics, the Ālhā-khānd also acquired a written component when, in 1865, one Charles Elliott compiled a recension by collating various oral versions, leading to a Hindi publication of the tale in 1871. This printed version has been used in various contexts, but it remains an inherently idiosyncratic and fixed recension of a ballad that has always thrived as a living and changing set of organisms in the oral tradition. (In that sense, it is somewhat akin to Homer's *Iliad* and *Odyssey*, although literacy was far older and better established in nineteenth-century India than it was in Homer's Hellenic world.)

The fate of the Ālhā-khānd in modern India is like that of many traditional folk arts. On the one hand, its popularity has been gravely and irreversibly eroded by the new forms of mass-mediated entertainment, as television and now commercial VCDs pervade rural as well as urban India. Hence, most North Indians, bred on Bollywood and its musical hit parade, would have no interest in listening to some wizened bard endlessly chant to the accompaniment of a wheezy harmonium about the squabbles of petty medieval chieftains. At the same time, however, modernity has also brought new sorts of performance contexts and even new sorts of meanings to the genre. Hence, versions of Ālhā have been marketed on cassettes (see Manuel 1993, 156), on VCDs, and on the radio, and it is still performed at various quasi-folkloric events that promote local folk arts. The mass media, while undermining the genre in various ways, offer performers new means of dissemination as well as exposure to other singers' practices.

While there is no documentation of the transmission of the Ālhā-khānd to the Caribbean, elderly informants of mine attested to its popularity as recently as the 1960s, and in the 1990s the genre was still recited by a handful of Hindi-speaking elders. It is clear, therefore, that the ranks of the indentured immi-

grants included several *alhets,* whether they were learned bards with extensive repertoires or amateur enthusiasts able to recite only a few battle scenes. In the days before television and radio, such singers were much valued for their ability to entertain Indians in villages and plantation barracks while providing a sense of cultural connection to the towns whence they or their parents had emigrated. (Continuity was further enhanced by retaining the tradition of singing the epic only in July and August, and some believed that proper renditions could cause rain.)

Given the lack of a critical mass of singers, not to mention of professional *alhets*, it was natural that the printed edition of the tale would acquire a new importance in perpetuating the tradition. In India, the thick tome would have been of little interest to the hundreds of *alhets* who were steeped in narrations of the tale since childhood and whose ability to memorize verse was not yet undermined by the mixed effects of the printed word. In the Caribbean, however, possession of the tome enabled any Hindi-literate individual to perform the entire ballad, using whatever simple stock tune he knew.

Boodram Jattan, quoted above, recalled of his youth in Trinidad:

Yes, I used to read Ālhā. We used to do it when there would be a scarcity of rain. One thing I still remember—in Ālhā, you have some of the best *sumirans* [introductory sung invocations]. People enjoyed Ālhā because it's very rhythmic, and the old people understood the language back then. Because of the style in which it was written, sometimes people listening would be tempted to become violent. It's about war. Usually there would be one or two people reading, from the book. No dholak, no instruments [though in some cases dholak might be used]. I myself used to have a copy of the book. They were very old books. Whether it was fact or fiction, there was something about Ālhā, it generates this kind of fighting spirit in people. It has a lot of vigor in it, and people would get agitated. Like, it says, just as a dog can only live twelve years, so Ālhā says that a kshatriya who lives beyond the age of eighteen is useless, because they're a warrior caste. That kind of spirited thing. Long before TV, not even a radio, that was village entertainment. Anyone could do it—you don't have to be an entertainer or a pandit. As long as you could read Hindi. But then, as people lost the ability to understand, the whole sense of it was lost. (p.c.)

By 2009, when I commenced my inquiries into Ālhā in the Caribbean, Jattan's explanation of the genre's decline could be interpreted as an autopsy. In Trinidad, I encountered a few elderly birha performers—including Sadho Boodram Ramgoolam and Lalram Jaggernath—who had tattered copies of the 1870s edition and still occasionally read it. In our meeting that year, Jag-

gernath mentioned that he had been "reading" the book just the night before; I found this unremarkable, until he clarified by adding, "and people were enjoying it."[34] Jaggernath was referring to an archaic form of "reading" which, while using print as an aid, remains essentially in an oral tradition—indeed, in accordance with the oral narrative nature of the ballad itself. To "read," in this sense, is not a solitary, silent act, but a chanted performance of a text done for an audience—in this case, a few of Jaggernath's peers who knew enough Hindi to follow and enjoy the narrative.

While I was impressed to meet learned individuals like Jaggernath, there is no doubt that the Ālhā-khānd's decline is terminal. (Jaggernath himself passed away in 2010.) As we have seen, both birha and *Mānas* singing have managed to survive in niches, despite the decline of Hindi comprehension, and the next chapter explores how chowtal—another Hindi-language antiphonal folksong—flourishes vigorously in the diaspora. But the various factors that enable birha and *Mānas* singing to limp along do not obtain with respect to Ālhā. As a purely musical genre, Ālhā is too simple and plain to sustain aesthetic interest, and it offers little scope for being innovatively syncretized and enlivened, as a few performers have attempted to do with birha by setting it to soca rhythms; instead, Ālhā is a thoroughly text-driven entity, with the repetitive stock tune serving merely as a vehicle for the narrative. Birha—aside from having a catchier tune—can traditionally be combined with dance and lively nagāra playing, in which context a singer might recycle a familiar snippet like the "Rāmaji ki bagiya" doggerel. While Ālhā audiences may have favorite chapters, there are no comparably familiar passages known to such a wide spectrum of lay enthusiasts. Nor can Ālhā be a vehicle for collective performance, in which a group of moderately competent singers responsorially echoes a knowledgeable leader.

Ālhā also lacks the sort of broad-based cultural presence of the *Mānas*, which enjoys wide popularity outside of its being sung by formal mandalis. As a cultural entity, the Ālhā-khānd has no such support, and even its importance to subcontinental Ahirs and Rajputs as an expression of their martial vigor has not survived in the Caribbean, where such caste identities have dissipated.[35] Ultimately, the Ālhā-khānd, as a Hindi narrative epic, is simply too dependent on linguistic comprehension to survive in a monolingually Anglophone society; it is precisely the sort of text-driven genre least likely to persist in a situation of diasporic language loss. To reiterate Jattan's postmortem, "As people lost the ability to understand, the whole sense of it was lost."

Conclusions: Narrative Ballad in the Age of Powder and Lead

Is Achilles possible side by side with powder and lead? . . .
Do not singing and reciting and the muses necessarily go out of
existence with the appearance of the printer's bar, and do not,
therefore, disappear the prerequisites of epic poetry?

—Karl Marx, *A Contribution to the Critique of
Political Economy*

In this chapter we have looked at three narrative folk-song traditions transmitted from North India to the Caribbean; each of these has declined dramatically in the last half-century, yet the degree to which they have done so has been conditioned by their distinct qualities and their subsequent abilities to adapt in the diaspora.

All three of the genres were, in their distinct ways, traditionally maintained by oral tradition. Birha was, both in textual and musical parameters, a thoroughly folk idiom, its texts generally transmitted orally, and set in a dialect (Bhojpuri) that itself had little existence, not to mention status, as a literary language. For its part, Tulsidas's *Mānas* is of course a literary work, written by a poet educated in a hoary tradition of devotional, narrative, and amatory literature; the *Mānas* itself is an original literary opus, rather than being, like a Homerian epic, a mere written recension of a fundamentally oral ballad. Nevertheless, the practice of *Mānas* singing, like other forms of *Mānas* dissemination, has itself been an oral tradition, even if it has relied on the written text itself. Finally, the Ālhā-khānd has evolved and thrived as a quintessential oral epic, told and retold by creative bards in myriad versions, among which the published version enjoys no particular primacy, not to mention originary status.

Birha, *Mānas* singing, and Ālhā came to collectively confront a set of grave challenges in the diaspora. One of these has involved the process—noted pithily by Marx above and discussed more expansively by Ong (1982)—in which literacy and print erode not only the popularity of oral epics, but also the entire worldview that generated and sustained them. A related and equally broad and inexorable sort of menace to the survival of the three genres has been modernity itself, whose various ramifications—from mass-mediated entertainment to globalization—have combined to erode traditions dependent on static, isolated, provincial folkways. Meanwhile, the most overt and palpable blow to the three genres has been the decline of Hindi—a wound that, as the case of chowtal illustrates, need not in itself be mortal, but in combination with other factors may indeed prove grievous.

As we have seen, birha, *Mānas* singing, and Ālhā have each been undermined by these developments, but their trajectories, although collectively downward, have not been identical. Birha was able to flourish through the mid-twentieth

century, as long as it could be sustained by a critical mass of Hindi-speakers. Even after that audience largely passed away, birha could eke out a meager afterlife as an accompaniment to Ahir-dance shows, as an ephemeral neotraditional fusion enlivened by soca-style drumming, or as a rustic but feisty curio sung at odd occasions in a fragmented form. For its part, *Mānas* singing, like birha, thrived until the 1960s, reaching a sort of apogee in Trinidadian competitions, but subsequently declined dramatically with the passing away of the last generation of people raised in Hindi-speaking households. However, the genre is not yet dead, and the handful of groups that perform it include at least one youth *gol*, some of whose members may go on to lead their own *mandalis*. Regarding the Ālhā-khānd, there is perhaps less to be said, as its decline is more definitive and irreversible, and its significance here is more as an illustration of the kind of oral tradition that stands little chance of survival in any form once its linguistic basis has eclipsed.

The diasporic trajectories of these genres exhibit a few trends that will also be discussed more expansively in this book's conclusion. One is that as Hindi language comprehension declines, written texts come to acquire a considerably greater importance than they might possess in the oral-tradition counterpart in India. Hence, the Trinidadian and Guyanese vocalists who might be able to sing a birha or two generally need to consult their handwritten notebooks of song lyrics. Similarly, *alhets* able to sing passages of the Ālhā epic from memory have long since passed from the scene; even those of the mid-twentieth century described by Jattan had to rely on the printed text.

Another concomitant of the decline of Hindi is a process of "musicalization," in which, insofar as the genre admits, the more purely musical features are foregrounded, instead of textual features. Such a process can be said to be operant when the ubiquitous "Rāmaji ki bagiya" fragment is sung to accompany an Ahir-dance show, with the birha serving essentially as a catchy folk tune rather than a vehicle for narrative content. In such a context, as in the odd soca-style setting, birha survives, but essentially as a ditty rather than a lyric idiom. A different sort of musicalization occurs when tassa drummers adopt and elaborate the typical birha drum accompaniment pattern in the form of the popular and basic "nagāra" hand (composite rhythm). For its part, the ability of *Mānas* singing to survive even in its limited capacity has no doubt been enabled partly by the purely musical interest and rewards that it offers, with its lively rhythms, dynamic ebb and flow, and antiphonal sociality. For its part, Ālhā singing is simply too plain and simple in musical terms and too reliant on its textual dimension to afford any scope for being elaborated, reinvented, or syncretized as a musical genre. In the next chapter, we look at chowtal, another Hindi folksong genre, that by virtue of some of these same trends has been able not only to survive but even to flourish in the diaspora.

Chowtal and the Dantāl

Finding Fertile Soil in the New Homelands

In chapter 2 we explored three genres—Ālhā, birha, and *Mānas* singing—which remained vital in Indo-Caribbean culture until the mid-twentieth century, after which the rapid decline of Hindi eroded their lexical basis. Until that period, and even insofar as they survive today, these genres have resisted any form of creolization, while also being wholly independent of whatever transformations their counterparts—especially birha—have undergone in North India. As such, Indo-Caribbean birha, although in terminal decline, has constituted a remarkable example of a marginal survival, in terms of its form. This chapter discusses two other traditional entities in Indo-Caribbean music culture, the antiphonal folksong genre called chowtal and the dantāl, a common metallophone. The pairing of these entities in this chapter might seem odd, not only because they are so distinct, but also because chowtal's close stylistic and sociomusical affinities with *Mānas* singing would suggest that those two genres be discussed together. However, chowtal and the dantāl, aside from their identical final syllables, share an important feature: although both derive from Bhojpuri North India, they have not declined, as have Ālhā, birha, and *Mānas* singing, but rather have flourished in the diaspora (including Fiji). In fact, they have become considerably more widespread, on a per capita basis, than their counterparts in North India. In the process they illustrate how the neotraditional stratum of the international Bhojpuri diaspora—including both the Caribbean and Fiji—can constitute an entity that shares features that, despite being of traditional Indian origin, nevertheless are distinct from the Bhojpuri ancestral culture. These phenomena illustrate how, in this sense, neotraditional Bhojpuri diasporic music

culture—that is, excluding its obvious creolized forms—is best seen not as a microcosm of its nineteenth-century Bhojpuri-region ancestor, but as an entity with its own distinctive features, in which inherited features may assume trajectories quite distinct from their North Indian counterparts.

Chowtal

In mid-February 2007, I attended some lively sessions of chowtal, a boisterous Bhojpuri and eastern Uttar Pradesh folk song genre, in a Hindu temple in a small town a few hours from Banaras (Varanasi), North India.[1] The following weekend I was singing chowtal, in an identical style, with an Indo-Guyanese ensemble in Queens, New York. In the subsequent season of the vernal Phagwa (Holi) festival, in March 2008, I found myself singing along with a group of Indo-Fijians in Sacramento, California, as they performed a similar version of one of the same chowtal songs. Despite the nearly identical styles of the three song sessions, they were separated not only by thousands of miles, but more significantly, by the more than ninety years that had elapsed since indentured emigration from the Bhojpuri region ceased in 1917. Subsequent cultural contacts between that region and its diasporic communities in the Caribbean and Fiji became minimal, and interaction between the latter two sites has been practically nil. Given such geographic and temporal remoteness, the similarities between the three chowtal renderings I witnessed are in themselves noteworthy, as are, in a different sense, the differences.

While concentrating primarily on Indo-Caribbean chowtal, this chapter aims at achieving a triangular perspective by incorporating reference to North Indian and Indo-Fijian practice. I provide a basic description and analysis of chowtal as performed in Indo-Caribbean music and, to a lesser extent, in India and Fiji. I further compare and contrast the traditions as extant today and offer suggestions as to how diasporic dynamics have contributed to the dramatically successful way the genre has taken root and flourished in the diaspora even as it declines in India itself.[2] However, the present study must be regarded as provisional rather than definitive, due to the incomplete nature of my fieldwork. Chowtal is in fact a vast genre, comprising many regional variants even in small countries like Suriname and Guyana, not to mention the immense and underresearched Bhojpuri region. It thus merits much more extensive documentation than I am able to provide here. An exhaustive study of chowtal would necessarily extend over several Phagwa seasons spent in different locales in India and the diaspora.[3]

Chowtal Context, Style, and Structure

Chowtal in India is primarily a Bhojpuri seasonal genre, linked to the vernal Hindu Holi or Hori festival, which in the diaspora is more commonly called Phagwa (Hindi, *phagwā*, or in Fiji, *fāg*). In India and the diaspora, Phagwa culminates in a day (usually in early March) of carnivalesque saturnalia, especially the throwing of colored powders and liquids, playful (but not unmeasured) violation of class and caste boundaries, performance of various forms of vernacular song, and a general spirit of sensuous abandon and fun.

In India's Bhojpuri region, song sessions of various genres associated with Phagwa occur in diverse contexts in the weeks leading up to the culminating day itself. Typically, groups of men and women agree to gather informally (and in India, usually separately) at someone's house or patio for an evening song session, the rowdy and boisterous character of which might occasionally be further enhanced by moderate consumption of *bhāng* or some other hashish-based libation.[4] Alternately, regular evening bhajan or Ramayan-singing sessions held in temples might, during Phagwa season, instead be devoted to Holi-related genres such as chowtal. Such groups might also be invited to sing at a Hindu acquaintance's home, which will be effectively blessed by the event. On such occasions, some people might gather to listen, but on the whole, chowtal singers, like bhajan groups, perform for their own entertainment rather than that of an audience. In both Indo-Caribbean and Indo-Fijian culture, chowtal may also be sung in the context of a formal *sammelan* (festival, convocation) involving several groups.

The term "chowtal" collectively designates a set of subgenres, including that specifically known as chowtal, all performed in a distinctive antiphonal format. In a typical Indo-Caribbean chowtal session, a rendering of the core subgenre chowtal (preceded by an initial invocatory *sumiran*) should properly segue to an attached and shorter *ulārā* (*ullāra*) and thence proceed freely to other chowtals or to the miscellaneous other subgenres sung in the same stentorian antiphonal style. These genres can include *dhamārī, kabīr, jogira, rasiyā, jāti, jhūmar, bilvariyā, baiswāra, lej*, and the farewell song "*Sadā-ānand*." These are distinguished variously by their prosodic schemes, melodies, and their characteristic sequences of rhythmic modulations and stanzaic repetitions, perhaps along with other criteria (which individual singers are unlikely to be able to articulate in abstract terms). Miller (2008, 219) astutely categorizes the subgenres as either "long-format" styles (especially chowtal and jhūmar) or "short-format" ones (such as kabīr, jogira, and "Sadā-ānand").[5]

Chowtal is sung in an antiphonal format very similar to the *Mānas* singing described in chapter 2. In both genres, two groups of vocalists (each ideally of

at least four people) sit facing each other or in a circle, with a dholak player at one end. As cued by a leader, one group sings a line, and the others repeat it, while also playing jhāl, perhaps along with other percussion instruments such as *kartāl* (*khartāl*, two pairs of short metal or wooden sticks), and *jhīkā* (a shaken wooden frame with jingles). In India and Fiji, harmonium and other melodic instruments (such as Hawaiian guitar) may also be played, although Caribbean groups shun such instruments out of a purist aesthetic.

Chowtal is rowdy and vigorous in character, rather than lyrical, and accordingly, is more often sung by men than women. Text lines are sung at full volume, with one group catching its breath while the other group sings. Most typically, in the "long-format" chowtal and jhūmar, a textual-melodic line is first repeated a few times at moderate tempo in seven-beat meter, which, as in chapter 2, I shall call "dīpchandi" for convenience; then it is rendered a few more times at a somewhat faster tempo in duple meter (like the North Indian kaharva, although that term is largely unknown in the diaspora). After a few repetitions, the tempo quickens again, and then yet again, such that the words come to constitute merely a garbled blur to listeners, and a tongue twister to vocalists themselves. By this point a spirit of exuberant frenzy often prevails, with vocalists singing and striking their jhāls at full volume, interjecting shouts and cheers, gesticulating, and perhaps rising to their knees. Then the excitement subsides as the line is rendered in its original tempo, segueing then to a new text line and melodic setting, which is repeated a few times in duple meter and then accelerated and intensified as was the opening line. Another verse line is then sung to the original melody and subjected to similar modulations, accelerations, and intensifications, in a similar series of climaxes and reposeful passages. Proceeding to the next verse, the group then repeats the entire process again, and then two or three times again, with a single "song" easily lasting fifteen minutes and sometimes as long as thirty minutes.

In its antiphonal format, its progression from seven-beat to duple meter, and its generally stentorian style, chowtal closely resembles *Mānas* singing, and traditionally, many Caribbean chowtal gols consisted essentially of *Mānas* groups that switch to chowtal during Phagwa season. Variations of the chowtal and *Mānas* format are also used in a variety of other Bhojpuri-region song genres. In a broad sense, the general practice of antiphonally repeating a given line is common to many genres of the region, including various women's folk songs and bhajan or *kīrtan* singing (see Slawek 1986, 123). Henry notes that the practice of alternating sections in quadratic and seven-beat meters also occurs in *khilauna*, a Bhojpuri/Maithili women's song form (2000, 85–86). For its part, the more specific pattern described here, with its dramatic accelerations and decelerations, also characterizes various specific other genres. Henry documents its use in the

Holi-season *chahkā* sung by villagers to the northwest of Banaras (Henry 1988, 124; see also Henry 2002). In the month of Chait following Phāgun, the song genres *ghāṭo* and *chaitā/chaitī* are also sung in a similar fashion, by antiphonal male groups alternating sections in seven-beat and quadratic rhythm (see, for example, Jain 1980, 69–71, 112–14, 126–30). A similar genre in Suriname and Bhojpuri-region India is *khañjri gīt*, in which vocalists sing Kabir or Siewnaraini bhajans while accompanying themselves on small tambourines called khañjri (not to be confused with the monsoon-season genre *kajri*).

The formal structure of chowtal itself, like that of the other subgenres mentioned, is distinctive and considerably more complex than that of a simple strophic song like a bhajan. The genre's name itself reflects its intricacy, as Indian informants claim that it derives from "*chār tāl*," that is, "four *tāl*s," reflecting the four rhythmic modulations it can be seen as running through. Chowtal groups can render the form even more elaborate by adding variations, sometimes cued by a leader while singing. Ideally, chowtal groups are either accustomed to performing a song in a given pattern, or else they are ready for whatever familiar variations the leader might introduce (either by singing or perhaps gesturing), such that they can adapt almost instantaneously. As the variations increase, the structure becomes more complex and potentially challenging, which can make the singing especially rewarding and exciting, as singers smoothly and collectively negotiate the transitions, variations, and dizzyingly fast renditions of lines. In such instances, the sense of collective exuberance and delight is palpable, as reflected in the animated shouts, gestures, and laughter that ensue.

The complexity of the chowtal form puts it beyond the scope of the average informal kīrtan group, whether in India or the diaspora. Chowtal requires the presence of at least one knowledgeable enthusiast, along with a few others who are familiar enough with the genre to follow his cues. The dholak player must also be sufficiently skilled to signal the rhythmic shifts (usually following the leader's signs), although it would be difficult for him to lead the session as a whole. Further, singers must either have written lyrics in front of them or else have memorized them through frequent performance. Confusion and distortions certainly occur; in a chowtal recorded in India by Edward Henry, the singers flounder at one of the transitions, resuming hesitantly and incorrectly in kaharva until, after some audible shouting, the leader steers them toward the proper line in 7/8. A subsequent chowtal, sung by this same understaffed group of merely four singers and a drummer, is ragged and disjointed throughout (and would not have won any awards at an Indo-Caribbean competition).[6]

Chowtal itself exhibits relatively little melodic variety; most of the *sthāī* (initial verse) melodies can be seen as variants of two or three recurring stock

tunes, similar to that shown in Ex. 4 below. Most other subgenres sung in a chowtal session are equally standardized, and their melodies are often even simpler, in many cases merely alternating tonic and second degrees. In general, for participants, aesthetic interest lies less in melodic richness and subtlety than in the excitement generated by the collective rendering of the rhythmic sections, with their modulations and intensifications. A good drummer can contribute greatly to the success of a song, both by signaling modulations and enlivening the music with his spirited playing. Many Caribbean and Fijian dholak players are prodigious virtuosos, providing a perpetual thumping, pumping, rollicking accompaniment adorned with machine-gun rolls, lively flams, slaps, and other effects, all at considerable volume in order to be heard through the boisterous singing.[7]

Although chowtal as a folk genre is unique to the Bhojpuri and Awadhi regions, chowtal texts are less often in the dialects of those areas than in Brajbhasha, or a Braj close to ("standard") *kharī-bolī* Hindi. Presumably, the authors of chowtal texts, though residents of the pūrab region, have composed their verses in Braj because of its greater prestige as a literary language. (The most common songbooks are published in Bombay but sell only in the pūrab region and the diaspora, as chowtal is unknown elsewhere in India.) In this sense chowtal contrasts with a "cultivated" local folk genre like birha, which is generally sung in the Bhojpuri dialect.

The poetic form of chowtals is in some respects typical of much Hindi sung verse, especially in the presence of an initial and recurring *ṭek* (refrain, pronounced like "take"), which punctuates two-line verses (*pad*, rhyming with "bud"), each of which comprises two grammatical phrases (separated in modern printed editions by a comma). Although the metrical scheme is somewhat flexible, lines must be regular enough to comfortably fit the conventional fixed tunes and rhythmic modulations. Thus, for example, verses of related but melodically and prosodically distinct genres, such as jhūmar or *dhamārī*, cannot be easily accommodated into a chowtal melody (and vice versa). The ṭek and *pad* typically end in "—ānī," "—ārī," or "—āī," as these fit the final melisma pattern nicely.

The lyrics of the ṭek and first *pad* of the song transcribed as example 4 are shown below, indicating pronounced inherent vowels (for example, "*hātha*" instead of the normally written "*hāth*"). The internal structures of chowtal ṭek and *pad* lines are distinctive. Chowtal ṭek and final *pad* lines typically have what could be regarded as an internal rhyme, with the final words—here, "*hāth pichakārī*" and "*kanchan kī pichakārī*"—effectively serving as tags. "*Hāth pichakārī*," which concludes the ṭek, is also appended to the second half of the *pad*'s second line in order to extend it to the appropriate length of its melody.

While the ṭek has a prominent internal rhyme, the other lines duplicate its ending ("*pichakārī*") rather than rhyme.

Hori khelata janaka dulāri // hātha pichakārī
rūpe ke thāra gulāba bhare hai; kanchana kī pichakāri
gore badana nīlāmbar sohata, aur mukha para besara dhāri //
    hātha pichakārī

Janaka's dear daughter [Sita] plays Holi with a pichkāri [squirt gun]
    in her hand
The silver plate is full of colored powder; the golden pichkāri,
Her fair-skinned body clothed in dark-blue shines, and she wears
    a nose-ring //
pichkāri in hand

Songtexts generally adhere to the familiar conventions of *rītī* poetry, the prevailingly secular, rhetorically oriented verse in which Krishna teases the cowgirls, charms them with his flute playing, torments Radha by his absence, overpowers the snake-demon, and so on. Many concern Holi itself, as celebrated by Krishna and Radha, Rama and Sita, or even Shiva and his consort Parvati. However, by no means are all songtexts saccharine and conventional. Both in the Caribbean and South Asian contexts (see, for example, Henry 1988, 125, 130), amateur composers have freely introduced ribaldry and irreverent social commentary, examples of which can be found even in popular chapbooks. One example still sung in the Caribbean is the dhamāri "Jogi anal tan jānā . . ." (from *Chowtāl Phāgsangrah*), which describes, in so many words, mendicant *jogis* bathing after so long that the water merely courses off the caked filth on their bodies as if off a duck's back. In another chowtal in the same volume, the young wife relates how her ardent husband treats her breasts as his toys.

In India, most verses not derived from common anthologies may be assumed to be written by amateur male poets, the likes of which abound in cities and small towns throughout North India. Such poets, writing in Braj or regional dialects for specific song genres, generally circulate their verse through local singing contexts. Thus, a poet might be active in a given *akhāra* or music club, or may perform cultivated genres like Mirzapur-style kajrī or Hathrasi rasiyā; or he might write on a semiprofessional basis for a Bhojpuri birhā group; alternately, he might merely popularize his lyrics among the local bhajan singers at the nearby temple, who might keep handwritten notebooks of his lyrics and those derived elsewhere. A few poets might have their verse published in cheap chapbooks such as are marketed by street vendors outside train stations and temples.[8] Chowtal singers, accordingly, either remember their lyrics from frequent usage, retain them in handwritten notebooks they compile, or get them from published

chapbooks. Aside from the short (sometimes ten-page) chapbooks found in India, two popular Indian anthologies used both in India and the diaspora are *Holī Chowtāl Sangrah* (Shrikrishandas 1985) and *Chowtāl Phāgsangrah* (Shri Sadholalji 1988). Informants told me that Sadholalji, the compiler of the latter anthology, collected his texts from oral tradition, although presumably they were originally authored by regional poets, some of whose pen names appear in concluding verses. Some songs derive from chapbooks that are considerably older; Guyanese drummer and music savant Ramnarine (Rudy) Sasenarine led his group in singing songs from a photocopied booklet, *Chowtāl Chandrika*, published in 1846. (In 2010 Sasenarine and I collated these and other songtexts and published them in a booklet titled *Chowtal Rang Bahar*.[9])

Chowtal in Modern India

A thorough study of chowtal in North India would require several Holi seasons' worth of fieldwork in the pūrab region, including in the extensive densely populated but backward and dangerous parts of Bihar. My own research, although far less comprehensive, has not been unproductive and has enabled me to make some tentative generalizations. For purposes of this provisional study, the most outstanding feature of chowtal in India today is that it does not appear to be as proportionally popular or widespread as it is in the Indic Caribbean or Fiji. Arriving in Banaras (Varanasi) in the Bhojpuri heartland in February 2007, I had considerable initial difficulty finding anyone who had even heard of the genre,[10] and the extant literature (whether in Hindi, Urdu, or English) on Bhojpuri folk music provided little guidance. Eventually, during that trip and a subsequent one in 2009, I was able to interview several knowledgeable informants and attend some lively performance sessions in Kachhwa Bazar, a market town a few hours west of Banaras. The latter of these was especially spirited, as my local contact (a gifted radio singer named Matuk Singh) had called knowledgeable local elders and enthusiasts to attend for my benefit the Saturday night song session at the Hanuman temple. In 2013 I met a young man from Allahabad, west of the Bhojpuri region, who sang chowtal and assured me that it was sung here and there in his district.

My research, though far from exhaustive, enables me to conclude with some confidence that chowtal is still avidly sung in many villages in the Bhojpuri and eastern Uttar Pradesh regions, stretching west to Allahabad district. However, its popularity has declined dramatically in recent generations, such that in many more villages not only is it not sung, it is also completely unknown. Formerly abundant provincial composers of chowtal lyrics are now rare, and publishers of chowtal chapbooks like Sadanand Press (Varanasi) have ceased to issue new booklets for lack of fresh material. Moreover, while extant groups may

sing with great zest, their repertoire tends to be limited to a few songs in the familiar, basic subgenres (chowtal proper, ulārā, jhūmar, baiswāra, and jogirā), such that more rarefied items like lej, jati, and rasiyā are forgotten. My informants attributed chowtal's decline primarily to the preference of the young for film music and especially for the light, often lewd commercial Bhojpuri songs (including newly composed Holi songs) now marketed on cheap DVDs and mp3 discs. They clarified that in various villages one might well find pockets where younger and elder enthusiasts still sing chowtal with zeal (as they do in Kachhwa Bazar). However, these are becoming fewer and farther between, and as one informant related, young people soon lose interest if the verses are not sufficiently ribald. Chowtal's obscurity contrasts with the familiarity of certain other neofolk genres like modern birha, which is well known throughout the Bhojpuri region, and kajrī, which, although a specialty of Mirzapur, is familiar well beyond that area, including in Banaras. My research also suggested that in the Banaras region, the genre chaitā, sung during the month after Phagwa, is considerably better known than chowtal, which it resembles to some extent.

In the realm of Bhojpuri folk music genres, chowtal enjoys—or perhaps suffers from—a sort of intermediate status. On the one hand, as mentioned, it is too complex to be sung by the average kīrtan group, but rather requires the presence of a core of knowledgeable enthusiasts. On the other hand, chowtal lacks the types of formalized patronage that sustains more cultivated folk genres like birha and kajrī. Birha continues to thrive as a formal entertainment genre performed by professionals, often to audiences of several hundred. For its part, kajrī is still performed in a variety of styles and contexts, and it has until the last generation been especially cultivated in Mirzapur as a sophisticated poetic-musical genre by the grassroots institutions of akhāras or music clubs, with their chief poets, specialized repertoires, and formal disciples and members.

Performances of Mirzapuri kajrī and Hathrasi rasiyā are ideally structured as competitions (*muqābilā, dangal*) between two akhāras, who, aside from insulting each other in song, pose riddles and questions—especially regarding Hindu mythology—which the opposing akhāra must answer (in appropriate rhyme scheme, meter, and melody). Although there are no formal chowtal akhāras, informants related that competitive chowtal performances of this nature also occasionally occur, with questions posed in the ulāra section to be answered in the other group's chowtal. Such events might be formally sponsored by some patron or organizing committee for the general public, to celebrate a wedding, the birth of a son, or the consecration of a new building. Competing groups might well be paid for such performances, though they would not constitute regular professionals like the singers of birhā, qawwālī, or *bilvariā* (*bilvariyā*), another Mirzapur-area genre, and would only perform chowtal during Holi season. Pre-

sumably, they would be more in the nature of the Birla Kirtan Samaj studied by Slawek (1986, 139), which might be invited to perform at local temples and other events (just as are temple-based chowtal gols in the Caribbean).

Meanwhile, chowtal has only minimal representation in the Indian mass media and is thus effectively marginalized by them. Commercial cassettes, DVDs, and mp3 discs of Bhojpuri music—including Holi music—abound, but these are primarily newly composed, studio-produced folk-pop songs, as rendered by stars like Manoj Tiwari or Kalpana Patowary, the honey-voiced, Assam-born songstress who has replaced Sharda Sinha as the leading female exponent of Bhojpuri popular music. Chowtal is not marketed on such commercial recordings, although given the extent to which melodies are recycled in India, it is not surprising to occasionally encounter chowtal melodies in birhā or bilvariā, which can be found in a few cassettes, and which, somewhat like chaitā and qawwālī, typically feature a male solo singer accompanied by a chorus. The standard three-section ulāra melody, rendered in similarly responsorial fashion, also surfaces in several modern commercial Bhojpuri Holi folk-pop songs marketed on mp3 discs.

Chowtal might also occasionally be sung in a stylized fashion on All India Radio (AIR) as a solo song. A vocalist wanting to become an "approved" singer of folk music on AIR must demonstrate familiarity with sixteen folk genres chosen out of a list of sixty-four, which includes chowtal. While such an AIR-style solo rendition of chowtal would be quite distinct from a more typical rowdy group song, two AIR "approved" Banaras folk singers (both educated musicians of bourgeois background) nevertheless demonstrated for me how chowtal could be sung solo, skipping the line repetitions and moving quickly through the verses and rhythmic modulations.[11]

Chowtal singing in India is primarily a male pastime, although, as will be discussed below, such is no longer the case in the Caribbean. Indian folk genres whose names describe formal characteristics (such as poetic meter or, in the case of chowtal, rhythm) tend to be associated more with male authorship and performance milieus (see Vatuk 1979, 38–47). Authors of chowtal verses appear to have been primarily, if not entirely, men. Almost all chowtals are "through-composed" texts rather than compositions that rely on the repetition and word substitution that typically distinguish women's folk songs (see Vatuk 1979, 46). In terms of performance, women generally do not attend the evening kīrtan or chowtal sessions held in local Hindu temples on regular weekdays (for example, in Hanuman temples, typically Tuesdays and Saturdays). As Henry notes, it might be inappropriate for respectable women in India to sing in the boisterous manner typical of genres like chahkā or, by extension, chowtal (Henry 1988, 144). Nevertheless, village women do sing chowtal in a more reserved manner

among themselves, as in the session recorded by Henry in 1972. Chaturvedi (1989, 245, 256) also notes that women and men might together sing *dhamār* and the chowtal-related *derhtāl*.

Chowtal in Indo-Caribbean Music

Chowtal—along with the closely related tradition of group Rāmāyan-singing discussed in chapter 2—occupies a singular place in Indo-Caribbean music culture.[12] Unlike local-classical singing or chutney-soca, Indo-Caribbean chowtal does not appear to have changed dramatically in the Caribbean context, such that it still closely resembles its South Asian counterpart. Moreover, unlike women's folk songs, chowtal is not only surviving, it is thriving in Indo-Caribbean culture. Indeed, the popularity of chowtal in the Indic Caribbean contrasts dramatically with its relative obscurity in India. It is safe to say that most Indo-Caribbean Hindu adults have a degree of basic familiarity with chowtal, being able to identify it, at the very least, as some sort of rowdy folk song that Hindu enthusiasts sing in temples during Phagwa season. (As discussed later, chowtal is equally popular and familiar in Indo-Fijian society.)

Given the minimal cultural contact between Bhojpuri India, Fiji, and the Caribbean since 1917, the parallels between the three chowtal traditions are remarkable. While numerous variants exist in all three regions, essentially identical versions of chowtal and its subgenres can also be found in each site, exhibiting the same form and style, with some of the same melodies and the same complex conventional rhythmic modulations. As mentioned elsewhere, versions of ulāra in the three areas are also basically identical, and they correspond to the form of chahkā recorded in 1972 by Henry in Ghazipur district. Further multilocale research would presumably reveal other equivalences. While it is seldom possible to ascertain the antiquity of folk songs in India or elsewhere, the documented parallels indicate that these song forms are at least a century old and presumably date back to the nineteenth century (if not earlier). They also indicate a remarkable persistence and stability in all three communities, coexisting, of course, with dramatic changes in other aspects of music culture. On the Caribbean side, the persistence of tradition has been aided by a conscious conservatism in chowtal performance. Hence, for example, while harmonium is widely used in other Caribbean genres, chowtal groups generally shun it, preferring a purist, more austere texture of only voices and percussion. Since Bhojpuri Indian groups currently have no objection to harmonium, its avoidance in the Caribbean can be seen as a sort of marginal survival—or perhaps better, a hypertraditionalist retention—of the Indian performance practice that predated the advent of that instrument.

My elderly Caribbean informants assert that chowtal was well established in their younger years and was sung by their immigrant parents in essentially the same style and contexts as it is today. One prominent sociomusical change has been the greater participation of women, both in the form of all-female groups (such as compete in Trinidadian contests) and in the occasional presence of women in temple and neighborhood groups (although women and men generally prefer to sing at different pitches). Such mixed ensembles would be exceptional in India and are also uncharacteristic in Fiji. A Guyanese informant related to me that even Afro-Caribbean neighbors might learn to sing chowtal as best they could, joining village ensembles. Another contextual development in both the Caribbean and Fiji has been the institutionalization of chowtal performance, especially in the form of nationwide competitions and festivals organized annually in Trinidad by Sanatanist Hindu organizations like the Hindu Prachar Kendra, Hindu Seva Sangh, and Sanatan Dharma Maha Sabha, and in Guyana by the Guyana Hindi Dharmic Sabha, which would each involve dozens of groups. In Trinidad, such institutionalized competitions have flourished especially since the mid-1980s. One organized by the National Phagwa Council typically features over sixty groups. Such events may be structured as competitions, with trophies or plaques awarded by panels of judges. Organizers and participants of such events may downplay the competitive aspect, although in the past, rivalries between Caribbean groups could be intense. Rudy Sasenarine lamented to me how such competitive sensibilities had often motivated erudite singers to hide rather than share their knowledge of recondite forms like lej and jati.

In Trinidad's 2012 National Phagwa Council's Chowtal Singing competition, the first prize was $10,000 TT (about US$1700); the several lesser prizes included those for best male and female drummers, best-dressed groups (male and female), and most promising groups (again, male and female). Each group was to consist of between fourteen and twenty-two members, having ten minutes in which to perform a chowtal and ulāra, and to "depict via portrayal (acting out) a synopsis of their rendition." In Guyana, formalized competitions have been less common, and Phagwa and chowtal singing have remained more rural and traditional in character, with neighborhood groups proceeding from house to house, singing and playing Holi (by throwing colored powder, hurling each other into canals ["trenching"], and the like). The competitive spirit, even if not institutionalized, can encourage groups to hone their renditions and cultivate esoteric subgenres like lej and jati. In the 2011 Phagwa season I accompanied Sasenarine to a chowtal session at a temple in the New York area, which was the home mandir of another well-rehearsed Guyanese chowtal

Figure 1. The New York Youth Ramayan and Chowtal Gol.
Photograph by the author.

group, led by a knowledgeable and welcoming enthusiast. In the previous year's gathering, that group's captain had led them in singing an obscure rasiya, in a manner which Sasenarine had interpreted as a veiled challenge to his own group. In 2011, determined not to be outdone, he gathered his core members in the temple parking lot and briefly reminded them how to sing a few of the more rarefied forms from the final pages of our published compilation. After they had reconvened inside, the singing commenced, with Sasenarine's newly formed all-women's group singing a spirited and well-received chowtal. Next, the host led his group in singing a familiar chowtal, and then, as Sasenarine had anticipated, proceeded to conduct them in singing a baiswāra, the likes of which would only be encountered from the best-trained groups. After a short break, Sasenarine's group then assembled and, after a familiar chowtal, segued to a seldom-heard lej. For the ethnomusicologist, the friendly rivalry provided a fine opportunity to hear these rare items.

Youth groups are another prominent feature of chowtal performance; day-long Phagwa sammelan festivals held at a temple in Queens, New York, typi-

cally include three or four such temple-based youth ensembles, each comprising more than thirty schoolchildren and teenagers who render (albeit with more enthusiasm than precision) various chowtals, kabīrs, and ulāras. Juvenile and teenage groups also abound in Fiji and in the Fijian secondary diaspora communities in California and Australia. In my research in Bhojpuri India, I neither found nor heard of counterparts to such groups. Nor are chowtal groups limited to the Caribbean, or to large communities like New York, as they are also found in such places as Atlanta, Georgia, and wherever a nucleus of Indo-Caribbean or Indo-Fijian enthusiasts and one or two competent guides can be found.[13] To Caribbean Hindus keen on preserving some sort of traditional religious and cultural identity, chowtal singing has come to serve as an entertaining and instructive temple-based activity that can unite young and old in a spirit of fun.

As mentioned above, a chowtal session in India today might occasionally take the form of a duel between two groups whose lyrics would respond to each other's posed questions or challenges. Contemporary Trinidadians and Guyanese lack the fluency in Hindi needed to engage in such repartees. However, as late as the 1960s there were many singers who, although born in the Caribbean, were raised in Bhojpuri-speaking families and used their linguistic fluency to compose chowtal lyrics. A few had booklets of their Hindi verses published in India (showing verses in both Hindi and Roman script) and imported to the Caribbean.[14] Some such chowtals, which may contain the *chāp* or pen name of their authors, are still sung by gols today. Some of their songs might adhere to the conventions of rītī verse, while others might be in the vein of the humorous, irreverent, and even risqué lyrics mentioned above. A favorite topic—at once contemporary and in the tradition of Kabir's sixteenth-century depictions of "topsy-turvy times"—comprises sardonic commentary on changing times and the downfall of Brahminical pretensions, such as this Guyanese chowtal:

Ab kal yūg sun lo bāyān suno nar nāri
Brahmin bābā murgī ko se khub bane kar kārī
Botal botal dāru mangāi, snāps snāps chāhī aī . . .

Listen to how Kali Yūg [the decadent present era] is these days
The Brahmin cooks his chicken, makes a nice curry
orders bottle after bottle of liquor, has his schnapps
His daughter has become a Christian and has changed her name to Lucy
And now she's shacked up with a black man . . .

In a similar vein is a 1950s Trinidadian chowtal by Bhil Pancharran Phulchan, describing Brahman pandits cooking fowl and drinking rum, and asking, "Women are dressing so lewdly, why not go all the way and walk about naked?"[15]

When such irreverent songtexts were common, they would traditionally be sung primarily after Shiv Ratri, with the earlier Phagwa period devoted to more conventional lyrics. Very few composers of chowtal lyrics are alive today in Trinidad and Guyana. Nowadays most groups rely on written texts, whether the aforementioned *Holi Chautāl Sangrah* and *Chautāl Phāgsangrah* or photocopied notebooks of romanized transliterations of them, or of lyrics written by an elder poet. (As with other Indo-Caribbean genres involving Hindi lyrics, niceties of pronunciation often suffer among the Anglophone Guyanese and Trinidadians.)

In Trinidad in 1993, an attempt to modernize chowtal was undertaken by Ravindra Nath Maharaj (Raviji), a cultural activist, newspaper columnist, spiritual leader, and director of the Hindu Prachar Kendra, which sponsors various cultural and religious events. Concerned that chowtal had ceased to be a vehicle for local poetic expression, he organized a competition for which groups were to compose English-language chowtals. During this period there seemed to be a particular intensity to the ongoing debates within the Indo-Trinidadian community as to cultural orientation. Those such as Raviji, in what might be called the "progressive" camp, encouraged not only traditional but also selected innovative art forms, in order to branch out to the creole community, reflect the reality of living in the West Indies and effectively revitalize Indian culture by contemporizing it. Conservatives—most conspicuously the often-inflammatory Satnarayan Maharaj, head of the Sanatan Dharm Mahasabha (SDMS)—denounced such undertakings as promoting "douglarization," that is, undermining the purity of Hindu culture through bastardization with the Afro-Saxon antagonist. Music often figured prominently in such debates (see Manuel 2000c). In the case of chowtal, Raviji's innovation proved to be so controversial that he organized a seminar to air diverse opinions on the subject. Sat Maharaj fulminated, "The Mahasabha will not be party to seducing chowtals into calypso singing," while another critic wrote, "If this practice started by the Kendra is not stopped, the age of soca, dub, and calypso tunes will obliterate all traces of Holiness in Holi."[16] While Raviji noted the popularity—and initially controversial nature—of Tulsidas's rendering of the Ramayan in vernacular Avadhi, a professor, Prakash Persad, retorted, "How do you think parang [a Spanish-language yuletide song form] will sound in English? The enjoyment comes from the Spanish words."[17]

From our present vantage point of twenty years later, we can observe that while English-language chowtals have not become widely popular, Raviji might nevertheless be pleased that chowtal remains vigorous, with competitions continuing to attract dozens of groups. Although singing parang in English has in

fact become increasingly common, the ongoing popularity of Hindi chowtal would seem to corroborate Persad's claim that much of the relish derives from the Hindi words.

Indo-Caribbean chowtal groups typically either coalesce during Phagwa season or else consist of temple-based kīrtan groups that switch to chowtal after Vasant Panchami, a few weeks prior to Phagwa. In the Caribbean and especially in Guyana, chowtal has also often been performed as a processional song, with a nucleus of core singers and a drummer walking through a village and being joined by (male) enthusiasts (with the women typically following behind); many may carry sticks. Once a group assembles at its destination, the sticks are added to a bonfire that commemorates the mythical immolation of Holika, around which the festival is based.

Some of the temple-based groups assume a fairly formal structure, with an elected or otherwise selected secretary, treasurer, public-relations man, and a "captain" who serves as general music director and assumes various responsibilities, such as providing jhāl cymbals and copies of songbooks to members who need them. The captain may also decide who gets to lead individual songs, perhaps nodding at the chosen person after a song ends. At that point, the designated leader of a song announces or simply commences the next, obliging some of the others to hurriedly flip through their notebooks to find it. (Ideally, participants have memorized songs, such that they can sing loudly with each other in merry visual communion rather than having to bury their heads in their notebooks.) In instances where there are textual insertions, the leader might cue his or her neighbors by quickly saying a key text word before it is to be sung. At anticipated rhythmic transitions, the drummer will be watching the leader closely for a glance or gesture indicating a shift, as most singers will follow the drummer's lead at such points. Various factors might influence the choice of songs. Some would say that only devotional rather than amatory "*rasikā*" songs are appropriate for a temple setting, and at a competition a group might well present some of its more specialized "technical" repertoire rather than a familiar chowtal like "Gokul bich janmeṅ" or "Shiv Shankar dīndayāl." Ideally, group sessions generate a sense of joyous camaraderie, to which I can attest as an occasional participant. However, human nature being what it is, some groups are rent by personal rivalries and enmities, which surface in such matters as choice of leaders and captains, and the degree of authority such personages command.

While certain core structures and melodies (such as that presented below) can be found throughout Trinidad, Guyana, and Suriname, distinctive versions of chowtal and lesser subgenres abound. Hence, for example, not only do fa-

vored Guyanese melodies differ somewhat from those of Trinidad, but within Guyana itself regional distinctions exist between, say, styles of Bath and Berbice districts. Some such differences may result from local innovations, but they may also derive from the influence of particular enthusiasts who immigrated from specific Bhojpuri-region locales, bringing their own distinctive homeland repertoires with them.

Chowtal in Indo-Fijian Music

From 1879 to 1916, some 61,000 Indians—predominantly from the Bhojpuri region—came to the Fiji islands as indentured workers. They now number some 311,000 in Fiji and around 145,000 in secondary diasporic sites, including California, Australia, and elsewhere. Indo-Fijian culture exhibits remarkable similarities to Indo-Caribbean culture, from its primarily Bhojpuri traditional base to the complex ethnic tensions involved in sharing the diasporic homeland with another population—in this case, the indigenous Fijians. Indo-Fijian society is perhaps especially similar to Indo-Surinamese society in that the indentureship program started a few decades later than it did in Trinidad and Guyana; as in Suriname, a version of Bhojpuri Hindi is still widely spoken. Knowledge of both Bhojpuri and standard Hindi has facilitated both perpetuation of traditional folk forms like chowtal as well as an easy familiarity with contemporary Indian culture, including film music and modern Bhojpuri commercial popular music. Such fluency allows Fijians, like Indo-Surinamese, to be adept at composing verses, both in the form of topical chowtals and jhūmars and in light, humorous genres like jogira.

Miller's insightful study of Fijian chowtal (2008), supplemented by my own limited fieldwork with Fijian immigrants in California, reveals close parallels with Indo-Caribbean chowtal, both in form and sociomusical aspects. Fijians, using the same Indian songbooks, sing some of the same chowtals, in the identical rhythmic structure and in closely similar melodies as can be found in India and the Caribbean. Their versions of several short-format subgenres like kabīr and ulāra are also essentially identical to Caribbean counterparts. Perhaps the most salient difference is that among most Indo-Fijians, while the term "chowtal" (or, in some contexts, "Faag") is used as a standard umbrella term, the common default long-format subgenre is a variety of jhūmar, rather than chowtal itself. Thus, for example, at the 2008 Faag Sammelan I attended in Sacramento, California, most of the items presented were jhūmars, with only two or three chowtals sung in the course of the event. The formal structure of Fijian jhūmar is essentially identical to that of chowtal, though the verses scan differently, and the stock melodies are also distinct (both from chowtal and from Caribbean jhūmars). Since jhūmars are less common in Indian chowtal

songbooks, Miller relates that groups tend to rely on texts published in sources such as Indo-Fijian newspapers (2008, 223).

Another difference from Caribbean chowtal is that Fijians, like their North Indian counterparts, are not hesitant to supplement the jhāl and dholak accompaniment with harmonium and other instruments, such as Hawaiian guitar, as might be available. The use of melodic instruments may contribute to the practice, by some groups, of modulating to a higher tonic pitch for the ulāra following a jhūmar or chowtal. Fijian Faag singing also has a somewhat more soloistic dimension, with the group leader alone singing a line at the start of a song and after key cadences. In a sammelan or competition, awards and announcements specify the leader rather than the group, and a given group might accompany different leaders in different songs. Meanwhile, the mixed male and female groups now common in the Caribbean are not typical of Indo-Fijian chowtal, although a few girls' groups participated in the 2008 sammelan I attended.

Chowtal Structure

A typical chowtal text, as indicated earlier, may be regarded as comprising an initial line (the ṭek) followed by three or four verses (pad), each essentially of two lines. The ṭek commences in what could be regarded as medium-tempo 7/8 meter, and after a few repetitions it adapts the same tune (the sthāī, or sthāyī) and text line to the quadratic meter, which Hindustani musicians might call kaharva, but which, as noted elsewhere, in the Caribbean is more likely to be called "chaubola," if it has any name at all; the singing then accelerates, and perhaps accelerates again, and then reverts to the original 7/8. After this rendering of the first text line, the pad is sung more or less as follows: the first line of the pad is performed four or six times (in other words, twice or thrice by each row of singers) to a new melody (tune #2) in chaubola, and then is accelerated, and then accelerated again once or twice. (Song collections like that of Chaturvedi [1989, 214] refer to this and subsequent lines as the antarā, but in its narrow and low range it has little of the character of a typical antarā. "Sthāī" and "antarā" are also musicological terms unlikely to be used or understood by chowtal singers.) The first half of the second line of the pad is then sung four or so times to its own tune (tune #3) and then sung faster. Then the second half of the second pad line, lengthened by adding the final words of the ṭek, is sung more or less in the same manner as line #1, that is, starting in 7/8 with the original sthāī melody, segueing to duple meter, and accelerating once or twice before reverting to a few renditions in 7/8. The subsequent pads are sung in more or less the same manner as the first one, such that the form is essentially strophic. This pattern may be schematized as follows:

tek, in tune #1 (*sthāī*) (6 mm):
4X in 7/8
4X in 4/8
4X in 4/8, faster
optional: 4X in 4/8, even faster
4X in 7/8 (original tempo)
1st line of *pad*, in tune #2, in duple meter (8 mm):
4X
2X, faster
2X, even faster
optional: 6X, even faster
1st half of 2nd line of *pad*, in tune #3, in duple meter (only 4 mm):
4X
4X, faster
2nd half of 2nd line of *pad*, in tune #1 (6 mm):
4X in 7/8
4X in 4/8
4X in 4/8, faster
optional: 4X in 4/8, even faster
4X in 7/8 (original tempo)

In practice, this pattern is subject to various kinds of alterations, whether in accordance with the conventions of a given group or with the signals given by the leader of a particular song.

Example 4 presents the ṭek and first *pad* of a chowtal, as recorded in a self-distributed cassette by the Mahatma Gandhi Satsang Society, the respected Indo-Guyanese gol based in Queens with which I studied and performed. The subsequent three *pad*s are sung in the same manner as the first *pad*, shown here. The form roughly follows that shown schematically above. The words "*bole Mahādev hara hara hara*" in the fifth staff (in the first line of the *pad*) are a nontextual interpolation, the likes of which might require cueing by the leader. The text derives from the *Holi Chautāl Sangrah* (Shrikrishandas 1985, 11), copies of which are regularly imported by some Indo-Caribbean bazaars. The initial sthāī tune is standard in the Caribbean, and is also notated in Slawek (1986, 263–65, 275–77) as performed by a Banaras group in 1981. (All notations in this volume are transposed to a tonic of C.)

Subsidiary Genres

As mentioned above, "chowtal," as a general synecdoche for a certain style or format of singing, comprises a set of several subgenres, of which the specific genre called chowtal constitutes the most important (except in Fiji). A typical Indo-Caribbean chowtal session might commence with an invocatory

Example 4. Chowtal. "Hori khelat janak dulāri"; ṭek and first *pad.*

sumiran, and/or *dohā*s (couplets, in the meter of the same name, sung in free rhythm). Subsequently one or two chowtals would typically be sung, each followed by an ulāra or dhamārī. The session might then segue to other genres, typically including one or more kabīrs and, in the case of house visits, ending with the farewell song "Sadā ānand," in which the host's name is mentioned. Repertoires of more knowledgeable groups might include lej, jātī, bilvarīyā, baiswāra, chahkā, jhūmar, rasiyā, jogira, and, in the Caribbean, perhaps some light chutney-style songs. The paucity of published descriptions, whether in Hindi or English, of the Bhojpuri versions of these subgenres is remarkable, especially in books purporting to survey the region's folk music. Even the most knowledgeable informants are generally unable to articulate the distinguishing criteria of these genres. What they know, instead, are particular songs with particular forms, which they may recognize as being in a certain genre, especially in accordance with being labeled thusly in the chapbook where they are found. By extension, a singer may be able to take a lyric found in a book, labeled a certain way, and set it to the mold of the designated genre. Most gol members will sing given songs without knowing or particularly caring which genre they represent.

Rasiyā and jhūmar are genres that exist independently of chowtal, being performed in various styles and contexts in the Bhojpuri region and elsewhere in North India. A few other genres, such as ulāra, exist only as components of a chowtal session. Whatever their structural differences may be, all acquire a certain homogeneity of style and texture when performed in chowtal, with its characteristic antiphonal format, instrumentation, and vocal style. Further, several of the subgenres—at least as performed in the chowtal context—adhere to the same limited repertoire of conventional melodies. Melodies of sumiran, kabīr, and rasiyā are (even) simpler and of more limited range than those of chowtal, typically alternating tonic and second degree, then foraying to the fourth degree and back to the tonic, all in kaharva, and subjected to accelerations and decelerations.

A chowtal is generally followed by an attached ulāra, which ideally is linked to that particular chowtal and corresponds in theme. As Mirzapur-area informant Suraj Singh noted, in the "duel" format, such as occurs occasionally in India, the ulāra—whose name derives from *ulārnā*, "to turn over"—is used to pose a question or challenge to the opposing group. Shorter than a chowtal, and set to up-tempo chaubola, ulāra has the character of a light dance song. Accordingly, among Fijians, ulāra might provoke dancing by women in a characteristic Bhojpuri style, with the same vigorous hip movements and graceful hand and arm gestures that also characterize Caribbean chutney dancing.[18]

Another common short-format genre is kabīr, which is also sung in other contexts in the Bhojpuri region (see Henry 1988, 125, 130). Although bhajans by the saint-poet Kabir are widely sung in Bhojpuri India and the Caribbean, knowledgeable informants note that the chowtal-style kabīr has nothing to do with that personage but is rather a corruption of the Hindi term *kabī* (poet). Kabīrs (along with certain other chowtal songs, confusingly) are preceded by the exclamation "Sun le morā kabīr"—"Listen to my kabir [poetry]."[19]

Chowtal and Diasporic Dynamics

In the more than ninety years that have elapsed since contacts between Bhojpuri India and the diasporic communities ceased, much has changed in their respective music cultures. Entire genres, not to mention songs, have died out, and new ones have arisen to take their places, whether under the influence of new technologies, new demographic contacts, or new socioeconomic conditions in general. The presence of identical music forms in South Asian, Fijian, and Caribbean contexts thus indicates a remarkable persistence within all three cultures.[20] Chowtal provides a particularly striking example of such continuity, with, for example, all three traditions containing versions of the basic structure described above and the melody shown as example 4. The panregional persistence of this tune and form reinforce a perspective that would regard the diasporic sites as microcosms of Bhojpuri-region India during the indentureship period.

Equally conspicuous, however, are the differences between the three communities. It is also these distinctions that most clearly pose questions relating to the dynamics of diasporic music and culture in general. Some of the most obvious differences relate to forces of creolization in the diaspora, as, for example, in the case of a hybrid genre like Trinidadian chutney-soca. However, both in the Caribbean and Fiji, chowtal singers have preferred to perpetuate the genre in its traditional forms, eschewing creolization. Thus, in comparing diasporic chowtal with its counterpart in the Bhojpuri region, the conspicuous distinction is not one of style but rather of degree of per capita popularity. While further research is needed to document conclusively the extent of chowtal's survival in North India, it seems safe to say that chowtal is not remotely as widespread (on a per capita basis) as it is in Indo-Caribbean and Indo-Fijian music culture, where it is universally familiar as a Phagwa-season folksong. Our ability to understand this contrast in degree of popularity is impeded by our ignorance of chowtal's history in India. Was it a widespread genre in the nineteenth century whose provenance subsequently shrank, or was it always based primarily in the Mirzapur/Allahabad region, somehow becoming general-

ized in the diaspora? My own surmise is that it was sufficiently common in the western Bhojpuri region such that it could disseminate amply to the diaspora. While chowtal's decline in India seems logical enough, what perhaps remains more challenging to explain is why it has spread and continues to flourish in the diaspora. Addressing this question raises broader issues of diasporic musical dynamics in general, and the factors conditioning the trajectories of other music genres and cultural entities. What seems likely is that chowtal—due to its distinctive features and the nature of the Bhojpuri diasporas—has turned out to be particularly well suited to flourish in the immigrant communities.

A major consideration in Indo-Trinidadian and Guyanese musical developments is that the decline of Bhojpuri Hindi in recent generations has vitiated text-driven musical genres (as opposed, for example, to tassa drumming) by eroding their linguistic base. Hence, among the Bhojpuri musical inheritance, narrative epic ballads like Ālhā have nearly disappeared, while women's folksong traditions formerly transmitted by oral tradition have also declined. As discussed in chapter 2 (and in Manuel 2000a, 77–82),[21] the only word-oriented traditional genres that can hope to survive in the Indic Caribbean are those in which performers can rely on printed texts. Hence, Trinidadian local-classical music, with its lyrics derived from old song anthologies, has managed to last, in however reduced a form, until the present. Bhajan groups continue to thrive, as their music is relatively simple and there is no shortage of songbooks, whether in Hindi script or Roman, and whether printed in India or the Caribbean.

Indo-Caribbean chowtal occupies a particular place in this continuum. As a site for competitive display of spontaneous versification, it no longer flourishes, if it ever did, and even the tradition of composing lyrics largely ended with the last generation. However, neither composition of new lyrics nor comprehension of existing ones is essential to the genre, such that chowtal groups, as mentioned, have been able to rely on booklets and notebooks, whose meaning can be explained by a knowledgeable pandit. Moreover, while it would be unfair to characterize bhajan singing as monotonous, chowtal certainly offers a different dimension of excitement and musical camaraderie to the enthusiast. The loosening of social inhibitions regulating male-female interaction has also enabled women and girls to augment the ranks of temple-based groups. Moreover, chowtal is particularly effective as a celebration of the devotional bhakti-oriented Hinduism (as opposed to Brahminical orthodoxy and ritual) that predominates in the diaspora. Hence, even if chowtal was originally brought by immigrants from one particular region, it proved to be well suited to the diasporic music culture, such that it could spread and even enjoy a greater durability than its Bhojpuri-region counterpart. Elder singers, to be sure, lament what they regard as the decline of chowtal, in terms of numbers of groups,

variety of subgenres actively sung, and the excellence and precision of rendering. Even in culturally vigorous Trinidad, informants like Suresh Kalladeen of the renowned Shri Krishan Chowtal Gol, state that the genre was weakened by the emigration and dispersal of many top musicians during the economic recession of the 1980s (p.c.).

Such factors may help explain chowtal's popularity and resilience and are perhaps more satisfying to the scholar than would be the attribution of music history to arbitrary accident. Most intriguing, the case of chowtal may suggest the existence of a neotraditional stratum of Bhojpuri diasporic culture—especially in Fiji and the Caribbean—that is not only relatively uniform but in some ways distinct from its counterpart in Indian Bhojpuri culture, past and present.

The Enigmatic Dantāl

Chowtal is not the only example of a neotraditional music entity that has become proportionally more widespread in the diaspora than it was in the ancestral homeland. Another instance of this phenomenon is represented by the dantāl, which has also constituted an enigma of sorts in Bhojpuri diasporic music culture. The dantāl is a metal idiophone consisting of a rod about four feet long, with one end tapered or roughly sharpened and the other bent into a small loop. The player, sitting cross-legged on the floor, rests the looped end in front of him and, holding the rod vertically, strikes it with a U-shaped clapper (which may be called the *tāli*) while grasping and releasing the rod with his other hand in order to dampen or prolong the sound. The most common pattern played is a simple *ching chickaching chickaching*. The instrument's name derives from the Hindi compound of *ḍaṇḍ* (stick, rod) + *tāl*, in this case a suffix denoting a percussion instrument, as in *kartāl* (a pair of short wooden or metal sticks struck together). The resultant compound *ḍaṇḍtāl* is pronounced "dantāl" in the Caribbean, with the conventional retroflex Trinidadian/Guyanese 't' in this case according with proper Hindi pronunciation. (Trinidadians, fond of inserting the letter *h* as an orthographical icon of Indianness, sometimes spell the word "dhantal," although the word contains no aspiration, as such a rendering might suggest.)

The dantāl (as we shall spell it) is an indispensable member of the standard Bhojpuri diaspora Ur-trio also comprising the harmonium and the dholak. This ensemble constitutes the conventional accompaniment for bhajans, filmsongs, local-classical music, "classical" chutney, and other miscellaneous folksongs. Indeed, it is perhaps simpler to specify the genres in which dantāl is *not* employed; these would include chowtal and *Mānas* singing (in which the more portable and easily accessible jhāls are instead played), tassa drumming (us-

ing a larger jhāl or jhānjh), the South Indian–derived drum ensemble used for Kali worship, and, of course, creole/Westernized or classical Hindustani ensembles. Strikingly (as it were), the dantāl is equally common in Indo-Fijian music, in the same range of contexts. While the dantāl is not exactly a "homemade" instrument, it is easily enough fashioned at a basic machine shop, using readily available automobile brake spring material for the rod. Many percussionists do in fact shape the rod and tāli themselves, if they have access to requisite tools.[22]

The ubiquity of the dantāl in the Bhojpuri diaspora obviously suggests a Bhojpuri-region or at least North Indian origin. However, the instrument is in fact almost unheard of in the Bhojpuri area, not to mention the rest of India, and therein lies an intriguing enigma, whose examination is revealing, in its way, of the dynamics of the Bhojpuri diaspora. The dantāl's origin and spread have in fact been the subject of considerable speculation, much of which has been weakened by an inattention to the status of the instrument in India itself.

One set of theories plausibly attempts to locate the instrument's origin in various tools or implements, surmising, for example, that it derived from a tool for stirring coals in an oven, or from the axle of an oxcart, or from a tether for domestic animals (comprising a rod driven into the ground, with a protruding ring to which a rope may be attached).[23] As discussed below, the origin of the instrument in a utilitarian object seems overwhelmingly likely, but this still does not resolve the mystery of its dramatically uneven distribution.

Several Trinidadians have claimed that the dantāl was invented in their country and spread from there to Guyana, Suriname, Fiji, and even back to India. There may be an element of ethnic nationalism animating this hypothesis, as many Indo-Trinidadians are sensitive to creole accusations that their culture is a mere derivative or imitation of India's, unlike that of the Afro-Trinidadians, with their celebrated invention of calypso and the steel drum, and Indians may be accordingly eager to claim local creation of cultural entities. At any rate, while it is not impossible that the dantāl was invented in Trinidad, there are good reasons to question this theory. First, as we shall note, there is strong evidence suggesting the prior existence of counterparts and predecessors in the Bhojpuri region. Second, even if the diaspora were to be claimed as the instrument's cradle, there is no particular reason to favor Trinidad as the site rather than British Guiana (Fiji and Suriname being somewhat less likely sites given the later commencement of their indentureship programs).

As I shall suggest, it may be impossible to arrive at a definitive answer to the enigma posed by the dantāl. However, some progress can be made by, at the very least, framing and posing the appropriate questions, with requisite attention to the status—past and present—of the instrument in India itself.

Figure 2. A dantāl in Fiji. Photograph by Kevin Miller.

An initial point is that the dantāl, by that same name, although obscure in India, is not entirely unheard of. In Banaras in 2009 I interviewed two elderly singers (of birha and chowtal) who were well familiar with the instrument, attesting that until recently it was not uncommon in the Bhojpuri region, being employed to accompany various sorts of folksong. At present, they related, it has declined along with various other folk music entities, and they were unaware of it still being used.[24] Ethnomusicologist Laxmi Tewari also noted the use of the instrument, by that name, to accompany Ālhā singing (1993, 16). Finally, the instrument is depicted and identified by name in Hiralal Tiwari's 1980 survey of Gangetic-plain folk music.[25]

Equally significant is that an essentially identical instrument, whether called ḍaṇḍtāl or not, has been used in the region, especially to accompany Ālhā-singing (whose proper accompaniment instrument may be called *gaj*, *sīnk*, or *sariya*, as well as ḍaṇḍtāl (Tewari 1993, 16). Similarly, Karine Schomer, in her writing on Ālhā performance, indicates the use of the gaj and jhīk, describing the latter as an elephant prod struck with another piece of metal (1990, 62, and p.c.). She also provides the basic gaj rhythmic pattern—"*tā* tika tā tika *tā* tika tā tika"—which is identical to the aforementioned standard pattern of the diasporic dantāl (1992, 67). These four terms designate implements designed for primary purposes other than music making. Platts's 1884 dictionary defines gaj (from Persian *gaz*, "a yard") as "a yard measure, a ramrod" (897); sīnk is "the hooked iron instrument with which bread is drawn from ovens" (714); and sariya is "a thin iron rod (used in making bars or fences, &c)" (658). Schomer's definition of jhīk as elephant prod might conceivably have derived from her informants, but more typically, and certainly in my own experience, the elephant prod is called *āṅkush* (or *āṅkus*, *āṅkas*), while jhīk or jhīkā denotes an idiophone consisting of a tablet-sized wooden frame with jingles attached, which is shaken and/or struck. The elephant prod might roughly resemble a dantāl, but more typically the sharpened point and the hook are both at the same end. When struck with a U-shaped tāli, the gaj, sīnk, or sariya could provide a metallic timbral supplement to the dholak, harmonium, and voice, and, unlike cymbals (jhāl, jhānjh, manjīra) can play crisp sixteenth notes as well as resonant longer notes. It is highly improbable that the musical use of these diverse traditional implements in the Ālhā zone could have derived from a differently named instrument invented in the Caribbean. In other words, evidence strongly suggests that the instrument was invented in India, if by "instrument" we mean to denote an extant implement played as an idiophone, with the same technique and the same typical rhythm as those of the dantāl. What was new about the dantāl was, first, the practice of constructing it specifically for use as a musical instrument, and second, the corresponding designation of it by the name ḍaṇḍtāl, a term akin to and obviously modeled on the extant instruments kartāl and the jhīk-like *kaṭhtāl*.[26] (The kartāl also appears in Platts's 1884 dictionary.)

We are thus in a position to pose the appropriate questions constituting the enigma of the dantāl. First, when and where did the practice of constructing the instrument and naming it "ḍaṇḍtāl" emerge? Second, and more important, why did this instrument become so common in the diaspora (especially the Caribbean and Fiji) while remaining (or becoming?) obscure in India?

An initial possibility is that the dantāl was common in India during the indentureship period and subsequently declined there, such that its popularity in the diaspora represents a marginal survival. However, there is no particular

evidence to support this scenario, given the complete absence of references to the instrument before the 1980s—as opposed, for example, to the kartāl, which is cited by Platts. A second possibility is that it was in fact invented in the diaspora—most likely Trinidad or British Guiana. In order to thence reach Fiji, the dantāl, or the notion and intent of making one, could conceivably have been borne to Fiji by Caribbean-returned workers who enrolled for subsequent indentureships, this time in Fiji. However, the numbers of such second-time multisite indentureds appear to have been relatively small.[27] More plausible is the dissemination of the dantāl through the embarkation depot in Calcutta, which might also well have been the locale for the instrument's "invention," that is, its deliberate construction as an instrument with a new name. At any given time during the indentureship program, a few hundred people would be residing, in some cases for several months, in this encampment, awaiting transport to whichever colony was their assigned or chosen destination. As there was no work to be done in the camp, the indentureds must have indulged in a considerable amount of collective music-making activities to pass the time. Neither in the camp nor in their destinations would there be any need for elephant prods, and it is entirely likely that in those sites sariyas and sīnks were not available in such quantities as to fulfill the demand for metal idiophones in the evening song sessions. It is easy enough to imagine an enthusiastic sariya player who has not brought such an implement to the depot with him and who does not envision obtaining one in the colony, where he will be cutting cane rather than baking bread. In order to contribute more actively to the song sessions during the unanticipated months of waiting, for a modest fee he engages a nearby blacksmith to fashion a sariya-like instrument, which he, or someone, baptizes with the neologism "ḍanḍtāl."

The spread of the instrument—manufactured as such, and bearing its new name—may have been expedited by the paucity of traditional implements like gaj, sariya, and sīnk (not to mention elephant prods) in the new homelands. In the colonies, it may simply have been more expedient—at least for the earliest immigrants—to have a local smith forge a dantāl than to locate, borrow, or otherwise obtain a traditional Indian-style implement for use in song sessions. Perhaps by the time that diasporic infrastructures—that is, local blacksmiths— were producing versions of sariya and sīnk, a tradition of fashioning dantāls and designating them as such, had already taken root and then grew apace of its own accord. Meanwhile, in India, the dantāl per se might find its way back to the Bhojpuri region, but it might be just as easy to adapt a sariya or sīnk for that purpose. That is to say, it is quite plausible that the origin of the dantāl— manufactured and named as such—was in fact associated with the diaspora.

At this point the reader may protest that this scenario, however plausible,

remains conjectural, and that it still fails to explain why the dantāl-type metal-lophone should become so common in the diaspora; why, that is, should the dantāl in Fiji and the Caribbean come to be considerably more widespread than are the ḍanḍtāl, gaj, sariya, and sīnk, combined, in India? It is this question, indeed, that constitutes the fundamental mystery of the dantāl. I suspect that the question may never be resolved, and in many respects my own hypothesis may constitute little more than one man's conjecture among many. I would, however, suggest two considerations.

First, it is customary in Bhojpuri folk music ensembles for the harmonium and dholak to be supplemented by some sort of metal idiophone, whether cymbals (manjīrā, jhāl, jhānjh), a dantāl-type instrument, or a *chimta* (a pair of loosely attached metal rods clinked together). As we have seen, Indo-Caribbean chowtal and *Mānas* ensembles, as well as tassa bands, still incorporate cymbals, but the manjīra is relatively uncommon, and the chimta is not used at all. It may be said that the dantāl has largely replaced the manjīra and chimta, as well as the gaj, sariya, and sīnk, in what could be regarded as a process of consolidation and streamlining of musical resources.

Second, it could be argued that the preference for the dantāl over these instruments, and its general spread, may accord with a tendency in Indo-Caribbean music—evident more in some genres than others—to highlight the rhythmic dimension of music. This tendency can to some extent be seen as a means of heightening purely musical interest in a situation where Hindi comprehension has declined. Hence, for example, the prominent and virtuoso dholak playing that accompanies local-classical music, and, it may be added, the remarkable abundance of dholak virtuosos in Trinidad, which surely exceeds that in India on a per capita basis. The dantāl, although not exactly suited to display virtuoso pyrotechnics, is capable of playing basic patterns—especially fast sixteenth notes—that are impossible on cymbals or the chimta. A competent dantāl player can provide a lively percussive complement to the rollicking dholak, with the two instruments together rendering an animated rhythmic accompaniment that might be considered superfluous, or even inappropriate, in various counterpart genres in India, where the intelligible Hindi text is instead the focus of aesthetic interest.

Chowtal and the Dantāl as Diasporic Icons

Such speculations and observations may not resolve the enigma of the dantāl's disproportionate spread in the diaspora relative to its presence in India. Abandoning further contemplation of this conundrum, we may return to the theme suggested in the introduction to this chapter, namely, the qualitative link be-

tween chowtal and the dantāl as diasporic entities, and their implications for Bhojpuri diasporic music culture. As we have seen, both chowtal and dantāl-type instruments derive from India and have been perpetuated essentially in their traditional forms in the Bhojpuri diaspora, including Indo-Fijian culture. Neither has undergone any particular process of creolization. Strikingly, both have become more widespread, on a per capita basis, than their counterparts in India have. As such they represent a distinctive feature of the Bhojpuri diaspora—from Fiji to the Caribbean—in which traditional, India-derived musical entities come to occupy greater proportional prominence than in the ancestral homeland. Clearly, certain factors—whose identification may be difficult—have made these entities particularly well suited to flourish in the diaspora. Hence they illustrate a sense in which even the neotraditional stratum of Bhojpuri diasporic music culture constitutes neither a microcosm of its North Indian ancestor nor a diluted or creolized version thereof, but instead a distinct entity in which certain traditional elements have, for various reasons, flourished to a greater extent than in the ancestral homeland.

At the risk of digression, a striking parallel may be noted, outside the realm of music, in another Bhojpuri-derived diasporic entity—specifically, the *jhaṇḍi*. A jhaṇḍi is a triangular flag mounted atop a bamboo pole, typically in sets of three or four, rooted in a dirt-filled pot. In the Bhojpuri diaspora, jhaṇḍis are nearly ubiquitous features in front of Hindu homes of the Sanatanist mainstream (that is, as opposed to Kali worshipers or Arya Samajis). Thus they abound not only in Fiji and the Indic Caribbean, but also in Queens (New York), Sacramento (California), and wherever Bhojpuri secondary diasporic communities exist. The jhaṇḍi is associated especially with Hanuman the monkey-god (a prominent figure in the Ramayan), who, among Bhojpuri diasporic Hindus, has the status of a patron saint akin to that of St. Patrick among the Irish. A Sanatanist family typically replaces their jhaṇḍis every few years, inviting a pandit to perform an accompanying ritual, and perhaps hosting a festive party to further commemorate the event (which may itself thus be called a "jhaṇḍi"). A ragged and faded jhaṇḍi, though better than no jhaṇḍi at all, is taken to indicate a household that is poorly maintained, whether due to poverty or indifference.[28]

Since jhaṇḍis are so ubiquitous in the diaspora, when I revisited the Banaras area in 2008 with eyes and ears newly attuned to the quest for diasporic roots, I naturally expected to see them fluttering in front of homes throughout villages and towns. However, I was surprised to see no domestic jhaṇḍis at all; further, informants from other parts of the region—such as hotel menials from Bihar—assured me that there was no tradition of erecting domestic jhaṇḍis in their areas. Jhaṇḍis, it emerged, are maintained primarily at Hanuman temples, rather than by private homes.

The conspicuous proliferation of jhandis in the Bhojpuri diaspora has been noted by a few other commentators, especially Vertovec (1992, 226) and Jain (1988, 139, cited in Vertovec). Jain notes how jhandis in Trinidad have come to serve as statements of material success, of "having arrived" both in geographical and economic terms. This interpretation, though probably accurate, does not entirely explain why jhandis should proliferate in the diaspora more than in India. In fact, it is likely that jhandi flags, although uncommon throughout most of the Bhojpuri region, came to be widely adopted in the diaspora because Hindus found in them a convenient way of proudly asserting their social identity in a new situation in which they had to coexist with other ethnic groups. Whatever the reason, their abundance constitutes another instance of the phenomenon noted with chowtal and the dantāl, in which a traditional entity brought from the Bhojpuri region acquires new popularity and vitality—and to some extent, new meaning—in the diaspora.

Bhojpuri Diasporic Music and the Encounter with India

Thus far this volume has focused on a set of traditional music genres—such as birha, chowtal, and Ramayan singing—that have flourished within the most conservative stratum of Bhojpuri-derived Indo-Caribbean music culture. Given the tradition-oriented nature of this cultural sector, I have made little mention of sociomusical influences external to the Bhojpuri core of Indo-Caribbean society, instead stressing the continuities with ancestral or parallel practices in India and even Fiji. Such an approach should not suggest, of course, that any level of Indo-Caribbean culture can be regarded as insular, hermetically sealed, and impervious to influence from or interaction with other cultures. Most obvious and extensive has been the relation of Indo-Caribbean communities with creole West Indian culture—an interaction that, whether in reference to music in particular or culture in general, has been the focus of a fair amount of scholarly literature (see, for example, Manuel 2000b), along with endless and ongoing journalistic and lay debate. Far less attention has been paid to the complex relationship with another cultural complex that could also be regarded as external to the traditional culture brought by the indentured immigrants, namely, the diverse forms of mainstream North Indian culture that began reaching the Caribbean in force a few decades after the indentureship program ended in 1917. Particularly prominent among these inputs were Hindi films and film music recordings, and the visits of diverse Hindu godmen and sectarian proselytists. Most Indo-Caribbeans welcomed these cultural inputs, especially insofar as they mitigated the bleak isolation following 1917, when ships from India stopped coming and the pressures to creolize or Anglicize intensified. Through the advent of Hindi films, records, and visiting gurus, local

Indians were able to renew and reinvigorate their sense of Indian identity, even as Afro-creole and Western elements—especially but not only in the realm of language—were inexorably threatening Indian traditions.

The influence of imported Hindi films was particularly profound. Indian "talkies" began to be produced in Bombay in 1931, and within a decade the Indian cinema industry was blossoming, churning out prodigious numbers of feature films that achieved mass popularity. Almost all releases featured song-and-dance scenes, and the rapidly evolving genre of Bombay Hindi filmsong, as produced by a tiny coterie of artists and marketed by a single record company, with the apt logo "His Master's Voice" (HMV), soon came to dominate and virtually define the field of commercial popular music in North India. Hindi films were of course produced primarily for their home South Asian audiences, but from the 1950s they attained wide appeal throughout much of the developing world. From Nigeria to Turkestan, audiences enjoyed the songs, dances, and extravagant sets, whether or not the particular Bollywood ideologies and aesthetics matched their own sensibilities. In the Indic Caribbean, the natural appeal of the Bombay blockbusters and their music was supplemented by their special value as links to the distant but still cherished ancestral homeland. After the success of the first imported Hindi talkie to the Caribbean, *Bala Joban*, in 1935, imported Hindi films and their music became basic constituents of Indo-Caribbean cultural life, even among second- and third-generation immigrants who could only partially understand the Hindi-Urdu dialogue and song lyrics in the films, which seldom featured subtitles before the 1970s. Narsaloo Ramaya (b. 1920), a musician and an astute chronicler of Trinidadian music culture, described the impact of Hindi films: "Before that we had only seen Hollywood films, with white people. Then seeing our own people in *Bala Joban* and the films following it, a certain amount of pride developed in us, and we became interested in Indian things, including Indian music" (p.c.). As he further related, the imported movies and records helped create a generation of "born-again Indians [who] sought their ancestral links and developed a passion to acquaint themselves with and appreciate the value of Indian culture and civilization" (1996).[1] Weekend film screenings in Chaguanas and other Indian-dominated towns became focal community cultural events, and the advent of television in the 1970s and videos in the 1980s increased film consumption. From the 1950s, the popularity of filmsongs was further intensified by radio programs, record sales, and visits of Bombay stars like dancer-actress Hema Malini and vocalist Hemant Kumar, whose performances were vividly recalled by several of my older informants. Consequently, by the 1960s Hindi filmsong had become the single most popular kind of music among Indo-Caribbeans. In many Indo-Caribbean homes and workplaces, Indian film music may be playing almost

constantly, and Indian films came to provide a new connection with India, in a medium that is at once colorful, alluring, idiosyncratically modern, and distinctively Indian.

The mid-century decades saw a dramatically increasing flow of goods from India, including household and religious items, books, and photographs of movie stars and Indian leaders, which came to adorn walls throughout the community. Alongside these came steady numbers of visiting Hindu holy men, whether proselytists of the reformist Arya Samaj sect or, more often, pandits purveying what was becoming a standardized, mainstream form of North Indian and Indo-Caribbean Hinduism, referred to as Sanatan Dharm. In effect, if the indentureship period of 1845–1917 constituted an initial, formative era of Indian input to the Caribbean, the stream of cinematic, musical, and religious entities intensifying from the 1930s comprised a second chapter, of quite a distinct character.

It may seem paradoxical, if not nonsensical, to regard such South Asian entities as foreign or external to a society of Indian immigrants who were only a generation or two removed from India and who eagerly welcomed these inputs as ties to their ancestral homeland. However, the reception and digestion of these imported entities were not unproblematic; rather, they were complicated by a fundamental tension resulting from the fact that the newly arriving Hindi films, records, and visiting swamis represented aspects of a mainstream urban North Indian culture that was in many ways quite distinct from the rustic Bhojpuri heritage of the indentureds and their offspring. This disjuncture—whether or not controversial or even acknowledged—has constituted a fundamental dynamic in the evolution of Indo-Caribbean culture since the late 1930s, and one that has received little scholarly recognition, whether in reference to music or other dimensions of culture.

There is in fact a set of distinct, if overlapping, aspects to the discontinuities between traditional Bhojpuri-derived Indo-Caribbean culture and the new complex of inputs arriving from the 1930s. One of these dimensions comprised the relationship between a local, regional tradition—the Bhojpuri folk culture brought by the indentureds—and the larger, panregional North Indian "mainstream" culture represented, in however different forms, by Bombay films and visiting pandits. The encounter also involved an interaction between traditional and modern forms of Indian culture, with the Indo-Caribbean cultural core comprising a heritage largely derived from nineteenth-century immigrants, now confronting a set of twentieth-century entities, from Bollywood hits to reformist repackagings of Hinduism such as the Sanatan Dharm. Third, alongside the traditional/modern and regional/panregional dynamics, the new inputs from India involved a disjuncture between a Bhojpuri heritage, which was largely of rural

peasant origin, and a new cultural complex based in an emerging urban and in many ways middle-class society. Collectively, these discontinuities meant that while a Hindi film such as the 1957 *Mother India* was welcomed, like other imported movies, as a link to the ancestral motherland, the culture that film represented was in many respects not a maternal one; it was not the Bhojpuri "mother" but rather more like a distant city aunt, whose attitude toward rustic Bhojpuri culture might have been, if anything, disdainful and condescending.

The cultural disjunctures were manifest in a number of spheres. Perhaps most overt was the linguistic disparity involved. By the turn of the century, if any South Asian language was domestically spoken or used as a lingua franca in the Caribbean, it would be Bhojpuri, or more properly, an amalgamation of similar Bhojpuri-region subdialects with elements of Awadhi. However, Bhojpuri had no place in the new cultural entities arriving in the 1930s; the imported Bombay films were in an Urdu-inflected form of panregional standard Hindustani, and the visiting pandits and pooh-bahs used a similarly mainstream idiom, albeit with a more Sanskritized lexicon, which would also be the language taught in various formal and informal Hindi classes. The advent of the standard panregional form of Hindustani in many ways served to devalue rather than reinforce the status of Bhojpuri in the Caribbean.

Paralleling this linguistic asymmetry was a disjuncture in the realm of religion. As mentioned in this book's introduction, the indentured immigrants could be regarded as very roughly approximating a cross-section of North Indians as a whole in comprising around eighty-five percent Hindus and the remainder Muslims. Moreover, many aspects of Indo-Caribbean beliefs and practices corresponded to those found throughout much of North India. At the same time, however, much of Indo-Caribbean Hinduism consisted of fragmented, localized Bhojpuri-region folk religion elements, such as village godlings (typically called "Dih") and superstitions, transplanted to the Caribbean. Most Hindus followed particular sects popular in the Bhojpuri region, especially those of the Kabir panthis, Siewnarainis (about which more will be said later), Agora panthis, and Ramanandis, along with the South Indian-derived Kali/Mariamman worshipers. To these was added the Arya Samaj reformist sect. Over the decades, however, and especially through the influence of visiting pandits from the 1920s and 1930s, the panregional North Indian Sanatan Dharm came to comprise something of an Indo-Caribbean mainstream, absorbing the Ramanandis, outnumbering the Arya Samajis and Kabir panthis, and effectively marginalizing the Siewnarainis and Agora panthis (see Vertovec 1992, 106–12).[2] All these religious sects and movements had their own associated music traditions, such that their trajectories in the diaspora had direct ramifications on musical practice, as will be considered below.

As mentioned in chapter 1, the various contrasting cultural practices outlined here, in their dynamics of region, class, and tradition-versus-modernity aspects, roughly correspond to a dichotomy common in South Asian studies, between great and little traditions. In terms of Hindu religion, the "little traditions" would comprise the myriad village godlings, superstitions, local-dialect incantations, and venerated sites such as trees and stones, all rooted in parochial oral tradition. These entities were in a perpetual and complex relationship with canonic, great-tradition Hinduism, which consisted of panregional practices and beliefs ultimately grounded in written and especially Sanskritic texts. The concept of great and little traditions has been productively, albeit with certain qualifications, extended to other aspects of South Asian culture, including music. Thus, for example, much of Indo-Caribbean traditional culture—including language, religion, and music—could be categorized as Bhojpuri-derived little traditions, which found themselves increasingly in a dialectic relationship, whether enriching or impoverishing, with mainstream North Indian great traditions, especially from the 1920s and 1930s. Although the notion of "great tradition" typically connotes an established body of Sanskritic religious belief, I believe that Bombay film culture—including music—can be aptly regarded as a new sort of commercial great tradition in its own right—panregional in scope, urban professional in origin, well established since the 1940s, embedded in mass-mediated "texts" (in this case, films) rather than unsupported oral tradition, and engaged in a complex dialectic with regional oral traditions.[3]

While the encounter between Bhojpuri-derived Indo-Caribbean traditions and the mainstream Indian culture arriving from the 1920s and 1930s can be seen as a confrontation between great and little traditions, this dynamic, far from being a purely diasporic phenomenon, has in many ways paralleled that extant in India itself. Hence, much of the discussion that follows might well be applicable to corresponding processes transpiring in India's Bhojpuri region. Within the Bhojpuri region itself, culture—from music to religion and cuisine— has long been animated by a dynamic interaction between the parochial and the panregional, the vernacular oral and the institution-backed scriptural, and, in modern times, the grassroots and the commercial corporate. As such, many of the interactions described in the following pages find counterparts within the Bhojpuri region itself. In my 1993 study *Cassette Culture*, for instance, I discussed aspects of the complex relationship between Bhojpuri regional folk and folk-pop music on the one hand, and Bollywood film music on the other, and the role that grassroots control of the means of musical production played in this changing dynamic. At the same time, however, certain features distinctive to the Indo-Caribbean diasporic situation should be noted. First, in an Indian setting like the Bhojpuri region, great and little traditions are engaged

in an ongoing dialectic of interaction and mutual influence. While the great tradition constitutes in many respects a hegemonic force, it can also absorb elements from little traditions, in a process Marriott termed "universalization"; meanwhile, a converse phenomenon of "parochialization" can occur, wherein regional subcultures can effectively indigenize great-tradition practices and beliefs by incorporating them into local structures. However, in the Indic Caribbean the rapport of little and great traditions has always consisted less of a genuine interaction than a unidirectional flow. That is, while India provided a steady stream of Bombay films, visiting holy men, commercial recordings, and other entities, there has been virtually no reciprocal output from the Caribbean to India (aside from one or two recent chutney songs that have enjoyed ephemeral popularity in India).

Another distinctive feature of the Indo-Caribbean diaspora has been the dramatic cessation of contact with the Bhojpuri region itself. As we have seen, some aspects of Bhojpuri culture in the Caribbean, such as chowtal, have proved to be remarkably resilient, but the geographic rupture has occasioned a variety of divergences from ancestral homeland practices. These include some marginal survivals, such as the standard birha tune, but more conspicuous is the decline of various traditions in the diaspora, especially the Bhojpuri language and related entities that expired unsupported in the third generation of immigrants. Further, while most Bhojpuri-derived traditions were not static, frozen artifacts in the Caribbean, their vitality, dependent as it is on inherited momentum, cannot be compared to that of their counterparts in the Gangetic plains, where Bhojpuri culture has continued to evolve as an organic and vigorously fecund entity animated by a living linguistic basis. Hence, for example, the thriving field of modern Bhojpuri-language commercial popular music, as sung by artists such as Kalpana Patowary and Dinesh Lal Yadav, which in the Caribbean has neither mass popularity nor a local counterpart, pop chutney notwithstanding. Finally, even in a discussion of Indian great- and little-tradition interaction, it bears mentioning that while Westernization is certainly a potent element in modern North India, it is obviously more immediate and ubiquitous a factor in the Caribbean, and it is present primarily in the particular form of Afro-creole culture.

The phenomenon described here is fairly unique among global diasporas, involving a situation in which a population transplanted from a particular backward rural hinterland is, after a few decades of relative isolation, subjected to a heavy and ongoing cultural infusion from a related but distinct urban culture. Such a sequence of events is different from the more typical disjunctures of multigenerational diasporas, where the elders adhere to traditional ancestral

homeland culture while the youngsters—often second-generation immigrants— acculturate, syncretize, and assimilate to the mainstream culture of the new homeland. There may be few other diasporic groups exhibiting the pattern evident in the Indo-Caribbean scenario, except on a much smaller scale, as in, for example, the Kurdish-speaking family from Tabriz, which, having emigrated to Miami, in the second and third generations remains isolated from its ancestral homeland but is eventually able to access cultural inputs from urban, Persian-speaking Iran. Alternately, to take a hypothetical example, a comparable situation might arise if members of Yoruba-derived subcultures in Cuba and Brazil found themselves inundated with cultural influences from modern Nigeria, centered around standard modern Yoruba language rather than the archaic koine amalgamated from rural nineteenth-century dialects spoken by their ancestors.

The Musical Great Traditions from India: Enriching or Impoverishing?

The relation between great and little traditions in the Caribbean, as in India, constitutes a complex dialectic conducive to several analytical perspectives. A particularly obvious set of questions involves whether the great traditions are best seen as culturally enriching or hegemonically impoverishing in relation to established little traditions. In my 1993 book *Cassette Culture*, I examined this problem with regard to commercial popular music in North India. In the opening sections of that book I suggested that Hindi film music, while in many ways richer and more varied than individual regional folk musics, constituted in some respects a sort of superimposed, corporate-produced common-denominator entity that, in its linguistic and stylistic uniformity and its domination by a tiny clique of producers, tended to thrive at the expense of the extraordinary diversity of regional musics. The hegemony of the commercial "great tradition" of Hindi filmsong, as monopolized by the EMI label, was ultimately thwarted by the emergence of cassette technology in the 1980s, which enabled the emergence of hundreds of cottage-cassette producers, large and small, who proliferated by marketing an unprecedented variety of new hybrid musics to diverse regional audiences.

In the Caribbean, the advent of Indian musical great traditions, from filmsongs to the Hindi bhajans sung by Sanatanist pandits, has had similarly mixed effects. From one perspective, the new musical inputs from India dramatically expanded and enriched what was a relatively finite and in some ways static Bhojpuri music tradition. Despite the variety of Bhojpuri music genres

transmitted to the Caribbean and the innovative vitality exhibited by genres like local-classical music and tassa drumming, a great proportion of Bhojpuri music could be characterized as relying on a quite limited set of melodies and rhythms. George Grierson, writing of Bhojpuri music in India in the 1880s, commented on this heavy reliance on stock tunes: "This paucity of melodies has often struck me. In the country districts I have never heard of a new tune being invented. There seems to be a certain stock of tunes ready made, to which the words of every song must be fitted. . . . So certain songs sung in the month of Chait are classed as *ghatos*, because they are sung to the tune called *ghato*, and the class of songs sung in the rainy season is called *kaj'ri*, which is the name of the air to which they are sung" (1886, 210). To Grierson's comment could be added the observation that most of the stock tunes themselves exhibited relatively little variety, relying overwhelmingly on obvious diatonic modes and especially simple sa-re-ga-ma (do-re-mi-fa) ditties like the standard birha tune presented in chapter 2. Also conforming to this pattern was the great majority of melodies used in devotional bhajans, chowtal, *Mānas* singing, and women's folksongs. Given such limitations, it is not surprising that Indo-Caribbeans avidly consumed and performed the Indian filmsongs that flowed into the region in the wake of *Bala Joban*, as they offered an incomparably greater degree of melodic and instrumental richness and variety. Hence Trinidadian singers achieved community renown as "a Local Mukesh" (a film singer) or "A True Imitator," and from the 1950s dozens of ensembles formed that specialized in film music, performing at weddings and other occasions. Narsaloo Ramaya was a core member and longtime violinist in one of these bands, the Naya Zamana group (founded in 1944). Although appreciative of local traditional music, Ramaya saw no comparison between that and filmsong in terms of musical quality. When I asked him if he lamented how film culture had hastened the extinction of Gopichand and Harichand local folk music-theater, he acknowledged that those traditional rustic entertainments had been enjoyed by their audiences, but he added, "If you only heard the songs . . .," groaning and rolling his eyes. As he explained, such folk theater presentations were colorful in their quaint way, but they had little to offer in terms of musical and especially melodic richness or variety. In such a context, it is not surprising that Indo-Caribbean music lovers and performers found in Bombay filmsong a music that both expanded their musical horizons and provided a link to the ancestral homeland, whose values and identity they still cherished.

At the same time, Bombay film music and mainstream Indian devotional songs have flourished to a large extent at the expense of local musics in the Caribbean—indeed, just as has happened throughout India itself. In the pro-

cess, folksongs created and perpetuated by regional communities came to be replaced by mass-produced, common-denominator filmsongs generated in far-off Bombay by a tiny handful of composers and vocalists. Regional folksongs, with their local dialects and references, and vocal production styles, gave way to a corporate-produced repertoire of film music sung in a single language, a single vocal style, and, in most cases, a single lyric theme, that of sentimental love. Moreover, despite a certain degree of amateur filmsong performance, the advent of film culture has often entailed the replacement of community-based, amateur performance by passive consumption of recordings. In some cases, as in Hindu weddings both in India and the Caribbean, women's folksongs are literally drowned out by film music blaring from loudspeakers. In my own experience, I have attended many temple functions (especially satsangs) with pass-the-mike sessions in which one young woman after another sings dreary, plodding film songs, hopelessly out of tune, while a skilled chowtal group, or a virtuoso local-classical singer, or even some veteran auntie with a repertoire of Bhojpuri traditional songs, sits patiently waiting to sing. To the reader who has not had occasion to sit through such an event, I can only say of the film-ditty renditions: "If you only heard the songs . . . ," while groaning and rolling my eyes. Nevertheless, both film songs and the "filmi" style of singing may be typically regarded as more cosmopolitan, modern, and sweet than the rustic Bhojpuri style of the "aunties."[4]

In the following pages I explore the dynamic between imported mainstream great-tradition musics and a variety of Indo-Caribbean, Bhojpuri-derived traditional musics. At this point, however, it is appropriate to stress a point mentioned in the introduction—namely, that the complex and sometimes competitive and problematic relationship between Bhojpuri traditional musics and imported mainstream Indian ones is only in certain contexts, and by certain individuals, regarded as an important theme. On the vernacular level, most Indo-Caribbeans see themselves as "East Indians" rather than "Bhojpuri people" per se. Many Indo-Caribbeans are indeed profoundly concerned about maintaining and as-serting East Indian culture, but relatively few reflect a sense of alarm or defen-siveness about upholding traditional Bhojpuri music culture itself.

However, in various contexts and to various persons, as I shall suggest below, several performers, impresarios, and commentators do articulate their concern about the vitality of the Bhojpuri music little traditions as well as lo-cal neotraditional styles, and about the problematic relation of these genres to contemporary Indian imports. Moreover, the dialectic in general remains a basic and underacknowledged dynamic in Indo-Caribbean cultural history—a consideration that, I believe, justifies its examination in this chapter.

Hindu Devotional Music:
Vernacular and Mainstream Traditions

In Indo-Caribbean society, a prodigious amount of music making is associated with Hindu devotional practice. Such music comprises both amateur and professional categories and may be performed in temples, private homes, and other locales. Devotional music itself encompasses considerable diversity in terms of genre, origin, style, and format. Accordingly, a variety of factors are involved in the selection of musics performed in any given context and the relationships between them; often these relations are not regarded as problematic by participants, but in some contexts they reflect ongoing sociomusical dynamics and may be subjects of negotiation and contestation. In many cases, these dynamics pertain to the complex relation between distinctive Bhojpuri-derived traditions and panregional song styles rendered in standard Hindi and disseminated by the commercial mass media, professional South Asian stage singers, and their local imitators. Some of the Bhojpuri-derived song traditions are associated with particular Hindu sects, which have their own complex and in some respects competitive relationships with what has become a local mainstream form of Hinduism. Accordingly, on one level the heterogeneity of music practices involves the dynamics between these forms of Hinduism, while on another level, the diverse forms may coexist—problematically or not—within the practices of an individual sect or worship context itself.

Many of the religious practices and beliefs brought by Hindu immigrants in the indentureship period were decidedly in the realm of little traditions. Many workers came from isolated villages with their own local godlings, spirits, and demons. Literate Brahmans, who would have the greatest exposure to Sanskritic, panregional, great-tradition Hinduism, would constitute a minority in such villages, and an even smaller percentage among the indentureds, who hailed overwhelmingly from the lower castes and classes. Meanwhile, most of the immigrants followed particular heterodox sects or cults, rather than being adherents of any sort of canonic, panregional, mainstream Hinduism. In the Caribbean, these sects naturally corresponded to those prevalent in the Bhojpuri region at the time, especially Ramanandis, Kabir-panthis, Agora-panthis, and Siewnarainis, all of whom had their own devotional song repertoires and styles, and all of whom found themselves interacting not only with each other but also with an emerging mainstream form of Sanatan Dharm Hinduism. As might be expected, many of these interactions had musical dimensions.

Steven Vertovec (1992, 108–27) has succinctly described the general process of homogenization that transpired in Trinidadian Hinduism from the latter

part of the indentureship period. This process was in some respects influenced by corresponding developments in India itself, but in most ways it was conditioned by the distinctive features of the diasporic context. The consolidation that transpired was to some extent a predictable development, as a smaller pantheon of Sanskritic gods replaced the assorted village godlings and ghosts, and the India-founded Sanatan Dharm Association assumed the character of a standard mainstream Hindu organization. Although conservative in some respects (especially in admitting only Brahmins to the clergy), Sanatan Dharm practice was in most ways flexible and adaptable to the new context. While temples in India are constructed primarily for individual acts of worship, Indo-Caribbean temples came to resemble Christian churches in being designed and built for congregational worship, irrespective of caste, with a raised dais (backed by idols) for the officiating pandit, and rows of seats or open floor space for the devout. A typical Sunday-morning service involves an *ārti* prayer ritual, a peroration by the pandit, and congregational or small-group singing (discussed further below), followed by a communal meal and socializing. In accordance with the increasing dissolution of caste barriers, Sanatan Dharm services have stressed bhakti devotionalism, with emphasis on group singing and devotion rather than arcane ritual and individual worship.

The alternative sects followed divergent trajectories in the Caribbean. The reformist Arya Samaj, reinforced by visiting missionaries from India, remained a resilient entity, explicitly opposed to the residual casteism of the Sanatan Dharm. Arya Samajis have their own repertoire of devotional bhajans, but these neither derive from Bhojpuri-region sources nor differ markedly in style or performance format from Sanatan Dharm counterparts, and hence will not be discussed here. The Shaivite Agora-panthis, with their asceticism and lurid practices, were ostracized and have largely disappeared. The other sects, founded on principles of bhakti devotion and opposition to caste, have tended to decline as caste distinctions evaporated in the New World. Thus, the Ramanandi sect, founded by the eponymous fourteenth-century saint, was largely absorbed into the Sanatan Dharm, which has also been able to comfortably accommodate Kabir bhajans, teachings, and devotees. However, the Kabir panth and Siewnaraini sects, with their distinctive music practices and demographic trajectories, merit some attention in these pages.

Kabir Bhajans

Kabir Das (1440–1518) was a mystic poet-saint of the Banaras area. Of indeterminate sectarian parentage, he was raised by Muslim weavers and became revered as a poet and spiritual guru. His philosophy sought to reconcile and

synthesize aspects of Islam and bhakti Hinduism in a transcendent message of harmony, spirituality, and opposition to caste, sectarianism, and dogma. Although he was illiterate, a substantial body of poetry is attributed to him, some of which may have been notated by his amanuenses. Over the centuries, however, this body of verse has grown considerably in accordance with the Indian practice of appending a given saint's name to a verse composed in the style of that model; hence, even Trinidadian poets have concluded some of their verses with the standard Kabir tag "Kahta Kabir suno bhāi sādhu" (Kabir says, listen, sādhu). With their simple, colloquial Hindi diction, their effective imagery, and their populist message, Kabir's verses (especially *doha* couplets and aphoristic *sākhis*) became popular throughout North India (including Pakistan, Rajasthan, and the Punjab) and have lent themselves well to rendition as song lyrics. Accordingly, Kabir bhajans have enjoyed considerable popularity—rendered in different tunes, styles, and regional-language translations—among diverse Hindus and Muslims as well as specific devotees of the Kabir *panth* (path, or sect, rhyming roughly with English "punt").

Kabir panthis comprised a substantial percentage of the indentured immigrants, especially since Kabir's homeland of Banaras and the Bhojpuri region had remained a stronghold of his sect. Trinidadian Kabir panthis cite Kedar Das Singh, an indentured immigrant, as an important figure in establishing the sect in that island. By the time of the indentureship period many Kabir panth practices had become generalized, with some local variations, throughout North India, including a focal ceremony (the *chowka*), officiated by a *mahānt*, involving coconuts, *diya* lamps, and other paraphernalia. In Trinidad, the Kabir panthis were among the first sects to establish a formal organization (the Kabir Panthi Association of Trinidad and Tobago) in 1932; in the 1950s the sect founded two largely nonsectarian public schools. The community remained resilient over the subsequent decades, especially in the area around Freeport, even though religious functions (satsangs) were held only in homes and small, makeshift temples. In the early 1980s the sect was invigorated by the visit of a mahānt, Huzur Uditram, from the Kabir ashram in Lahartara, near Varanasi, and, perhaps more important, by a general spirit of awakening and mobilization among Trinidad Hindus, fueled in part by the island's new affluence (see Vertovec 1992, chapter 3). Informants related to me that Uditram trained several local mahānts and was generally appreciative and respectful of Trinidadian ritual and worship practices, even if they differed somewhat from those in his home ashram in India. Manifestations of the Trinidadian revival included the construction of four capacious temples ("ashrams"), including the Chaura Mat Ashram in Penal, the Kabir Lotus Ashram in Williamsville, and

the Kabir Updesh Ashram in Freeport. A stone's throw from the latter, a self-made trucking magnate (founder of Ramdass Transport) constructed a large domestic Kabir worship center. The Updesh Ashram is packed on Sundays and special events, and several of its congregants attested to me that the presence of such ashrams had lent a new strength to the sect (even if assessments of its demographic resilience are contradictory; there seem to be no Kabir ashrams in Guyana or the secondary diasporas). Sunday-morning Kabir-panth services have come to resemble those of Sanatanist Hindu temples in their combination of a sermon by the pandit/mahānt, interspersed with bhajan singing, an ārti, and finally, a communal lunch.

Kabir bhajans—that is, settings of Kabir verses to song—have always played central roles in devotional functions and have attracted many to the sect, both in India and the Caribbean. In the Caribbean, as in India, Kabir bhajans are sung in a variety of styles, the interrelations of which can be seen to reflect broader dynamics within Indo-Caribbean music culture. The most distinctive traditional Indo-Caribbean style of Kabir bhajan comprises a variety of what could be regarded as a broader format called "*khaṅjri gīt*" or "*sadhua bhajan*" (sadhu-style bhajan). The khaṅjri, as mentioned in chapter 2, is a hand-held circular-frame drum, like a tambourine, but with a smaller head and deeper frame, and without jingles. It is traditionally associated with religious songs, whether rendered by sadhus (mendicants) or lay devotees. In the Caribbean, the term "khaṅjri gīt" (khaṅjri song) came to imply a distinctive format and rhythm, which was used for Kabir bhajans, Siewnaraini bhajans, and a few other devotional genres. Khaṅjri gīt is typically performed by two rows of vocalists (usually men), who play khaṅjri as they sing, and are perhaps supplemented by a dholak player. They sing antiphonally, as in chowtal and *Mānas* singing, but the style is not so boisterous and rhythmically complex as in those genres. Rather, the typical "khaṅjri drum" employs a simple ostinato during the verses, which could be schematized as xx-x-xx-; in between the verses, the song's first line (the ṭek, or refrain) is repeated, and the rhythm changes to an irregular "limping" beat that could be crudely described as "long-short-short / long-short-short" and so on. If scrutinized in greatly decelerated form, this ostinato reveals itself to be more like 10/8, or 4+3+3. In local-classical parlance, this brief, rhythmically more intense section would be referred to as the "barti" (like the *laggi* in Hindustani genres like thumri), though that term is not current among khaṅjri-gīt singers.[5] Typically, the ṭek is sung a few times, then the first line of the next dohā couplet is sung responsorially to the same melody (which could be called the sthāī); the second line of the dohā is then sung to a higher melody (which could be called the antara), which then segues to the ṭek, which is repeated a

few times to the accompaniment of the "limping" rhythm (whose adaptation by tassa drummers in the "Kabir Das bhajan hand" will be further discussed in chapter 5). The subsequent dohās are sung in the same fashion.

The khañjri gīt format presumably derives from the Bhojpuri region, though it is one of several idioms that have yet to be studied there (like chowtal and *Mānas* singing, which through my efforts are better documented in the diaspora than in the homeland). Some of the tunes bear clear resemblance to those sung in Mauritius. Today, in Trinidad and Guyana, although the odd Kabir panthi might be seen playing a khañjri, the antiphonal khañjri gīt format appears to have effectively died out. It is, however, occasionally encountered in Suriname.[6] Its decline might seem surprising, given the resilience of the antiphonal chowtal. One factor may be the smaller demographic community of knowledgeable Kabir-panthi singers, compared with the larger pool of mainstream Sanatanists who could learn to sing chowtal, aided by photocopies of popular songtexts in roman script. Thus, it seems that despite the presence of spacious ashrams amply attended by the devout, the diminished number of inspired and informed singers has been unable to sustain the performance tradition, to the extent that it is no longer being passed down at all. Instead, songs are typically performed in a more soloistic format, with or without accompaniment by the congregation.

In my own experience attending Kabir-panthi services in Trinidad, I could not help but notice another factor inhibiting collective singing in general. At such functions, as in many Sanatanist counterparts, it has been the custom for some time to use microphones and speakers to amplify the music-making to levels that are thunderous and even physically painful to those such as myself whose ears are not already damaged by regular attendance at such events. Although such amplification may be considered an emblem of status and modernity, it renders congregational singing essentially pointless and impossible. At one service at the Updesh Ashram, the young mahānt, while singing into a mike and playing harmonium, attempted to lead the congregants in singing a series of bhajans, accompanied by a dholak player. Although he repeatedly exhorted his minions to lend their voices to the song, his own voice and harmonium were amplified to such a deafening level that even the most vigorous singing by others would have been inaudible. Although many familiar songs are well known to congregants, I was not surprised to note that no one responded to his exhortation, aside from two or three women who listlessly mouthed the words and tapped their fingers on their seats for a minute or two. For a few minutes during one song, the electric power went off, and I noticed that several women took advantage of the opportunity to sing. Later, a sister of the mahānt fondly reminisced to me about earlier decades when devotees used to sing all night; when I commented that the amplification seemed to discourage congregational

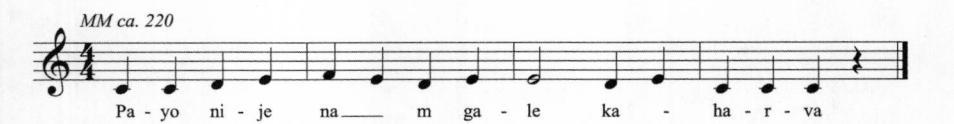

Example 5. Kabir bhajan refrain.

singing, she replied, "Yes, it's a problem, we need more microphones." (Meanwhile, the decline of all-night religious functions, weddings, and other cultural events is widely attributed to the deteriorated law-and-order situation—especially rampant kidnappings of Indians—due to which Indians no longer feel safe moving about after dark.)

The use of amplification and the attenuated number of knowledgeable singers have together led to the replacement of congregational khañjri gīt by more soloistic formats. One of these is what could be regarded as a hybrid format that retains the traditional repertoire, distinctive rhythm, and responsorial format of the khañjri songs while relying on a skilled lead singer rather than a substantial number of knowledgeable vocalists. In this style, the lead singer—with obligatory microphone—is answered by three or four other singers, who may share a mike. In place of the collectively played khañjris, a trained drummer renders the traditional khañjri beat on dholak. In Trinidad as of 2014, the most prominent vocalist in this style is Balliram Bala Ramroop (b. 1941), who, aside from being a senior and recognized local-classical singer, is a Kabir-panthi mahānt. Most of Ramroop's Kabir bhajan repertoire is "traditional" in being acquired from local elders. As is the case with much of the local-classical repertoire, it may be impossible to trace their origins either to India or the Caribbean. There is a greater reliance on a few stock tunes than is the case in local-classical music. Ramroop is often accompanied on dholak by his son, who is well versed in the distinctive khañjri-derived rhythmic style. (Occasionally one hears less knowledgeable drummers play vague approximations of this beat.) A typical ṭek refrain from this repertoire is shown in example 5.

Other forms of Kabir bhajans may also be heard at satsangs, especially in the absence of a skilled traditional singer like Ramroop. These forms are essentially sung solo (with dholak and dantāl), though the vocalist, as mentioned above, might encourage others to join in. The repertoire might juxtapose traditional melodic settings (such as derive from the khañjri-gīt tradition) with songs from the pop stage bhajan style of modern India. The latter genre, with its tuneful, soloistic, polished renderings of original settings, rose to particular prominence in India in tandem with the cassette boom of the 1980s, especially as rendered by Anup Jalota, Jagjit Singh, and Hari Om Sharan (see Manuel,

Cassette Culture, chapter 6). Kabir bhajans, with newly composed tunes, figure prominently in the repertoire of these singers, whose music has been widely disseminated in India and the Caribbean on cassettes and, later, CDs and mp3 discs. As I have suggested, in their panregional popularity and corporate mass-media promotion these songs could be likened to a quasi-pop-music variety of "great tradition," as opposed to the decidedly little tradition of Caribbean sad-hua bhajans. At Kabir satsangs, these songs may be sung by the mahānt, who, like Hindu pandits nowadays, is often expected to be a presentable singer. The mike might also be passed to others, who may take turns singing familiar songs from the repertoire. Such songs might even be sung after a skilled traditional vocalist like those Ramroop has performed, perhaps while most congregants are chatting and enjoying the complimentary lunch.

The traditional khaṅjri-gīt repertoire could be said to be in a state of competition with the commercial stage-bhajan from India. At a given satsang, one genre or the other may predominate, depending on the talents and tastes of those present. Certainly there are many Indo-Trinidadians who regard the Jalota/Sharan/Jagjit repertoire as more modern, sophisticated, and musically rich than the traditional local style, with its finite set of stock tunes. As one Trinidadian amateur vocalist—a self-described "Jagjit singer"—told me, "Jalota's music will never be exhausted, it will never be killed off by film music the way our traditional music has been." As knowledgeable traditionalist singers like Ram-roop retire or pass away, there is a genuine danger that the Trinidadian repertoire may decline. Ajeet Praimsingh, motivated by such concerns, produced a cassette of Ramroop singing in the traditional local style.[7] However, Ramroop himself, in chatting with me, did not articulate such a sense of competition or pessimism; rather, he opined, the two repertoires could comfortably coexist, and even he might occasionally sing a Jalota setting if requested.

Another category of Kabir bhajans comprises original settings by local-classical singers. Indeed, Kabir's lyrics have long been favorites of the local-classical vocalists, due to the verses' accessible diction and pithy messages, and the easy availability of text anthologies (see Manuel 2000a, 98). Local-classical vocalists—who sing solo (with instrumental accompaniment) rather than in a group format—do not feel obliged to use traditional khaṅjri-gīt tunes; rather, they use original settings, whether newly composed or heard from elders. Hence a given Kabir verse could be rendered in the distinctive local style of a thumri, a ghazal, a lāvni, or virtually any other subgenre, with its standard rhythmic accompaniment and formal structure. A local-classical singer might perform such a Kabir song at any song session, such as a wedding; alternately, a Kabir enthusiast like Jairam Dindial might participate in a Kabir satsang. Finally, in enumerating Kabir bhajan styles, mention must be made of the aforementioned

tassa adaptation of the Kabir-style khanjri rhythm, which will be discussed in greater detail in the next chapter.[8]

The gamut of Kabir bhajan styles—from the neotraditional style of Balliram Ramroop to the Jalota settings sung by pandits—represents one way in which diverse styles can coexist. While the future of the former style is uncertain, for the time being the relative resilience of the Kabir-panth and the healthy amount of music-making therein has allowed local traditional as well as imported South Asian contemporary styles to persist. Meanwhile, the Kabir sect in general has clearly been invigorated by contact with its counterpart in India. Caribbean Kabir-panthis, rather than feeling isolated, are aware that they are part of a global network of co-religionists surviving not only in India but also in various diasporic communities.

The Siewnaraini Tradition

If the Kabir panth and its bhajan tradition illustrate how a Bhojpuri-derived little tradition can manage to coexist with competing Sanatanist and mainstream Indian counterparts, a less successful trajectory is illustrated by the Siewnaraini sect in Trinidad. The sect's founder was a Rajput named Shivnarayan (Shiv Nayaran, Siewnarain, 1716–1790) from Ghazipur district, east of Varanasi, who flourished during the reign of Mughal ruler Mohammad Shah (r. 1719–1748), whom he is said to have befriended. Inspired by Kabir, Shivnarayan preached a message of bhakti devotionalism, monotheistic unitarianism, and opposition to caste and sectarianism. Although allegedly illiterate (like Kabir), through a scribe named Ramdas he authored several books, especially the *Bijak*, printed recensions of which are focal objects of worship in the sect's rituals. Shivnarayan established a wide following among Bhojpuri-region Rajputs and especially lower-caste Chamārs.[9] Much of his literary output consists of verses whose musical rendering has always constituted a central devotional practice.

As mentioned, Siewnarainis, together with Ramanandis and Kabir-panthis, constituted a majority of indentured Hindu immigrants to the Caribbean, in accordance with the popularity of these sects in the nineteenth-century Bhojpuri region. While the Ramanandis were largely absorbed into the growing Sanatanist mainstream, and the Kabir panthis retained some resilience, the Siewnaraini community has dwindled dramatically in Trinidad and, to this author's knowledge, is largely defunct in Guyana and Suriname as well. Some of the reasons for the decline also obtain in India, where the sect has experienced a similar attenuation. One factor, noted by Vertovec (1992, 112), is that the sect's once-distinctive and central tenet of bhakti devotion and opposition to caste has ironically become less crucial in the Caribbean, where caste distinctions

have largely evaporated and collective bhakti-oriented worship has become a mainstream practice. Another factor is that the decline of the Siewnaraini sect in India has left the Caribbean followers wholly isolated, lacking the sort of encouragement that, for example, a revered visitor like Huzur Uditram was able to provide the Kabir panthis.

Further insights regarding the sect's status were offered to me by Mukram Sirjoo, a Siewnaraini pandit with whom I spent an afternoon in 2011. When I arrived at his modest home and temple in central Trinidad, Sirjoo was consulting an Afro-Trinidadian couple who were seeking his spiritual assistance regarding some matter. The three were seated on humble folding chairs in a yard cluttered with diverse *murtis* (statues) of Hindu deities, and even a painting of Christ, with whose teaching Shivnarayan is surmised to have been familiar. Sirjoo, rather than being an otherworldly ascetic, devotes much of his spare time to his hobby of tinkering with motorcycles, several of which were propped up in various states of disrepair. Like the Kabir-panthis, he explained to me, the Siewnarainis had established a formal association whose activities included outreach, publication of songbooks, new editions of Siewnarain's Hindi books, and some coordination of activities of the several active temples. After the mid-twentieth century, however, the sect declined dramatically, such that at present only a few temples in south Trinidad are active (especially that in Debe). Aside from the lack of support from any fraternal organization in India, Sirjoo noted that the sect's tradition of humility and lack of ostentation had discouraged followers, whether in India or the Caribbean, from building extravagant temples. He himself followed this practice, stating:

> This place is a little bit run down, but I like it so; it keeps the pride out, the ego out. My son-in-law wants me to take this house down and put up a two-story building, something posh, but I say no. I want it to be humble. Religion is commercialized now, everyone wants to build a nice mandir, and people have to donate. I want to remain as I am; people come here for my assistance and they don't have to pay anything. I don't want any cash donation.

Sirjoo noted that both the Debe temple and he himself had adapted to the dilution of the Siewnaraini tradition by adopting a more inclusive approach that incorporated elements of Kabir-panthi and Sanatanist devotional practices.

As with the Kabir panth, a Siewnaraini samāj or devotional session comprises a focal ritual (the *guru gaddi*) around a low altar, in which the teachings and sacred books of the saint rather than particular deities are venerated, with bhajan-singing playing a central role. The traditional Siewnaraini bhajan style corresponds to the "sadhua bhajan" format shared by Kabir-panthis, with antiphonal singing and beating on khañjris in the distinctive rhythm described

Example 6. Traditional Siewnaraini bhajan refrain.

above. The melodies are essentially similar in style—diatonic, syllabic, and in a conventional sthāī-antara format. Sirjoo himself takes an active interest in music and even studied Hindustani singing under H. S. Adesh, the first teacher of that art in Trinidad. (Hence, he referred to the three-stroke "limping" barti-style khañjri rhythm as "dādra.") Like Indo-Caribbean exponents of various other Bhojpuri-derived genres, he feels sufficiently confident in the tradition to compose his own settings of Siewnaraini bhajans, which he teaches and sings alongside traditional ones of unknown origin. Among the latter, a very few stock tunes are common, such as that presented in example 6, which is essentially the same as the Kabir bhajan tune shown in the preceding example. The lyrics derive from traditional songbooks, including the *Lau Parvānā Hukm Nāmā* and *Shabd Granthshabdāvli* (published in Kanpur) and the *Swami Shiva Narayan Bhajan Mala*, a chapbook compiled and printed by Sirjoo himself in Trinidad.[10] Like Kabir bhajans, the lyrics may mention deities like Ram and Krishna, but most are philosophical or spiritual, with the author's *chāp* (Kabir, or Shivnarayan) occurring in the penultimate line.

As with Kabir bhajans, the decline of the traditional antiphonal sadhua bhajan style has led to a more responsorial style with a lead singer, such as Sirjoo himself, or a local-classical singer such as Sam Boodram, who is a follower of the sect. Meanwhile, a few tassa groups play an adaptation of the "Siewnaraini bhajan." (Sirjoo was amused to hear of this practice from me.)

The trajectory of the Siewnaraini tradition contrasts in some respects with that of the Kabir-panth in the Caribbean. The complete absence of contact with Siewnarainis in India has meant that there has been neither external competition nor reinforcement in the realms of music and the religion. Siewnaraini bhajans, deriving from a regional, declining, and now low-caste tradition, are not sung by the likes of Anup Jalota or Hari Om Sharan; no cassettes of Indian Siewnaraini songs exist in the Caribbean, such that sect members have no sense of being part of any sort of international community. As the few remaining mahānts like Sirjoo retire, the persistence of this sect and its musical tradition

appears dubious, and the musical energy once devoted to it could already be seen as being directed instead toward mainstream and filmi bhajans.

The Secular Sphere:
Bollywood and Local Music in Mastana Bahar

If traditional Bhojpuri devotional genres like the sadhua bhajan have fared poorly in the confrontation with more modern bhajan styles, the complex and often problematic dynamic between film and local musics is even more pronounced in the realm of secular entertainment music. Particularly illustrative has been their interaction in the realm of a Trinidadian music and dance forum called Mastana Bahar. Mastana Bahar (roughly, "joyous spring") is an amateur competition network that, since its founding in 1970, has become an institution in Trinidadian culture. The forum was created and energetically directed largely by Sham (Shamsuddin) Mohammed, part of a veritable entertainment dynasty notably featuring his brothers Kamal (Kamaluddin), a politician and radio show host, and Moean (Moeanuddin), who dominated the fields of Indo-Trinidadian music recording and, to some extent, concert production from the 1960s through the late 1980s. (As impresarios, Moean and Sham were particularly influential in promoting the emergence of chutney in the 1980s.) While being a commercial enterprise, Mastana Bahar's averred goal has been the promotion, cultivation, and showcasing of diverse forms of local Indian music and dance talent through an island-wide annual competition. Over the space of roughly half the year, each weekend a competition ("audition") show is held at some site in the island, leading up to final events in which judges select winners of substantial prizes. By the mid-1970s Mastana Bahar had become prodigiously popular and successful. Although inspired by and to some extent modeled on the Calypso Monarch competition, Mastana Bahar has consistently attracted private sponsorship—especially from Indian businesses—enabling it to offer prizes that surpass in value those of the calypso revue. Further, while oriented toward Indian genres, the show's weekly broadcasts on national television (TTT) came to be widely viewed not only by Indians but also by Afro-Trinidadians, a number of whom have competed in and even won awards in the forum. Several of the island's successful performers began their careers in Mastana Bahar, including the young Jameer Hussein and Sham Yankaran (d. 2011), who went on to become skilled local-classical vocalists, and vocalist Parvati Khan (b. 1962), who subsequently moved to Bombay and sang in several Hindi films (such as "Disco Dancer").

The Mohammeds sought from the start to promote a variety of performance genres, including local-classical singing, tassa drumming, instrumental music,

chutney, miscellaneous newly composed "local songs," Indian classical and film-style dance, and Hindi film songs. However, while a typical Sunday-morning audition might contain a few such items, it soon emerged that each audition and show was thoroughly dominated by a parade of amateur filmsong crooners (many of them quite incapable of carrying a tune) and dancers.[11] To both critics and fans, both Mastana Bahar and the Indian Cultural Pageant (ICP) organized by the Mohammeds came to be seen primarily as forums for film song and dance, featuring local talent (or lack thereof), but not local content. Local-classical singers were particularly critical of the forums for promoting "Local Mukesh" imitators rather than their own sophisticated and unique art form. As one of them told me, "It's Mastana Bahar that has promoted all this film trash; a local-classical singer can never win that competition."

The Mohammeds, along with their musical producer Harry Mahabir, although justifiably proud of the extraordinary success of the competition, have on occasion expressed dissatisfaction with the direction their shows have taken. In a conversation before one audition in 1994, Moean explicitly voiced to me his dismay with the filmsong hegemony.[12] For his part, Mahabir had arrived at a critical perspective through a personal experience in 1965, when he was a member of an ensemble sent to perform in London. As Sharda Patasar related, Mahabir and his colleagues "went with a repertoire of Indian films songs originally sung by the great film singers Lata Mangeshkar and the late Mohammed Rafi from India. On arrival in London the Trinidadian artistes were confronted by the contingent from India, which included the very singers whom they were trying so desperately to imitate" (1998, 35). Traumatized, Mahabir quickly added some Trinidadian folk songs to the group's act and vowed to work toward the promotion of distinctively Trinidadian songs in the future. Sham, the most intimately involved with Mastana Bahar production, shared the same concerns, which were further voiced by his son Shamoon, a broadcast promoter who authored a book on Mastana Bahar (1982). Shamoon offered various explanations for the disproportionate popularity of filmsongs:

> In the first case, it may be due to the fact that most people gather some idea of the meaning of film songs through the English subtitles [in films].[13] . . . Secondly, this phenomenon might be due in part to the increasing use of western instruments in Indian music, giving it a more varied and attractive dimension. Thirdly, more and more people can lay their hands on records from films they have seen; the same does not apply to all the [local] "classical" and devotional types. To these, one may add the overwhelming preponderance of modern film songs on local radio programmes. (67)

About the results of this preponderance, he lamented:

Already the writer has noted the tendency of many contestants who are merely content to immerse themselves in the naked copying of the songs of famous Indian and Pakistani singers. Surely imitation has its values, especially as a springboard of the development of budding artistes and for those who are learning and desirous or mastering various song types. But once artistes have attained some reasonable degree of maturity, one would expect them to utilize the skills gained through imitation to display their creative and imaginative propensities. This does not seem to be the case of songsters appearing on Mastana Bahar. (69–70)

To address the problem, in the early 1980s Sham inaugurated a separate competition category for "local songs" to be composed in mixed Hindi and English, using Indian-style melodies. This attempt to stimulate the local muse resembled the subsequent endeavor by Raviji (discussed in chapter 3) to promote English-language chowtal composition and melodically nondescript "pichakaree" songs during the Hindu Prachar Kendra's Phagwa festivities. Like the pichakaree songs, the Mastana Bahar "local songs" did not achieve great success, either in quantity or quality, and both Mastana Bahar and the ICP have continued to be dominated by Bollywood imitators. A fundamental problem in composing "local songs" is that ignorance of Hindi, coupled with the inability to use film tunes and unfamiliarity with local-classical music, has left singers and would-be singers without any particular melodic models or tradition to build upon, except nursery-rhyme-like chutney ditties and, even more problematically, calypso and soca style. Sham Mohammed noted this trend:

This definitely seems to be a retrograde step, especially at a time in our history when every step should be made to encourage a greater knowledge of the oriental languages not only among local Indian artistes, but among Indians as a whole. It can also cause local Indian composers and musicians to swing over completely to pure English compositions, which only assist in the unpalatable process of westernization of East Indians and a consequent loss of cultural identity. . . . One clearly observes that local Indian composers are trailing far behind their Trinidadian African counterparts in terms of production and creativity in local songs. In this respect, the local production of calypsos dwarf [sic] that of local Indian compositions. (71–73)

Further, as with the English-language chowtals, the local-song category, whose products sometimes resembled second-rate calypsos, provoked indignant protests from purists who felt that it promoted degenerate "douglarization" of Indian tradition (a dougla being an Indian-creole mulatto). Hence Sham felt obliged to repeatedly defend the project:

The Local Song Contest has been designed particularly to represent a Trinidad and Tobago situation. . . . We are not in Bihar state. . . . We are living in

Trinidad and Tobago, which could be drowned up so many times in India. So what must I do in Trinidad and Tobago? Must I wear dhoti and phagri [pagri, traditional Indian village attire] and carry on every single thing they do in India? I totally reject that idea. . . . We can't go on imitating [film singers] Mohammed Rafi and Mukesh at all times. We use them as inspiration. . . . We don't want to do away with anything, but it is merely to add an "addendum" as we call it, to the range of songs that we have in our community . . . Some people say, you want to creolize this! [But] the local songs are fifty percent in Hindustani with an Indian tune! Those are the requirements. We are living in a mixed community, and we have to be friends with everybody. We want to get the rest of the community to accept what we are doing, and to participate. Culture is something that should cut across all barriers. (144–45)

In a 1983 ICP brochure, he continued:

Can we therefore create something to suit our particular situation? . . . Can we not carve a new channel that will flow into the same river of Indian culture? . . . What is Indian culture? . . . Does it mean a continuous imitation of India? Is this what we opt for as an independent nation? Is it wrong to seek to develop our own as we attempt to do in the pageant? Have we observed that India is imitating Trinidad in song and music via Kanchan and Babla?[14]

In such exhortations Mohammed was articulating a fundamental challenge facing Indo-Caribbean musicians and dancers, and by extension, Indo-Caribbean society as a whole. How can Indo-Caribbean performers—and Indo-Caribbeans in general—cultivate an identity in a way that is at once Indian, modern, and reflective of the reality of living in the West Indies? In the realm of music, little-tradition Bhojpuri genres like birha and chowtal, for all their rustic charm and vigor, ultimately cannot constitute vehicles for contemporary musical or lyric expression. The new Indian pop great tradition of film songs and stage bhajans constitutes a natural resource of far greater variety and richness than a population of a million Indo-Caribbeans could generate, but cultivation of these ultimately foreign genres typically takes the form of mere imitation rather than interpretation, not to mention creation, and fails to engage with the reality of living in the West Indies.

Local-Classical Music and the Encounter with the Indian Great Tradition

The complexities of the Indo-Caribbean encounter with importations from India are illustrated in a distinct way by the interaction—or lack thereof—between the Indian great traditions of classical and film music with the decidedly "little" tradition of Trinidadian and Guyanese local-classical music. Indo-Caribbean

local-classical music (including its variants of Guyanese tān-singing and Su-rinamese *baithak gānā*) evolved as an idiosyncratic genre developed by musicians drawing from old songbooks, imported records of qawwālis and other styles, and the garbled and fragmentary knowledge of Hindustani classical and light-classical music brought by some indentured immigrants. After the immigration of indentureds ended in 1917, the genre, in its regional variants, coalesced into a unique idiom, performed at weddings, religious functions, competitions, and other occasions, evolving as a genre without any further influence from North Indian classical music. While Guyanese tān-singing is in terminal decline, Trinidadian local-classical music remains reasonably vital, despite the inability of contemporary audiences to understand its Hindi texts. Local-classical music is not a quintessential component of the Bhojpuri legacy, as its Braj Bhasha songtexts and light-classical elements derive from panregional North Indian traditions, and certain features—such as aspects of the Trinidadian thumri rhythm—are Caribbean inventions. Since I devoted several pages in my earlier volume, *East Indian Music in the West Indies* (2000, 104–10), to the genre's interaction with Indian great-tradition musics, I will only briefly recapitulate some of my observations here.

After the last ships bearing indentured immigrants came in 1917, local-classical music developed in almost complete isolation from South Asian influences, save the handfuls of qawwāli recordings by singers like Kalloo Qawwal and Pyare Qawwal that reached India goods stores. The vogue of imported films and film music from the 1940s had a largely negative effect on the genre, as many patrons at weddings and other events came to contract film music bands like Naya Zamana rather than the more rustic local-classical singers. However, some singers did commence their artistic endeavors singing film music, whether in such ensembles (as did Sohan Girdharrie and Dev Ramdass) or, later, in Mastana Bahar (as did Jameer Hossein). As mentioned earlier, classical singers have tended to regard forums like Mastana Bahar essentially as film music competitions that marginalize their own distinctive art form.

A different sort of North Indian great tradition appeared on the Trinidadian scene in 1966, when former Indian embassy staffer and amateur vocalist H. S. Adesh started a school of Hindustani music, the Bharatiya Vidya Sansthan (BVS). Over the years, several hundred students learned the rudiments of Hindustani vocal music from Adesh, who remained in the island until 1984, becoming a Trinidadian citizen and composing some patriotic songs. A few local-classical singers—notably Issac Yankarran and Abdul "Kush" Razack—studied at the BVS, though the impact of their training is unclear, as they continued to sing primarily in the local style. Further, since the 1970s, increasing numbers of Indo-Caribbeans have been able to study Hindustani music, whether, in the

case of a few, by visiting India or, more commonly, by taking classes from such people or from Indian teachers at institutions like the Indian Cultural Centre in Guyana (founded in 1972). Classes offered at the BVS and elsewhere have enriched the island's music scene in various ways. Hindustani music is certainly a richer, more substantial, and more prestigious art form than local-classical music, and it also offers students a standardized and systematic pedagogy that has no counterpart in local-classical music, whose exponents are largely innocent of music theory. Accordingly, perhaps, the Hindustani music presence in the Caribbean has tended to further marginalize and devalue local-classical music.[15] This relationship parallels that of the Hindi classes, now common in the Indic Caribbean, to the rustic Bhojpuri of local folksongs and vernacular extant discourse. Like the BVS curriculum, the language classes—which impart only standard Hindi—purvey an aspect of mainstream North Indian culture while marginalizing or even devaluing rustic Bhojpuri, which is condescendingly referred to as "broken Hindi" (even by some of the "aunties" who speak it), despite being as venerable and old an idiom as the Delhi-region dialect that was adopted as a North Indian lingua franca around 1900.

On the whole, however, it must be said that Hindustani music and local-classical music tend to operate in distinct spheres, and local-classical musicians would regard film music and chutney as more overt menaces to their art. In general, local-classical musicians have been isolated from Hindustani music for too long for it to be meaningful to them. They are neither familiar with it nor particularly interested in it, and when exposed to it, they generally deem it boring.[16] As one told me, "That music ain't got no spice to it." As I related in my earlier book, local-classical musicians may also be quick to take umbrage at any perceived condescension exhibited by visiting performers from India. Such attitudes could be said to reflect not only the isolation that has nurtured local-classical music, but also a healthy sense of the legitimacy of their own art. Conversely, local-classical singers, despite the unique charm and vigor of their art, could be said to have a fairly limited repertoire of melodic ideas, and they could well enrich and strengthen their music by introducing into it some of the variety and richness of Hindustani melody.

Singing Along With, or Against, His Master's Voice

Indo-Caribbean Bhojpuri-derived musics can be seen as facing a set of alternative means of engaging with the challenges posed by great-tradition musics from India. The diverse forms of negotiating these alternatives have consistently been debated, and no doubt actively influenced, by outspoken intellectuals, pandits, impresarios, and others who carry on running arguments in newspa-

pers and other forums.[17] Ultimately, however, the directions taken by musical developments are conditioned more by broader architectonic developments, as reflected in popular tastes, than they are by newspaper columnists. From the present vantage point, one might interpret the last few decades as illustrating three ways in which local little traditions interact with the imported great traditions. One of these comprises the development of original, dynamic, uniquely Indo-Caribbean neotraditional arts—in particular, local-classical music and tassa drumming. Of these, the former has never been destined to enjoy mass appeal, while the latter is flourishing vigorously.[18]

A second "strategic" development has been the vogue of chutney and especially chutney-soca, the pop hybrid that fuses simple Bhojpuri-type tunes, mixed Hindi-English lyrics, and soca rhythms to accompany dance styles that combine Bhojpuri moves with the pelvic "wining" of Afro-creole dancing. As I have discussed elsewhere (Manuel 2000a, chapter 5), chutney provoked much controversy within the Indo-Trinidadian community when it flowered in the 1980s, but by the early 1990s its popularity had effectively silenced or marginalized its critics who had disparaged it as, again, "douglarization." Chutney, of course, is a dance music that does not reflect the full potential of Indo-Caribbean musical creativity (nor could any single genre do so); in terms of sophistication, I would assert that it cannot compare to local-classical music or tassa drumming. Its lyrics, though occasionally droll, are light and trivial; its rhythm is generated by pressing the "soca" button on the synth keyboard; its melodies generally follow the simplest Bhojpuri-style ditties, like that of birha, which often resemble Western nursery rhymes; and its singers seldom seem to possess anything beyond the most ordinary level of talent. Despite the theatrical smoke, fireworks, and stage effects that can animate its concerts, most of the songs retain the character of throwaway music and, accordingly, seldom enjoy more than ephemeral popularity. Meanwhile, the excitement generated by chutney-soca in the 1990s seems to have waned somewhat, and in New York dance clubs frequented by Indo-Caribbeans chutney-soca may even be played before the venue closes in order to hasten the departure of attendees.

However, as a sociomusical phenomenon chutney-soca has been undoubtedly significant and, indeed, reflective of a certain coming of age for Indo-Caribbean—and especially Indo-Trinidadian—culture. Its effective "triumph" on the Trini scene in the mid-1990s at once coincided with, dramatized, and actively contributed to a dynamic moment during which an Indian prime minister and Indian-oriented political party took power, and a new paradigm of multiculturalism replaced the former hegemony of creole culture, with its trinity of creole steelband, calypso, and Carnival (see Manuel 2000c). Despite the fulminations of negrophobic and increasingly isolated critics like Satnarayan

Maharaj, chutney-soca came to be recognized as reflecting a new spirit of creative syncretism on the part of Indians that at once affirmed and bridged East Indian and West Indian identities, and also came to be enjoyed and even performed by significant numbers of Afro-Trinidadians.[19]

Alongside the neotraditional vitality manifest in local-classical music and tassa, and the syncretic energy of the chutney phenomenon, a third and distinct sort of musical response to the distinctive challenges of the Indo-Caribbean condition is evident in the form of the pluralistic coexistence of diverse genres. In this situation, the "Local Rafi," the local-classical singer, the singer of Bhojpuri wedding songs, the chutney star enjoying her fleeting renown, the Bharat Natyam dancer, and even the Indian member of a steelband all occupy their niches, however unequal and unstable, in the cultural scene. To be sure, certain genres—especially traditional folksongs—fare poorly, and local-classical musicians cannot but lament the dominance of filmsongs and the chutney they are obliged to sing at weddings. However, while any music culture naturally sustains diverse genres, the nature of coexistence in Indo-Caribbean and especially Trinidadian music constitutes a particularly salient feature.[20]

The relative success of Trinidadian musical pluralism is enabled partially by the sheer amount of music-making on the island. Between the Mastana Bahar contestants, the legions of chowtal and tassa ensembles, the congregants singing bhajans at temple functions, and even the high school students in steelbands, it could be said that the Indo-Trinidadians who do *not* regularly perform some sort of music must constitute a distinct minority. While statistical evidence is wanting, my own impressions leave me convinced that the prodigious amount of per capita "musicking" in Trinidad—whether amateurish or polished—considerably exceeds that in India. It is estimated, for instance, that around ninety thousand people have competed in Mastana Bahar since the show's inception. This ability of diverse genres to survive and even flourish also mitigates what might otherwise be a sense of alarm about the decline of certain traditional idioms. The demise of birha, Siewnaraini bhajans, and Ramayan bāni may be inexorable, but several other forms of traditional song may endure, albeit in reduced and modified forms.

The diverse and changing roles of Bhojpuri traditional musics and modern trends are particularly manifest in the context of Indo-Caribbean Hindu weddings. Since the 1940s these focal community events have been primary sites for both traditional folksongs and modern musics. In most weddings, particularly prominent would be Bhojpuri women's songs, sung during particular events, especially during the Friday evening maticore (matkor, maṭkor, matkorwa) at the bride's house, the Saturday evening preparation of *lāwā* (parched rice) at the groom's house, and on Sunday, most of the extended ceremony itself at the

bride's house and a smaller, parallel women's gathering at the groom's house.[21] As discussed in the next chapter, tassa drumming accompanies the Friday matikor and occurs at various points during the Sunday event. If the groom's father is an enthusiast of local-classical music, the festive Saturday night batwān ("cooking night") party might feature one or more such groups, which since the 1980s might also be requested to perform chutney so that people can dance. More often, the cooking night features a band and/or a deejay ("mike-man") proffering modern pop music. As noted earlier, filmsong bands have proliferated since the 1940s, though a modern mike-man could play a potpourri of chutney-soca, upbeat Bollywood hits, reggae, and other danceable genres. Thus, neotraditional local-classical music has clearly suffered from the competition with these modern Indian, creole, and Western sounds, but tassa remains indispensable.[22]

For their part, the Bhojpuri women's songs have over the decades followed a pattern of dramatic but incomplete decline, with some of the repertoire surviving in a repackaged form. During her 1977 research in Trinidad, Myers found this music tradition to be surprisingly resilient, with a fairly large number of songs still being sung by ordinary women, despite their only fragmentary knowledge of Bhojpuri Hindi. Since then, however, amateur knowledge and performance of this repertoire have decreased dramatically, and it may be rare to find ordinary women singing such songs, except in Suriname, where Sarnami/Bhojpuri is still spoken. Even there, as in North India itself, the tradition of women's songs has suffered markedly, especially with sound systems blaring filmsongs throughout much of the wedding.

Despite such trends, in Trinidad and to a lesser extent in Guyanese communities, it has become fairly common to hire professional troupes of female singers (with sound system, and dholak and harmonium accompaniment) to sing at Sunday weddings. Typically, these groups perform at several appropriate points during the extended wedding ritual, perhaps preceding songs with spoken explanations of the relevant ritual and the songtext. Several of the Trinidadian groups use the songbook *Vivaaha Geet: 108 (Appropriate) Traditional Hindu Wedding Songs*, collected and edited by Rukminee Holass-Beepath. Holass herself is the sort of dedicated and knowledgeable enthusiast who can make a significant impact in a finite, bounded site like Trinidad. Her parents—second-generation immigrants from the Bhojpuri region—were active folksingers, and her brother Budram is a skilled exponent of folksongs, chutney, and local-classical music. Rukminee teaches regular classes wherein she imparts the folksongs she collected from her parents and others. Her students have founded around ten professional troupes who perform at weddings, birthdays, Ramayan yajnas, *janeus* (sacred-thread donning ceremonies), funerals, and other events. These troupes typically use one of her three books, which

Figure 3. A folksong troupe at a Trinidadian wedding. Photograph by the author.

contain romanized versions of the songs, with translations and explanations.[23] She has also recorded commercial cassettes of several of the songs. Although she wrote in the preface to *Vivaaha Geet* that she was motivated by concern about the survival of the repertoire, in June 2011 she seemed quite confident of the ability of her troupes, and those of others, to keep the songs alive, even to a greater extent than in previous years. "My own group is booked solid through March," she told me, "and before us, there was nothing, only the remaining aunties who could sing." While Bhojpuri songs constitute most of her groups' repertoire, she does not hesitate to sing filmsongs if requested, and sees no particular threat to the traditional repertoire from such eclecticism. Her confidence in this respect echoed that of Balliram Bala, who, as mentioned above, does not mind singing an occasional Anup Jalota bhajan, as requested, amid his renderings of traditional Kabir bhajans. Meanwhile, at many Guyanese and Trinidad weddings, requisite songs may be provided by a smaller group, whether amateur or semiprofessional, perhaps centered around a single vocalist who has learned the material by one means or another.

There is no doubt, of course, that performance of folksongs by an invited professional troupe differs in various qualitative ways from traditional informal

renderings by ordinary amateurs; the same applies to the staged choral performances of folksongs—often with whimsical skits or theatrics—presented by student groups from the more than thirty primary schools run by the SDMS in Trinidad.[24] Nevertheless, such staged enactments do provide a certain afterlife to the repertoire, which thus remains at least familiar to a broad sector of the community. Moreover, although some of my informants have claimed that the presence of invited singers at weddings is declining, it is also possible that this new tradition may prove durable, as it has already outlasted the effective extinction of Bhojpuri as a living language among Guyanese and Trinidadians.

Dancing between Antipodes

The complex dynamics involved among Bollywood, local-traditional, and creole arts are also evident, in similar ways, in the realm of dance. While space does not permit—nor is the author qualified to present—an expansive discussion of this subject, a few general observations may be of use.[25] As with music, Indo-Caribbean dance culture can be seen as site of interaction of a set of antipodal genres, whose relationships may be variously competitive, mutually enriching, and the subject of ongoing negotiation and contestation.

As in the case of music, it is the Bhojpuri folk stratum, in its diverse constituents, that constituted the bulk of traditional popular dance in Indo-Caribbean society through the mid-1900s. Some of these dances were the provenance of men, such as the athletic "bare-back" *ahirva kā nāch* noted in chapter 2, and the potpourri of styles that would be presented in a staging of Harichand and Indersabha music-drama. In British Guiana an idiosyncratic style called "rajdhar"—perhaps a local reconstruction of North Indian kathak—was cultivated by a handful of dancers (see Singh 1994), but on the whole, no consistent Indo-Caribbean "local-classical dance" style evolved as a counterpart to local-classical singing. Since respectable women in traditional Indian society did not dance in public, some dances in folk dramas, as well as the gyrating of the *launḍā* (transvestite dancer) at weddings, were performed by men in female attire, in accordance with North Indian convention. However, actual women were perhaps the most important carriers of tradition at the domestic level. Particularly important were weddings and matikor festivities, when women, liberated from the leering or disapproving gaze of men by their exclusion from the environs, would dance in an uninhibited and often bawdy manner to light songs or perhaps to drumming by a tassa group whose members would stand at a respectful distance. The Bhojpuri women's dance style is distinctive, featuring graceful hand and arm gestures and a judicious amount of hip rolling, combined with certain characteristic poses, such as that with one hand behind

the back and the other behind the head (asserted by Mungal Patasar to mimic the demon Bhasmasur, who was tricked into immolating himself by assuming that posture).

A new force arrived on the scene with the advent of Bombay films in the mid-1930s, and especially with the coalescence of a distinct Bollywood style of dancing in the 1940s. Even more so than was the case with film music, the film dance style, despite being from "Mother India," had little in common with the Bhojpuri legacy (or with any regional Indian dance); instead, its style (aptly described by one Indian critic as "jerky calisthenics") was largely a creation of the Bombay studios, drawing only tangentially from the Indian folk and classical traditions that had evolved organically over centuries. Nevertheless, the new film dance style soon came to be widely popular and extensively cultivated in the Caribbean, especially as Indian film dancers like Hema Malini began touring the region. By the mid-1940s Trinidadian ensembles like Naya Zamana were incorporating film-style dancers into their performances. In the 1950s, Champa Devi (Fatima Khan, 1923–2010?) became the first female professional dancer to achieve broad acceptance,[26] heralding a new liberalization of attitudes and a decline of male transvestite dancing (with the launda tradition persisting only in more "provincial" Suriname). Meanwhile, just as the film ārtī song "Jay Jagdish Hare" came to be sung in temples throughout India and the Caribbean, similarly did the writhing "snake dance" from the film *Nagin* become so widely imitated in Trinidad as to achieve a certain sort of "folk" status (Maharaj 2010, 326–27). As with Bollywood music, film dance at once stimulated and enriched the local performance scene while devaluing local Bhojpuri-derived traditions.

From the 1960s Indian classical dancing—especially but not only North Indian kathak—began to have some presence in the Caribbean scene. A few local dancers, such as Trinidad's Rajkumar Krishna Persad, Hansraj Ramkissoon, and Polly Sookraj, and Guyana's Gora Singh—were able to study in India, and several others have followed in their paths. Meanwhile, various institutions and individuals—both South Asian and local—commenced teaching Indian classical (and even stylized folk) dances in the Caribbean, paralleling the teaching of North Indian classical music by H. S. Adesh and others. Compared to local arts—from chutney to rajdhar and local-classical singing—Indian classical dance could attract students not only by its greater prestige but also by its standardized theory and pedagogy. Meanwhile, increasing numbers of young East Indians might on various occasions dance in the local creole styles, especially those associated with soca, with its pneumatic pelvic pumping.

As was to some extent the case with the diverse local and imported music styles, the heterogeneous dance styles came to predominate in discrete and

parallel arenas. Although the traditional dance styles of folk drama and Ahir dance are defunct, the Bhojpuri-derived women's style (whether done by men or women) has remained vital in the contexts of the matikor, the wedding, and the chutney fête, with matronly "aunties" often constituting the most graceful, expressive, and exuberant dancers. Such dancing enjoys no particular prestige or institutional recognition, but the evaporation of traditional inhibitions has allowed for a considerably greater amount of per capita social dancing than one would encounter in an Indian village. If women in the Bhojpuri region enjoy few socially acceptable opportunities to dance, many Indo-Caribbean women and men seem to be ready to dance at the drop of a hat.

For its part, filmi dance has little presence in social dance contexts, but tends to pervade the realm of "presentational" dancing. This dominance is particularly conspicuous, for example, in Mastana Bahar, paralleling that of film music. Hence, since the 1970s a considerable portion of any Mastana Bahar audition or show has consisted of teenage girls rendering popular film dances from current Bollywood hits, perhaps having learned their choreography in local film dance classes taught by former Mastana Bahar winners. Over the decades, the girls who have performed film dances in Mastana Bahar are estimated to number in the tens of thousands. Ironically, some of the filmi dances consist of artificial Bollywood-style "folk dances," while local Bhojpuri-derived dance styles are neglected. In his book on Mastana Bahar (1982, 104–27), Shamoon Mohammed lamented this hegemony of film dance, as he did that of film music. One objectionable feature, he noted, was the way that much suggestive film dancing had become a vehicle for the introduction of Western-style vulgarity into Trinidad. Another problem, as with filmsongs, has been the obsequious imitation of Bollywood rather than attempts to choreograph new folk dances based on local traditions. He asked, "Why not locally created dances that reflect the social and economic activities of our people: fishing and seine-pulling at Mayaro, Maracas or Charlotteville, or fishing, oyster, crab catching and hunting in our swamps?" (110). However, as with film music, his exhortations do not seem to have great effect, despite his admirable intentions and his ongoing involvement with Mastana Bahar, whose dancing remains dominated by Bollywood imitations. It is perhaps not surprising that few dancers have pursued his ideas, given that seine-pulling and crab-catching, though perhaps picturesque, are not activities familiar or meaningful to many modern Trinidadians.

To a considerable extent, the contemporary Indo-Caribbean dance scene—especially in Trinidad—has accommodated a sort of pluralistic coexistence of styles comparable to that of the local music scene, similarly aided by the sheer amount of dancing by the public. Film and classical dance are pervasive, but primarily in stage contexts like Mastana Bahar. On the vernacular level, the

dynamic chutney-soca scene has promoted not only musical syncreticism but also a lively fusion of traditional and creole dance styles, especially the frontal pelvic pumping called "wining."[27] While much dancing to chutney may be essentially free form, the Bhojpuri-style graceful gestures and "Bhasmasur" pose remain common, often in combination with wining. The presence of a certain amount of hip rolling in traditional Bhojpuri women's dance has facilitated incorporation of the athletic creole-style wining, just, indeed, as the compatible chutney and soca rhythms blend easily.[28] In any case, dancing may be done solo, or with a partner of either sex. (The sort of homophobia that would prevent two Afro-Caribbean men from briefly dancing with each other is less operant in Indo-Caribbean society. In Trinidad, the only local genre featuring couple dancing in ballroom posture is Yuletide parang.)

Meanwhile, if few dancers have taken up Shamoon Mohammed's suggestions for new mimetic folk dances, a spirit of lively innovation has nevertheless animated local stage choreographers, especially Michael Salickram and Satnarine Balkaransingh. Under their guidance, since around 1990 their Shiv Shakti Dance Company and Nrityanjali Theater groups, respectively, have presented many shows artfully combining or juxtaposing kathak, chutney, bhangra, Michael Jackson shines, creole moves, and other elements, accompanied by similarly diverse sorts of local and foreign music.

Concluding Perspectives:
The Local "Little" versus the Far-off "Great"

Indo-Caribbean music culture, with its relatively modest size but impressive vigor and diversity, can be seen as drawing from three larger music cultures that function like antipodes, with the inherited Bhojpuri-derived folk music legacy serving as a kind of baseline substratum. Although resilient in some ways, because this tradition has lost its linguistic core and is isolated from India and thus unsupported, it has been under constant erosion from other local and imported music idioms.

Of these, the musical great traditions imported from North India have had the most overt impact. As noted, these include Hindustani music, the "stage bhajans" of Anup Jalota et al., and, above all, the modern commercial great tradition of Bombay film music. Representing different aspects of mainstream, panregional North Indian culture, all these benefit, in the Indo-Caribbean world, from their mass-media presence, high prestige, links to the ancestral homeland, pedagogical networks and systems, and the ways they each (including even Hindustani music) embody a certain sort of modernity.

A second and different sort of antipode is represented by local West Indian

Afro-creole music culture, which constitutes an immediate presence embodied by living individuals rather than a mass-mediated import from remote South Asia. While calypso, Carnival, and steelband—the familiar Trinidadian triumvirate—have constituted conventional icons, more popular and influential, especially among the young, have been the popular dance and music genres soca and dancehall reggae.

Finally, Afro-American popular musics occupy a distinct sort of presence, while not exerting the hegemony that is often ascribed to them in commentary on global culture. Neither contemporary hip-hop nor R & B is widely cultivated or performed in the West Indies, though they are popular and well established in the media (including maxi-taxi sound systems). Indo-Caribbeans in secondary diaspora sites like New York may be particularly drawn to such genres.

On the vernacular level, it could be said that most Indo-Caribbeans do not regard the interactions of these musical spheres as problematic or controversial; rather, they cheerfully choose their own preferred entertainment musics without vexatious consideration of sociopolitical implications, and they move comfortably between consuming and often performing various idioms. Hence, for example, an Indo-Trinidadian high school student might play in the school steelband, dance to soca and chutney-soca at parties with her friends, "get on bad" to tassa drumming at weddings, sing bhajans at the Hindu temple on Sunday mornings, and passively hear and perhaps idly sing along with the Bombay filmsongs that may be playing on the radio at home. Accordingly, instead of explicit concern about the fragility of the Bhojpuri-derived little traditions, a more typical lay attitude is that traditional folksong, modern filmsong, pop chutney, and commercial bhajans from India—to take a few examples—all have their places in culture, and that the Bhojpuri tradition is sufficiently resilient as to obviate any sense of alarm about its survival. Hence, at the Sunday satsang, the chowtal group will eventually get its turn, once the legion of amateur Lata Mangeshkars have crooned for an hour or so.

However, if such an easy cosmopolitanism characterizes much lay experience, the relationships of diverse musical genres are in fact the subject of ongoing controversies, polemically argued in Trinidadian and Guyanese newspapers, academic conferences, and YouTube flame wars. In most cases these heated exchanges involve not aesthetics per se but rather questions of ethnic identity, of which music is seen to constitute a preeminent symbol. Such sociomusical polemics have taken place either between antagonistic parties of Indians and Afro-creoles, or else they have been internal controversies involving different factions of Indo-Caribbeans. In the former category, particularly lively and acrimonious in Trinidad and Guyana have been debates over the amount of media devoted to Indian music, the often negative representations of Indians

in calypso, and the question of whether the harmonium, together with the steel drum, should enjoy the status of being Trinidad's "national instrument."

As Mark Slobin has pithily remarked, "Nothing is simple in the world of diasporic music-making" (1992, 46), and relations of diasporic populations to their ancestral homelands can be especially complex, contradictory, and laden with tension. As we have seen, such ambivalences inhere particularly to the asymmetry between the Bhojpuri-derived little tradition of Indo-Caribbean culture and the imported mainstream great traditions, from Anup Jalota bhajans to Bollywood kitsch. Central to their relationship are the ways in which the great tradition imports can be seen variously to enrich or to stifle extant Indo-Caribbean music culture.

The enriching and impoverishing forces are often inseparable. As we noted, the distinctive "little tradition" of sadhua bhajans once cultivated by Kabir panthis and Siewnarainis has increasingly been replaced by a bland style of congregational singing derived from mainstream North Indian practice; often, collective singing itself is undermined by the use of a sound system that blares the Jalota-style singing of the pandit or mahānt. At the same time, the Kabir panth and, indirectly, its associated music have in general been reinforced and invigorated by renewed contacts with India, especially in the form of visits by respected mahānts. While contact with India has tended to promote a mainstream stage bhajan style rather than the Bhojpuri-derived khañjri gīt, the continued vitality of the sect does allow space for the distinctive "little tradition" to survive, as rendered in a hybrid form by a few singers like Balliram Balroop. By contrast, the Siewnaraini sect has been totally unsupported by its declining counterpart in South Asia. Accordingly, while no "competing" form of Siewnaraini bhajan has been imported from India, the isolation of the sect as a whole has contributed to its general eclipse, together with that of its distinctive song tradition.

As we have suggested, the traditional music culture of a million descendants of Bhojpuri peasants can scarcely be expected to rival in richness the music emanating from greater India, with its billion souls and its prodigious commercial- and classical-music scenes. For Indo-Caribbeans isolated from their ancestral homeland, consumption and performance—whether skilled or inept—of imported South Asian mainstream musics have also constituted a fundamental means of maintaining Indian identity. Hence, most Indo-Caribbeans do not regard imported Indian music as a stultifying hegemon; they see it, rather, as an inexhaustible potential resource that can provide a cultural depth and continuity unavailable to Afro-creoles, alienated as they are from the traditions of their African forebears. Further, it could be noted that the Indo-Caribbean enjoyment of film music and stage bhajans does not entail any considerable

drain of capital to India, nor does it necessarily replace local performance with passive consumption, given the prodigious amount of amateur renditions of Bollywood fare, Jalota bhajans, and other imported genres at Mastana Bahar, temple functions, and other events. Perhaps most important, enjoyment and performance of contemporary South Asian musics afford Indo-Caribbeans a way to cultivate an Indian form of modernity that cannot be found in rustic traditional genres like chowtal, birha, and women's wedding songs. Accordingly, as we have seen, relatively few Indo-Caribbeans have expressed concern over the way that Indian great-tradition musics have thrived to some extent at the expense of Bhojpuri-derived traditional music. Hence it is primarily the folklorist, the ethnomusicologist, or the veteran performer of some archaic genre who laments how modern pop musics, whether local or imported, vitiate traditional genres that had evolved organically over generations to suit the particular sensibilities of a given community.

Various individuals, as noted, do in fact criticize the hegemony exercised by Bollywood fare in some contexts, although their primary complaint is generally not the threat posed by these genres to Bhojpuri-derived folksong. Instead, their criticisms have centered on two distinct issues. First, cultural activists like Sham and Shamoon Mohammed have lamented how amateur performers have overwhelmingly opted for rote imitation of Indian film fare rather than active creation of distinctly local and original songs and dances. Second, they and others have disparaged the way that Bollywood has served as a conduit for vulgar and kitsch Western culture, whether in the form of lewd dancing or sensuous pop songs. I recall, for example, chatting at a Guyanese wedding with an elderly tān-singer, who, lamenting the lack of interest in his art, said of the raucous filmsong blaring from the loudspeakers, "All this disco noise—this all came from India!"

The disgruntled vocalist was in effect articulating a viewpoint that recurs in Indo-Caribbean discourse—namely, that Indo-Caribbeans are in some ways more genuinely Indian than are people from India itself. Since Indo-Caribbeans have virtually no exposure to Indian folk culture, including that of the Bhojpuri region, their image of modern India derives mostly from films and the similarly Westernized engineers, doctors, and businessmen from South Asia whom they encounter in New York, Toronto, and other secondary diaspora sites, or occasionally in the Caribbean itself. Although "NRI's" (non-resident Indians) in Queens, New York, tend to regard their Indo-Caribbean neighbors as deculturated half-breeds who have lost their caste and language, many of the latter see such "India people" as shallow materialists who have little involvement with their own traditional culture. As one Indo-Caribbean wrote in a YouTube polemic on this theme, "when u go in a temple in nyc nearly all the ppl come

from trinidad or guyana. indians who came from india who live here don't keep half the traditions that we do. for example they don't celebrate diwali, holi and other hindu festivals like we do." The notion that Bollywood imagery represents Indian culture as a whole can lead by extension to an occasional stigmatization of even neutral Indian entities. Accordingly, at one Guyanese wedding I attended the pandit explicitly pointed out that he was referring to the wedding canopy by the Bhojpuri term "*māro*" rather than the standard Hindi "*maṇḍap*," saying, "We don't want any Bollywood culture here."

As I have suggested elsewhere, such perspectives, whether grounded in insight or misunderstanding, can be seen as latter-day perpetuations of an ambivalence toward India that dates from the first period of indentureship itself. Although many of the indentured workers were tricked into emigrating, others left in order to escape caste discrimination, exploitation by landlords, or other iniquities. Those who remained in the Caribbean did so out of choice, and some who did not subsequently returned there in disgust to tell of the expensive purification rituals that hometown Brahmans demanded they undergo (Vertovec 1992, 73).

Generations later, while Bollywood films and film music remain popular, a latent ambivalence toward India and Indians persists, which surfaces on diverse occasions. More important, the emergence of a distinct, lively, syncretic Indo-Caribbean pop culture has offered local Indians an alternative form of modernity, leading to a palpable and occasionally noted decrease in the popularity and cultural centrality of Bollywood culture in the Caribbean. The chutney-soca scene, with its youthful exuberance, its combination of Bhojpuri and Afro-creole elements, and its attendant videos and extravagant concerts, has played a key role in the emergence of this competing modernity. Another important musical constituent of Indo-Caribbean modernity has been tassa, which features its own sort of syncretism and fashionable appeal to youth, as well as a unique sort of musical sophistication. To this important, dynamic, and uniquely Indo-Caribbean genre we may now turn.

Tassa Drumming from India to the Caribbean and Beyond

Tassa drumming is an Indo-Trinidadian art form of extraordinary originality and richness, combining technical virtuosity and innovative dynamism over a solid base of traditional repertoire and style. With more than one hundred semiprofessional groups performing on the island, tassa is heard at competitions and various other functions, and it is indispensable at Hindu weddings and the Muslim Hosay (Muharram) commemoration. Originally a transplant from North India, tassa has flourished to the extent that repeated calls have been made for it to be enshrined alongside the steel drum as a "national instrument," and on the vernacular level it certainly merits being included in the traditional description of Trinidad as "the land of calypso, Carnival, and steeldrum." However, despite its popularity and musical richness, tassa drumming has never been adequately documented in published form, either as flourishing in India or the Caribbean.[1]

Tassa and Related Drum Traditions in India

The tassa is a medium-sized kettledrum, about eighteen inches in diameter, suspended at waist level and played with a pair of flexible sticks, and combined, in Trinidad and India, with one or more heavy cylindrical bass drums called *ḍhol* or, more commonly in the Caribbean, simply "bass," and a pair of brass cymbals, six to twelve inches wide, called jhānjh or jhāl. The typical Trinidadian band (or "side") consists of a quartet comprising a "cutter," or lead tassa, a supporting (but identical) tassa called "foulay" or "fuller," a bass, and jhāl.

Although some Indo-Trinidadians, inspired by ethnic pride, have claimed that the tassa was invented on their island, the tassa ensemble was clearly brought to the Caribbean from India, and in fact the tassa drum originated prior to that in the Middle East. The Arabic-script orthography of the word (*to'e-sīn-he*) indicates a Persian or Arabic lexical origin; Platts, in his erudite 1884 Urdu dictionary (1930, 750), suggests that the word originated in Arabic (perhaps as *tāsat*) and spread thence to Persian and Urdu. Arabic would presumably be the source for the Spanish homonym *taza* (bowl, cup, pronounced "tassa") and the French cognate *tasse* (as in "demi-tasse"). In India tassa—to use the standard Trinidadian orthography in place of "tāsa"—is often pronounced "tāsha" (see Wolf 2000, 87.) In Yemen and other Arabic-speaking places, the word denotes both a drum and a bowl. Certainly the instrument itself is of considerable antiquity, as is suggested by depictions in the Persian Tāq-i-Bustān reliefs (590–628 c.e.; see Farmer 1939, cited in Wolf 2000, 87). The tassa, by that name, has spread as far as Indonesia. Outside India, it is particularly common in Yemen, though its playing there has clearly been reinforced or reintroduced by immigrants from India, especially Bombay.[2]

Despite such geographical peregrinations, there is no doubt that the tassa ensemble rose to prominence in North India in the early and mid-1800s, and especially in the city of Lucknow, at that time the most dynamic center of Indo-Muslim culture, including music. A list of instruments in an 1832 chronicle by one Jaffur Shurreef mentions the tassa drum, adding that it is invariably accompanied by the ḍhol-like *murfa'* barrel drum (50)[3]; a few years later, British historian R. M. Martin provided a brief description and drawing of a tassa, with a clay body (1838, 600–601).[4] In the early 1900s, Abdul Halim Sharar (1860–1926), a chronicler descended from a family of courtiers to the nawabs, penned an artful and much-cited contemporary portrait of "Lakhnavi" society at its peak, which included an informative description of tassa drumming. Noting that the "ḍhola tasha" ensemble is one of six kinds of groups that accompany weddings and other processions, Sharar relates:

> In Lucknow bands there are usually three or four large ḍholas and at least one man, though occasionally two or three, beating tashas. There is also at least one man playing the jhanjh, cymbals. The jhanjh can be traced to Persia and neighboring countries and the tasha is common in and around Egypt, but the ḍhol is purely Indian. This type of band was introduced into Lucknow from Delhi mainly by the military. In Delhi there were only ḍholas and jhanjh; tashas were added in Lucknow and very soon were considered so important that a band without them seemed to lack life. (Sharar 1975, 151)

Describing the style of these groups, he continues:

They [the tassa players] establish the rhythm and the ḍhol players go on following them. In the tassa playing method, the beats should fall with such rapidity that one stroke cannot be distinguished from another [in other words, "buzz rolls"]. Rhythmic patterns and compositions are produced from these continuous and incessant strokes, which are low and high, and from the contrasting registers of the drums. In Lucknow these bandsmen were so skilled that ḍhol players from other cities cannot [or would be ashamed to] play in front of them. (151, adapted from translation by Wolf 2000, 91)

Sharar goes on to relate how tassa ensembles accompanied processions of tāzias—mobile cenotaphs of the Shia martyrs—during Muharram; the tassa groups were among the ensembles that "were surrounded by admirers and stood in one place for hours on end, issuing challenges to all and sundry to rival them at playing music . . . Among these musicians, the tasha players were the most skilled and were always introducing innovations into their music." Even the last nawab of Lucknow, Wajid Ali Shah, was a skilled tassa drummer; after the British exiled him and his retinue in 1856 to Matiya Burj in Calcutta, Sharar had occasion to marvel upon seeing him play, surrounded by singers playing ḍhols (151–52).

The devastation wrought upon Lucknow during the Revolt of 1857–58 did not attenuate the widespread presence of tassa drumming in North India, although the instrument does not seem to have enjoyed such prestige since then, and the Mutiny may have contributed to the decline of tassa within Lucknow itself (which has been further exacerbated by the Shia-Sunni brawling that often erupts during Muharram). Since the nineteenth century the tasha-ḍhol ensemble has in fact spread throughout North India, from Calcutta to Bombay, or rather, Kolkatta to Mumbai.

Considering how widespread the tassa-ḍhol ensembles are in North India, the lack of scholarly attention to their music is remarkable. Aside from myself, the only investigator to have studied tassa drum traditions in South Asia is ethnomusicologist Richard Wolf (2000, 2014), who has researched the Muharram drumming of tassa groups in Delhi, Lucknow, and elsewhere, including Pakistani drummers of *mohājar* immigrant communities from the Agra-Bharatpur area. In 2009 I studied the playing of drummers in and around Banaras, with the assumption that drumming in the Bhojpuri area might be especially relevant to whatever traditions were transplanted to the Caribbean. (In 2013 I also researched "ḍhol-tasha" drumming at the Ganesh festival in Pune, quite far from the Bhojpuri region.) Tassa playing in distant parts of the subcontinent certainly merits attention, though its direct relevance to Indo-Caribbean drumming is questionable. In Kolkatta, for example, tassa drums are part of the *dhāk ḍhol* ensembles that play during Durga Puja each fall; it is conceivable that such

Figure 4. Tassa player in Lucknow region, mid-1800s.
Adapted by the author from mica print.

playing traditions may have constituted one source for Caribbean drumming, but the absence of Durga puja celebrations—or any other substantial Bengali cultural entities—in the Indic Caribbean might cast doubt on such connections. Similarly, in Maharashtra, extravagant "ḍhol-tasha" competitions are held during the Ganesh festival, where massive amateur ensembles—incorporating as many as a hundred ḍhols and tashas—perform conventional and new rhythms

with elaborate choreography and costumes. The core of these rhythms is a sequences of "hands" (composite meters, with lead tassa improvisations) devised in the 1960s and 1970s, alongside adaptations of Indian filmsongs and international tunes like "We Will Rock You."[5] Intriguing and worthy of study as this music is, its relation to Indo-Caribbean tassa drumming is dubious, both for the modernity of its origin and the unlikelihood that any indentured immigrants hailed from Maharashtra. However, there is no doubt that regional North Indian tassa drumming styles in nineteenth-century North India may have evolved as an eclectic set of traditions, with certain sorts and degrees of stylistic connections. Moreover, as we shall discuss, the eclectic practice of adapting rhythms from diverse sources certainly finds parallel among Trinidadian tassa drummers, some of whom merrily adapt rhythms from all manner of sources, be it a Bollywood hit, a traditional folksong style, or the theme of "George of the Jungle." In general, regional tassa drumming traditions in India—and their interconnections—require further study.

Given the inadequate documentation of tassa drumming in India, it is only with qualification that one can hazard generalizations about traditions in the areas whence the indentureds came to the Caribbean. However, on the basis of research conducted by Wolf and myself, some tentative observations can be made, including some general comments presented here and some more specific details noted further below.

Tassa drumming can be regarded as part of a stratum of "vernacular" drumming in North India (and Pakistan), which also comprises nagāra, ḍhol, and dholak playing. These sorts of percussion traditions lack the formal theory and some of the richness and variety of classical tabla music. Their tendency to be patronized by lower rather than upper classes also situates them in the category of "folk" music. However, some of these styles share certain features that distinguish them from the more rudimentary forms of amateur drumming, such as the desultory thumping a peasant woman might provide on dholak to accompany an informal courtyard song session.

Vernacular drumming might be provided by paid professional specialists trained in their art. Typically, such drummers do not concern themselves with the sort of formal theory that would enable them, for example, to enumerate beats (or *mātras*) in a given meter that they play. Similarly, in this stratum there may be a general lack of terms for abstract musical concepts. Hence, in place of the conspicuously absent Hindustani "*tāl*" for "meter," one encounters a plethora of inconsistent and (to the investigator) confusing terms, such as *lay* (in Hindustani music: tempo), *jāti* (type), *tarz, dhun* (melody), *lakri* (wood), *chāl* (motion), and *hāth* (hand)—the latter term being commonly used in Hindi in Suriname, and in English in Trinidad and Guyana. Despite such ambiguities,

Figure 5. A ḍhol-tasha ensemble in Pune's Ganesh festival, 2013.
Photograph by the author.

musicians in this milieu typically know and play a variety of named composite meters, some of which have no counterparts in Hindustani music or other
drum traditions. Thus, for instance, tassa drummers in Banaras play not only
familiar panregional rhythms like *kaharva* and *bhangra* but also the distinctive
local meters *chakli* and *langāra*. For their part, nagāra drummers in that region,
as discussed below, play a variety of composite rhythms, including *lāchārī*,
jhūmar, *devi ka gīt* (named after song forms), *dihbari* (named after a goddess),
ahirva, *khari kalaiya* (dance styles), and *khemta* and *bhartalla* (specific rhythm
names). Some of the meter names seem to enumerate formal features, however
ambiguously, such as the *ektāl*, *dotāl*, and *tīntāl* of Pune tassa drummers, the
"*das ki ginti*" ("ten-count") and *bāsath jarben* ("62 [ḍhol] strokes") of Delhi
tassa players encountered by Wolf (2014, chapter 3), and the Trinidadian "tīn
chopra" (three strokes) and "chaubola" (four *bols*). In some cases, drummers
may be specially appreciated and remunerated for their virtuosity.

Since the tassa and ḍhol (in contrast to the nagāra) are typically played
standing, supported by straps around the player's neck, tassa-ḍhol ensembles

141

are favored for ambulatory occasions, including processions associated with Muharrum, Hindu weddings, and miscellaneous street events like parades, protests, and political marches. In Hindu weddings in the Bhojpuri region, tassa-ḍhol players might walk in a *barāt* (groom's party procession) with a brass band, either accompanying them or playing separately.[6]

While neither I nor anyone else appears to be qualified to generalize authoritatively about the quality of tassa drumming throughout the Gangetic plain, I will nevertheless venture a tentative observation, to the effect that on the whole, tassa drumming in that region seems to compare unfavorably with its Trinidadian counterpart in terms of vitality, richness, and status. In North India, many tassa drummers—including those who turn out for Muharrum processions—are either amateurs (and often even children) or else specialists in other instruments (including tabla) who merely play tassa casually at this annual event. In Jaipur, where Sunni Muslims pride themselves on the beauty of their tazias and the size of their tassa ensembles, I met several individuals who told me they joined such groups, for which neither practice nor talent was required; as one told me, "Anyone can get a drum and play." Even the professional drummers I recorded in Banaras had a very limited repertoire of meters—essentially, *langāra*, *kaharva*, *bhangra*, "disco," and two simple Muharram beats. There was little internal variety to these meters, which instead consisted of simple vamps, unlike some of the Trinidadian hands, with their conventional sequences and variations; *bhangra*, by far the most popular Banaras-area rhythm at present, is a recent borrowing from Punjabi music. The drumming of the semiprofessional lead tassa players I heard was unimpressive in terms of technique and variety. Many of them, I noticed, were not even able to play a buzz roll, which is otherwise the forte of the tassa as an instrument and was clearly the technique at which Sharar marveled in his description of Lucknow drummers. To some extent like the brass bands they might accompany, the function of the modern tassa groups I saw seemed to be merely to provide a festive, loud, and rhythmic noise, whose particular musical merit was not essential. Aside from the massive amateur ensembles of the Maharashtra Ganesh festival, there seems to be no North Indian counterpart to the Trinidadian tassa milieu, with its cult of virtuosity, its competitive spirit, its dynamic combination of tradition and innovation, and the celebration of tassa drumming as a cherished and prominent aspect of culture. Wolf (p.c.) relates that Lucknow—celebrated in the mid-1800s for its tassa tradition—seems to be conspicuously and pathetically bereft of presentable players.[7] As well, in accordance with the sheer material poverty of Indian drummers, I noticed that in place of the sturdy wood and goatskin ḍhols obligatory in Trini ensembles, many Indian groups use aluminum bass drum shells with flimsy plastic heads

that lack both the volume and the durability of proper ḍhols. My admittedly superficial impression is that tassa drumming in the modern-day Gangetic plain has never regained the richness and the prestige that it evidently enjoyed in nawabi Lucknow. The variety and vitality of Trinidadian playing may represent both a marginal-survival perpetuation of that former glory, as well as a fresh dynamism enlivened by the particular nature of the Indo-Trinidadian cultural milieu.

In some respects, Indo-Caribbean tassa drumming finds a counterpart less in contemporary Bhojpuri-region tassa playing than in nagāra music, which thus merits some discussion here. The nagāra (nakāra, naqqāra) is a drum pair of considerable antiquity and geographical provenance. By the name naqqāra (from Arabic), it is found throughout much of the Muslim world. In India, it is depicted in numerous Mughal-era miniatures and is mentioned in several texts. Most notably in this respect is the sixteenth-century *Ain-i-Akbari* (Fazl 1927, I: 52–53), which describes the *naqqāra-khāna*, an ensemble of naqqāras, shahnāis, and other instruments, which constituted an important ensign of royalty, marking times of day at the palace and at military encampments and dignifying various formal events. Emperor Akbar himself played the naqqāra. At present, the drum pair is played throughout much of North India (and even parts of South India), whether as a vestige of palatial ceremony in Rajasthan or for rustic folk entertainment. It was an essential feature in the nautanki music and dance theater that flourished from the late 1800s to the mid-twentieth century (an early version of which was performed in the Caribbean).

Of particular relevance here is the use of the instrument in the Bhojpuri area, which is most likely to have contributed to Indo-Caribbean drumming. In general, nagāra drumming in the Gangetic plain merits further study; the data presented here derive from a passage in a book about Banaras folk music by Onkar Prasad (1987, 54–59) and sessions I conducted in 2009 with Natay Ustad, the leading professional nagāra player of Banaras. While hardly affording a comprehensive understanding of nagāra music, these corroborating sources have sufficed to illustrate that Bhojpuri-region nagāra drumming in fact exhibits striking affinities with Indo-Caribbean tassa music—more so, in some ways, than does North Indian tassa drumming, given what appears to be its rather rudimentary, or perhaps degraded nature.

Like the tassa and other North Indian nagāra formats, the Bhojpuri-region nagāra forms the core of an eponymous ensemble, in its case generally consisting of a lead nagāra pair, a supporting pair (which might be called *bharne-wāla*, "filling out" [the sound]), a cymbal or other metallophone, and a large frame drum called *dafla*. The nagāra pair itself consists of a large earthen or metal kettledrum (itself called nagāra), and a smaller drum (*kurkuriya*, *gīl*), both of

which are struck with a pair of simple wooden sticks (*chob*). Although the nagāra, unlike the tassa, is ideally rested on the ground and played while sitting, it may be affixed to shoulder straps and played while standing or walking. Further affinities with Caribbean tassa drumming are numerous. The nagāra is played to enliven or dignify a variety of occasions, including matrimonial or funeral processions, or festive dancing. The level and sort of theoretical knowledge articulated by nagāra drummers are roughly akin to that of tassa players; while drummers do not count beats, nor do they make systematic use of names for different strokes, they do designate specific rhythms by appropriate names and are readily able, for example, to demonstrate such meters on request. The nagāra's repertoire, like that of tassa, consists of composite meters (for which the most common generic term is *lakri*—"wood," as in the drumstick). As with tassa, some of the meter names (mentioned above), such as *lāchāri* and *jhūmar*, designate the song forms whose accompaniment patterns they imitate in stylized form; others, like *khemta*, *rela*, and *bhartalla*, are strictly musical terms. Like such tassa hands as dingolay and "nagāra," some of the nagāra *lakris* are designed to accompany vigorous dancing, especially by Ahir men; invigorated by liquor and the drumming, Ahirs dance athletically, even performing cartwheels to the *khari kalaiya* beat.[8]

Nagāra drumming bears a number of specific similarities to Trinidadian tassa music. Several of the *lakris*, like some tassa hands and other North Indian drum styles, embody sequential sections, and drummers may segue from one *lakri* to another in suite format, in accordance with the context. While we need not present detailed analyses of nagāra meters here, some of the *lakris*, such as *nautanki* and *rela*, often reiterate a "TA-tikaTA-tikaTA-" beat that is essentially identical to the standard ostinato in Caribbean nagāra drumming, such as accompanies birha singing, and also pervades the popular eponymous Trinidadian tassa hand that imitates that beat. The *khemta* rhythm played by Banarsi nagāra drummers also closely resembles the hand by the same name of Indo-Caribbean local-classical and tassa music, with its distinctive, "limping" long-short-short / long-short-short pattern (discussed below). Further, both Banarsi nagāra drumming and tassa music often feature strikingly similar ensemble "break" patterns, especially that shown in example 13 below. Finally, the supporting nagāra drum pair, like the supporting foulay in hands like steelpan, often plays a steady sixteenth-note pattern. Wolf (2014, chapter 4) notes that in some North Indian ḍhol-tassa Muharram styles, the accompanying tassas play similar patterns.

While in the Bhojpuri region the nagāra typically forms the core of an ensemble, in the Caribbean it has more typically been played solo. In that sense, the subcontinental Indian nagāra ensemble bears closer affinities with Caribbean tassa, with its similar ensemble of supporting drum, metallophone, and low-

Figure 6. A nagāra player in Pune. Photograph by the author.

pitched bass drum. It is clear that certain specific rhythms—as in the case of the "nagāra" hand—were adopted by Trinidadian tassa drummers from nagāra playing. On a broader level, it is likely that during the indentureship period, nagāra and tassa ensembles coexisted in the Bhojpuri region and shared many features; since tassa drumming in that region appears to have declined in rich-ness, affinities with and counterparts to Trinidadian tassa drumming are in some respects more evident in Bhojpuri nagāra drumming than in tassa music.

Tassa in the Caribbean

The early history of tassa in the Caribbean, like that of essentially every other form of Indo-Caribbean traditional music, is obscure and undocumented. Given the evident prominence of tassa-ḍhol ensembles in Lucknow and, presumably,

its environs during the indentureship period, it is not surprising that the tradition was brought to the Caribbean, where drummers would have been in demand for Muharram processions, weddings, and other festivities. Tassa players could have come from Lucknow itself, or from surrounding areas where the tradition had taken root. While the British preferred hardy farmers to frail musicians, it is not inconceivable that the ranks of the indentured might even have included some underemployed musicians from Wajid Ali Shah's entourage, since Matiya Burj, the site of their transplanted court, was adjacent to the depot where, at any given time, a few hundred indentured emigrants would be encamped awaiting the next outgoing vessel. It is known that some workers brought drums with them on the ships,[9] but in any case, artisans in the Caribbean could relatively easily make tassas and ḍhols, whose components of goatskin, clay, and mango wood were readily available. One can only speculate as to whether those who brought tassa to the Caribbean included trained specialists as well as casual amateurs with only an incomplete knowledge of drum technique and repertoire.

Specific references to tassa drums are wanting in the historical record. As will be discussed below, Muharram processions—evidently with tassa drumming—had become major cultural events by the 1860s in Trinidad and British Guiana, enlivened by the participation of many Afro-Caribbeans. Indo-Caribbean Muharram, as documented from the 1850s, clearly replicated key aspects of Lucknow-area Muharram, especially in its towering tazias. Since tassa ensembles were a familiar component of North Indian Muharram, it is logical to assume that they were played in the Caribbean processions as well, although no specific references to them from the nineteenth century have emerged.[10] In general, it seems quite likely that the very first generations of immigrants included drummers who fashioned drums locally and played them at Muharram and, subsequently, at weddings and other festivities where loud and festive percussion was in demand. It is also likely that these first tassa drummers were Muslims of urban rather than rural provenance.

A certain sort of historical data is offered by oral genealogies provided by members of some of the five surviving Trinidadian "yards," or hereditary centers of Muharrum activities in the St. James neighborhood of Port of Spain (which will be further discussed below). Of these, the two oldest are the Panchayati and Ghulam Hussein yards. The Panchayati yard was founded as a neighborhood entity, as suggested by its name (*panchāyat* being a sort of traditional village council). The Ghulam Hussein yard, by contrast, developed as the patrimony of a particular family lineage. Raiaz Ali, currently the patriarch of that yard, traces his Shia ancestry to his great-grandfather, Musahib Ali, a drummer from India who, according to Raiaz, brought the art form to Trinidad and commenced playing at weddings as well as at Hosay commemorations. According to Raiaz,

Musahib's brother, Ali Hussein, settled in Rio Claro and Princes Town in south Trinidad and established the tassa tradition there. In St. James the tradition was perpetuated by Musahib's son Yusuf Ali and his brother Ghulam Hussein; Raiaz's maternal uncle Kalal moved to San Juan, in the suburban "corridor" east of Port of Spain, and established tassa drumming there, especially at weddings and miscellaneous festivities. Yusuf's son Ibrahim Boboy Ali perpetuated the tradition and handed it down to his son Raiaz.

The Boodoosingh family of south Trinidad also traces its lineage to an immigrant drummer from India. According to family informants, this man's son, John Kuar Singh, started a family-based tassa group in 1917, that was then perpetuated by his own son, Boodoosingh, whose Petrotrin Boodoosingh Tassa Group, as currently staffed by younger family members, has been one of the top ensembles of recent decades. Due to personal differences, Boodoosingh's eldest son, Lenny Kumar—also a top drummer—formed his own band, the Trinidad & Tobago Sweet Tassa Group, which is one of the foremost ensembles in the country. (Despite tassa's thunderous volume, the standard term of praise for good tassa drumming is that it is "sweet.") Most of the prominent groups have formed within the last generation or two. Thus, for example, the Malick Tassa Drummers group was founded in 1956, by Soogrim Ramkissoon, and the Hummingbird Tassa Group was established in 1954.

As with several other Indo-Caribbean music genres, there is no reason to believe that any contact with drummers in India occurred after the last ship arrived in 1917. Hence the Caribbean tassa traditions flourished entirely on their own, in isolation from their South Asian progenitor. Tassa drumming thus persisted and evolved alongside other percussion traditions employing dholak, nagāra, and khañjri. The earliest extant recordings were those made in 1956 by Emory Cook, followed by others made by Alan Lomax in 1962. Playing in these recordings, insofar as subgenres can be correlated, is essentially cognate with present-day drumming, suggesting that most of the basic styles and hands were effectively in place by that period. Later in this chapter some speculative comments will be made about particular aspects of the evolution of drum styles and hands.

In British Guiana a tradition of tassa drumming existed until the 1960s or 1970s, but it does not seem to have ever been cultivated in such an elaborate way as in Trinidad. A few players of the younger generation have taken up the art, but for the most part they play the simple Trinidadian rhythms like dingolay and nagāra. (Meanwhile, in secondary diaspora sites like New York City, several Guyanese youths play tassa, and tassa bands may be hired for Guyanese as well as Trinidadian weddings.) As discussed below, Muharram commemorations disappeared, for various reasons, in that colony in the late 1800s, after which the

tradition of tassa drumming never spread. In south Trinidad, the once-massive Hosay celebrations were violently repressed by the British in 1884 but were allowed to continue, on smaller scales, in St. James (a neighborhood of Port of Spain), in certain communities in the suburban corridor east of that city, and in the southwestern coast town of Cedros. It is conceivable that the nuclei of drummers associated with these centers played crucial roles in teaching and inspiring the players whose ranks came to proliferate in the twentieth century. This essential role of Hosay drummers is also suggested by the somewhat dis-proportionately high number of Muslim drummers in Trinidad.

In neighboring Suriname, neither tassa drumming nor Muharram appears to have taken strong root at any point. Informants[11] relate that in both Suri-name and British Guiana, handfuls of tassa drummers have always existed, but neither were they numerous nor their drum traditions distinctive; in recent decades, more ensembles have sprung up in both countries, but their playing is essentially imitative of Trinidadians.

The eclecticism of tassa drumming is reflected in the associated drum no-menclature, which derives from a mixture of sources, exhibiting both North Indian archaisms and evident borrowings from Afro-creole and even locally encountered West African roots. The words tassa, jhāl, jhānjh, chōb, and ḍhol come from Hindi; "bass" is English, and "cutter" and "fuller/foulay" appear to derive from various converging sources. An English origin of the latter term is suggested by drummers' observations that the supporting tassa "fills out" the sound, making it "fuller." Such a usage, indeed, could be seen as a calque, that is, a translation of Hindi terms describing supporting drum pair in a nagāra ensemble, which my Banaras informants called the "*bharne-wālā*" or "filling-out" instrument. However, drummers generally pronounce and sometimes write the term as "foulay" (foolay, fulé), which strongly suggests a distinct—and especially West African—etymology. "Fulé" is the name of a medium-range instrument in the Afro-Trinidadian tamboo-bamboo ensembles that became popular processional percussion groups after the British banned neo-African camboulay drumming in 1881. Winer, in her erudite dictionary of Trinidadian creole (2009, 359), notes that the term has various relevant meanings in West African languages, including "flute" (in Manding), hammer (in Kikongo), and "two/second" (in Bamana—such as might conceivably denote the "second" drum in a group). For its part, the cutter, as tassa drummers note, does indeed "cut" through the ensemble sound, but that term might also derive from West African sources. As Winer (2009, 278) observes, in Fon "*katá*" designates a type of drum, while in Kikongo it means "to hit forcefully." Katá also designates drums used in the Haitian vodou ensemble, in the Trinidadian Orisha drum set, and in the tambrin frame-drum ensemble of Tobago.[12] A 1790 chronicler

in Jamaica referred to "a cotter, upon which they beat with sticks" (in Abrahams and Szwed 1983, 289; see also Gerstin 2004, 23), and the term "cutting" is still applied to drumming in that island's Kumina religion. The use of the terms "cutter" and "fulé/fuller" by tassa drummers is doubtlessly a case of convergent etymologies, involving the adoption of terms that come from different languages but have compatible meanings.

Tassa in Contemporary Trinidad

Since the mid-1900s the island of Trinidad has come to host an extraordinary amount of music-making, animated by relative affluence, political stability, and a proud self-awareness of the island's renown as "the land of calypso and steelband." Most of this "musicking" is on the amateur or semiprofessional level. In creole (Afro-Trinidadian) society, most conspicuous are the abundant steelbands, numbering more than one hundred, whether organized by neighborhoods, schools, or semiprofessional institutions. Also proliferating in recent decades are "rhythm bands," in which amateur enthusiasts guided by a teacher play wholly invented genres of "African music" on assortments of djembes and other percussion instruments (sometimes in conjunction with "African dance," which is equally unrelated to any specific tradition).

The amount of music-making in Indo-Trinidadian society is no less impressive, and it might to some extent, on some level, be invigorated by a sense of competition, however seldom articulated, with creoles. Certainly music, more than any other activity, has come to be the most prominent marker of national identity and of ethnic identity. Increasing numbers of Indo-Trinidadians have joined steelbands, but the more conspicuous Indian musical activities would comprise the chowtal groups, the bhajans sung collectively in temples, the filmsongs crooned in the vast Mastana Bahar competition network, and the miscellaneous Bollywood hits sung solo, with harmonium, dholak, and dantāl accompaniment, at domestic or temple satsangs and even weddings, giving these events the nature of amateur talent shows.

Last but not least, there are the tassa bands. Some of these might be purely amateur groups, but most seek and obtain at least occasional paying gigs at weddings and other events. It might be impossible to enumerate the groups on the island, but their number would certainly exceed the eighty-eight named on the website www.tntisland.com (dated 2009). To this tally should be added the numerous groups active among Trinidadian—and now Guyanese—communities in North America and the U.K., especially New York, Miami, and Toronto. A competition in 2010 in New York City featured eighteen local groups, several being as skilled and professional as the best ensembles in Trinidad.

Many tassa drummers come from informal hereditary lineages, learning the art from playing in family bands and being guided by a father or uncle. Most groups, however, emerge as conglomerations of friends who cultivate an interest, purchase drums, and learn to play by one means or another. Generally, the group includes a knowledgeable cutter man who can lead the others in playing the basic "breakaway" hands like dingolay and nagāra, and also a few obligatory more complex hands like tikora and wedding hand. Once a group has reached this basic level, it can give itself a name, a business card, and matching t-shirts, and make itself available for weddings and other occasions. Veteran players lament that too many groups fail to progress beyond this elementary stage. In order to do so, a knowledgeable player—usually the cutter man—generally needs guidance, whether formal or informal, from a more experienced player. Some drummers take lessons from professionals like Lenny Kumar, but most learn more through imitation, osmosis, and informal guidance. Band members also study extant CDs of drumming, though these seldom number more than half a dozen and as pedagogical tools are far from ideal, with their sometimes idiosyncratic and even incorrectly labeled items. YouTube postings of groups offer another source of models. Those few drummers who do give formal instruction often complain about the inadequate training their students seem satisfied with. Lenny Kumar told me, "I will teach a class, people will take ten classes, they may only know five beats, but then they start a band and play, and the standard goes on dropping."

The better bands acquire local renown through being heard regularly and through placing presentably in competitions. Several of the professional bands, like the larger steelbands, obtain some sort of corporate sponsorship, enabling them, among other things, to pay for dancers and stage effects at competitions. In return, the bands include their sponsors in their names, as in the case of the Petrotrin Boodoosingh Tassa Group, the Monas Industrial Premsingh Tassa Group, the RBTT (Royal Bank of T&T) Dragon Boys Tassa Group, the Caribel [Wireless] Fun Lovers, the Naipaul Extra Foods Power Star Tassa Drummers, and the Point Lisas Steel Products Rhythm Crew Tassa Group.

Both the status of tassa drummers and their remunerations have appreciated dramatically over the last half-century. Unlike some percussionist castes in India, tassa drummers do not seem ever to have been stigmatized as pariahs, but in previous generations they enjoyed no particular respect and, if anything, might be seen as amateurish noisemakers excessively fond of the bottle. Drummers today, by contrast, are respected and appreciated, and playing in a band might well enhance a young man's image as "sexy." Groups are paid accordingly. Raiaz Ali (b. 1962) notes: "It's only since my youth that the tassa drum

has become economically feasible. My father and grandparents, they used to play for a drink, or some food, or to have a good time, whatever, and it was more family-oriented and friendly, you know, like 'Let's play some tassa for the guys.' Now it has become a business. Like I'm playing at Zen nightclub tonight—it's just a job. You can raise a family with it, I know people who live off it." Nevertheless, for all but a very few tassa players, drumming is only a secondary source of income. Vishnu Ramnarine, leader of the St. John's United Tassa Players, explains:

> You really have to love tassa to be in tassa; when we play at a wedding sometimes we get around $1,000 [ca. US$170], when you have to divide that four ways and pay transport for your instruments sometimes you end up with just $100 [US$17] for the day. The National Title has given us immense popularity, and we are now in demand to play at weddings, government functions, and we have played in Barbados for the 2005 Crop Over, but it can cost a Tassa side between $5,000-$10,000 [US$850–1700] a year to maintain equipment, and sometimes the money you make is barely even enough to maintain our operating costs. (http://tassa.biz/)

The increased status and popularity of tassa are reflected in the histories of many groups. As we have seen, while a few family lineages, such as that of the Ghulam Hussein yard, clearly date back to the indentureship period, most of the respected groups formed far more recently.

Tassa is appreciated on various levels. At appropriate points during wedding festivities, tassa drumming provokes energetic dancing, and enthusiasts, whether young or old, certainly do not regard it as old-fashioned or folksy. For their part, audiences at competitions—many of whom might be friends of performers—can be loudly appreciative and partisan. Comments on YouTube tassa clips often articulate such enthusiasm, as in the following:

> i LOVE you guys, continuing our legacy, and in some cases
> even doin it better
> buss up shut, doubles [Trini foods], tassa, pepperz pot, fine gyalz winin
> west indies where it's at

Meanwhile, among a core of aficionados—most of whom are drummers themselves—there exists a definite sense of connoisseurship (which may have no counterpart among tassa and nagāra players in Bhojpuri-region North India). The spirit of this taste culture is also well conveyed in YouTube comments. These may often be appreciative, such as the remark of "taal290," who particularly enjoyed a prominent group's artful transition from one hand (rhythm) to another:

taal290
baddest ting was at 50 seconds when they switched from tikora to wedding
hand, dat ripped a hole in the space-time continuum

The standard layman's praise, however, is that the drumming makes one want
to dance, as in these comments on a clip by the Hummingbird Tassa Group:

tesha1310
thumbs up if u luv listenin 2 dis tassa tune. .:) nd wanna make yuh dance
nd wine. .:)
2706winston
god damn this is bad, dancing with coronas in my hands
DJChaos Bradley Rutendra Ganouri
meh feel strong again damn cyah stop wine meh backside woi
Annie Dennison
Phew! Need OXYGEN after dancing to this!!!
tas1790
this music hav my hips an waist moving from one end of trinidad to the next!!!

Just as often, YouTube comments on tassa clips, as on so many other subjects,
take the form of "flame wars" in which anonymous partisans hurl colorful invec-
tive at each other, as in these comments on a posting of the "Trinlando" band:

realriddim08
"Trinlando" LOL
What a dotish [doltish] name.[13]
shivamoonian
dotish name yuh say, the ppl who does pay we mega bucks all d time doh
tink so. so leh meh see . . . mak+ wit yuh kindergarten education . . . FUCK
DAT!!! SHOW ME THE MONEY!!! TrinLando Tassa
rajsoogrim1975
yo shiva, you got a bunch of haters who don't know anything about tassa
. . . all they could do is try to play in nagāra and dingolay and that is it. . . .

The latter post articulated a common complaint about the many amateurish
groups who have failed to progress beyond crude renditions of the most familiar
breakaway hands. Such bands may indeed manage to inspire lively dancing,
but if shown on YouTube, critics will be quick to disparage them, as in one
comment, "this group has no clue what the hell they're doing. . . . . its a shame
people actually paid money for this performance."

In other less vitriolic posts, drummers seek advice and exchange thoughts
on equipment, instruction, and competitions. As with so many other taste cultures, the internet, and especially YouTube, have provided forums for a virtual

community of drummers and enthusiasts, whether residing in Trinidad, New York, Guyana, or elsewhere.

Instrument Construction and the Social Consequences of Modernization

Although the tassa ensemble as a concept and tradition was imported from India, the drums themselves, like dholaks, nagāras, and dantāls, soon came to be made by local artisans rather than being imported from India (as is still the case with harmoniums). Most of these artisans have been performers themselves, making drums and/or components for themselves, friends, or, in some cases, for public sale, using local materials, informally acquired skills, and labor-intensive techniques. In recent decades synthetic, store-bought products—especially plastic tassa heads—have come to replace traditional organic materials, entailing significant changes not only in musical sound but also in the social aspects of drum manufacture and maintenance.

Martin's 1836 description of the Indian tassa—"a drum made of potter's ware"—indicates that its body was of clay (1838, 601), but modern Indian tassa bowls are invariably of light metal. Similarly, according to informants such as Raiaz Ali, the early Caribbean tassa drum body was a shallow copper or tin pan, called a "taireen,"[14] resembling and perhaps even fashioned from a cooking pan or pot. Such flat shells are still the norm in North Indian tassa, affording a sound that, although reasonably loud, is not particularly resonant. At some point—probably the mid-twentieth century—it became more standard in Trinidad to use clay "*ḍabbu*" pots, of a considerably deeper shape.[15] The clay dabboos provide a more full, resonant, and "sweet" sound, but they are heavy and somewhat fragile. In the late 1990s they came to be replaced by steel pots, of a similarly deep, rounded shape. The metal bowls are equally resonant, and they are also lighter, louder, and indestructible. The bass drum has always been wooden, typically mango or cedar.

The tassa is played with a pair of flexible sticks called "chōb"; formerly made of cane, pessy vine, or mamoo liana (Mahabir 1984, 4), these are generally of plastic nowadays. The chōbs are held with the top end protruding between the thumb and forefinger, and the lower end emerging between the third finger and ring finger; this grip is in contrast to that which I have generally encountered in India, where the lower end emerges below the little finger. For his part, the bass player holds in one hand a heavy stick (*danka, dhanka*[16]) with a ball of tape (cloth tape, covered by electrical tape) on its tip, and strikes the other, higher-pitched drumhead with his bare hand. The brass cymbals are

larger than the jhāls used by chowtal and Ramayan singers, and according to some, should properly be called jhānjh (or "jhainch," from Persian *sānj*), but the term "jhāl" has nevertheless become standard. They are locally fashioned or can be purchased in India goods stores.

The drums are manufactured at the artisanal rather than industrial level. Most of the makers of the various components are themselves drummers. Over the past two generations, the most prominent "throwers" of clay shells have been the Chase Village drummer Gurcharan and his father, who hail from the *kumhar* traditional potter caste. The metal shells that came into vogue in the 1990s can be made without too much difficulty from a sawed-off propane or air-conditioning canister, or even a buoy. In *Tassa Thunder*,[17] master drummer Lenny Kumar demonstrates how he makes the drum bodies, sawing off the butt of the A-C canister with a hacksaw, shaping and cutting the metal strips to which the head will be attached, and then welding them on. Some drummers inscribe the names of their bands on the tassa heads.

Manufacture of the bass drum, like that of the tassa, involves no more than machine-shop technology, though it does demand skill and a considerable amount of labor. The shell is made from a thick log, which is hollowed out, first by a buzz saw and then, painstakingly, by a hand chisel. Most of the makers of drum shells have access, in one way or another, to the necessary tools. Thus, Lenny Kumar acquired his skills and tools in his former work as a machinist. Master cutter-man Sunil Mathura, shown making a bass drum in *Tassa Thunder*, used the construction and hauling equipment belonging to the family of his bandmates, the Ragoo brothers, to cut the mango log, transport it to their compound, and saw out the core.[18]

The goatskins formerly used for tassa heads and still used for bass drums (and dholaks) can be obtained from an abattoir or an individual agriculturalist (or latter-day goatherd) who markets them to drummers; depending on one's source, they can cost as much as US$25. The skins need to be dried and scraped free of hair, perhaps using an empty bottle. Various techniques can be used for attaching them to the shell of the tassa. Normally they are tied, using synthetic or hemp rope, or, formerly, deerskin. Different patterns of tying may be used, including a crisscross pattern stated by some informants to be borrowed from Shango drums (although it is certainly encountered in India). Alternately, they may be attached to metal lugs such as those affixed to the steel canister by Lenny Kumar. In *Tassa Thunder*, Sunil Mathura is shown attaching the goatskin to a bass drum. After moistening it, he cuts it to the appropriate size, perforates it with holes around its edges, and attaches it to the drum with the aid of a cane or PVC strip made into a hoop (or "lock") and by weaving the waxed and stiffened end of a rope through the holes and around the shell. Once

Figure 7. Two styles of affixing drum heads. Photograph by the author.

dried overnight, the skin is lifted off so that a "masala" paste (whose recipe may be a trade secret) is applied to the inside to improve the sound. Deerskin has sometimes been used for bass drum heads, but players find it to be stiff, heavy, and taxing to the bare hand that strikes it. Those unable to manufacture bass drums can buy them from makers for around US$600. A finished bass drum weighs thirty-five to forty pounds and can take a toll on the back and shoulders of its player. Mukesh Ragoo explained to me that he moves around animatedly while playing, partially in order to distribute the burden on his back.[19]

While simple strap systems suffice to tighten skin heads on bass drums (and dholaks), a higher tension is required for goatskin tassa heads, which must be heated over a fire in order to dry and tighten. After being played for an hour or so, the skin loosens and must be heated again. In an outdoor event such as a wedding or Hosay procession, drummers or their teammates would gather combustible trash and build a curbside "campfire" over which the tassa player would hold his drum to "stand it up," tapping it all the while to monitor the tension. In such outdoor events, this practice would constitute a manageable

nuisance, but in a site like a nightclub, it would be an outright impossibility. Further, the skin heads can simply break after several days of playing, from the drumming and the stress of being continually reheated. As Raiaz Ali told me, "After a few days and nights of playing at Hosay, where they takin' heat, and they are pull tight, expanding, then you release it and play, and it dries and crips [gets crisp]—there's no way that skin won't burst." Hence the switch to synthetic plastic drum heads, easily imported from American suppliers, was a natural development. Once adopted by Vijay Mallick and Krishna Soogrim-Ram of the Mallick Tassa Drummers around 1996, the plastic heads and metal bodies soon became standard throughout the island. The synthetic heads are strong, relatively inexpensive, easy to apply, and even louder than the already deafening skin heads; their timbre is also somewhat harsher. Sunil Mathura told me, "If it burst, you just unbolt it and put the next one on; but I seen cases where the plastic send people to the hospital from a wedding with a headache, it so loud." Moreover, drummers observe that Trinidadian goats are nowadays raised on feed rather than living free-range, such that their skins are thin, fatty, and weak; although satisfactory for dhols and dholaks (and for the goats themselves to inhabit), they are unable to withstand the sharp hammering of the chōbs and break far too readily.[20] Hence, goatskin heads are seldom encountered, although a few drummers, such as Ryan Ali Boodoosingh, may use one on special occasions, perhaps heating it with a hair dryer. Accompanying the trend toward synthetic materials is the replacement of cane or mamoo liana drumsticks and the bamboo "lock" by plastic PVC.

The transition to synthetic heads, despite its clearly beneficial aspects, has had various sociomusical ramifications which have been less unambiguously positive. These were stressed to me in particular by Raiaz Ali, a leader of the respected Ghulam Hussein yard of Hosay drummers in St. James. For Raiaz, the adoption of synthetic heads put an end to an entire set of interpersonal relationships that had been centered around tassa manufacture and maintenance. These relations involved both his father and elder male relatives, and the broader group of yard members, who would fill the family compound in St. James much of the year with their activity and their camaraderie. When I first visited Raiaz in 2009, the yard (an extended patio and courtyard) was deserted, and Raiaz was openly despondent about the technological change that had led to its emptiness.

> When you had tassa makin' from the goatskins, you had a lot of guys here, who growed up with that part of it, shavin' the skin, stretchin' the skin, checkin' to see how this one will sound, "this skin lookin' good," "better pull that one . . ." This whole department [the drum making and maintenance sec-

tion, aside from the tazia section]—it used to be very active, it was as big as the section that was building the tazia. It had people working on it every day. You had a companionship within the camp, everybody laughin,' but when the plastic came, the whole section died, became null and void. It's become a museum. You lost that whole bunch of fellas; they've strayed, resigned, dropped out, because they came to feel left out, there was nothing to do.

Raiaz was particularly nostalgic about the way the drum preparation had involved familial ties.

I grew up doin' all that with my dad and uncles, and it was fun. We used to wake early Sunday morning, go to the different abattoirs, to the countryside, purchase the goatskins, come home, stretch them in the yard, put them in the sun. When I was a boy my work was to make sure that they dry good, then take it off the board in the afternoon, or the day after. I had to get up in the morning, take them off the board, turn them around, and you would have inspectors. Even the bamboo for the hoop—I grew up knowing bamboo. My grandfather used to go cut it and bring it here for us to strip. And during Hosay it was a whole different concept, you would abstain from certain things, it was family-oriented.

Aside from strengthening family and social relationships, he noted, the preparation and maintenance of the goatskin head, precisely because of being so laborious, generated a certain affective bond with the drum. This bond was further intensified by the fragility of the goatskin head and clay body and the according care with which the drum had to be treated.

The plastic head, you can leave it on for about three years. But the skin one, the breeze blow on it and pow!—it burst. But you'd get a traditional feelin' with the skin, and with this [gesturing contemptuously at a nearby plastic drum head], you don't get anything, you don't be satisfied playing it. You could express yourself with a goatskin, but not with this, you could play to the meanin's with the goatskin, but not with this. It's entirely different. So nowadays I play "bam bam," and then I say, "OK Joe, take a hand," [play some] whatever, and I give him the drum. But with your goatskin and clay drum, you have to be careful who you givin' it to, because it can crack like an egg. And if you tālkin' to someone with the drum hangin' by your side, and a nex' fella walkin' by you, you have to move the drum so he don't bump it and break it. And you cannot rest it face down, because the head will get scratched and that's the end of it, crack! Because it's heated. And if someone's drinkin' water, and the water spills on the hot drum, crack! Or the drum will get cold, and you have to run back and heat it. That used to keep you involved in the playin' of the drum. The drum was like your baby, you have to be careful with it. Caring for the drum, it was like the way you

take care of yourself. But all these things gone, and we had a lot of fun, it was nice when it lasted.

Raiaz further opined that the loss of social engagement with the drumming community and with the drum itself has also undermined the quality of drumming today, such that young players fail to develop the discipline, dedication, and knowledge that older drummers did.

> Young people are not willing to learn the artistry, because it has developed into an easier art, with the plastics. In my day I had to take my drum and pull it, and my grandfather would give me a pair of sticks and tell me how to heat it, and I have to develop my song, my instincts, my abilities, as I am listening.

Skin heads, as mentioned, are still used for the bass drum, but these require less maintenance, since they need not be heated to obtain proper tension, and further, they typically last three or four years. However, in my own experience, I had the good fortune to get some sense of the social aspect of drum preparation when I spent the aforementioned evening with Sunil Mathura and the Ragoo family while he affixed the head on a bass. The process took several hours and effectively constituted a "lime" (convivial hanging-out), during which the many-talented Mathura also cooked a fine curry goat over an open fire and the rest of us assisted, chatted, drank beer, and, in my case, shot video footage.

The undermining of the artisanal tassa yard community through the advent of plastic heads and metal shells, far from being an isolated phenomenon, is a quintessential example of how modernity, in the form of industrial technology, can destroy community ties. Marx and Engels wrote eloquently of this process in their *Communist Manifesto* of 1848, and the vaporization of the Ghulam Hussein social network epitomizes the way "all that is solid melts into thin air" under the inexorable force of modernity. Tassa drummers today have their own social networks, marked by both camaraderie and rivalry, and it could be argued that the advent of synthetic materials has enabled more enthusiasts to take up the art. Nevertheless, there is no doubt that an entire dimension of interpersonal interaction has disappeared as imported industrial products have replaced local artisanal ones.

Performance Contexts: Hindu Weddings

Tassa drumming has become a common feature of the Trinidadian soundscape. On any given weekend, whether day or evening, whether in towns or in the Indian-dominated rural areas, it is not uncommon to hear the sound of tassa drumming wafting from some festivity, like distant thunder. Tassa groups are also

increasingly booked for events that are not specifically Indian in orientation, and creoles may be just as likely as Indians to "jump up and wine" to the drumming.

The most common context for tassa drumming is the Hindu wedding. A proper Hindu Trini wedding stretches over a full weekend, commencing with a party at the groom's house on Friday night. (The typical Trinidadian house is raised on pillars, with the ground floor being an essentially empty open space that can be devoted to storage or, as the case may be, fêtes.) A tassa group is generally booked for the weekend, or more specifically, for Friday night and Sunday. The Friday party might typically feature a deejay who plays current hits (soca, chutney-soca, and the like) and a tassa group that plays during interludes. The central ritual event, however, is the maticore (maṭkor), in which the womenfolk perform a set of rituals; after anointing the tassa drums with various items, they walk to a field or someplace where water is available, dig a bit of earth (the maticore proper), and then sing and dance in a ribald fashion to the accompaniment of the tassa drummers, who stand at a discreet distance. The event being merry rather than ceremonial, the drummers play dance rhythms like dingolay and nagāra, provoking animated wining by young and old. However, trained drummers aver that properly, at least five "fine" or "classical" hands should be played before moving on to breakaway dance hands; these more serious hands could typically include tikora, Hosay tikora, nadidin, tillāna, thumri, chaubola, and khemta. Further rituals are performed upon returning to the house. On Saturday night, or "cooking night," a fête is held at the bride's home, often with a dance band or—if the parents are of more traditional tastes—a local-classical ensemble of singer with harmonium, dholak, and dantāl. Typically this group performs thumris, tillānas, and the like until youngsters start clamoring for chutney, at which point the group acquiesces and wild dancing ensues until the wee hours (see Manuel 2000a). Meanwhile, some auntie ceremonially cooks puffed rice (lāwā).[21]

Sunday is the occasion for the wedding proper, which occurs either at the bride's home, a rented space at a temple, or elsewhere. Folding chairs, a ritual fireplace, and a canopy for the bride and groom have been set up. Womenfolk are busy preparing an afternoon repast for the guests, who may easily number a hundred, and who may include friends, family, miscellaneous neighbors, and perhaps the odd unknown ethnomusicologist accompanying the musicians. Another panoply of rituals is conducted, at both the bride's and groom's homes. The tassa group is present from around 10:00 A.M., usually sitting and chatting outside until they are called to perform. Sometime around noon, the groom's party, or barāt, arrives with as much fanfare as is possible. While in India the ideal traditional vehicle for the groom is an elephant, in Trinidad the

barāt generally consists of a car caravan, often with the groom in a stretch limo; sometimes another car fitted with external speakers is blaring music.

Ideally, the barāt also includes a tassa group. If such is the case, the car caravan might stop a hundred yards or so from the wedding venue, and the entourage would proceed thence on foot for the *agwānī*, or meeting of the two families. At this point, the two groups, with the pandit among the bride's family, walk toward each other, and upon meeting, the bride's father gives the groom's father a tray with some items. During this process, the tassa group is playing, or if there are two, they approach each other, playing. As the drummers meet, a friendly group duet ensues, which is called a "jassal" (jassle). The etymology of this term is uncertain. Although it is presumably from "jostle," one informant opined that it may derive from "joust." (The word is occasionally written "jhassal," with the "h" serving as the customary icon of Indianness.) In this preliminary jassle, the two ensembles usually join in playing wedding hand, an important rhythm whose distinctive structure is described below. The two lead drummers, or cutter-men, from the respective groups might take turns "cutting," or soloing, during this session, which might last twenty minutes or so.[22]

In other cases, depending on locale and other factors, the barāt, with its stretch limo, stops in front of the wedding venue and waits until the appropriate time for the groom to exit. As other guests are filing in, the tassa band plays a suite, typically segueing from tikora and wedding hand to other "fine hands" like thumri, khemta, and tillāna, that are not necessarily used for dancing. Once the guests and the groom's party have entered and seated themselves, the drumming stops, and the wedding proper commences. This event takes several hours, and it will not be described in detail here. The pandit performs various rituals and may give an extended peroration into the microphone. An invited troupe, also with amplification, may sing traditional wedding songs at various occasions. Eventually the bride appears from inside the house, at which point the drummers might be asked to play briefly. Generally, however, the drummers retire to the street curb and "lime," that is, hang out and chat, often for several hours, perhaps snacking and drinking beer or rum. At some point in the early afternoon, while less important parts of the ritual are taking place, guests and the drummers may proceed to where food is being served, whether on paper plates or banana leaves. The atmosphere is informal and friendly. For the drummers, most of the time at a given gig is spent liming, though they would be ill advised to drift away, since they might be called to play at any interlude. Traditionally, specific tassa hands would be considered appropriate for specific ritual points in the protracted wedding process; several tassa players are aware of these conventions, and may even follow them, but they are largely forgotten nowadays.

Figure 8. Jason Nandoo, tassa, with accompanists and dancers at a wedding in Queens, New York. Photograph by the author.

Eventually the wedding proper concludes, the couple is pronounced man and wife, and the drummers are again requested to play. If only one group is present, they typically play festive rhythms, again provoking merry dancing. If two groups are attending, a second, more distinctive sort of jassle may later ensue, perhaps across the street from the wedding venue. Traditionally, in this jassle the groups would trade off playing some of the more esoteric classical hands. Amidh Mohammad describes this style of duel, "In a jassle I used to like to play fine hands against the other group; I play one, you play one, you play one for me, if you can't play what I play, then I'm the winner, then we hug each other and go and drink." Often, however, the jassle may involve the two groups crowding together, each playing a different rhythm, in a different pulse, and attempting to overpower the other group by sheer volume and stamina. The intensity and zest of their playing are enhanced by the liberal amounts of liquor that they may have consumed while liming.

This sort of jassle is a unique sort of musical event. In its thunderous volume and its jumble of asynchronous rhythms, it lends new meaning to the word "ca-

cophony." For the tassa enthusiast, it is not an occasion to savor sophisticated playing, for unless one stands right in the thick of one ensemble, one can barely distinguish one group's rhythm from the racket generated by the other. Nor is the jumbled roar particularly well suited for accompanying dance. Rather, the jassle is typically most enjoyed by the players themselves and the handfuls of enthusiasts standing around drinking rum. As time passes, the duel format may break up and the session can turn into an informal jam. Some drummers may retire, and others materialize, perhaps from a wedding nearby. Various amateurs, from an aspiring youth to the pandit himself, might commandeer a tassa or a bass and join in.[23] Eventually the hired drummers collect their pay and drift off, and peace is restored.

This ruckus, however, may not be the end of the festivity. Indians, though renowned as thrifty and industrious, also "love to fête" as much as do creoles, and hence it has become common for the bride's family to host yet another party, called a "second Sunday," the following weekend, as if to burn off residual steam. This event typically features a hired deejay and a tassa group, and allows for further dancing, drinking, eating, and merrymaking.

One prominent drummer described to me a typical Sunday wedding format:

Sometimes we're playing weddings every Sunday for three or four months straight. For a wedding we might charge about $3000TT (ca. US$500). More, depending on the distance, and if we have to provide our own transport. And we gotta bring an extra drum, because sometime the plastic head might burst. We might bring some food and cook it. A temple wedding can be boring. Maybe we go down the road, relax, lime, take a little drink, and then they call us again. Or we lie down and sleep, then they call us, "Wedding done, time to play drum."

Although Muslim weddings are generally more serious and sober than Hindu weddings, tassa groups are occasionally called to enliven both Muslim and Christian weddings.

The dancing to tassa merits some comment. In India, outside of the Westernized bourgeoisie, occasions for social dancing per se are limited, and men and women would seldom dance together. Indo-Caribbeans, no doubt influenced by creole culture, have largely shed such inhibitions: they dance often, with much relish, and in many cases, with marvelous grace. Enthusiasts dance to tassa drumming in the same manner as they would to chutney. As music, compared to chutney-soca, tassa drumming certainly has a more traditional character, but it nevertheless generates at least as much excitement and can bring to their feet several people who may have been sitting bored during the deejay's session. When creoles dance to tassa, as they often have occasion to

do, they typically emphasize wining and do not attempt the "Oriental" hand gestures. Occasionally, stage shows might feature some sort of "tassa dancing," by which is generally meant something more akin to the Ahīrva nāch or nautanki-style Harichand dance traditionally accompanied by nagāra.

Competitions

In Trinidad, formal stage competitions have become familiar parts of music culture, enlivening a wide variety of genres, including not only the celebrated calypso and steelband forms, but also soca, chutney-soca, parang, local-classical music, and tassa. Competitions also structure many forms of nonmusical cultural activity, including various sorts of costumes associated with Carnival. On the Indian side of culture, competitions have been organized for all manner of activities, from dance and music to the preparation of foodstuffs like roti and "doubles."

Indo-Trinidadian music competitions draw from both local creole and subcontinental Indian inspiration. Well before the modern era, musical duels in India had become features both of regional genres like Marathi lāvni as well as classical singing, with the legendary joust between Tan Sen and Baiju Bawra becoming part of musical folklore. In the early twentieth century—perhaps somewhat after the end of indentureship in 1917—formal duels (called *muqābila* or *dangal*) became standard features of regional "professional folk" genres such as birhā, rasiya, and kajri. In the Caribbean, as mentioned in the previous chapter, soirées of birha and Surinamese qawwāli also often took the form of duels in which participants would attempt to outdo each other in displays of Hindu erudition or musical-poetic skill. All such competitions, however, were generally diadic affairs involving only two contending parties. The format of having several competitors, by contrast, seems to have been initiated in creole culture, and in particular in association with the calypso competitions in vogue from the 1920s. These contests themselves to some extent represented extensions of the diadic duels between opposing stick-fighting teams, each of which featured a chantwell who would lead his or her supporters in singing responsorial songs boasting of their team's prowess and lewdly insulting the others. Many early calypsonians were chantwells who effectively transferred their art from the street to the tent.

In the 1920s, formal competitions began to be staged for local-classical singing, and by the 1950s, competitions were being held in Trinidad for other genres as well, including, as mentioned before, *Mānas* singing and chowtal. Competitions for tassa appear to have started considerably later. Like calypso competitions, they commenced with small, privately sponsored forums and

gradually grew to become more national in stature, in some cases acquiring government subsidy. In general, however, state support has been reserved for the creole—though putatively "national"—art forms of calypso, steelband, and Carnival masquerade bands. Indian competitions, from Mastana Bahar to chowtal contests, have been overwhelmingly funded by private sponsors. Such sponsorship increased in the 1980s as Indians emerged as the most vigorous sector of the economy aside from the state-owned oil industry.

In 1984 Republic Bank established a well-funded annual competition, originally called "Tassarama" and subsequently, "Tassa Taal." In 2001 the Tassa Association of Trinidad and Tobago (TATT) established an annual "National Tassa Competition," which, together with Tassa Taal, has become a central event for tassa performers and fans. The TATT competition is partially subsidized by the government. Meanwhile, various smaller competitions are held on irregular bases in different parts of the island at different times of year. Prominent among these is the "Junior Tassa Rama" held by Mere Desh (Our Country), an organization founded and led by Ajeet Praimsingh, an indefatigable and creative promoter of local Indian culture.

The competitions tend to follow a fairly standard format, with some variation. Typically, each group is allotted eight or ten minutes, during which they must play a specified series of hands. At the 2009 National Tassa Competition, for example, the prescribed sequence was tikora, chaubola, nagāra, dingolay, and steelpan, which are in fact the most familiar and basic hands in the repertoire. In some cases, slightly more esoteric hands might be called for. Often, innovation is promoted by requesting groups to also play an original hand, of their own invention. (As with calypso, such an item must be fresh, rather than recycled from a previous year.) Occasionally, a "test piece" will be created and then made available on cassette or CD to contending groups, which must master it by rote. As with calypso and steelband contests, a semifinal competition is held, which might feature some twenty or thirty groups. Of these, ten or fifteen might be selected for the final round (which might require a different set of hands). The competitions are generally held in some open-air venue, such as an amphitheater or a field where a stage has been erected. As such, they are vulnerable to disruption by inclement weather. Although the drums themselves are loud, they are further amplified via massive speakers, which are also used by deejays or, occasionally, live bands that play during interludes. Attendance at the larger competitions is generally free; as at the steelband "Panorama" competition, audiences turn the event into a leisurely "lime," at which they drink, eat, socialize, and cheer for their favorite competitors.

Tassa groups are motivated to compete for a number of reasons. The top cash prizes in a forum like Tassa Taal are of course attractive in themselves. Perhaps

even more valuable is the prestige that accrues to winners, and the remunerative engagements that ensue. Many families who host weddings want to impress their guests by offering "nothing but the best," including a tassa group that can claim preeminence by having won a recent competition. Hence, for example, chatting with the Country Boys group at the 2009 TATT semifinals, I learned that they had cut short a European tour in order to return for the competition, in the hopes of winning and boosting their subsequent earnings. (They placed second, winning first prize the next year.) However, competing involves risks as well as rewards, as it can be profoundly humiliating for a respected group to place poorly. Meanwhile, many groups—and especially those who do not anticipate winning—participate primarily for the pleasure of performing on stage for an attentive and appreciative audience that has gathered to listen to drumming for its own sake, unlike the wedding context. Thus, one drummer told me that despite all the frustrations and problems involved in the competitions, he would continue to compete, just for the pleasure of showcasing his group on stage. Another, Laki Bhagan, commented, "The competitions are nice; family and friends come to support, and we all lime" (p.c.).

The competition is adjudicated by a panel of three to five judges. Selection of a panel that is at once knowledgeable and impartial is inherently difficult. Usually, at least one of the judges is himself a player and is thus able to bring an insider's knowledge to the evaluations. However, since players are products of the community of tassa drummers, they are often either biased by personal or family ties to certain groups, or at any rate they are liable to be accused of such favoritism.[24] At one recent youth competition, for example, the head judge—one of the island's top cutter-men—awarded first prize to the group led by his own son; this act generated such outrage that the organizer felt obliged to nullify and entirely revise the rankings, an action that itself precipitated further dismay and frustration for competitors. Partly to avoid such acts of apparent favoritism and also to attempt to lend a certain prestige to the panel, organizers may select judges, such as college music professors, who are outsiders to the tassa circuit and thus presumably more impartial. However, such individuals often have limited knowledge of tassa drumming and are unable to spot mistakes or niceties that experienced drummers themselves would recognize. An uninformed judge might be inclined to rank a group highly based on its stage antics and superficial appearance of "energy," while failing to notice, for example, that the band played only one of the three conventional tāls in nagāra hand, or that the jhāl player missed the entrance of a group tāl, or that the cutter-man was playing dingolay patterns in steelpan hand.

In an attempt to standardize judging, the organizers—again, in a manner probably originally modeled on calypso competitions—direct the judges to award

points according to fixed criteria, as specified on a scorecard. Thus, for example, the 2009 Tassa Taal competition awarded points on the following basis:

Dress: 15
Purity of hand: 25
Rhythm and harmony (cutting, and coordination): 30
Presentation and performance: 20
General conduct and behavior: 10
Total: 100

Parameters in other competitions might include "breaking of tāl and changing from one hand to the next," and "overall discipline." Awards are also typically given for distinct categories, as in the Tassa Taal's 2009 prizes, shown below:

Best group: 1st place, $15,000 TT (around US$2500)
2nd place, $10,000 TT (around US$1650)
3rd place, $7500
4th place, $5000
Best dressed: $1000
Best appearance: $1000
People's choice: $1000
(appearance fee: $400)

From the perspective of drummers and cognoscenti, primary among judging criteria should be an informed evaluation of the playing. First, a given hand should be played correctly, in terms of what should and should not be present. Thus, the cutter should not play patterns too strongly redolent of other hands, and conversely, the essential patterns of a given hand should all be performed. For example, dingolay and nagāra, though festive "breakaway" hands, both have a fair number of typical "cuts" (cutter patterns) and tāls (cadences); a group that fails to play these may be regarded by cognoscenti as deficient. Further, transitions between hands, although somewhat flexible in their form, must be smooth, the bass and jhāl players should be in synchrony, and the group must in general play with flair and finesse. Particularly important, of course, is the expertise of the cutter-man, who effectively solos throughout the set.

In recent years, it has become common for groups to present various sorts of theatrics on stage. At the most minimal level, these might involve wearing elaborate Indian-wedding-style costumes instead of street clothes or playing in a particularly showy manner, with much waving and twirling of sticks, playing cutter while on one's knees, and other antics. Many groups go considerably further in order to present a visual spectacle. Dry-ice smoke machines and fireworks are increasingly common, and several groups hire semiprofessional dance troupes to perform some sort of inventive choreography, typically combining

Bollywood and creole styles. Skits might be presented, such as reenactments of a maticore, or of a matrimonial circumambulation (*kānya-dān*) to accompany wedding hand.[25]

The competitions, whether despite or because of the participants' zeal, invariably generate prodigious cynicism, anger, and ill feeling, with the use of props and theatrics constituting one of the most controversial aspects. Critics feel that judges may naturally tend to favor those groups that present visual extravaganzas, as opposed to those who just stand there and play, foregrounding only their sheer musicality. Thus, for example, in one recent nationwide competition, the winning group (Malick Rhythm Boys) was also the only one to present theatrics, in the form of elaborate fireworks. However, not all groups can afford such spectacles, and relatively few groups are able or willing to hire a dance troupe (which might typically cost around US$1000); the bands that can do so are generally those with some sort of corporate or private sponsorship. When theatrics are presented, both audience attention and judging criteria shift from excellence of drumming to visual spectacle.[26] One acquaintance of mine, a group leader and an insightful commentator on the competition scene, voiced these reservations about a TATT competition on a Facebook posting: "Once again, this competition reeked with poor judging and the same old thing year after year. We had numerous meetings with the organisers for this event and a lot of the same things happened again. One is having a whole dance school on the same stage as the drummers, blocking them from view, and putting full attention to the gyrating dancers." Drummer Mukesh Ragoo has astutely argued in such meetings that the points awarded for stage theatrics should be relegated to a special category with a separate prize, distinct from the criteria for judging the purely musical merit of a group. Similarly, he and others have argued that the dancers should be on a separate stage, such that the drummers remain visible.[27]

Conversely, various arguments are offered in favor of the theatricalization of the shows. As a member of the Country Boys group pointed out to me, the sequence of one drum group after another, all playing the same hands, can become tedious for both audiences and judges, and a modicum of visual display can provide welcome entertainment. Organizers also emphasize that the event must be not just an erudite performance for drum connoisseurs, but a "show" for the public—especially if it is financed by ticket sales, as is the case with some of the smaller events. Further, combining dance or other theatrics with tassa drumming can certainly be regarded as a fresh art form in itself, with considerable potential for innovation, creativity, and richness. Satnarine Balkaransingh, who leads an innovative dance troupe and has also judged tassa competitions, emphasized to me that the collaborations between

his dancers and the St. John's United Tassa Group were edifying and enriching for both parties. Such considerations, however, are not incompatible with Ragoo's argument for relegating theatrics to a separate ranking category.

Balkaransingh has also argued for various other reforms: instituting a judging category specifically for transitions between hands; expecting drummers to know how to comport themselves to use microphones effectively; requiring that outfits be color coordinated or somehow matching—even a "rustic" look, if cultivated, should be done convincingly. Points should be awarded for a separate category of visually entertaining stick work, but judges should nevertheless be able to reward those groups who play with expressivity and "soul," rather than those who emphasize technical flash (including interminable cutter rolls). Balkaransingh also opines that some competitions should require drummers to play more varied and demanding hands, including those associated with Hosay processions. However, such a practice would be offensive to some Shia Muslims who feel that those hands should be reserved for commemoration of the deaths of their martyrs, not for entertainment of a beer-drinking, dancing crowd at a fête.

Tassa connoisseurs often argue for the inclusion of more "classical" hands in competitions, in order to promote learning of these rhythms and to weed out the amateurish bands whose repertoire scarcely extends beyond dingolay and nagāra. One virtuoso drummer told me,

> For the Monarch, they tell you come and play five hands, tikora, chaubola, weddin' drum, nagāra or dingolay, and the makeup hand. Now how you goin' to judge somebody on a makeup hand? We're all playin' something different, three different rhythms, if they all good, who is the winner? That is stupidness. You wanna see something, you hold a competition and invite island drummers to come, you tell them to play tikora, wedding hand, and nagāra, and the two compulsory hands you judge them from is tillana and rag bhajan [esoteric classical hands], and see how much of them gonna enter that competition. Dem is classical hands, they won't know it. But organizers of competitions have to give the crowd what it wants, and they don't want to hear classical. Nagāra, steel pan, dingolay, mash up [mess up] a hand, and they're done.

Detractors of the competitions also voiced to me various other criticisms involving general suspicions of bias of one sort or another. In order to prevent excessive dominance of one group, the TATT competition judiciously stipulates that any group who wins three years in a row cannot compete for five subsequent years. However, even such well-intentioned regulations cannot prevent abuses, or at least, accusations of impropriety. For example, the Malick Rhythm Boys—a group that is universally respected for its musicianship—won

TATT's first prize in 2005 and 2006. Had they won again in 2007, they would have been barred from subsequent years, but instead they placed second (to the Country Boys), while in fact winning a few other categories. In doing so they actually garnered more award money than the Country Boys, and were allowed to go on to compete—and win—in 2008. In 2009 they earned second prize despite playing an incorrect hand in the stipulated sequence during the semifinals. Meanwhile, for the original piece that was required in 2008, they played an item called "Unity." In 2009, this same piece was again presented as an original composition by another band, who was awarded first prize by a panel of judges that included the actual creator of the piece. Whether or not such events reflect actual bias is of course unclear. However, the impression they give, as one drummer told me, is "smelly," and it is this sort of irregularity that breeds a pervasive cynicism and frustration, as well as a sense of rivalrous rancor among drummers whose relations would otherwise be entirely amicable.

Informants like Balkaransingh corroborate that the competition organizers appear to be well-meaning individuals who want their events to be respected and enjoyed (as well as profitable) and who are well aware of the criticisms, problems, and challenges involved, including the need to attract audiences with some kind of spectacle and the need to find judges who are both informed and impartial. Hence, as noted above, organizers of the larger competitions hold public meetings where drummers can voice their concerns and suggestions. I myself had occasion to reflect upon the difficulties involved when I was approached by an organizer of a New York competition and asked if I might be willing to serve on the judging panel. Presumably, my status as a university professor and as a supposed "outsider" to the tassa community would lend an air of prestige and impartiality to the process. Fortunately, I was out of town and unable to adjudicate, and the event itself impressed upon me the impossibility of my being able to do so in a satisfactory way. First, perhaps because my sensitivity to nuances and niceties is inadequate, I would have found it quite impossible to rank the five or seven better groups whose performances all seemed to me equally brilliant and flawless. Second, I could by no means have pretended to be "impartial," since several of the drummers, of different groups, are individuals whom I would like to count as friends (as well as informants), and I am well aware of the anger that the competitions inevitably generate. Indeed, at a New York competition the previous year, when the prizes were announced, a fight broke out, a drink was thrown in a protesting woman's face, the bouncers had to eject an irate contestant, and, in general, prodigious rancor was generated among certain drummers and their minions. (In other respects, however, the event was successful, as the venue—the Tobago Club—was packed, and the audience was wildly enthusiastic.) A competition held the

Figures 9 and 10. Drummers at Phagwa Parade in Queens, New York. Photographs by the author.

previous year had its own irregularities, with a member of the winning group telling me, "We won the trophy but never got the promised $700."

Mukesh Ragoo, leader of D'Evergreen Tassa Band, is one of the drummers who disparages the competitions in general for the suspicion and acrimony they generate. Instead, he argues, there should simply be tassa festivals, where groups play hands of their own choosing, and performers and enthusiasts gather to enjoy the art form without any destructive sense of rivalry or bitterness. Organizers, however, tend to insist that audiences prefer the competition format; for entrepreneurs who lack state or corporate subsidies and depend on ticket sales, such considerations are crucial.

Finally, mention must be made of the irregular participation of tassa bands in competitions not specifically devoted to that idiom. In Trinidad, competitions are held for virtually every category of music, from calypso to parang, and some competitions—especially the Best Village forum—incorporate all manner of categories and genres. Hence a tassa group might enter such a contest, in which the band would find itself competing against a belé dancer, a gospel choir, and a djembe-based "African" drum ensemble. Judging in such events would be based more on showmanship and impact rather than punctiliously correct execution of hands.

Hosay

Hosay is the Trinidadian term for Muharram, the first month in the Muslim lunar calendar, and, more important, the commemoration of the martyrdom of the Prophet Mohammad's grandsons Hussein and Hassan. Tassa drumming plays a prominent role in both Trinidadian and South Asian Muharram processions, and correspondingly, Hosay has constituted an important component of the Trinidadian tassa scene since the early decades of the indentureship period. Evidence suggests that Hosay drummers and their rhythms played seminal roles in the development of Trinidadian tassa playing in general.[28]

Although both Hosay and South Asian Muharram are occasionally referred to as festivals, Muslims note that they are properly regarded as sober commemorations of a tragic event, specifically, the battle at Karbala in 680 C.E., in which henchmen of the Umayyad caliph Yazid slew Imam Hussein, who was the son of Muhammad's daughter Fatima and her husband Ali, and a rival contender for the title of caliph, or spiritual and political leader of the faithful. As if in accordance with the Quranic celebration of righteous warfare, fighting over the title of caliph had commenced in the generation after the Prophet, with Ali himself being killed in 661. Hussein's subsequent slaying became a seminal event in the founding of Shia Islam, whose followers regard the Um-

mayad caliphs and their Sunni successors as usurpers, and who foreground the killing as a paradigmatic event. Shia Islam thus came to place special emphasis on the redemptive power of lamentation and mourning—especially of the martyrdom of Hussein. Shi'ism became especially well established in Persia/ Iran, and Shias came to constitute around 15 percent of Muslims in South Asia, and, by extension, in the Indo-Caribbean diaspora.

In Iran, by the tenth century Muharram had come to be the occasion for dramatic reactualizations of the Karbala battle, together with various forms of chanted lamentation. The dramatizations would provoke intense emotional responses, although reports of actors portraying the villains being killed by enraged audiences may be apocryphal. In the eighteenth century these traditions fused to become what is known as *ta'ziyeh*, which centers around public processions. Muharram commemorations also took root in North India, acquiring particular prominence and their essentially modern forms in Lucknow and its environs in the mid-nineteenth century. The primary Muharram events came to comprise public chanting of Urdu laments, especially in the monumental *imāmbāras* constructed by the nawabs, and massive outdoor processions. Both practices still take place in several North Indian sites, including such Bhojpuri-region cities as Banaras and Patna, whence many of the indentureds emigrated.

At various places in the streets of these cities, young men will flagellate themselves with metal whips, but the focal elements in the processions are imaginative models of tombs, called taziyas, of the martyrs. Artfully decorated with mirrors, multicolored tiles, Styrofoam trimmings, and minarets, these cenotaphs are fashioned with great care and nicety each year by community craftsmen and are carried through the streets by devout and sturdy men. They often tower thirty feet high, such that attendants with long poles must push up the tangle of power and telephone wires that would otherwise obstruct their passage. Accompanying the tazias are tassa drummers, who, as mentioned before, often consist of casual amateurs rather than trained professionals, or else professionals who mostly perform other drums, such as dholak or tabla, but play tassa every Muharram. While skilled drummers may stop in front of shops and play showy rolls to solicit tips, most play simple, somewhat lugubrious Muharram beats.[29] As discussed below, in Delhi and other cities the more knowledgeable ensembles will play asymmetrical rhythms whose dhol patterns articulate lexical phrases, such as the *kalma* (*"La ilaha illa Allah . . ."*).[30]

Although the Karbala battle has had special significance for Shias, the sectarian status of South Asian Muharram is far from simple and unproblematic, in accordance with the ambiguous status of Shi'ism within the larger Muslim community, and the sense in which the martyrdom was at once a tragedy and a generative event to be celebrated. Many Shias (as well as Sunnis) disapprove of

the self-mortification, which they see as morbid and, too often, an occasion for young men to show off. Some disparage the tassa drumming as being inappropriately festive; as Wolf notes, such criticisms are especially common in areas where tassa is commonly heard at weddings, reinforcing the drum's association with saturnalia. Some Shias may tolerate or appreciate the tassa music, while feeling that it is inappropriate for Shias themselves to play it; as a result, the drummers tend to be Sunnis and even Hindus (see Wolf 2000; Wolf 2014; and Korom 2003, chapters 2 and 3). Meanwhile, many Sunnis, Sufis, and Hindus may join in the processions and might even build tazias, diluting the event's specifically Shia character[31]; conversely, in cities such as Lucknow, Shias and Sunnis may seize the opportunity to attack each other. Further, although many Shias insist on the fundamentally lachrymose nature of the commemoration, Muharram may in some cases acquire a decidedly—and controversially—upbeat tenor. In Banaras, whose population is famously given to parades, fairs, and festivals, Muharram is the occasion not only for tazia processions and self-flagellation but also for a family-fun-oriented carnival (*mela*), with merry-go-rounds, Ferris wheels, and street vendors hawking snacks and souvenirs. Thus, depending on his preferences, a man may spend the day carousing with friends and family or whipping his back into a bloody pulp with a cat-o'-nine-tails.

Colonial accounts indicate that Muharram processions had become a lively feature of cultural life in Trinidad and British Guiana by the 1860s. As in India, craftsmen lovingly fashioned towering tazias, which were carried along roads (then felicitously free of overhanging wires), accompanied by crowds and tassa drummers. Since most Indians lived on rural plantations, the tazia processions took place on country roads, though they sometimes converged on towns, especially south Trinidad's San Fernando, through whose streets they would be paraded with much excitement and pride.

As in most of India, Shia Muslims played central roles in Muharram, but the status and ethnic character of the event were complex and contested, albeit with a somewhat different gamut of interest groups involved. In British Guiana, by the 1860s tazia processions were thriving, swollen by the avid participation of Shias, Sunnis, Hindus, and Afro-creoles. A British observer wrote of the latter in 1862, "They marched along with [the Indians], in procession, assisted them to carry their gods, beat their breasts in the same manner, uttered with them the same words and helped to swell the demonlike yells of those poor idolatrous" (in Moore 1995, 223). To some extent, the event had clearly become a site for the amicable interaction of the two subaltern communities whose relations could otherwise be fractious. This same inter-ethnic harmony perturbed the British colonial authorities, who feared that the processions—with their thunderous tassa drumming and regiments of stick fighters staging mock

battles—could become occasions for blacks and Indians to unite in insurrectionary mayhem against their white masters. Hence in 1869 the British passed an ordinance regulating the processions. Meanwhile, evidence suggests that the avid participation of fête-loving Afro-creoles in the processions had grown to such an extent that Indians themselves increasingly withdrew from them. These developments, added to the expense of constructing tazias, collectively led to the decline and ultimately the complete cessation of Muharram processions in that colony by the 1880s (see Moore 1995, 222–26). Concurrently, whatever tradition of playing tassa had existed in British Guiana also declined or failed to develop.

In Trinidad, Muharram had come to be celebrated at least as extensively and earnestly as in British Guiana, and there is no evidence that the creole presence was discouraging Indians from participating, or that it was undermining the event's primarily Indian character. While tazias were taken out wherever there were concentrations of Indians, the epicenter was the southwestern town of San Fernando, upon which dozens of processions would converge from the surrounding plantations. As with the rowdy Afro-creole camboulay processions enlivening Carnival, local whites regarded the event with ambivalence, being at once entertained by the colorful spectacle and anxious about the perceived potential for chaos as urban thoroughfares were taken over by capering, stick-wielding subalterns. Apprehensions had increased in the early 1880s, as British exploitation of Indian workers became significantly harsher and labor unrest had increased accordingly. Restrictions on creole Carnival processions in February 1884 provoked the violent "camboulay riots." Subsequently, in an atmosphere of heightened tension, British authorities decided to repress the October Muharram processions in San Fernando, which they did by having troops fire at close range into the peacefully advancing throngs, killing at least sixteen people. The Muharram Massacre effectively put an end to tazia processions throughout most of the island. They survived primarily in the "eastern corridor" towns of El Dorado, Arouca, Tunapuna, and Tacarigua, in the sleepy southern fishing village of Cedros, and, more substantially, in the Indian-dominated "Coolie Town" of St. James, whose processions were easily blocked from entering Port of Spain at a bridge and thus were not seen as dangerous. The eastern-corridor tazias processions thrived in the early twentieth century, with their focal site being a "holy ground" savannah off the Main Road, where the processions would meet. However, all died out by the 1970s, evidently due to attrition of knowledgeable and motivated tazia makers, and the expenses involved. However, the St. James Hosay flourished, and in fact came to be appreciated by the government, which since the 1950s has publicized and modestly supported the commemoration for its potential as a tourist attraction.

The colonial government had also granted a site at the Queens Royal College grounds, on the outskirts of Port of Spain, to which the tazias could be taken on the final day for the "janaaza" ritual. Somewhere along the line, the event came to be called "Hosay," presumably from the practice of shouting "Hussein," as is done in North Indian *nauhās* and chants.

In St. James, the tazia (tadjah) processions, with their attendant drummers, came to be led by neighborhood hereditary organizations called "yards." As Donald Hill (1993, 22–23) noted, in Trinidad the physical yard adjacent to a house has long constituted a focal site for social life, especially in a temperate tropical climate, where the actual domicile may be a mere shelter from rain. In the steelband culture that developed out of tamboo-bamboo bands in the 1930s, the "panyards"—open spaces in an urban neighborhood—served similarly central roles, not only for rehearsals but also as sites where locals and gang members would "lime." As Korom (2003, 128–33) has insightfully discussed, domestic yards have functioned somewhat similarly in St. James Hosay culture. At the same time, they can be seen as reconstituting the neighborhood (*mohalla*) organizations that construct tazias in India. Further, it could be added, a few of the yards, such as Ghulam Hussein, could be likened to North Indian musical *gharānas*, or family musical lineages. In St. James, there were five main yards—Cocorite, Balma, Bay Road, Panchayati, and Ghulam Hosein—each of which constructed a tazia and hosted its core of accompanying tassa drummers. In the 1990s drummer Noble Bisnath left Balma and founded the Bisnath yard. Meanwhile, two other somewhat more secretive and esoteric yards would construct the two crescent-shaped "moons" that are also taken out in procession and made to "dance" by the sturdy men who bear them. All the yards are located along the axis of Western Main Road, which bisects St. James, except for the Cocorite yard, based in that adjacent community and allegedly founded in the early 1900s. Physically, most of the yards consist of concrete-floored spaces, perhaps partly sheltered from the elements by a tin roof, adjoining the home of the hereditary headman. During the period leading up to Hosay, the yard serves as a workshop where the tazias are constructed and the tassa drums are prepared. As discussed earlier, prior to the advent of synthetic drum heads in the 1990s, throughout much of the year drummers would be present, tinkering with the tassas and skins, and of course, socializing.

As Korom discusses, a spirit of friendly competition exists between the yards, both in respect to the grandeur and craftsmanship of the tazias and the vigor and size of their accompanying tassa ensembles. The Ghulam Hosein yard—the oldest, together with Panchayati—is generally regarded as preeminent in the latter category, as its ensemble often includes as many as ten basses and fifteen tassa drummers, most of whom might belong to other professional quartets or

Figure 11. Hosay in St. James, 1993. Photograph by the author.

are perhaps unaffiliated. The ranks of drummers—especially bass men—may include Afro-creoles. Raiaz himself is a distinguished drummer, leader of the yard's tassa ensemble, and teacher of three or four younger groups. His ancestors are said to have instructed other community players. In order to play with a yard ensemble like that of Ghulam Hussein, one must be a more or less regular member who attends practices; that is, a drummer, even if competent, cannot simply show up and expect to be allowed to join in the procession.

Korom describes in some detail the activities of tassa drummers during Hosay itself (2003, 176–91). In the week leading up to Muharram, drummers hold evening practice sessions in the yards, rehearsing the distinctive Hosay hands

Figure 12. Drummers at a recreation of Hosay in Queens, New York, 2011.
Photograph by the author.

and attracting onlookers and enthusiasts while the tazias are being completed
and various rituals performed. The first public procession is Flag Night, when
the yards, in a specified order, wheel platforms bearing flags to the western
end of Main Road, accompanied by throngs and the "drum rooms," that is, the
tassa players. As the drummers slowly make their way down the thoroughfare,
they play the various Hosay hands (excluding chalta kabulkhana), which evoke
for knowledgeable listeners their particular associated moods and events. Also
present may be assorted Indian and creole revelers who drink rum, make merry,
and in doing so provoke orthodox Muslims to disparage the entire event as irreverent. As the yard entourages reach the end of the strip, the drum ensembles
may face off and stage sonic clashes in which, playing the mahātam war hand
and evoking the Karbala battle, they attempt to overpower each other, egged
on by cheering supporters. Eventually the processions turn and slowly make
their way back to their yards before the 4:00 A.M. curfew.

The following night is "Small Tadjah" or "Small Hosay" night, repeating
the previous night's activities but adorning the flag carts with tazias about two

or three feet tall. The following afternoon, the large tazias are wheeled out of their yard workshops and crowned with their elaborate domes. That night, after a series of rituals and chants of "I say, Hosay!" the tazia entourages and their drummers retrace the route of the previous nights, animated by crowds who admiringly compare the ornate cenotaphs and savor the drum battles. The next day the processions make their way—for the first time in daylight—toward the Queens Royal College grounds, conceived as the local Karbala, and the tassa drummers eventually play the lugubrious chalta kabulkhana "dead hand." After an imam recites the janaaza funeral prayers, the tazias are wheeled back to their yards, accompanied by tassa drummers playing "breakaway" hands like dingolay. Finally, the following day, the tazias are partially disassembled and wheeled to the sea, where they are further dismantled and unceremoniously immersed, to the accompaniment of festive drumming.[32]

The Cedros Hosay resembles that of St. James, although it is smaller and has more the character of a fête. Accordingly, it is deprecated as shallow and inappropriately festive by St. James people, whether they have seen it or not. Both in Cedros and St. James, the expense of constructing a tazia—around US$5000—constitutes an ongoing obstacle that must be surmounted each year.

Meanwhile, in the 1980s and 1990s, "Manhattan Hosay" was commemorated in New York City, animated by the presence of a tazia maker from St. James and a core of knowledgeable drummers (the members of the US #1 Tassa Band). Around 2000, the tazia maker retired and the tradition died out, despite the arrival of several other knowledgeable drummers.

Tassa Rhythms

Tassa drumming is an art form of considerable complexity and richness, and as such it merits analytical description for its own sake. Formal analysis of tassa can also illuminate various conceptual musical and sociomusical phenomena, including dynamics of retention and invention, of creolization and orthogenetic elaboration, and of the processes by which tassa drummers creatively adapt and transform rhythms from diverse forms and incorporate them into a coherent although eclectic art form. In the following pages I provide basic description of the most common hands and explore some of these more interpretive themes. My presentations of the rhythms are descriptive rather than prescriptive in intent, and they fall far short of constituting a comprehensive documentation of tassa music. Among other things, I do not cover regional variants, such as the south Trinidad style of wedding hand; further, I restrict myself to the more standardized and traditional hands, thus omitting, for example, the various new

inventions generated for competitions demanding such items. Finally, I limit myself to schematizing the basic and typical cutter patterns in a given hand rather than elaborate improvisational strategies.

Since many tassa rhythms are metrical entities of essentially North Indian character, one might assume it logical to analyze them as variants of the tāls (tālas) of Hindustani music. However, because tassa hands differ in certain fundamental ways from tāls, this approach would be misleading and inappropriate. First, tassa hands, unlike tāls quintessentially executed on a tabla drum pair, are composite rhythms, involving specified patterns not only for the lead cutter, but also for the bass, jhāl, and, in several cases, the accompanying foulay. Secondly, while a Hindustani tāl consists essentially of a meter with internal structural subsections, a tassa hand also includes a set of conventional cutter patterns that may be played, with flexibility, within the basic rhythm, sometimes in typical sequences; a hand is in that sense a more specific, standardized, and elaborate entity than a tāl, which is a simple metrical skeleton. Further, several hands contain discrete sections through which the ensemble must move; several have accelerated barti sections, and wedding hand and tīn chopra can be regarded as a set of modules deployed in conventional sequences. Moreover, the latter two hands contain sections that, although quasi-metrical, have irregular beat counts, in contrast to contemporary Hindustani tāls. In these passages the sense of a downbeat is also obscure, again in contrast to tāls, in which the *sam* or first beat has an exclusive and generally clear primacy. Finally, while tassa drumming has (for enthusiasts such as myself) a prodigious expressivity and appeal, one cannot compare the music of a skilled tabla player and a "cutter-man" in terms of variety and richness; in cutting (improvising) in rhythms like dingolay and wedding hand, even the best cutter players deploy a quite finite set of rhythms. In that sense, indeed, they resemble local-classical singers, who tend to have a fairly limited repertoire of melodic ideas for deployment in quasi-improvised sections of songs. Hence, tassa hands, and tassa music in general, are more productively likened to counterparts in vernacular North Indian drumming, especially those played on tassa and nagāra, as discussed above.

Tassa drumming bears a certain resemblance—primarily coincidental—to various Afro-Caribbean drum ensemble musics, especially the typical format in which two or three drums together with one or two idiophones (a bell, or hardwood sticks) render composite rhythms, primarily for dance accompaniment. As with tassa drumming, the Afro-Caribbean composite meters bear names (for example, *guaguancó*, *sicá*, *yanvalou*) and encompass standardized ensemble parts as well as conventional lead-drum patterns. Most such drum traditions in Trinidad were either effectively stamped out by the British or else

died natural deaths, such that the tradition of kalinda drumming (accompanying stick fighting) constitutes the only Afro-Caribbean drum music that may have contributed directly to the tassa repertoire.

Despite the superficial similarities between tassa and Afro-Caribbean percussion musics, the formal differences between them are pronounced and provide good reason not to seek to combine them in some putative family of "creole Caribbean drum ensemble music." At this point it may suffice to note one salient, albeit technical distinction. Afro-Caribbean percussion music is particularly distinguished by its pervasive syncopation, whether in the form of explicit 12/8 polyrhythms or, more often, various "three-against-two" patterns within a duple framework that are either introduced by a soloist or are structurally present in the composite ostinatos themselves. Syncopation is certainly present in Indian and Indo-Caribbean musics, and in North India one has little difficulty finding the "three-three-two" beat that is often taken as an icon of African influence. Nevertheless, I would assert that in tassa music, as in the related vernacular drum traditions of North India, syncopation per se is not a pervasive feature. Tassa drumming may be fast, intricate, varied, and kinetic, but it generates musical interest largely by other strategies, as will be discussed.

The basic strokes and sonorities available to the tassa drummer are relatively few, especially, for example, compared with those that can be generated on the tabla and dholak. On both heads of the dholak, and both drums of the tabla pair, the player can produce both resonant, ringing strokes as well as damped ones; the tassa, by contrast, can generate only resonant strokes. Further, much of the expressivity of both tabla and dholak playing derives from the pitch variation available on the lower-pitched head (in the dholak) or the *bāyan* drum (of the tabla pair); no such variation is possible on the tassa or bass dhol. The only pronounced timbral contrast available on the tassa is that between strokes more or less on the center of the drum, and rim shots, in which the middle of the stick connects with the rim of the drum, generating a metallic, reverberating bang. Similar tones are available on the nagāra, and find rough counterparts in the *tīn* and more ringing *tā* strokes on the tabla. Perhaps the most distinctive timbre available on the tassa is that not of a particular stroke but of the buzz roll (called simply "rolling"), in which the stick bounces a few times on the head before the other stick hits. Skilled dholak and especially tabla players, to be sure, can generate exciting, fluttering rolls (primarily via damped "kitatakatirekata"-type strokes), but these are qualitatively different from the buzz roll, which sounds less like a series of individual strokes than a thunderous roar. (To reiterate Sharar's description penned in the early 1900s, "In the tassa playing method, the beats should fall with such rapidity that one stroke cannot be distinguished from another.") The buzz roll, of course, can

be overused, especially by immature players, but its deployment, in judicious alternation with slower, articulated strokes, is basic to the tassa's timbral palette.

For its part, the bass drum sonorities are more limited, consisting primarily of the resonant strokes on the higher-pitched right-hand side, struck with the heavy mallet, and on the left-hand, lower-pitched side, struck with the palm of the hand. Muted strokes can also be played on either head, but these tend to be softer and less audible.[33] Finally, the jhāl can produce three sounds: a relatively staccato tone, obtained by holding the cymbals together after striking them; a sort of "sizzle," generated by gently keeping an edge of one cymbal in contact with the other cymbal after striking; and—least often used—a resonant "clang," produced by separating the cymbals after striking them together. The "sizzle" technique can require some practice and skill.

A standard tassa ensemble, as mentioned, comprises two tassas (cutter and foulay), a bass, and a jhāl. In several hands, including tikora and chaubola, the foulay does not play. Instead, the player "shadows," that is, silently pretends to play eighth or sixteenth notes. Given the formidable racket that even the other three players generate, most listeners would fail to notice that the foulay drummer is not really playing. They would, however, notice if he were physically absent, and might make ignorant complaints about the band being understaffed; hence the practice of foulay "shadowing," both at competitions and hired engagements.

Some disclaimer about notation practice used in this chapter is necessary. Since tassa drumming is entirely an oral tradition, there are no extant conventions of transcribing it. Hands like nagāra and dingolay, while basically duple, could be notated in various ways, that is, in either 2/4/, 4/4, or cut time, and even within such parameters, placement of bar lines is often arbitrary. In some cases, as the reader will note, the rhythm seems to suggest a quadratic (4/4) meter, which, however, may be subsequently disrupted by a certain pattern, such as the standard tāl of what could be regarded as eighteen beats (four and a half bars of 4/4). In the pages following I also make little attempt to indicate actual stroke patterns, but, especially with regard to cutter patterns, instead aim for skeletal representations of the audibly salient rhythms. Meanwhile, transcribing percussion music in staff notation invariably involves arbitrary decisions regarding note values, such as whether to transcribe a stroke as a quarter note or an eighth note with a rest; in most such cases, I have endeavored to notate in the manner that is easiest to read. Hence these notations, far from being prescriptive, are only descriptive in the most approximate sense. (Note that in the idiosyncratic transcriptions given here, a diamond above a note indicates a metallic rim shot.)

Tassa drummers are accustomed to conceiving of their music as an autonomous art, and they are often able and willing to discuss or demonstrate particular

hands and tāls. If chowtal and birha singers often tended to direct the conversation away from my tedious questions about musical form and toward spiritual and mythological matters, many tassa drummers with whom I conversed were quite comfortable demonstrating rhythms for me, often by tapping their fingers on a table. However, tassa players, with very few exceptions, have no formal training in music, whether Western or Indian, and thus do not command the sort of explicit music theory that would enable them to enumerate ("check") beats and meters, identify downbeats, or specify lengths of rests. As a result, for example, a drummer would be unlikely to recognize that the bihāg hand could be regarded as being in seven beats. As I suggest below, this "lack" of explicit theory, rather than limiting the music's richness, in fact allows it to accommodate certain expressive asymmetries and idiosyncrasies that would be uncharacteristic of, for example, tabla drumming, which must adhere to a framework of fixed meters. For my own task of analyzing and transcribing tassa drumming, however, rhythms like wedding hand and tīn chopra posed particular analytical and notational challenges, as drummers were not able to recognize or interpret their inconsistent rest lengths, asymmetrical ostinato patterns, and seeming lack of clear downbeats. Hence, as discussed below, in transcribing such rhythms I found myself obliged to make judicious etic interpretations, while endeavoring as much as possible to incorporate or intuit what seemed to be emic sensibilities.

Finally, the following descriptions do not attempt to cover variant versions of hands, especially the distinctive south Trinidad renditions; instead, they are based on the north-central mainstream, particularly as I have gleaned or interpreted it, however idiosyncratically, from informants such as Sunil Mathura, Mukesh Ragoo, Jason Nandoo, Amidh Mohammad, Laki Bhagan, and others. A comprehensive study of tassa drumming would also cover the diverse recently invented hands, only a few of which have come to be played by groups other than their creator.

Tāl and Barti

Before describing the individual tassa hands, it may be useful to outline two features that recur in several hands, namely, the pattern called "tāl," and the barti section. In North Indian classical music, "tāl" means meter, but in Indo-Caribbean music—both tassa and local-classical music—it designates a cadential pattern. In Trinidadian and Guyanese local-classical music, this can occasionally take the form of a syncopated phrase consisting of three beats, or pairs of beats, the last of which falls conclusively on the downbeat; in this form, the local-classical "tāl" is equivalent to a simple *tihāī* of Hindustani

music. The term *tihāī*, however, is not known by traditional Indo-Caribbean musicians (and its use in North India may not have been common until the decades around 1900, toward the end of the indentureship period).[34] Actual tihāīs are in fact rare in tassa drumming; essentially, drummers do not know them or play them, and in that sense their playing resembles that of folk nagāra and tassa playing in the Bhojpuri region. Rather, the tāl of tassa drumming is a sort of standardized cadential pattern that, once familiar to listeners, has its own logic and conclusiveness. The idiosyncratic use of the term "tāl" finds parallels in North Indian vernacular music, as in the drumming of Mundas in Chotanagpur (south of the Bhojpuri region), where it designates a particular kind of rhythmic sequence (Babiracki 1991, 189, 271–74).

The Trinidadian tassa tāl is an ensemble pattern in which the bass and jhāl players diverge from their basic ostinatos to join the cutter in emphasizing the structural beats and rests; the tāl thus serves to vary the musical texture. Different hands have their own distinctive tāls, some of which should not be played in other hands; in nagāra, for instance, at least three distinct tāls can be played. However, a single tāl pattern, represented as in example 7 below, or slight variants thereof, recurs in several hands. As the brackets indicate, this tāl pattern could in fact be regarded as an introductory measure leading to a genuine two-bar tihāī (bracketed), whose conclusiveness, by Hindustani standards, is then frustrated, as it were, by the addition of a six-beat tag. Hence, while the hands wherein this tāl is used, such as tikora and chaubola, can be generally regarded as quadratic meters, the tāl effectively ruptures this pattern with its six-beat conclusion. Needless to say, the "Hindustani perspective" is irrelevant, and the pattern fulfills its cadential function in its own effective manner. In "classical" tassa hands like tikora and chaubola, a knowledgeable ensemble will play or "break" tāl three times, with the original hand resuming after the first two renderings; after the third tāl, the drumming segues to the barti or another hand. Meanwhile, the concept of tāl is used somewhat unsystematically to designate other patterns, especially, for example, in wedding hand, as discussed below.

Several hands have intermediate or closing sections, called "barti" (or "daur") in a faster tempo with a distinctive, more intense beat. Barti is a basic

Example 7. Basic tāl.

feature of many subgenres of local-classical song, as discussed in my volume on that music (2000a, 127–29). In song forms such as bihāg, ḍanḍak, holi, and especially Trinidadian thumri, typically after three verses (with their ṭek refrains), the singer signals the dholak player to shift to a barti section, during which the drummer plays flashy pyrotechnics while the vocalist reiterates earlier text lines in a floating, free-rhythmic manner. Regardless of the meter of the original section (such as the 7/8 of bihāg, ḍanḍak, and holi), the barti is always in quadratic meter. After a few minutes of barti, the vocalist sings the ṭek to signal a brief return to the original tempo and meter, and the song concludes. In such contexts, the barti corresponds closely to the *laggi* of Hindustani semiclassical genres thumri and ghazal. (The term laggi, however, is unknown in the Caribbean and may constitute, like *tihāī*, a relative neologism in the Hindustani music lexicon.)[35] However, both the Hindustani laggi and the barti of local-classical music may be assumed to derive from a corresponding, and certainly older, practice in Bhojpuri-region folk music (with certain counterparts elsewhere in North India) in which a song proceeds through a few *pad-ṭek* sets and then segues to a faster section in what could be called kaharva. Several variants of this pattern can be found; thus, as discussed in chapter 3, chowtal can be seen as moving from a predominantly 7/8 section to an ulārā in fast quadratic meter; on the more local level, an individual chowtal verse itself (like a Ramayan *pad* in *Mānas* singing) proceeds from a 7/8 section, through a quadratic barti, and then reverts briefly to the ṭek in 7/8, before moving to the next *pad*. Chowtal and other folksong types with barti sections are common in Indo-Caribbean music.

The barti of tassa drumming recapitulates that of Bhojpuri folksong, but as used in the thumri hand, and the less common bihāg, it derives more directly as stylized imitation of the local-classical namesake. However, as discussed below, barti is also a feature of the chaubola hand, which has no direct counterpart in local-classical music, and thus can be said to derive from a more general practice. Further, the barti of chaubola is in a distinctive "limping" rhythm, unlike the quadratic local-classical bartis.

Tassa Hands

The tassa repertoire, as the reader will have gleaned by now, is based on a set of composite rhythms or hands. A hand comprises and is distinguished by: a standard bass and jhāl pattern, combined with one or more theka-like cutter patterns (collectively establishing a groove); a set of typical "cuts" or quasi-improvised cutter patterns or variations; conversely, avoidance of certain patterns too suggestive of other hands; and, in the case of some hands, standard

tāls and bartis. Some of the hands have one or more typical, basic composite rhythms, which are referred to as "theka" by some drummers—especially the very few that have had some exposure to tabla music. Hence, for example, it might be convenient to regard cutter playing in nagāra hand as comprising a theka (shown in example 11), a set of typical, quasi-improvised patterns and variations, and a few conventional tāls. However, in such hands as chaubola, as shown below, there are more than one—in fact, four—basic cutter patterns, problematizing the use of the term "theka" to specify a single one.

Both bass and jhāl patterns may be varied to a certain extent, in conventional ways. Jhāl playing is particularly flexible; often, the basic pattern consists of a series of quarter notes, alternating damped and "sizzle" strokes, although these might be rendered in either order. On the whole, the jhāl player follows the bass drum patterns.

Tassa hands are to some extent flexible entities that resist definitive standardization or description. Aside from jhāl and bass variations, cutter playing involves considerable improvisation, although within the conventions of the given hand. Further, individual cutter players have their own distinctive styles, to some extent. Patterns like the standard tāl, shown in example 7 above, are in fact played in different ways by different groups, and such variants may be regarded as legitimate to an extent, especially if they are executed smoothly by the ensemble. Finally, there exist regional differences, especially between north (and central) Trinidad and the south. While some bands based in the south play essentially like their northern counterparts, others play certain hands—especially wedding hand—in a distinctive form (which northerners acknowledge as a legitimate variant). Such flexibility, however, is not without its limits, and drummers—and knowledgeable competition judges—will not hesitate to criticize a performance they consider incorrect or deficient.

Most of the hands are basically duple metered, with the notable exceptions being the 6/8 nabi sarbat, the "limping" rhythm of khemta and the chaubola barti, the irregular wedding drum and tīn chopra, and the 7/8 employed in bihāg, chaiti, and holi.

A survey of tassa hands might organize them in various ways, according to formal features, sources, performance contexts, or degree of popularity. A fundamental "emic" categorization distinguishes traditional "classical" (or "fine") hands, such as tikora and wedding hand, from more festive, dance-oriented ones like dingolay and steelband, which bear creole names. (The "classical" hands bear no relation to North Indian classical music.) Tassa hands are in fact much more diverse in character and structure than are, for example, the tāls of Hindustani music. Some, like chaubola, have fairly standardized cutter parts, while others, like wedding hand and dingolay, offer more scope for improvisa-

tion. The subsequent analysis, while incorporating this distinction, groups the hands in a somewhat pragmatic rather than rigidly systematic fashion. I commence with seven of the most popular and basic hands. I then proceed to a set of hands that can be regarded as creative adaptations of rhythms employed in other genres, including Kabir bhajans, local-classical sub-genres, and "Madrasi" Kali/Mariamman drumming. I then discuss the Hosay hands and conclude with wedding hand, which appears to derive from Hosay tīn chopra hand.

Tikora

Tikora enjoys a certain elevated status among tassa hands. It is generally the first played in a suite, whether at competitions, other events, or even recordings, segueing on to chaubola and other hands. It is thus a basic hand, with a more rigorous and serious character than light, "breakaway" hands like dingolay and nagāra, which dominate the repertoires of noisy amateur players. While tikora might provoke dancing at a wedding or other festivity, it is not a dance-oriented hand per se. With its relatively standardized set of cutter patterns, it has a fairly defined and distinct character, especially in relation to a mere skeletal tāl like tīntāl or kaharva. A cutter-man's artistry in rendering tikora lies less in flamboyant displays or innovations than in the expressivity with which he plays the conventional patterns. While these are matters of nuance, players can nevertheless earn renown for their renditions, and a nicely rendered tikora has a unique, almost melodic flow and charm.

Tikora's venerable status is embodied in its name, which dates at least as far back as the 1830s. In that decade the term *tikara* denoted a single-headed drum pair, akin to a nagāra; Martin provides a line drawing of a tikara and offers a description: "Tikara, a drum made of potter's ware, and nearly of the same form with a kettle-drum. Two are always used at the same time, the performer beating with a small stick, on one with his right hand, and on the other with his left. It cannot therefore be used in processions" (Martin 1838, 601). Shurreef (1832, 50) also mentions takori as a "bass kettle-drum."[36] Platts, in his 1884 Urdu dictionary, defines "ṭakora" as "a fillip, tap; the sound of a drum; the treble end of the Moorish kettle-drum (cf. ṭankur, ṭankor)" (1930, 358). The "Moorish kettle-drum" in question is obviously the tassa, although the meaning of "the treble end" (of a single-headed drum?) is less clear than the other glosses.[37] While I cannot say that the term "tikora" is entirely unknown to any of India's 1.2 billion people, I have never encountered anyone—including the various tassa and nagāra drummers I met and interviewed in the Banaras area—who was familiar with it, such that I believe I can assert that it is certainly obscure there, and is perhaps extinct; its persistence in the Caribbean thus constitutes a striking marginal survival.

Example 8. Tikora: typical patterns.

In the words of Mukesh Ragoo, "Tikora is basically about rolling," and rolling indeed forms the basis of the hand's signature cutter pattern. More specifically, the pattern can be described as a steady roll with a rim shot on each quarter note, with the resulting typical composite theka schematized in the first bars of example 8.[38] Typically, the roll lasts two bars, giving way to some bars of eighth and sixteenth notes, as shown. These then segue to a crescendo roll either starting or intensifying from beat 3, itself followed by further rolling or else resolving in the former manner. Often, as shown in example 8, the roll from beat three is rendered three or four times, giving something of the effect of a tihāī. The bass player might perform either the one-bar pattern shown in mm. 1–4 below, or else the two-bar pattern shown in the subsequent bars. In *Tassa Thunder* (Manuel, from 44:48), Ryan Ali and accompanists provide a brief but exemplary rendering of tikora. In typical fashion, the bass player (Aron Ali) performs some variant patterns before settling into the standard accompaniment. Ryan Ali, on cutter, plays some standard variations, including the roll segueing to eighth notes, mentioned above; the jhāl player loosely follows the cutter parts. A standard tāl, as shown above, leads the transition to chaubola.

There are other subvarieties of tikora, with the standard hand described above being more specifically referred to as "wedding tikora." Some drummers designate certain wedding tikora passages as "bete drum" (baytay, bhatee, and so on, or "run dem down"), typically using the bass pattern: ‖♩♪♩♩♪‖♩.♪♩♩‖. Another tikora variant, called kālināth or nadidin (na-di-din), uses the bass pattern: ‖♩.♩♪♪♪‖♩♩♪♪‖.[39] Lakiram states that ideally and traditionally, during the agwāni, the group should commence with tikora and move through bete drum

and kālināth, although few people nowadays appreciate such conventions. Two other tikoras are Hosay tikora, played during the Hosay commemoration, and Madrasi tikora, played at Madrasi weddings and ceremonies. In Hosay tikora, unlike wedding tikora, the foulay plays rather than "shadows," and the bass pattern is also different, being roughly: ‖♩.♩♪♪‖. Raiaz Ali, of the Ghulam Hussein yard in St. James, regards Hosay tikora as a spurious hand introduced by "wedding drummers" from elsewhere. He told me, "Since I a little boy, I never hear my father or grandfather say anything about Hosay tikora."

Chaubola

Tikora most typically opens a suite, and is often followed by chaubola (chowbola, chaubola bhajan), another "classical" hand, not necessarily associated with dance. Like "tīn chopra," "chaubola" is a term denoting formal features, though originally in reference to prosody rather than music. Platts (1884, 447) defines the term as "a verse of four lines—a play," with "*cau-bola chand*," meaning "a kind of metre." Platts is clearly referring to the use of the term in the vernacular dance and music drama that in the early 1900s came to be known in North India as *nautanki*. While that latter term did not take root in the Indic Caribbean, the most popular plays in the repertoire—especially *Raja Harishchandra* and *Gopichandra*—were fairly widely performed by amateur and semiprofessional enthusiasts in the region. These were rustic renditions of swashbuckling costume dramas, using chapbooks obtained from India and featuring varied songs and dances, typically with nagāra and, later, harmonium accompaniment. In India, such dramas constituted significant conduits for transmission and mixing of folk and light-classical styles, as they combined unpretentious folk songs with stylized, vernacular versions of ghazals, thumris, taranas/tillanas, and kathak-like dance. Thespians in the Caribbean did their best to render these varied genres, as called for in the chapbooks, which seem to have exerted much influence on the formation of local-classical music as well (see Manuel 2000a, 21–22, 28–31). Aside from the specific song forms specified in chapbooks, the most common format for song and stylized speech was the sequence of *dohā-chaubola-daur*, in which a passage commenced with a dohā (couplet) sung in free rhythm, proceeded to a chaubola, punctuated with nagāra accompaniment, and then a faster, dance-oriented section called daur. "Chaubola," while properly designating the prosodic meter of the middle section, among Caribbean local-classical dholak players came to denote the standard quadratic meter—ubiquitous in North Indian folk and light music—which Hindustani musicians might call "kaharva"—a term that is, however, not used in the Caribbean. The chaubola of tassa drumming bears a rough resemblance to

kaharva in being a quadratic rhythm with a bass drum (or drum head) anacrusis on the fourth beat leading to a stroke on the downbeat. Meanwhile, however, the specific and distinctive tassa patterns of chaubola do not bear any particular resemblance to those heard in local-classical dholak playing.

Chaubola is typically rendered in medium tempo, around MM120, and occasionally slightly slower than the tikora, which usually precedes it. Like tikora, it is not a "breakaway" dance rhythm, nor one that accommodates flamboyant cutter playing; instead, it has a somewhat restrained, rigorous character, although with an insistent and infectious rhythmic drive. The chaubola cutter part can be regarded as comprising four basic patterns, which are often rendered sequentially, although with some flexibility. The salient feature of the first of these, schematized in the first two bars of example 9, is the pronounced flam on the "and" of beat one, providing a sort of syncopated kick to the measure, whose tension is not resolved until the downbeat of the next bar. (The remainder of the bar, indicated as a rest here, is in fact a series of softer eighth notes.) The second pattern (mm. 5–6 of the same example) is a roll essentially identical to the basic tikora pattern of example 8 above. The third pattern, shown in mm. 7–8, is a simple series of eighth notes with alternate rim shots, rendered as a "one-hand knock" (enabling showy drummers to raise their left aloft); were handy names desired for such patterns, I would call this one "chugging," or "chugging along," suggestive as it is of a steam engine. The fourth typical chaubola pattern (mm. 9–10) is the same as the basic nagāra hand pattern, also shown below as example 11. The bass part may vary, sometimes to a pattern of: // ♩♪♪ // The jhāl pattern is flexible and can typically alternate damped and ringing quarter notes, in either order.

Chaubola, unlike tikora, has a barti section that, as mentioned above, employs a particularly distinctive rhythm that defies analysis in terms of beat counts. The rhythm, as tapped on the cutter, corresponds to that of the barti of traditional khañjri-gīt Kabir bhajans, as described in chapter 4. As mentioned, this beat could be aptly described as "long-short-short-long-short-short." Close analysis reveals that it corresponds to 4+3+3, but musicians certainly do not conceive of it thusly, and its tempo is too brisk to admit such enumeration. The basic cutter rhythm could alternately be regarded as a 2/4 beat consisting of a quarter note—slightly shortened—followed by two eighths, but given its three-stroke pattern, it is more likely to be heard as 3/4, with a slightly elongated first beat. The same rhythm is used in the khemta of tassa drumming and local-classical music, and also in the *devi ka gīt* of Bhojpuri-region nagāra playing, and various rhythms played by Mundas of Chotanagpur (Babiracki 1991, 272–74); it also crops up in a tassa style documented by Wolf, of Pakistani descendants of immigrants from Agra (2014, chapter 4). Variants of it can also be found in

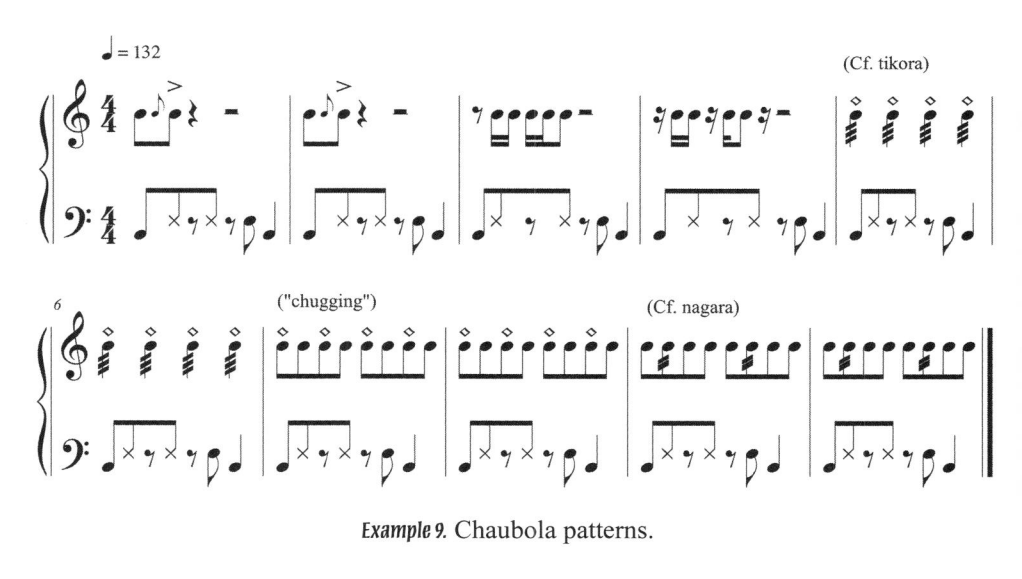

Example 9. Chaubola patterns.

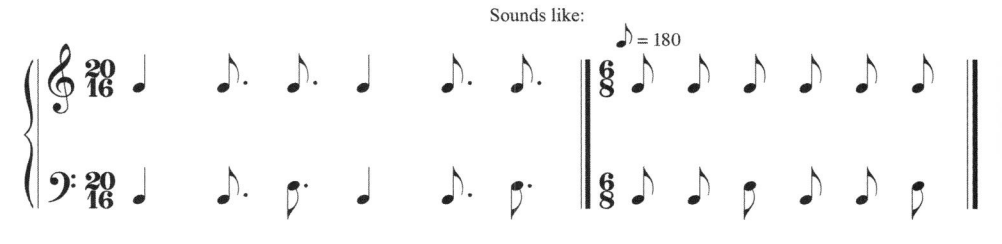

Example 10. Chaubola barti.

various other music cultures, as in the typical harp accompaniment to Andean *huaynos*. Incompatible as it is with any system based on an ability to enumerate beat-counts, it is precisely the sort of rhythm that is conspicuously absent in Hindustani music but present in vernacular musics not encumbered, as it were, by such theoretical constraints.

In chaubola, the cutter player introduces the four basic patterns, with some variation, punctuating them with two tāls. The third tāl segues to the barti, in which the basic "limping" pattern is played by cutter and bass, with some cutter variation; typically, the distinctive barti pattern lasts only a few bars, after which an exit tāl leads back to the original chaubola pattern. All these features are evident in the rendering of chaubola by Ryan Ali and accompanists in *Tassa Thunder* (Manuel, at 45:35). Ryan moves quickly through the four theka-like patterns, plays a tāl, reiterates the theka patterns, plays another tāl, returns to theka patterns with variations, and then proceeds via a tāl to the barti, and thence

with a tāl back to theka patterns. Another tāl leads to a brief pause, and then to dingolay. Perhaps more commonly, chaubola segues to nagāra, and thence to dingolay and steelpan.

Nagāra

As discussed above, the nagāra drum pair has been widespread in North India since the Mughal era and is still commonly encountered in the Bhojpuri region, where its music bears salient parallels with tassa drumming. The nagāra was obligatory in nautanki vernacular theater, which Caribbean enthusiasts cultivated in the form of "Gopichand" and "Harichand dance." More commonly, in the Caribbean the nagāra was associated especially with Ahirs and often accompanied Ahir dance and birha singing. While a North Indian ensemble might typically feature two (or even more) nagāra pairs, in the Caribbean it is generally played solo. Nagāra drumming in the Bhojpuri region, as mentioned above, comprises many rhythms, and even in the Caribbean a good nagāra player (such as were documented on some old Surinamese recordings) might move through a variety of patterns in accompanying song or dance. However, in such contexts most drummers have played a standard default pattern corresponding to the cutter pattern schematized in example 11. This also serves as the basic and defining pattern (and the obvious model) of the tassa hand called nagāra.[40]

Nagāra is a light, "breakaway" hand, rendered at fast tempo and suitable for festive dancing. Such quasi-improvised "cutting" as occurs tends to follow a few standard patterns. The basic theka ostinato is further varied by introducing tāls, of which three distinct varieties can be played, as schematized in examples 12, 13, and 14.[41] In the second of these, textural variety is achieved by having the bass and jhāl drop out during the rests (during which the cutter may actually play soft sixteenth notes). (A very similar "break" pattern can be found in Bhojpuri-region nagāra ensemble playing.) Nagāra has no barti.

The tassa group recorded by Alan Lomax in Pasea Village in 1962 played a version of nagāra with the same basic beat as that heard today, along with a tāl that could be described as a rudimentary version of the first tāl shown above.[42]

Some drummers play a similar hand called "birha," especially if a birha singer is present. Lakiram Bhagan relates, "If we're at a wedding, and a guy come up and say he want to sing a birha, I love that. When he's singing you play soft, but then when he stop you play nagāra [hand], Ahirwa nagāra, and that's the dancing part, because whoever's singing birha, he's supposed to have the dancers with him, or he dances; then the drummer make a tāl, make it soft, and then he come back singing" (p.c.).

Example 11. Nagāra basic pattern.

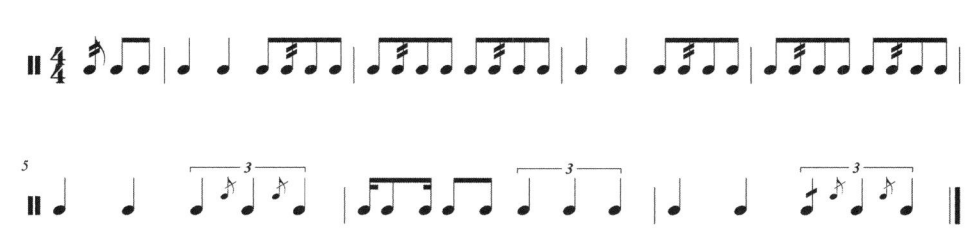

Example 12. Nagāra tāl #1.

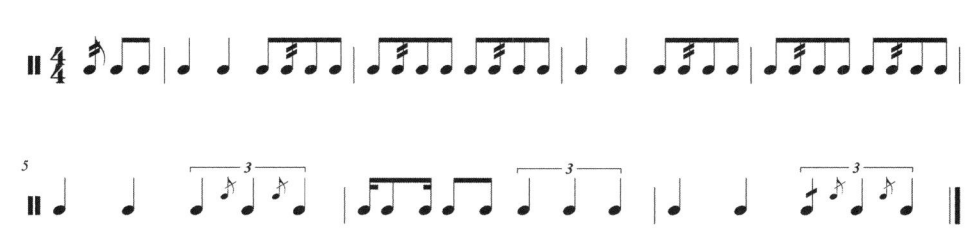

Example 13. Nagāra tāl #2.

Example 14. Nagāra tāl #3.

Dingolay

Dingolay, which typically follows nagāra, is a similarly light and dance-oriented hand, usually in a slightly brisker tempo. The word derives from local creole, in which it connotes "to dance with joyful abandon," as in "Ah gwan dingolay tonight." Winer plausibly traces the term to a Kongo verb meaning

"twist, turn, gyrate" (2009, 298). The word might thus suggest an Afro-creole origin of the rhythm; however, the term "dingolay" does not appear to have been used to denote any particular Afro-Trinidadian rhythm per se, and there is nothing in the hand itself that is atypical of, for example, Bhojpuri-region nagāra playing. The basic dingolay pattern, indeed, closely resembles Bhojpuri nagāra beats such as *nautanki*, *rela*, and *bhartāla*. Given its relative simplicity, it may also have developed in Trinidad as a generic up-tempo beat, to which the local creole term was applied, in keeping with its festive character. The hand had certainly assumed its modern form by 1962, when Alan Lomax recorded a rendering cognate with its present form (and featuring a version of the tāl #2 shown in example 17).

The gist of dingolay's cutter pattern is a steady, rollicking, sixteenth-note series, often with a buzz roll toward the end of what could be regarded as a two-bar pattern, as schematized in example 15. The foulay plays a similar pattern, without rolls. As in nagāra, the bass player may vary his pattern somewhat; while he might commence with a dotted quarter followed by a sixteenth, the difficulty of rendering this pattern at high speeds typically leads to its being "evened out" to the less syncopated pattern shown in example 15. As Amidh Mohammad told me, "It's all for dancing, so you can bring in whatever rhythm to make it better. And different drummers have their own styling; Emamalee's dingolay, which is one of the best, is quite different from Laki's (in other words, Emamalee Mohammad and Laki Bhagan), and they're both good players." Two distinct dingolay tāls are shown in examples 16 and 17; the first of these—whose notation here is especially approximate—varies considerably from drummer to drummer, though its distinctive eight-note lead-in remains prominent. The second tāl, a north Trinidad pattern, is especially effective in energizing dancers. The jhāl pattern varies. Dingolay could be notated and conceived either as a one-bar or two-bar pattern; the pattern of tāl #2 below might seem to suggest a two-bar entity, but the resumption of the sixteenth-note series could also be seen as the commencement of a one-bar basic pattern rather than the end of a two-bar pattern.

Nagāra, dingolay, and steelpan are played by all tassa groups, especially given the popularity of these hands with dancers. At a party with animated dancing, a band might play these hands, perhaps with kalinda, for an extended period, switching back and forth. However, knowledgeable drummers often disparage raucous youth groups whose repertoire seems to be limited to these hands, and to the simpler patterns therein. Savants also complain that competitions typically overemphasize these simple, crowd-pleasing hands rather than the musically richer classical rhythms like wedding hand.

Example 15. Dingolay basic pattern.

Example 16. Dingolay tāl #1.

Example 17. Dingolay tāl #2.

Steelpan

Typically following dingolay in a dance-oriented or competition suite is the hand variously called steelpan, steelband, panhand, ironhand, or calypso. Tassa players generally aver that the hand evolved, or must have evolved, as an imitation of the rhythm of steelband music. However, there has never been any single characteristic rhythm to steelband songs, although it is possible that in the 1950s and 1960s, many pan songs featured typical accompaniment patterns that provided the inspiration for the eponymous hand. Perhaps accordingly, the hand's bass drum pattern can be seen as an up-tempo version of the hoary creole "habanera" beat, which surfaces, in various forms, in such diverse genres as reggaeton and soca. Nevertheless, the steelpan rhythm, like that of dingolay, is not incompatible with Indian rhythms, including those of the Bhojpuri-region nagāra.

Like dingolay and nagāra, steelpan is a lively, dance-oriented hand, which tends to feature a fairly finite set of cutter variations. Although, like those hands, it has no barti section, it may accelerate. It incorporates a prominent foulay pattern, consisting (like the accompanying drum-pair in Bhojpuri-region nagāra drumming) of a steady sixteenth-note series. The entrance of the foulay can in

Example 18. Steelpan, basic pattern.

Example 19. Typical steelpan cutting patterns.

fact be a lively moment in a drum suite, provoking hoots, hollers, and intensified dancing. Example 19 shows some typical cutting patterns, including the
pronounced flams; also common are passages of thirty-second-note triplets
(which some drummers call "prattlin'" or "girgiri").

The tassa "steelband drums" recorded by Lomax in 1962 resemble the modern tassa hand. Some sources assert that the steelpan hand (and synthetic plastic
head) was created by one Cyril Raymond, which, if true, would make it perhaps
the only standard hand with a known inventor.[43]

Kabir Bhajan (Kabirdas Bhajan)

I have mentioned above how some of the basic hands of Bhojpuri-region nagāra
drumming are adaptations from characteristic rhythms of certain folksongs,
such as *devi ka gīt* and *lāchāri*. Trinidadian tassa drumming includes similar
borrowings, as in the case of the Kabir bhajan hand. As discussed in chapter 4,
singers of Kabir bhajans in Trinidad and Suriname would traditionally accompany themselves on the tambourine-like khaṅjri, playing a distinctive "khaṅjri
beat" during the verses; in between verses the rhythm segues to a barti section
in the characteristic three-stroke "long-short-short" rhythm similar to that of
the chaubola barti. The tassa Kabir bhajan hand can be seen as an idiosyncratic
adaptation of the first pattern. The basic pattern is rendered in medium tempo
with a triplet syncopation, affording a rhythm that strikes this author as somewhat sensual and sultry, despite its origin in devotional song. The pattern is
played for several bars, with some variation and "prattlin'," and then proceeds
to a dramatic fortissimo cadence, bringing the playing to an abrupt break, after

Example 20. Kabir bhajan: basic pattern and tāl.

which the cutter player leads the group in, tapping the pattern softly, almost tentatively. Kabir bhajan is ideally played at a moderate tempo, but it can also be played at a brisk pace.[44] Example 20 shows a few bars of the basic pattern and this cadence.

A few groups play a somewhat similar hand called "Siewnaraini bhajan," which has similar tāl, although less triplet syncopation; if played in fast tempo, it tends to blur with dingolay, though it has a distinctive barti section. Another obscure hand, lacking a barti, is kirtan bhajan, whose bass pattern can be schematized as ‖♪ ♩♩♪♩‖.

Kalinda

The term "kalinda" (calinda, calenda) has been documented as being used to denote a variety of neo-African Caribbean dance and music genres since the eighteenth century, when Jean Baptiste Labat described a Martinican line dance by that name, and L. M. de Saint-Mery portrayed Haitian kalinda as featuring couples taking turns dancing amid a ring of onlookers. Various genres called kalinda were subsequently documented in Carriacou, New Orleans, Puerto Rico, and elsewhere, and at least three forms of kalinda are currently performed in Martinique (see Gerstin 2004, 7–8). Gerstin, in his thorough study of the kalinda complex, relates that by the nineteenth century in various places the term had also come to denote topical, often satirical songs.

In Trinidad, the term has been used with a corresponding diversity of meanings. An 1881 newspaper article referred to it as a traditional dance, and in 1932, Katherine Dunham saw a couple-dance by that name (Gerstin 2004, 8, 14). Most commonly, however, Trinidadian kalinda has been known as a song, in French creole and/or English, with drumming, accompanying stick fighting. In 1962, Alan Lomax recorded several such songs (including the chestnut "Fire Brigade, Water de Road") in Maraval and other sites; these items represent a drumming and song repertoire that has dwindled dramatically, although a few songs are still performed—led by a chantwell singing in French creole—at stick fights during Carnival. Kalinda could also be performed solely as a drumming item, as in the item recorded by Cook in 1956.[45]

Kalinda is also a traditional tassa hand. Since the term "kalinda" is no longer familiar in Afro-creole musical discourse, it is perhaps not surprising that tassa drummers (at least, in my own experience) tend not to know its origin. It might seem logical to assume that the hand derived, in some fashion and at some point, from Afro-creole drumming. Nevertheless, the tassa kalinda—a duple composite rhythm with a fast triplet feel—does not closely resemble the most common Afro-creole kalinda, which, as played today and as recorded by Lomax, is a simple, nondescript beat in straight fours. A possible source for the tassa hand may be a tradition represented by a kalinda recorded by Emory Cook in Port of Spain, in which one drum reiterates a fast ♪♪♪♪♪♪ ostinato over which a second drum plays fast (conflicting) triplet rolls (and a third drum improvises). A tassa kalinda recorded by Lomax in 1962 could be seen as a variant of this rhythm, combining cutter patterns in fast triplets with a decelerated (and thus more compatible) version of the bass pattern: ♩♪♪♩♪♪. Modern tassa drumming more commonly features a brisk version of the creole "habanera"-style bass pattern: ♩♪♪♩♪.♪♪. , over which the cutter plays triplet-based "prattlin'" patterns.

It is interesting that the kalinda hand retains an association with "fighting" even for tassa drummers unfamiliar with the Afro-creole stick-fighting rhythm. Hence, kalinda is often used to enliven fight scenes in Ramdilla (Ramlila) theater.

Rag Bhajan

Rag bhajan is a "technical" and "classical" hand, played only by more knowledgeable drummers. Its somewhat inscrutable name is redolent of the sort of idiosyncratic jumbling of terms that one encounters in Indo-Caribbean local-classical and vernacular North Indian music. Its prominent bass (and duplicating jhāl) pattern is reminiscent of wedding hand, while its jerky cutter theka is unique. Since there is no local-classical song-type called "rag bhajan," and

Example 21. Rag bhajan.

the tassa hand does not resemble any particular local-classical or folk rhythm, the derivations of both name and rhythms are obscure. While rag bhajan has no barti, it has a particularly distinctive tāl, whose essence corresponds to a simple Hindustani tihāī, which is otherwise rare in tassa drumming and in Indo-Caribbean music as a whole. However, by North Indian standards, the cadential closure of this tāl is idiosyncratically ruptured by adding another loud cutter beat immediately after what should be the final stroke; then, after a flexible pause during which the pulse is interrupted, the basic pattern resumes. The tāl may also be played at a somewhat slower tempo than the theka, as suggested in example 21. As with other classical hands, the tāl is played three times in all, each time ending a passage of cutting. Although confounding by North Indian standards, the mannerism of adding an accented beat after the conclusion of a tihāī resembles the barti commencement of the Trinidadian local-classical thumri, and, more generally, the way local-classical drummers typically add a few desultory strokes after the conclusion of a song, as if an engine were sputtering and knocking before shutting down. It is as if the form of a tihāī were incompletely transmitted to the Caribbean, without its metrical logic. As

a result, the tihāī pattern acquired a new sort of musical logic. Example 21, adapted from a demonstration by Sunil Mathura and Mukesh Ragoo, schematizes some typical basic patterns, leading to the tāl at bar 11.

Khemta

Khemta is a venerable meter in North Indian vernacular drumming, and, by extension, in Trinidadian local-classical music. In the latter genre, its distinctive feature is its "limping" beat, which as described above, also characterizes the barti of chaubola and khañjri-gīt Kabir bhajan. The most common khemta of tassa drumming replicates this form in a manner similar to the barti of chaubola, as shown in example 10 above. Khemta, however, has its own barti, which roughly resembles dingolay. Khemta's ideal performance occasion is during a wedding, when the bride is given a bracelet to try on.

Chaiti, Holi, and Bihāg

In Trinidadian local-classical music, bihāg, holi (hori), and chaiti are three song-types with similar rhythmic structures; in each, the verses (or *pads*) are sung in up-tempo 14/8 or 7/8 (here called dīpchandi), segueing thence to a standard barti in duple meter, and ending with a short reprise of the ṭek in dīpchandi. Bihāg is the most common of the three; holi generally consists of the standard Hindustani Kafi holi (hori) tune, which has been familiar in various North Indian contexts since the mid-1800s. Its popularity in the Caribbean may have

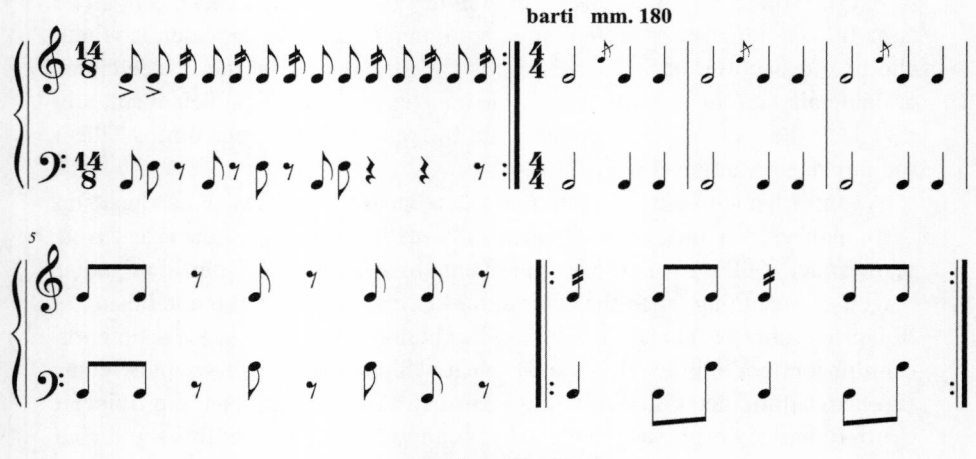

Example 22. Chaiti.

been reinforced by a 1930s recording by K. L. Saigal (see Manuel 2000a, 164). Chaiti (another seasonal Bhojpuri region folk song form) is more obscure but would be sung in the same form. The Caribbean forms, like their North Indian counterparts, segue to barti sections in duple meter and then reprise to the original theka. In Trinidad tassa music, chaiti and holi constitute obscure and seldom-heard "classical" hands, consisting of relatively literal adaptations from the song-types; thus, for example, the barti commences with the standard figure of quarter-eighth-eighth-quarter-eighth-eighth before gathering steam and accelerating. However, in the process of this adaptation, aside from acquiring bass drum parts, these rhythms also underwent some idiosyncratic alterations; most notably, while chaiti segues directly to the barti section, holi features a tāl—consisting of an accented, stripped-down theka pattern—before that segue.[46]

Tillāna, Mārfat, and Durpat (Dhrupad)

The tillāna and thumri of tassa drumming can be regarded as idiosyncratic adaptations of local-classical song types that are themselves idiosyncratic versions of North Indian genres. In South Indian classical music, tillāna is a song genre for dance accompaniment, distinguished by the nonlexical (or choreographic) syllables comprising its text. In North Indian music, the corresponding genre is "tarāna," but before the modern period that term was used interchangeably with "tillāna," including in the nautanki chapbooks that made their way to the Caribbean. In local-classical music, tillāna came to constitute a subgenre with a distinctive, unsyncopated quadratic dholak rhythm, and melodies most typically consisting of the standard Kafi melody in tīntāl, such as abounded in North India during the nineteenth century (see Manuel 2000a, 164). The tassa tillāna, however, is quite unique, with two distinct theka patterns, which alternate in sections of a few bars each. Then the second of these accelerates dramatically before segueing via a tāl to an even faster barti (which eventually reverts to the theka). Sunil Mathura and Mukesh Ragoo demonstrated tillāna roughly as in example 23.

A somewhat similar though more obscure hand is "mārfat," which bears no particular resemblance to the Trinidad thumri form of that name (for which see Manuel 2000a, 151). Mathura explains that traditionally, mārfat might be played at a wedding when the bride's mother first emerges from the house.

Durpat (dhrupad) hand, like tillāna and thumri hands, is a loose adaptation from its namesake in local-classical music which appears to have evolved as an idiosyncratic derivative of temple dhrupad singing traditions in provincial North Indian towns. I was unable to hear consistent versions of this somewhat obscure tassa hand.

Example 23. Tillāna.

Thumri

Thumri is perhaps the single most basic and common subgenre of Trinidad local-classical music. It has a particularly distinctive and structured form, with dholak thekas and tāls marking a conventional series of verses and refrains (*pad* and ṭek), segueing via a tihāī-like tāl to a barti, and ending with a reprise of the ṭek and theka pattern. The transition to the barti involves a rupturing of the quadratic meter via an "extra" beat that is also included in some tassa thumri renditions, as notated in example 24 with a one-beat bar.[47] The tassa thumri, as an instrumental idiom, is unable to reproduce the vocal lines central to the local-classical thumri form, but it very loosely approximates the thumri theka and then segues to a standard barti, like that of chaiti shown above. As befits a loose adaptation, the thumri basic pattern is heard in variant forms; some cutter men play it more or less like a medium-tempo nagāra hand and many omit the "extra" note prefacing the barti; the style shown below is that demonstrated by Sunil Mathura. Thumri, like such hands as Kabir bhajan, has no particular contextual association, though it might be played in the course of a wedding.

Madrasi Hand

The ranks of indentured immigrants, especially in the mid-1800s, included many thousands of workers from villages in Madras presidency (state) in South India who brought their own religious and musical traditions. Due to their smaller numbers and the natural pressures to assimilate to both Bhojpuri and

Example 24. Thumri: transition to barti.

creole English cultures, the "Madrasis" (a general North Indian term for South Indians) were unable to maintain either their secular music traditions or the Tamil language. However, various factors have enabled their core religious practices to survive and even thrive, in a modified form. At the heart of these is veneration of the goddess Mariamman, whose worship in the Caribbean may overlap with that of the more mainstream North Indian goddess Kali. If Bhojpuri-derived Indo-Caribbean Hindu forms have been considerably influenced by mainstream North Indian Sanatan Dharm over the course of the last century, Indo-Caribbean Mariamman/Kali has persisted in much greater isolation from in subcontinental counterpart. As a result, it has retained the earthy and unpretentious character of the lower-class rural cult that it was in the mid-nineteenth century. Its religious services, whether in village Guyana or Queens, New York, often involve goat sacrifice, vigorous playing of *ṭappū* frame drums, and animated spirit possession. While many mainstream Sanatanist Hindus disparage the sect, it appeals to those Hindus who, like Shouter Baptists or Pentecostalists, enjoy intensity and fervor in their religious ceremonies, especially in contrast to Sanatanist services, with their lengthy sermons followed by amateur renditions of filmi bhajans.

Since the corps of ṭappu drummers have long included semiprofessional dholak and tassa drummers, it is not surprising that the most characteristic ṭappū rhythm was adapted as a tassa hand. On the ṭappu, this beat is a jerky, tense, and kinetically driving ostinato with interlocking strokes played by a thin stick held in the left hand and a thicker one in the right. When played by

Example 25. Madrasi hand.

a tassa group, the cutter approximates the ṭappu parts, while the bass provides a simple accompanying pattern, effectively rounding off the asymmetrical ṭappu ostinato to a familiar quadratic beat, as shown in example 25. The hand may accelerate and accommodate diverse variations, though it has no barti. More precise notation would be required to indicate how the basic pattern has a distinct feel from that of nagāra.

Hosay Hands

As discussed above, Hosay (Muharram) has been a seminal context for tassa drumming in Trinidad, and its rhythms may have constituted significant models for other hands played at secular events. The distinctive Hosay repertoire is generally seen as comprising five or six hands, each with particular extramusical associations, which are not, however, entirely standardized. Korom (2003, 167) gives two alternate listings:

First consensus	*Second consensus*
kabulkhāna: the marching hand or drum of peace	*tīn chopra*: peace hand
mahātam: the war hand	*kabulkhāna*: marching/fine hand
nabi sarbat: the burial hand	*mahātam*: war hand
tīn chopra: the sorrow hand	*chalta kabulkhāna*: burial/dead hand
chalta kabulkhāna: walking kabulkhāna	*nabi sarbat*: lamentation hand

The hands themselves, like their supposed affective qualities, are not standardized. My own informants did not distinguish kabulkhāna and chalta kabulkhāna. Some groups play Hosay tikora, associated with the preparation for battle, and a rhythm called "country Hosay," representing the victory celebration of Yazid's men. In practice, most Hosay drumming consists of tīn chopra, mahātam, nabi sarbat, and Hosay tikora, which are played in succession—perhaps enlivened by an occasional dingolay—by the various groups as they

process slowly down the main thoroughfare in St. James, and, on the final day, on the road to Queens Royal College. In this context, their supposed specific extramusical emotive associations may not be operant for most listeners and players. Such associations are more overt in the case of the lugubrious chalta kabulkhāna, which is played only at the end of the commemoration, as the tazias are wheeled toward the sea to be dismantled and immersed. After that, the event becomes relaxed and upbeat, and the drummers play unabashedly festive hands.

One drummer, who performed for Cocorite yard, described to me the playing for that procession:

> We proceed down the flyover from Cocorite to reach the Western Main Road in St. James. There's a special hand we play when we reach the road. Then the rest is mostly four hands: Hosay tikora, which is a slow hand when you're preparing for war; mahātam, when you're trotting, going to war; then there's nabi sarbat, where the war is going on and the moons [large crescents affixed to a pole] are dancing, and tīn chopra, when you defeat the other side. Only at the end you play kabulkhana, and we play country Hosay, a fast celebration beat for the side that wins, celebrating the deaths, even though it's a sad thing.

Drummer Sunil Mathura laughed when I asked, "During the main processions, would you ever play something festive like dingolay?" Bass player Mukesh Ragoo explained, "Well, some people might object, but you see, the Hosay is such a long thing, that's why you change hands, otherwise it would be boring, so you can spice it up a little so people don't get bored. But mostly it's those four hands."

Hosay drumming differs from that in typical contexts: the ensemble may include many more players than the standard quartet. Many individuals who are not professional or fully experienced drummers may turn out to play bass, jhāl, or foulay in the procession of the yard with which they are affiliated. As such, an ensemble might easily include eight or more bass drummers and as many foulay players. Experienced core players within the yard, however, would take turns cutting and leading the group. The large ensembles perpetuate North Indian traditions, as described, for example, by Sharar in relation to nawabi Lucknow (1975, 151).

Tīn Chopra

Tīn chopra is a particularly distinctive rhythm. It bears striking similarities to wedding hand and is most likely the source for that rhythm. Drummers variously define "chopra" as meaning "beat" or hand" and tend to agree that the term

"tīn chopra" implies "three beats." However, as with other vernacular music terms suggesting formal features, such as "chowtal" and "chaubola," there is no clear relation between the name and the rhythm it designates. (Some of my informants referred to the hand as "tīn chopa.")

Tīn chopra can be regarded as having a basic pattern or theka, over which the cutter improvises, and which is punctuated by an extended tāl. Both patterns are essentially articulated by the bass drum(s), which thus plays an especially prominent role in this hand. The theka can be regarded as being in seven beats, although it does not have a strong sense of a downbeat, such that my place-ment of bar lines in example 26 (hearing the first bass stroke as an anacrusis to the second) is quite arbitrary. My attempts to ask tassa drummers about their interpretation of this pattern were largely fruitless, both because they do not articulate such analytical concepts and, more important, I suspect, precisely because this pattern lacks a clear sense of downbeat. It thus contrasts markedly with Indian classical tāls, with their stressed first beat or *sam*. This ambiguity was corroborated by Jason Nandoo, one of the very few tassa players who is conversant with theoretical concepts, being a skilled tabla player well versed in Hindustani tāl theory. Nandoo, in response to my questioning, opined that the downbeat could be heard as falling on the first bass stroke but that it could also be heard as falling as I have notated it.

During this theka ostinato, the cutter player "cuts," that is, improvises. Typi-cally, while the bass drum is beating, he plays "swung" eighth notes (that is, with a triplet feel), like the foulay, and then plays more prominent improvised patterns during the rests. These often consist of flams, prattlin' rolls, and other patterns, which may build sequentially on the patterns played during previous rest sections. After an indeterminate amount of cutting, he signals the basses by looking at the lead bass player and whacking several quarter-note beats dur-ing the rests, either in flams, or perhaps with one hand, while ostentatiously raising the other hand. The subsequent tāl, as shown in example 27, consists of a five-beat pattern, followed by a pause of five, six, or seven beats, played twice, followed by a nine-beat pattern played twice, followed by a reiteration of the first pattern, with its flexible number of subsequent rests. After the tāl the theka resumes. These irregular beat counts of the tāl further confound any sense of metricity or downbeat. Throughout the entire hand the foulays play slightly swung eighth notes.

Tīn chopra is played by the group as it stands before the tazia or as the en-tire unit progresses slowly down the street. Due to the participation of several bass drummers and the indeterminate length of the pause in the tāl, entrance of the basses may be occasionally ragged. The hand may continue for an ex-tended period, during which different tassa drummers may take turns cutting.

Example 26. Tîn chopra theka: bass pattern.

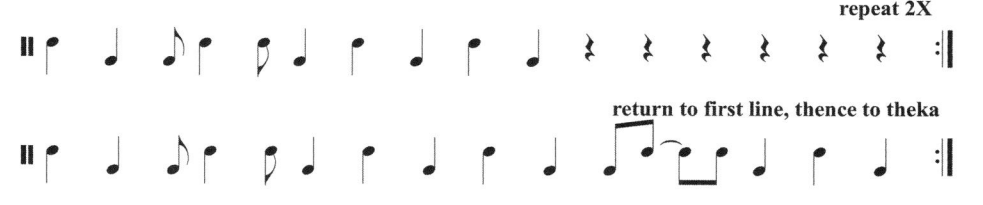

Example 27. Tîn chopra tāl: bass pattern.

When they shift—again by a visual cue from the current cutter—there may be a leisurely transition during which the basses are silent and only the tassa and jhāls are heard.

Both by North Indian classical standards and compared with other tassa hands, tīn chopra—along with its probable descendant, wedding hand—is unique and even enigmatic. Unlike such hands as dingolay, nagāra, and steelpan, tīn chopra lacks a simple, driving rhythm; in fact, it lacks even a clear downbeat. Nevertheless, like wedding hand, it has a distinctive appeal, and drummers enjoy it for the cutting opportunities it presents.

Tīn chopra's unique structure—so unlike the folksy grooves of vernacular drumming—strongly suggests an equally unique and idiosyncratic origin wholly independent of the quadratic or seven-beat rhythms of the Bhojpuri region. Richard Wolf, in his research with North Indian tassa drummers in the Delhi region, and with their descendants in Pakistan, has documented rhythmic practices so strikingly similar that they and Caribbean tīn chopra (and wedding hand) must indubitably be assumed to derive from a common North Indian source—with the South Asians being closer to the original model. Wolf has described some of the relevant Muharram tassa traditions in an informative 2000 article and in his thorough monograph (2014), and shared with me further materials, including video footage of Pakistani drummers in Hyderabad descended from *mohājirs* who emigrated to there from the Bharatpur area (near Agra) during Partition. Most of these players were not professional tassa drummers but rather were amateurs who played tassa solely during Muharram commemorations.[48]

The drummers filmed by Wolf, like most other South Asian tassa players, hold their *chobs* in the distinctive South Asian grip and play military-style bass drums with flimsy plastic heads. In other respects, some of their Hosay drumming bears remarkable resemblance to that in Trinidad. Like "tīn chopra," the names used by the Hyderabadi and Delhi drummers for their distinctive rhythms refer to specific formal features, whether these are clearly recognizable in playing or not. These names include "*N ki ginti*" ("N counts") and "*N ka mātam*" ("N laments")—for example, "*das ki ginti*" (ten counts) and "*tīn ka mātam*" (three laments, or a lament of three).

Of particular interest are rhythmic sequences in which a Muharram tassa ensemble commences with the supporting tassa drummers (the counterparts to Caribbean foulay players) playing swung or slightly swung eighth notes, while the lead drummer (the "cutter") improvises, playing buzz rolls and other patterns, with the ensemble sounding like the bass-free transitions played by Trinidadian tassa and jhāl players. Then the basses enter, playing an asymmetrical pattern: ♩♩♩♩♩♩♩♩♩♩ followed by several—typically seven—quarter rests; the pattern, with rests, may be repeated a few times and then can be repeated again, but with a longer bass pause—around nineteen or twenty beats; this entire set is repeated a few times, during which the supporting tassas and lead tassa continue their patterns. The bass drum strokes, in accordance with what might seem to be their want of musical or expressive logic, in fact are understood by knowledgeable drummers to be an articulation of a lexical text, specifically, the first half of the *kalma*, that is, "La ilaha illa Allah . . ."—"There is no god but Allah." In different cities, ḍhol patterns may in fact articulate a variety of diverse textual phrases (Wolf 2000: 100–101, 111). Wolf relates that some drummers in other ensembles play similar patterns without knowing their lexical significance or origin.

There need be little doubt that this sort of rhythm, or its nineteenth-century antecedent, is the source for the Caribbean tīn chopra. In the Caribbean, the lexical meaning of the bass drum strokes was definitively forgotten, and the rhythms came to be cultivated for their own purely musical expressivity, in a process suggested by Korom (1994). The bass pattern changed somewhat, and slightly new conventions of pausing and resuming developed, but in other respects the basic format remained the same. As I shall suggest, this format came to be perpetuated in wedding hand. The evolutionary link to wedding hand can be said to be represented by the rhythm called "wedding tīn chopra," which differs from Hosay tīn chopra in having four distinct tāls instead of one. As Wolf discusses, and as I explored in an early article on semiclassical tabla playing (1983), such rhythms constitute a form of meter defined by a particular

series of strokes rather than a consistent mātra count. The persistence of these particular patterns in Trinidad also strongly suggests that the drummers who introduced them to the island came not from the Bhojpuri heartland but from the Delhi-Agra region to the west.

Nabi Sarbat

The name "nabi sarbat" is as etymologically obscure as those of the other Hosay hands; "nabi" means "prophet " (Mohammad), and "sarbat" is cognate with "sherbet," the sweet dessert or juice. Drummer Raiaz Ali interprets the term as meaning "sweet water."[49]

Nabi sarbat is perhaps the only tassa hand in clear triple meter. In accordance with the length of its bass ostinato, I have notated it in 6/4 in example 28, although the proper placement of bar lines is somewhat ambiguous, as one might alternately choose to hear this notation's fourth beat as the downbeat. As with tīn chopra, less important than a sense of downbeat is the recurring bass ostinato that defines the hand. Other structural similarities with tīn chopra may be noted. During the extended theka sections, the cutter-man improvises, primarily by filling in the quarter-note rest and its adjacent beats with sequentially structured flams and rolls. Eventually, he signals a tāl, primarily by visually cueing a lead bass drummer. The tāl could be said to resemble a simple Hindustani tihāī in consisting of a threefold repetition of the original bass pattern. Throughout, the foulays either play more or less straight eighth notes or (by eliding the fourth and sixth beats) duplicate the bass pattern. As in tīn chopra, however, the foulay pattern can exhibit some microrhythmic distension, sounding somewhere between straight and swung eighths. Drummer Lakiram Bhagan states that in this hand, the foulay and bass are in fact harder and more important than the cutter (p.c.).

Example 28. Nabi sarbat: bass theka pattern and tāl.

Mahātam

The third common processional Hosay hand is mahātam. "Mahātam" would appear to be a corruption of the Urdu "mātam," or, more specifically, the Arabic root word "mā'tam," which denotes various forms of mourning (including chanted poetry) in which Shias indulge during Muharram. A slower, and less common variant of this rhythm is "sada mahātam."[50] Despite the meaning of "mātam," this hand is associated not with lamentation but rather with marching, or with battle, and its character is lively rather than lugubrious (as is, for that matter, the eponymous breast-beating associated with South Asian *nauhā* chanting). Mahātam, indeed, sounds much like the festive steeldrum hand, with the most prominent difference being its foulay pattern. Example 29 shows what could be regarded as a typical theka of bass and cutter; when played at a more moderate tempo, the rhythms can be slightly swung, that is, in triplet syncopation.

In mahātam, the cutter-man improvises extensively within the conventional patterns of this hand. Particularly common are sequences wherein a given pattern is subjected to diminution, as schematized in example 30.

Example 29. Mahātam theka.

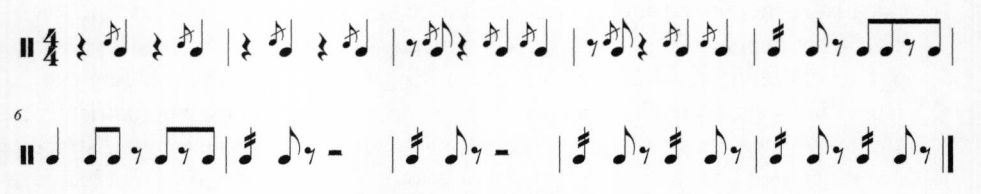

Example 30. Mahātam: typical cutter patterns.

Kabulkhana, Kabarkhana, Chalta Kabulkana

Kabulkhana (kabulkana, kabarkhana) is a dolorous funereal hand played while the tazias are being symbolically "buried" and later taken to the seashore, dismantled, and dragged into the water. Although often pronounced "kabulkana," some drummers call the hand "kabarkhana," which would more correctly indicate the term's likely etymology, from *qabr* + *khāna*, "burial place." Similarly, some drummers evidently distinguish a hand "chalta kabulkhana," but those with whom I worked play only one hand, kabulkhana. It is not a vehicle for showy cutting. Its iconic feature is the bass pattern: ♩♩|♩♩♩♩|♩♩♩♩|♩♩♩♩♩|♩. Chalta kabulkhana might also be played at a Muslim funeral.

Wedding Hand

Wedding hand is, by any standards, a remarkable rhythmic entity. It is a common and basic hand, being played regularly at Hindu Trinidadian weddings and, increasingly, at Muslim weddings and at Guyanese weddings in New York. At the same time, its structure, even more so than that of the tīn chopra from which it derives, is recondite, complex, and resistant to any sort of conventional metrical analysis, incorporating, as it does, segments of variable and asymmetrical beat counts, which lack clear sense of downbeat, and which may proceed in a variety of alternative directions according to the players' predilections. Analysis is further confounded by the relative absence of consistent terminology for the sections or practices, not to mention the inability of tassa drummers (with very few exceptions) to enumerate beats or identify downbeats. Wedding hand's evident evolution from tīn chopra also illustrates how an idiosyncratic rhythm based on a lexical pattern can shed that verbal dimension and evolve into a purely musical entity that has a unique charm, sophistication, and appeal to listeners and drummers.

Wedding hand may be played at various points during the Sunday nuptials. The initial and most essential occasion is during the arrival of the barāt at the wedding site (either the bride's family home, a temple, or other suitable venue). Ideally, as mentioned above, both families have their own tassa bands, and the two groups engage in a friendly jassle, typically playing wedding hand together for several minutes while the barāt and other guests file into the wedding site. Sometimes, the two bands will play with a common basic pulse, but metrically out of sync, perhaps hoping to confuse each other.[51] (This jassle is thus distinct from that in which two bands trade hands, or play completely different hands at close quarters.) After the arrival of the barāt—with the agwāni in which the bride's family walks out to greet that of the groom—the tassa drummers gen-

erally "lime" for several hours by the street, but during breaks in the rituals they might be called to play for a few minutes, when they might again play wedding hand. (At the conclusion of the wedding, they would also play, but more festive hands suitable for dancing.)

Wedding hand is best regarded as constituting a somewhat flexible sequence or "set" (as Jason Nandoo calls it) of modular patterns. Some musicians have names for some of these patterns, although these names are not used entirely consistently. Some players designate certain parts as belonging to wedding hand per se, and other parts to "lāwā"—i.e., rhythms originally played during the ritual cooking of puffed rice. Some parts might be referred to as "theka" (indefinitely repeating ostinatos) and others as tāls (cadential patterns punctuating theka sections). However, if the "theka" sections are short and the "tāls" long, the distinction becomes far from clear. Finally, some prominent sections have no particular or consistent names, obliging the analyst to invent section names for convenience, as I have done with the rather colloquial-sounding onomatopoeic terms "baDOOM" and "bah-doom." The following description combines my own idiosyncratic terms and approaches with those used variously by Amidh Mohammad and Jason Nandoo. I make no attempt to describe the somewhat different forms of wedding hand that may be encountered in south Trinidad, for example, by such well-known groups as Country Boys and Fun Lovers.[52] Rather, this description applies only to the more "mainstream" wedding hand of central and north Trinidad.

The similarities between wedding hand and tīn chopra are striking. In both, the bass drum pattern essentially defines the distinct sections of the rhythm, and the bass player may also introduce certain variants. Both hands—although especially wedding hand—offer considerable scope for cutting. Both hands are based on a slightly swung rhythm, whose basic steady eighth-note pulse—somewhere between swung triplet and straight eighths—is perpetually hammered out by the foulay and often, in an embellished form, by the cutter as well. A prominent and key section of wedding hand, which I refer to here as "wedding hand tāl," is essentially identical to the tāl of tīn chopra. The primary difference between the two hands is that while tīn chopra essentially alternates between theka and extended tāl sections, wedding hand features several additional sections. As I suggested, the practice of playing a variant of tīn chopra, called "wedding tīn chopra," at weddings could have provided a further evolutionary link between these hands. Presumably, tīn chopra, as a ceremonious, processional hand not associated with dance, or with lamentation or war, came to be performed at weddings—especially during the arrival of the barāt—and then was elaborated over the generations into wedding hand with the addition of new sections. In accordance with the relatively recent recontextualization and

development of the hand, it was given an English name rather than a Hindi (or Afro-creole) one.

Keeping in mind that my nomenclature and analysis are in some ways idiosyncratic, a conventional wedding hand "set" may be regarded as comprising the following sequence, which includes a specific rhythm called "wedding hand":

1. Wedding hand (without bass): cutter improvises, with foulay and jhāl accompaniment, while bass player is silent, awaiting the cutter signal to enter;
2. Wedding hand tāl: essentially identical to tīn chopra tāl, featuring an eight-beat bass pattern and a pause of five, six, or seven beats, played twice, followed by a similar seven-beat bass pattern played twice, segueing to the eight-beat pattern and pause; alternately, wedding hand tāl #2 (whose initial bass pattern consists of the nine-beat pattern otherwise used in the baDOOM intro) may be played instead;
3. The "baDOOM" pattern, featuring an eight-beat introductory bass pattern played thrice, leading to a quadratic, theka-like section, whose rhythm could be articulated as "baDOOM, baDOOM, baDOOM, baDOOM" and so on, segueing after a few bars to an exit pattern;
4. Lāwa tāl, featuring the same eight-beat pattern as the wedding hand tāl, but with only two quarter-note rests (making a ten-beat pattern), usually played thrice;
5. The quadratic "bah-doom" pattern, featuring the bass in quarter-notes, roughly as: bah-/doom-rest-rest-bah-/doom-rest-rest-bah-/doom;
6. Lāwa tāl.

At this point a few alternatives are possible, especially the following:

- repeat the entire set, starting with a return to wedding hand (without bass);
- baDOOM and lāwa tāl (again), and then repeat the entire set with a return to wedding hand (without bass);
- lāwa theka (a ten-beat bass pattern), and then lāwa tāl;
- repeat all, but with wedding tāl #2.

Eventually, these patterns segue to a final duple-metered section, featuring a nagāra-like bass pattern (quarter, eighth-eighth, quarter, and so on) combined with steelpan-like cutting.

These patterns are schematized in examples 31–36. I refrain from introducing bar lines in some patterns whose sense of downbeat is conspicuously lacking. Tempo throughout is MM ca. 170. Note that wedding tāl, the lāwa tāl, and the baDOOM introduction contain thrice-repeated phrases that are akin to Hindustani tihāīs, although followed by further sections that disrupt a regular meter.

Example 31. Wedding hand tāl.

Example 32. Wedding hand tāl #2.

Example 33. BaDOOM pattern.

Example 34. Lāwa tāl.

Example 35. Bah-doom theka.

Example 36. Lāwa theka.

Newly Invented Hands

As mentioned, several tassa groups have invented their own hands, especially for competitions that call for such innovations. Some of these might consist of whimsical renderings of rhythms derived from familiar songs. While the Punjabi bhangra rhythm has not pervaded tassa music in Trinidad to the extent it has in India, a few groups do perform their versions of this infectious beat. The few groups that have recorded CDs generally showcase their inventions, such as "Countryboys Mix" and "Cool Down" (Country Boys); "Culture Mix" (Petrotrin Boodoosingh); and "We Own Ting" (Fun Lovers). Tassa drummers balance their solid grounding in tradition with a healthy spirit of innovation and eclecticism. Lenny Kumar's approach is representative:

> I can play thirty-two different traditional beats (hands) that my father taught me, and then I have four new ones I made, including chutney, bhangra, and one from "George of the Jungle." I use them at special times to entertain people, and I have a few beats from the African side that I pick up from hearing djembe and all, because I'm an entertainer. People must enjoy what you do, and I may have a mixed crowd with Africans, so I play things for them too. Like any music I hear, if I hear something on the radio, I sit down and start to work with it, I will start to work with my part as the cutter, then I will formulate a bass line, then the cymbals. I pull the band together. Like samba and all that, I put that on tassa.

Naturally, it is difficult for new inventions and adaptations to enter the main-stream repertoire, although versions of bhangra and "chutney soca" are increasingly heard. However, to enjoy the status and appeal of a genuine hand, such rhythms must comprise not only catchy basic theka patterns but also a distinctive repertoire of tāls and cuts. The same principle, indeed, applies to all tassa hands that are inspired by other song forms, whether Madrasi chants, Kabir bhajans, or the thumri and tillana of local-classical music. A tassa adaptation of such a subgenre cannot in any form render the melody or text, which may constitute structural elements in the original genre. Instead, iconic features of the rhythmic accompaniment are loosely adapted, in stylized form, and then, in a typically invisible and gradual oral-tradition process, they are supplemented with various characteristic cutting patterns that may have no particular roots in the original genre, but which then become conventional.

Syncretism and Creolization

Much scholarly discussion has been devoted to the question of the degree and extent to which Indo-Caribbean culture has been creolized, whether in the restrictive sense of incorporating elements of Afro-creole culture, or in the

broader sense of exhibiting a general, quintessentially Caribbean openness and flexibility. In the next chapter I shall discuss these questions and their often contentious sociopolitical ramifications in relation to tassa and the other musics considered in this volume; at this point I wish to bypass such considerations and look more specifically at tassa drumming in terms of its relation to Afro-creole music.

There is no denying that Trinidadian "tassa culture" exhibits certain sorts of Afro-creole influence and inspiration. An obvious example of such influence can be found in the formal competitions that have enlivened the tassa scene from the 1980s. The immediate predecessors and models for these were the other Indo-Trinidadian music competitions, especially in chowtal and local-classical music and the vast Mastana Bahar pageant. However, these themselves—as Moean Mohammad assured me in reference to Mastana Bahar—were originally modeled on the island's renowned calypso and steelband competitions.

Another overtly Afro-creole element in the tassa scene is the presence of Afro-Trinidadian drummers. To be sure, none of these have attained particular prominence, and their numbers remain few, but they have been visible enough—especially at Hosay—that their presence raises no eyebrows. Meanwhile, Afro-Trinidadians do not hesitate to "jump up" at occasions where they encounter tassa drumming, and tassa groups are routinely booked for a wide variety of events—whether a shopping mall opening or a credit union banquet—that are attended by the general, ethnically mixed public rather than primarily Indians.

In the realm of tassa music itself, drummers pride themselves on their eclectic ability to incorporate inspiration from diverse sources, including local Afro-creole music. Lenny Kumar, for instance, was quoted above regarding his innovative adaptations of elements of samba and "African" rhythms that he might have occasion to hear. Such eclecticism, as I discuss in the next chapter, may be celebrated by certain cultural and political activists and spokespersons who wish to claim a certain distinctively local status for tassa and Indian culture in general vis-à-vis Trinidadian national culture. In the present discussion I seek to look as dispassionately as possible at tassa drumming itself and assess the nature and extent of its incorporation of Afro-creole elements. In brief, I advance the viewpoint—however popular or unpopular it may be in certain circles—that tassa drumming remains fundamentally Indian in character and that its debt to Afro-creole music is relatively minor.

An initial and obvious point to be made is that the rhythmic vigor and kinetic intensity of tassa drumming need not be attributed to Afro-Caribbean influence. One occasionally encounters the uninformed notion that any "hot" drumming in the Americas must be animated by African roots. Alan Lomax, for example, while recording tassa groups in 1962, made an offhand remark to the effect that the evident "hotness" of the drumming should surely be at-

tributed to Afro-Trinidadian influence, as exhibited by the presence of a few black tassa drummers he saw. If the notion of "hot" drumming implies fast, loud, ostinato-based percussion ensemble music designed to generate excitement and somatic drive, then it should scarcely need to be pointed out that India itself has no shortage of such music. Aside from the pyrotechnics of Hindustani tabla music, examples from regional musics would include Punjabi ḍhol music, Keralan *chenda* drumming, and, in the Bhojpuri region, nagāra and tassa drumming (such as can be heard in Manuel, *Tassa Thunder*). Africa and Afro-America by no means enjoy global monopolies on hot drum music traditions or even on music that is primarily rhythmic in orientation.

Second, as suggested earlier, one should not assume that the organological similarity of a tassa band to Afro-Caribbean drum ensembles indicates influence of the latter on the former. The tassa band, with its three drums and idiophone, does indeed resemble a standard format of neo-African musics found throughout the Caribbean in, for example, ensembles of Cuban rumba and *batá* music, Carriacou "big drum," and Jamaican kumina music. However, it should be noted that the three-drum-plus-idiophone format is also familiar in Bhojpuri traditional music, especially nagāra and tassa drumming. While the resemblance of these traditions is in some respects coincidental, the format can also be said to have its own musical logic, with a relatively high-pitched lead drum accompanied by two timbrally distinct drums and a metal (or wooden, in the case of the Cuban *clave*) idiophone, whose sharp, staccato tone cuts through the ensemble sound and serves a time-keeping function.

The most obvious possible evidence for black input in tassa music comprises the various terms of Afro-Caribbean origin, notably for the foulay drum, and the dingolay, kalinda, and steelpan hands. The word "foulay," as discussed above, appears to be of West African origin, presumably entering the Trinidad vernacular lexicon via the Afro-French-creole connection and converging with the English "fuller." Of greater possible importance than such lexical creolizations is the extent to which mainstream tassa hands have incorporated or been inspired by Afro-creole music, as would certainly be suggested by the names dingolay, kalinda, and steelpan. I would contend that while these rhythms are certainly compatible with Afro-Trinidadian rhythms, such as they exist, they are equally compatible with traditional North Indian folk rhythms and need not be regarded as borrowings from external music traditions. To examine these rhythms individually, a few points should be noted or reiterated. The dingolay tassa hand, to start with, is a festive, "breakaway" rhythm that does not appear to derive *directly* from any particular Indian (or Afro-creole) source, such as Kabir bhajans or tillana. However, it may not derive directly from any particular Afro-Trinidadian rhythm either. There is no Afro-creole

rhythm named "dingolay." Further, there is nothing in the form of dingolay that is uncharacteristic of North Indian vernacular drumming, and some of its specific patterns—including what I have presented as "tal #2" in example 17 above—can be assumed to derive directly from Bhojpuri-region nagāra music. Such evidence strongly suggests that drummers developed dingolay as a lively, dance-oriented hand, with much scope for flashy cutting, and came to call it "dingolay" in accordance with its festive character, rather than to denote any particular rhythmic features borrowed from black music.

A somewhat stronger case for Afro-creole inspiration could be made for the kalinda hand, which might have some relation to the traditional Trinidadian stick-fighting rhythm by that name, even if its current form does not resemble the tassa hand. As mentioned, while Afro-creole music might have constituted a sort of source for the "habanera"-type bass, that pattern is not uncharacteristic of North Indian drumming and can be seen as a variant of the 3–3–2 syncopation quite common in Indian folk drumming (especially the rhythm denoted as kaharva in light music).

Finally, there is the question of Afro-creole inspiration for the steelpan hand. Such inspiration might seem self-evident, given the hand's name and the opinion, easily solicited from tassa drummers, that the rhythm must have been adapted from steeldrum music. Further, the steeldrum hand, like kalinda, exhibits the familiar creole "habanera" bass pattern. However, it is very difficult to find evidence for further and more substantial creole influence. As mentioned above, there has never been any single distinctive steelband rhythm; rather, the steelband repertoire has traditionally consisted of arrangements, whether simple or intricate, of popular current calypsos (or, nowadays, soca songs). These vary in rhythm and tune; insofar as one can identify typical rhythmic features, the most prominent such pattern would be what Cubans call the *cinquillo* (x-xx-xx-), which enjoys no special prominence in the steelband hand of tassa. As with kalinda and dingolay, there is nothing in the steelband hand that is particularly uncharacteristic of North Indian folk drumming. Again, it seems most likely that the steelpan hand was developed by drummers interested in exploiting a particular syncopated, rollicking fast beat with the "habanera" bass they recognized as a feature of Caribbean creole music. Since the rhythm bore no special resemblance to any named Indian folk rhythm, in a spirit of multiethnic eclecticism drummers gave it a name associating it with a festive aspect of creole culture.

Hence, in general, there is nothing in hands like dingolay, kalinda, and steelpan that is foreign to the style and aesthetic of neotraditional North Indian vernacular drumming, and if a Trini tassa group playing these hands were transplanted to a Bhojpuri-region wedding procession, I suspect that all those

present would marvel at the group's skill but be otherwise nonplussed by the repertoire. Trinidadian tassa drumming, for example, does not incorporate the structural polyrhythms or even transitory three-against-two cross-rhythms that are so essential to Afro-Caribbean traditional drum traditions (although these are in any case not prominent in any Afro-Trinidadian music); rather, Trinidadian tassa drumming—much like Bhojpuri nagāra drumming—can be said to feature only a modest amount of syncopation in general.

A spirit of open-minded eclecticism certainly animates an innovative drummer like Lenny Kumar when he speaks of idiosyncratically adapting "African" rhythms like samba, "Swazi," or the now-rare Trinidadian version of belé.[53] Such innovations, while clearly marginal to the mainstream tassa repertoire, do enliven the scene in their way, even if the model for something like "Swazi" may be some recent concoction of the (pseudo-)"African" drum ensembles of djembes and congas that have emerged in recent years.

On the whole, these considerations suggest that tassa drummers have indeed selectively incorporated a few elements from Afro-creole music—but that these elements are not extensive or substantial, and have been chosen and adapted in ways that are wholly consistent with the fundamentally Indian aesthetics and rhythmic principles of traditional and neotraditional Indian music as locally cultivated. These borrowings can be seen as instances of a process that Korom characterizes as "decreolization," meaning, in his terms, a "grafting of local [Afro-creole] elements and lexical labels . . . onto a structural substrate derived from historical precedents originating in India" (2003, 12–13). In this manner, for instance, the Afro-creole term "dingolay" is borrowed, and effectively decreolized, to designate an essentially Indian (or more specifically, Indo-Trinidadian) rhythm.[54]

There is a certain irony in the strength of tassa drumming in comparison to the weakness of Afro-Trinidadian percussion music. Afro-Caribbean music, from rumba to bomba, has long been justifiably celebrated for its rhythmic power, complexity, and richness. As products of traditions brought from Africa and reworked by creative musicians over the centuries, the rhythms of Afro-Caribbean music, more than other elements, are what have made modern genres like salsa, the mambo, and merengue popular around the world. Evidence suggests that in the nineteenth century Trinidad was a lively regional center in this cauldron of rhythmic dynamism, with its flourishing neo-African traditions of camboulay and kalinda drumming, Yoruba-derived Orisha songs, and bongo wake music. And yet by the late twentieth century these music traditions were weak and marginal, if not wholly extinct. Camboulay drumming was effectively stamped out by direct British repression from the 1880s. Orisha music and religion were marginalized by the hegemony of Christianity and an Afro-Saxon rather than

Afrocentric sensibility; although they are currently undergoing something of a renaissance, their drumming styles are fairly simple and straightforward, exhibiting little of the polyrhythmic complexity of Yoruba diasporic drumming in Cuba and Brazil. In 1962, Alan Lomax recorded a remarkably rich and extensive body of calinda and bongo songs, mostly sung in local French creole, but little remains of this repertoire, with the extinction of that language as a living tongue and the disappearance of bongo wake music. Even the kalinda drumming that accompanies occasional stick fights today, although lively, is simple and straightforward in style. In effect, Trinidad has ceased to host vital neo-African drum traditions, though an interest in creating such musics has led in recent decades to the proliferation of djembe-dominated "African" drum ensembles whose fanciful arrangements have little or nothing to do with any local neo-African tradition. Instead, it has been the Indians who have been able to maintain and develop a vigorous neotraditional percussion music, in the form of tassa. Even if Indian drummers were open to borrowing from extant Afro-Trinidadian percussion traditions, after the banning of camboulay there would in fact have been little to borrow from. Some Afro-Trinidadians view the loss of neo-African tradition as a positive phenomenon that spurred creole creativity; as one told me, "I'm *glad* the British banned our traditional drumming, because it inspired us to invent the steel drum." The British, however, did not ban tassa, such that it went on to thrive with great vigor; it could well be that at a certain level some Afro-creoles find it awkward that it is not they but the Indians who are the bearers of the island's "hot" drumming tradition.

The Dynamics of a Drum Tradition:
Tassa as Quintessentially Indo-Trinidadian

In the first chapter of this volume I discussed some of the diverse trajectories and processes that can result when a music tradition is transplanted and then isolated from its parent culture. Outlining Nettl's enumerations of possible responses to Westernization, and extending these to cultural contact in general, I argued (contra Kartomi) that a close examination of retentions, coupled with a sensitivity to innovations and rearticulations, could afford a deeper understanding of the dynamics animating the evolution of a genre like tassa drumming. The present chapter's survey of tassa rhythms allows us to make more specific comments on such dynamics and on the general character and status of tassa as an Indo-Trinidadian art form.

While Nettl enumerated eleven possible responses to culture contact—and a few others could be added—particularly relevant in the case of tassa are three or four processes. These might include the phenomenon of *decline*, although

the absence of documentation of nineteenth-century tassa drumming in India renders impossible any definitive statements about the extent to which this process may have occurred. For example, as suggested above, it seems very likely that the prominent asymmetrical and idiosyncratic bass drum patterns in tīn chopra derived from renderings of lexical phrases—especially the *kalma*—which have since been forgotten. However, Trinidadian drummers' ignorance of conceptions of Hindustani tāl theory need not indicate any process of decline or amnesia on their part, since their tradition would have derived from a vernacular rather than classical North Indian source.

One can with greater certainty identify various retentions or persistences of North Indian elements, involving both general and specific features. Among the former are such obvious entities as the instrumental format of the tassa ensemble, the performance at Muharram and diverse other outdoor occasions, the general status as a vernacular tradition maintained by professional or semiprofessional "folk" performers, and an approach to rhythm that is broadly typical of that stratum of vernacular drumming (including nagāra drumming), with its repertoire of named composite rhythms ("hands") featuring a lead drummer and two or three accompanists. More specific retentions would include terms like "chōb" and "tāl," techniques like the buzz roll, kaharva-like hands such as chaubola, and a variety of idiosyncratic rhythms whose persistence over the generations is remarkable. Particularly notable, for example, is the limping "long-short-short" beat of khemta (and various North Indian counterparts), which is the sort of orally transmitted vernacular drumming entity that would be inadmissible in a classical metrical system like tabla music. Some of these diverse retentions appear to constitute marginal survivals, including the term "tikora," the use of the cylindrical bass rather than the barrel-shaped Punjabi-style ḍhol, and the popularity of the lexically derived tīn chopra and wedding hand rhythms, whose counterparts are rare in South Asia today. The development of these two hands illustrates a significant dynamic of the Indo-Caribbean musical diaspora, in which a text-driven musical entity—in this case, a set of asymmetrical bass patterns—loses its lexical dimension due to language decline, but instead of dying out becomes rearticulated and cultivated for its purely abstract musical qualities.

The most important generative phenomenon guiding the evolution of Trinidadian tassa music has been a process of creative development and elaboration occurring on purely Indian structural and aesthetic lines. This process—equally evident in local-classical music—generates musical idioms in some ways distinct from anything found in India, but which are nevertheless overwhelmingly Indian in character rather than acculturated or creole. This sort of musical

development could be characterized as "orthogenetic" or "endogamous"; in linguistic terms, its counterpart would be the evolution of a koine—that is, a lingua franca emerging from a set of closely related languages or dialects—as opposed to a creole deriving from the mixture of unrelated tongues. Tassa drumming in this sense has evolved as a syncretic, even omnivorous entity, but drawing overwhelmingly from diverse Indian rather than Afro-creole sources; these sources include Madrasi-derived drumming, the idiosyncratically Indo-Trinidadian local-classical music, and Bhojpuri-derived folk traditions (such as birha drumming) not previously associated with tassa.

This chapter's examination of tassa rhythms reveals how tassa is overwhelmingly Indian rather than Afro-creole in character, while at the same time being a thoroughly Trinidadian entity. Tassa drumming does indeed display a variety of "retentions" and "persistences" of North Indian features, but these have all been rearticulated into a musical system that, while consistent with North Indian stylistic and structural principles, is nevertheless original and distinct. Hence, like local-classical music, tassa drumming contains various features, such as the use of the word "tāl" and the particular rhythm it denotes, which could be regarded as jumbled-up recyclings of fragments brought from North India, but they have become constituents of a distinct, coherent, and idiosyncratic Trinidadian system. Meanwhile, tassa drummers have eclectically borrowed from various other Indian traditions present in Trinidad, but these have all been borrowings that could not have occurred elsewhere. For example, the incorporation of Madrasi rhythms would have been unlikely in the Bhojpuri region, where such music would probably not have been extant and available for adaptation. Further, the thumri, tillana, and dhrupad hands are adaptations not of the traditional North Indian versions of these genres, but of the distinctively Trinidadian local-classical song forms by these names, which differ dramatically from their Hindustani namesakes. Tassa, in a word, is thoroughly Indian without being a mere retention (like chowtal); at the same time, it is thoroughly Trinidadian, while owing very little to Afro-creole influence. It is thus quintessentially Indo-Trinidadian, and perhaps more than any other aspect of culture, it illustrates how vital and dynamic an entity in that category can be. It also reflects how a spirit of eclectic openness, adaptation, and innovation can characterize Indo-Caribbean culture and need not be associated with Afro-creole society. We shall return to these themes, and their sociopolitical implications, in the next chapter.

Concluding Perspectives

In recent decades the academic interest in syncretic popular musics has come to dominate much of the fields of cultural studies and ethnomusicology. Having contributed to this trend myself, especially with my 1988 volume *Popular Musics of the Non-Western World*, I at once appreciate the importance of this field while noting that many of the themes repeatedly belabored—about identity, hybridity, and resistance—have become rather commonplace and overworked. The perpetually growing interest in commercial popular musics, while of clear merit, runs the risk of marginalizing studies of traditional and neotraditional musics. The present volume has attempted to show that the rewards of such studies can be significant.

There is, first of all, a value in basic descriptive documentation and analysis of traditional genres that are actively performed by tens of thousands of enthusiasts each year, as is the case, for example, with chowtal, whether by Indo-Caribbeans, Fijians, or Bhojpuri-region dwellers. My own studies of chowtal in these three communities reveal a vital genre that has maintained remarkable continuity and stability despite the complete absence of musical contact between these three groups since 1917. This continuity across space and time also indicates with considerable certainty the form of chowtal in India in the latter nineteenth century. Similarly, the form of the standard birha melody pervasive throughout the Caribbean—though obscure in India itself—enables us to identify that tune as the ubiquitous stock melody mentioned, but not notated, by Grierson in 1886. Diasporic traditions thus provide unique information about otherwise undocumented folk music traditions in nineteenth-century India.

The value of basic analytical documentation is even more overt in the case of Indo-Trinidadian tassa drumming, a marvelously complex, rich, and idiosyncratic system nurtured by generations of drummers, performed by more than a hundred groups today and enjoyed by a broad spectrum of West Indians. With its well-established set of hands, each comprising composite ostinatos and conventional cutter patterns, tassa drumming lends itself well to—and indeed, demands—formal description. In fact, tassa rhythms merit much more detailed analysis than the basic schematic guides that have been provided in this volume. Meanwhile, it is worth reiterating that although tassa is a neotraditional genre grounded in aesthetic and rhythmic principles brought from India a century ago, in its idiosyncratic form, eclectic borrowings, and prodigious popularity, it is vitally contemporary and even downright fashionable among young Indo-Trinidadians.

Close examination of musical form yields its own insights about the dynamics of musical and even broader cultural developments in the distinctive, although not totally unique, conditions of the Indo-Caribbean diaspora. I have termed this diaspora an "isolated transplant," given the almost complete cessation of contact with the particular ancestral Bhojpuri homeland after 1917, counterbalanced by the community's ability and determination to perpetuate many aspects of traditional culture, despite the decline of Hindi/Bhojpuri and the inexorable pressure to acculturate to West Indian creole culture. Under these conditions, as we have seen, different musical genres have followed a variety of trajectories. Birha—a text-driven form with little purely musical substance—has declined predictably in tandem with command of Hindi. However, chowtal, its Hindi verses notwithstanding, has fared quite well, serving as a vehicle for lively and often competitive group singing, and for affirmation of Indian and especially Hindu identity.

The vitality of chowtal illustrates how a text-driven oral tradition can survive erosion of its linguistic base under certain conditions, including, in this case, written supplements in the form of cheap Hindi songbooks that can be informally romanized and circulated. The potential resilience of oral traditions is also evident in the survival of specific musical entities, such as the limping "long-short-short" ostinato found in both Bhojpuri and Indo-Caribbean drumming, which has no counterpart in or reinforcement from Hindustani music or Bollywood fare, not to mention Afro-creole music.

Particularly striking among diasporic Bhojpuri-derived culture is the phenomenon in which a transplanted traditional entity or practice—such as chowtal, the dantāl, or jhaṇḍi flags—becomes more widespread in the diaspora than in the ancestral Bhojpuri region, as it acquires new meaning and enhanced value in

the new social situation. Hence chowtal, despite its largely unintelligible texts, turns out to be a fine vehicle for Hindu choral singing; jhaṇḍi flags become proud symbols of Hindu identity in multiethnic societies; and the dantāl—for reasons that remain enigmatic—assumes the role of the standard, multipurpose idiophone in combination with the harmonium and dholak. Particularly remarkable is the occurrence of these same developments in Indo-Fijian society, which is geographically remote but in many ways similar, including in its Bhojpuri roots and its complex and often contentious relation with an established population of darker-skinned locals. The similar cultural responses of Indians in these sites illustrates how one can speak of a rhizomatic stratum of diasporic Bhojpuri culture that shares traditional and neotraditional features and at the same time is distinct from that of the ancestral homeland.

The spread of entities like chowtal, jhaṇḍi flags, and the dantāl among Indo-Caribbeans and Fijians in a manner disproportionate to North Indian models illustrates how even the traditional stratum of Bhojpuri-derived culture in the diaspora has not constituted a straightforward cross-section or miniature version of that transplanted from the plains of North India. Rather, in the new conditions of the diaspora its constitutive elements have taken a variety of trajectories, including decline, consolidation, compartmentalized persistence (including as marginal survivals), creolization, extensive growth, and development and elaboration along neotraditional Indian lines of evolution. Especially intriguing is the process of what can inelegantly be called "musicalization," whereby a musical entity with a lexical component—whether a song form or a mnemonic drum pattern—loses that dimension and becomes cultivated and elaborated as a purely musical idiom.

While Indo-Caribbean traditional culture has perforce been confronting and interacting in various ways with the Afro-creole "mainstream," since the 1940s the Bhojpuri-derived "little tradition" represented by genres like birha, chowtal, and women's wedding songs has also been engaged in a complex dialectic interaction with "great traditions" imported from India. In the realm of music, predominant among these have been Bollywood filmsong and the "stage bhajans" of singers such as Anup Jalota. Such cultural flows from "Mother India" helped stimulate interest and pride in all things Indian, and in that general sense indirectly promoted a degree of attention to Bhojpuri song traditions. At the same time, however, Bollywood culture and music undermined local traditions by presenting an attractive means to be modern and cosmopolitan without being creole or Western; accordingly, Bhojpuri-derived little traditions, such as the old wedding songs occasionally warbled by elderly aunties, came to be viewed as rustic and quaint. And indeed, there is no doubt that in terms of musical richness and complexity, the plain and simple stock tunes of

birha and women's songs do not compare with the slick and alluring musical products of Bollywood. Hence the inevitable appeal of filmsong, which soon came to dominate amateur performance forums, especially Mastana Bahar.

Meanwhile, acculturation to Afro-creole music has constituted another logical alternative way to be modern, whether in the form of consuming reggae and soca or via the hybrid of chutney-soca. It can also constitute a form of progressive resistance to traditional Indian culture, which can exert its own sort of hegemony within Indian communities and families. The creolization option illustrates how Indo-Caribbean music culture can be seen as a set of diverse genres and practices drawing from three fundamental antipodal resources: the Bhojpuri-derived little tradition, the imported Indian great traditions (especially that of Bollywood), and Afro-creole music.

Occupying a special place in this dynamic are tassa drumming and local-classical music. Although the two genres sound nothing alike, and local-classical music is less overtly eclectic, they are both products of a process of endogamously Indian development, in which fragments of transplanted music traditions were creatively forgotten, recombined, rearticulated, and elaborated into a new, unique, and dynamic music genre. As such, they are both quintessentially Indo-Caribbean, being distinctively local creations lacking substantial Afro-creole elements. They could also be regarded as comparable in their level of sophistication. While the two genres constitute pairs of a sort, tassa drumming is incomparably more popular and thus amounts to a more central element of Trinidadian mainstream music culture. Indeed, its popularity and its status as uniquely Indo-Trinidadian—rather than creole or purely Indian—have significant implications for the status of Indo-Caribbeans in Trinidadian national culture. They also call for a reassessment of current concepts of creolization and their centrality to West Indian culture.

Tassa, Creolization, and West Indian Identity

Indo-Caribbean culture, including music culture, can be seen as an ongoing dialectic product of three primary cultural realms—specifically, the transplanted but deeply local Bhojpuri little tradition, the imported North Indian great traditions (whether of visiting godmen or Bollywood blockbusters), and Afro-creole culture. (Euro-American mainstream culture and music would constitute a fourth but in many ways lesser influence, largely brokered by local Afro-creoles.) As discussed especially in chapter 4, the relation between the local Bhojpuri little tradition and the imported Indian great traditions is complex and in some ways competitive, but it is not a source of explicit ongoing debate, contestation, or general sense of alarm. Hence, while some cultural activists,

such as Shamoon Mohammed, do lament the hegemony of imported filmsong over local music, others, such as Rukminee Holass, seem to feel that both Bhojpuri traditional songs and Bollywood fare can comfortably coexist, even, for example, at the same wedding. In contrast, the relationship between Indian and Afro-creole cultures, in Guyana and especially Trinidad, has for decades been a subject of constant and immediate concern, polemically argued in newspapers, YouTube comments, and halls of parliament. What is at stake, indeed, is the social and even political status of Indo-Caribbeans in Trinidad and Guyana, whose national identities have traditionally been associated with their politically once-dominant but increasingly outnumbered Afro-creole populations.

The cultural, political, and economic relations between blacks and East Indians in Trinidad and Guyana have been subjects of considerable journalistic debate in those countries, as well as in scholarly literature in the academic world at large. In the American social sciences the countries—together with the Caribbean as a whole—have served as veritable laboratories for analysis, and in many ways they have provided social models paradigmatic for elsewhere in the world. Hence, for example, M. G. Smith's 1965 characterization (recapitulating that of Froude in 1888) of British Guiana as a "plural society"—in which Indians and blacks coexist without mixing—has been extended to other countries such as Malaysia. Even more broadly applied to global cultural dynamics has been the concept of creolization, as quintessentially embodied in the Caribbean; notions of creolization also lie at the crux of both lay contestations and academic exegeses regarding the status of Indians and their culture and music, in Trinidadian and broader West Indian society.

Such discussions have been rendered more complicated by the diverse meanings that have obtained to "creole" in the past, and even in the present. Around 1600, the term came to be used in Spanish and Portuguese to denote an Iberian born and raised in the Americas. In Peru, the word was subsequently applied to a black person raised locally, as opposed to a fresh-off-the-boat *bozal* slave. Over the following centuries, "creole" generally came to imply a person, entity, or practice of distinctly local New World—as opposed to African, Indian, or European—provenance. In linguistics, the term was retooled to denote a contact pidgin that becomes a mother tongue. More specifically—and of particular relevance in this volume—a creole language is defined as the syncretic product of languages from different families, as opposed to a koine, which derives from the mixture of related dialects or languages within a given family.

In discourse about the modern Caribbean, the notion of creolization came to be used in two general senses, whose ambiguous relationship has inspired much commentary.[1] The more general of these definitions is that associated with Sidney Mintz, who characterizes creolization as a distinctive spirit of cul-

tural openness, flexibility, accommodation, and syncretism that has animated Caribbean culture as a whole over the centuries. This Caribbean sensibility has been explicitly celebrated by some (for example, Glissant 1989), and has been characterized as a paradigmatic precursor of the modern global ecumene, with its incessant and omnidirectional cultural flows (see, for example, Mintz 1996, Hannerz 1987). In this academic sense the term has also come to be roughly synonymous with syncretism, hybridity, transculturation, interculturation, poly-culturalism, transversality, and other neologisms promoted by academics who hope to transcend the polysemies and ambiguities of extant terms. If in past centuries and in certain contexts creole entities might be disparaged as bastard impurities, they are now more often hailed, whether by postmodernist scholars or West Indian governments.

A second conception of creolization, more dominant in West Indian vernacular, journalistic, and academic discourse, associates the process more particularly with Afro-Caribbean culture. The seminal text in this tradition is Kamau Brathwaite's 1971 *The Development of Creole Society in Jamaica, 1770–1820*, whose model of Jamaican creolization as a syncretic Afro-Saxon process came to be more or less standard in subsequent West Indian thought. Hence, for example, in Trinidad, "creole" (although sometimes denoting a local white person) is generally used to describe local black culture—especially as centered around the iconic trinity of Carnival, calypso, and steelband music. These are quintessentially creole in that they were created as distinctly unique, new, and original entities by black communities long alienated from ancestral African roots. The realm of the "creole"—conventionally identified with national identity—would thus exclude the neo-African Shango/Orisha religion, which would be regarded as an idiosyncratic Old World transplant; it would also largely exclude East Indians and most of their culture—and therein lies a problem.

East Indians constitute around 20 percent of the population of the Anglophone West Indies; they form the largest ethnic group in Guyana and Suriname, and in Trinidad—of greatest interest in this text—they are roughly equivalent to Afro-Caribbeans in number. Since their arrival Indo-Trinidadians have been responsible for most of the island's agricultural output, and in recent decades for its business activity as well. Although Afro-Trinidadians are still commonly referred to as the "indigenous" population, many (such as celebrated calypsonian Mighty Sparrow) are in fact immigrants or descendants of people who arrived from elsewhere in the West Indies after the Indian indentureship period. Indo-Trinidadians, on the whole, are proud of their South Asian ancestry, but they regard themselves as Trinidadians rather than as immigrants or Indian nationals.

Relations with Afro-Trinidadians, and the status of East Indians in the island, were problematic from the early indentureship period, when Indians were im-

ported by planters essentially to undercut potential demands for higher wages by black former slaves. As subsequent generations of Indians, through legendary thrift, industriousness, and family cohesion, expanded into land ownership and business, many Afro-Trinidadians came to regard them as a menacing foreign element that was "taking over" the country. This perception intensified as Indians increasingly urbanized, even if that process also generated much amicable interaction. With independence in 1962, relations were further strained by the emergence of political parties that formed largely along ethnic lines, specifically, the PNM and the UNC, associated, respectively, with blacks and Indians.

Central to East Indians' status in national identity has been their relation to national culture and the definition of what constitutes that culture. Until the 1990s, Afro-Trinidadians had effectively defined national culture as Afro-creole, as quintessentially exemplified by the locally invented calypso, steelband, and Carnival. Historian and eventual prime minister Eric Williams seemed to endorse this notion and to renounce multiculturalism in an oft-quoted but ambiguous 1962 passage, stating, "There can be no Mother India for those whose ancestors came from India. . . . There can be no Mother Africa for those of African origin" (Williams 1982, 279). More generally, the familiar slogan "All o'we is one," while implicitly acknowledging diversity, at the same time seems to suggest that all Trinidadians are expected to acculturate to a unified mainstream culture, and it glosses over the realities of pervasive anti-Indian discrimination, whether by the state or gangs of Afro-Trinidadian kidnappers. Insofar as this putative mainstream culture is identified as creole—and implicitly or explicitly Afro-creole—it naturally excludes East Indians except insofar as they acculturate to that norm. In effect, the notion of creolization—implying, in the broader sense of the word, openness and accommodation—came, to some extent following Brathwaite's formulation, to be identified quintessentially, and then exclusively with Afro-Caribbeans. Thus, Afro-West Indians, unable to perpetuate their African traditions and unwilling or unable to wholly adopt European culture, fashioned an original, syncretic, creole culture, which then became in some respects a coherent and closed entity. East Indians, who have been both willing and able to maintain much of their Old World culture, are distinct from this (Afro-)creole culture and—insofar as it constitutes a national culture—are doomed to remain marginal except insofar as they assimilate.[2] Further, while creolization inevitably pervades many aspects of Indo-Caribbean culture, many Indians are deeply ambivalent about the process, which is often disparaged as "douglarization"—a "dougla" being an Indian-black mulatto.

The challenge these issues pose to national identity are nowhere more clear than in the realm of music, and accordingly, it is in reference to music that the competing conceptions of nationhood are most often argued and discussed. On

the one hand, there are the Afro-Trinidadians, who, turning cultural amnesia into an incentive to invent, created calypso and steelband, the celebrated products of an Afro-creole expressive genius. On the other hand are the East Indians, who devote much of their musical energy to singing chowtals from colonial India and filmsongs from the Bollywood hit parade. And yet these same Indians identify as Trinidadians and resent being excluded from a national identity that would mark them as foreigners. It is not their fault, some of them say, that unlike decultured plantation slaves, they were able to sustain cultural continuity and selectively chart a new course on their own terms.[3]

In a previous article (Manuel 2000c) I discussed several aspects of the complex imbrications of music in Indo-Caribbeans' quest for acceptance in the national fabric. In the present context I wish to focus more particularly on the roles that traditional and neotraditional musics have played, and could arguably play, in this dynamic. Tassa, as I shall argue, has particular potential as an icon of Indo-Trinidadian culture, but purely traditional genres like chowtal also have their own sort of sociopolitical significance. An initial consideration is that while ongoing performance of such music might be seen as an archaic retention motivated by a blinkered, stubborn attachment to Old World ways, it could also constitute a form of East Indian resistance to encroaching Afro-creole culture. Indo-Caribbean cultural activists have also invoked traditional music entities in arguing various agendas, often without having clear understanding of the origins of these entities. Knowing little of either the Bhojpuri region or other related diasporic sites like Fiji, spokespersons have built various ideological arguments on confused claims for local genesis of cultural entities or practices, or, conversely, a misattribution to Indian origin. Hence, for example, the problematic celebration of the dantāl and even the tassa as Indo-Trinidadian inventions. Thus, in clarifying terms aspects of origins by distinguishing transplanted persistences from local inventions, the study of "retentions," far from being a pointless antiquarian fetish, can in fact have contemporary sociopolitical ramifications.

Meanwhile, however, it is natural that genres of broader popularity figure more prominently in debates about national identity. Scholars, journalists, and cultural spokespersons have lavished particular attention on chutney-soca, especially as an example of Indo-Trinidadian creolization. Chutney-soca, its celebrants contend, illustrates how Indians have finally "arrived," creating a local hybrid that is danced to and even performed by Afro-Trinidadians as well as Indians, and that, for the latter, constitutes a departure from mere perpetuation or mimicking of musics from India (see Manuel 1998; Manuel 2000, chapter 6). As a creolized entity, chutney-soca can be seen as representing one kind of solution to the issue of Indian incorporation into the national identity of

Trinidad, which is already being hailed in some contexts, in a newly inclusive fashion, as "the land of calypso, steelband, and chutney-soca." Thus, if Trinidadian national culture is defined as creole, Indians can now claim chutney-soca as proof of genuine citizenship.

Sri Lankan anthropologist Viranjani Munasinghe is one scholar who has articulated the argument that Indo-Trinidadian culture should be recognized as fundamentally creole, and that definitions of creolization that associate the phenomenon with Afro-West Indians are discriminatory. Hence she faults Brathwaite for asserting that "it is the Caribbean black [rather than the East Indian] who has been most innovative and 'radical,'" and she disparages other scholars who have implicitly or explicitly treated Indo-Caribbeans as "peripheral to the creolization process" (Munasinghe 2006, 556). She points to various ways in which Indo-Trinidadian culture is effectively creole, such as typical behavior and attire at Hindu weddings. In a somewhat similar vein, Shalini Puri, another American-based scholar of South Asian descent who has written insightfully about this issue, judiciously stops short of outright advocacy but suggests how chutney-soca can embody a "dougla poetics" that could constitute a progressive and inclusive answer to the problem (Puri 1999).

On one level, the arguments of Munasinghe and Puri are well taken, and it is obvious that many aspects of Indo-Trinidadian culture are thoroughly creolized. At the same time, however, various problems can be seen to beset the agenda—articulated by these non-Trinidadian commentators—of Indians claiming Trinidadianness on the basis of their being creolized. First, as mentioned above, and as Munasinghe acknowledges in a footnote (2006, 559), many, if not most, Indo-Trinidadians consciously resist aspects of creolization, and they resent implicit or explicit demands that they must creolize in order to be fully Trinidadian. Munasinghe herself, indeed, seems not to question the notion that one must creolize in order to be Trinidadian; rather, she seeks to include Indians as Trinidadians by pointing out the ways they are in fact creolized. But many Indians want to be accepted as Trinidadians while maintaining their ethnic identity and creolizing only selectively, and on their own terms; what they want, rather than inclusion in an expanded concept of "creole" national culture, is a new paradigm of multiculturalism in which their distinctly Indian ethnicity would be not only accommodated but embraced.

A second and related problem with championing Indian creolization as a solution to the question of inclusiveness is that especially in the realm of expressive culture, Afro-Caribbeans have been far better exemplars of creolization, and conversely, much Indian cultural activity is in fact not markedly creole. Munasinghe (2006, 560) asks, "If 'creole' is the primary analytic to under-

stand Afro-Caribbean cultural creation, why is it not equally significant for the analysis of Indo-Caribbean forms?" The obvious answer is that creolization is simply far more overt, fundamental, and pervasive in Afro-Caribbean culture—especially in art forms like calypso and steelband—and that many important Indo-Caribbean cultural forms, including not only the "retention" chowtal but also the dynamic tassa, are *not* significantly creolized. Further, one might well argue that tassa is a considerably richer art form than chutney-soca, which, while hailed as creolized, could be faulted by cynics for its trivial lyrics, nursery-rhyme tunes, amateurish singers, and artless accompaniments churned out on drum machines and cheesy-sounding synth textures. Is chutney-soca the most worthy icon of Indians having belatedly "arrived" as Trinidadian citizens? Are tassa, and those who play it, to be regarded as somehow less Trinidadian than chutney-soca and its performers and fans?

My goal in this discussion is not to single out Munasinghe for critique but rather to highlight the problems of attempting to base a Trinidadian national identity on creolization, even in an expanded and more inclusive conception thereof. What has more potential, and is more in accordance with the expressed desires of Indians themselves, is a paradigm of multiculturalism. Traditional and neotraditional musics—and above all, tassa—could play key roles in this formulation of national identity.

A multiculturalist conception of Trinidadian national identity—which is already coming to be adopted—accommodates both the Yoruba songs of Orisha religion and the chowtals brought from the Bhojpuri region (as well as the filmi fare of Mastana Bahar). More important, it could have a special place for neotraditional genres—especially local-classical music and tassa—which have developed in Trinidad itself, albeit along orthogenetic Indian lines of evolution. Both these genres are art forms of considerable richness, although tassa is far more popular. As we have seen, in its formal aspects tassa is not markedly creole. Indeed, using Korom's terminology, its incorporation of terms like "dingolay," "foulay," and "steelpan" to designate essentially Indian entities can be seen as instances of decreolization, in which "what might seem like acculturation on the surface may simultaneously be a valid form of resistance to total cultural absorption" (Korom 2003, 12–13). In linguistic terms, both genres, in their eclectic borrowing from other Indian genres, are better viewed as Indo-Trinidadian koines than as Indo-African creole hybrids. Tassa, in particular, illustrates how a genre can be innovative, eclectic, complex, popular, and distinctly (Indo-)Trinidadian without being creole. While extramusical aspects, such as the formal competitions and personal behavior of its performers, may certainly be creolized, in its musical aspects it is a neotraditional

koine. It epitomizes the process presciently described by Brathwaite in 1971: "The Indian's modernization . . . is taking place largely in an endogamous and exclusive manner, *in-* rather than *inter-*culturation" (54).

The nature of tassa's evolution raises the question of whether its endogamous eclecticism should be seen as animated by the broader conception of creolization suggested by Mintz, which would see such openness as a feature of Caribbean culture in general, and which might implicitly occur without acculturation to or inspiration from Afro-creole patterns. That is, if we accept the fundamentally orthogenetic, Indian nature of tassa, should we nevertheless regard its innovative eclecticism as reflecting a distinctively Caribbean sensibility?

In my opinion, there should be no doubt that the Caribbean context, including the pervasiveness of Afro-creole culture, has promoted a similar eclecticism among generations of tassa drummers, even if they have chosen to develop that art form along primarily Indian aesthetic and structural lines. However, caution must be exercised in exalting the Caribbean in this fashion. It could be well argued, for example, that the tassa drummers of Pune, near Mumbai, exhibit a similar spirit of merry eclecticism, combining traditional rhythms like *gāvthi* with innovative adaptations of "We Will Rock You" and other contemporary tunes. And lest one counter that such eclecticism reflects a "creole" sensibility relatively unique to a cosmopolitan, modern city like Pune, and unrepresentative of greater India, one would do well to recall Sharar's comment on mid-nineteenth-century tassa drummers in Lucknow: "The tasha players were the most skilled and were always introducing innovations into their music" (1975, 151).

The special dynamism of tassa and its recognition as a quintessential Indo-Trinidadian art form have not gone unnoticed by cultural spokespersons. In recent years a few individuals—especially Vijay Ramlal Rai, president of the Tassa Association of Trinidad and Tobago—have called for the government to officially recognize tassa as a second "national instrument," alongside the steeldrum, which currently enjoys that unofficial designation. The steeldrum, of course, is justly celebrated as an entirely local invention, which is currently played in diverse countries around the world and constitutes Trinidad's outstanding gift to world music culture. Accordingly, steeldrum music receives various sorts of state support, including in the context of Panorama, the steelband competition at Carnival. In a quest for multicultural recognition, in 1994 some Indian activists—especially the often-provocative Hindu leader Satnarayan Maraj—had voiced a demand that the harmonium, as the most popular instrument in the Indian community, receive similar recognition and support. The case made for the harmonium—a humble instrument of European origin—was inherently weak, and Maraj's shrill demand generated more bemusement

than earnest support (see Manuel 2000c, 326–30). The repeated calls by Ramlal Rai and a few others for official recognition of tassa have also failed to generate mass mobilization and have involved some rather problematic historical claims. Advocates, attempting to liken it to steeldrum, have argued (incorrectly) that tassa was invented in Trinidad, or that although invented in India it is now extinct there (see, for example, Kangal 2003), or was never played in a quartet ensemble as it is in Trinidad. More cautiously, but still problematically, Ramlal Rai argues that at least tassa instruments are locally manufactured, unlike the oil drums used for steel pans.[4] Unfortunately, as Ballengee notes, even this claim is erroneous, as the canisters used to make tassa shells are in fact imported.

As a non-Trinidadian, I myself am not in a position to engage in advocacy, and I further appreciate that most Indo-Trinidadians are more exercised about other issues—such as the abominable law-and-order situation—than a campaign to have their own national instrument. Still, as a relatively dispassionate musicologist I will allow myself to suggest that were a call to be made for officially recognizing tassa, it could be articulated on stronger grounds than those that have been advocated. Although the tassa quartet is an Indian import, it may well be the case that tassa playing in that small-ensemble format, with much scope for virtuoso cutting, has reached a higher level of richness, complexity, popularity, and skill in Trinidad than has any counterpart in India. Although overwhelmingly a product of the Indian community, tassa is commonly performed at racially mixed events, and Afro-Trinidadians do not hesitate to "wine" and "get on bad" to its thunderous rhythms (unattached, as they are, to any incomprehensible Hindi lyrics or other overtly Indian baggage). Several Afro-Trinidadians also join the tassa groups that play during Hosay. Trinidadian-style tassa has gained its own sort of international presence, forming the model for nascent (or revivalist) tassa scenes in Guyana and Suriname and spawning a few dozen groups in New York, Toronto, and Florida, where it is widely played at Guyanese as well as Trinidadian functions. At the risk of being blasphemous, one might even argue that tassa is more popular than Trinidad's famed calypso, which seems to generate less interest (especially among the young) with each passing season. Meanwhile, standards for tassa players are certainly higher and more professional than they are for chutney singers. On the whole, the case for tassa could be made on the grounds that it is a dynamic and original art form that is wholly Indo-Trinidadian, and that it merits special recognition in the increasingly multiculturalist rather than creole-dominated model of national identity. On a broader level, the vitality and richness of tassa—as an entity that is at once neotraditional and contemporary—might suggest that creolization should not necessarily be upheld or celebrated as a dominant paradigm for either Caribbean or global culture.

Notes

Preface

1. As of 2014, ethnomusicologist Stephanie Jackson is conducting groundbreaking research on Madrasi music culture in the Indic Caribbean.

Chapter 1. Introduction

1. Kartomi also disparages the use of biological metaphors such as "transplant," on the grounds that they "imply negative survival prospects" (1981, 233); however, the botanical metaphor is too obvious and apt to eschew.

2. Although there is a town in Bihar called Bhojpur, that toponym is not generally used to designate the region as a whole.

3. This situation constitutes another parallel with the use of the modern term "Yoruba" to denote what has become the dominant ethnic group and lingua franca in Nigeria and, retrospectively, the derivative ethnic group and liturgical song dialect in Cuba, formerly called *lucumí* in that island.

4. The inability of singers and listeners to fully understand song texts is not solely a diasporic phenomenon. Grierson wrote in his 1884 article, "Some Bihari Folk-Songs," "The uneducated, and especially women, have a great reverence for the unintelligible. . . . Hence many an obscure word is retained, simply because it is not understood, and finally after generations of ignorant attrition becomes a sound and nothing more, having no meaning in itself, but interesting simply for its unintelligibility" (1884, 198).

Chapter 2. The Trajectories of Transplants

1. George Grierson commented on this feature in his 1886 essay; see chapter 5 herewith. See also Marcus (1989, 99).

2. Although *birhā* means "separation," as a song form the word evidently derives from *bīr*, designating a martial hero of the Ahir caste (Prasad 1987, 94). Given birha's close association with Ahirs, Platts presumably erred in describing it in his 1884 dictionary as "a kind of song peculiar to washermen" (150).

3. For footage of Ahir dancing, see Manuel, *Tassa Thunder*, from 9:28.

4. Vertovec (1992, 97) cites statistics suggesting that Ahirs constituted around 8 percent of immigrants, who numbered around 420,000 in Trinidad, Suriname, and British Guiana.

5. On occasion I have heard the major third degree replaced by its minor counterpart.

6. See Manuel, *Tassa Thunder*, from 12:55. A variant of the tune also appears in a responsorial birha sung by a rural entertainment troupe, recorded by Edward O. Henry in the 1980s on *Chant the Names of God: Village Music of the Bhojpuri-speaking Area of India* (Rounder Records 5008), side 2, track 2. However, the "field holler"-style khari birha on the same record (side 1, track 7) is quite distinct, as is that transcribed by Henry (1988, 305).

7. Examples can be heard at http://www.beatofindia.com/beatsofindia/babunandan_dhobi/3-babunandan-sasure_patoiyan_mein.mp3 (accessed February 27, 2014). Onkar Prasad, in his survey of Banaras folk music, also notates a similar birha tune (1987, 96, item, IV), while providing further data on contemporary Bhojpuri birha.

8. See the Laxmi Tewari's CD *Folk Music of Uttar Pradesh*, track 7. Various YouTube postings illustrate the *dhobi gīt* tune, including: http://www.youtube.com/watch?v=0yOqLfQuk1I&feature=related (Accessed February 27, 2014).

9. These subgenres include *bandha birha*, *phūldār birha*, *chaukaria birha*, and other types.

10. The alternate possibility is that nineteenth-century Ahirs both sang birha and played nagāra, but in the twentieth century, perhaps as a "Sanskritizing" strategy of seeking higher status, they gave up playing that drum, at least in professional contexts, relegating it to the lowly Chamārs.

11. Hiralal Tiwari provides this text as an example of a *binphūliā* birha, that is, an extended birha with only one simple melody (*phūl*, lit., flower, or *kari*, verse—a term also used in Suriname).

12. On *Praimsingh Presents Biraha Singing Trinidad Style*, track 6.

13. Siewnarine sings this birha in Manuel, *Tassa Thunder*, at 11:20.

14. On *Praimsingh Presents*, track 5. Both this birha and the aforementioned one by Ramdeen Chotoo, on the same CD, are in simple standard Hindi rather than Bhojpuri per se.

15. *Tassa Thunder* (Manuel) depicts one such rendering, at 10:30, in a Paramaribo temple, by Ramoutar Ramkhelawan.

16. See Manuel, *Tassa Thunder*, from 15:00, for a YouTube posting of Ramgool-

am's group, with dancing to the perennial favorite "Ramaji ki bagiya." In the *Mānas*, Sarvan (Shravan) Kumar is a model son mistakenly killed by King Dasrath, who is then cursed by the youth's parents. The use of this lachrymose episode as a frame for song, dance, and comedy is in some respects odd.

17. See Manuel, *Tassa Thunder*, at 16:30.

18. On *Dodo Popo: Hot Caribbean Dance Tracks*.

19. Although progressive in its use of a vernacular language rather than Sanskrit, the *Mānas*, as has often been noted, is "conservative" in its disparaging attitudes toward women and lower castes. See Lutgendorf 1991, 394–401.

20. Another significant medium has been the phenomenally popular cinematic series produced by Ramanand Sagar for Indian television in 1986.

21. See, for example, Laurence 1994, 252.

22. A jhāl is slightly larger than a manjīrā, typically around 3½ inches in diameter.

23. Lutgendorf (1991, 69) discusses the *līlā vānī*, and also demonstrated it for me.

24. Although extant in Suriname, *Mānas* singing is not mentioned by Arya in his 1968 study, though as his title (*Ritual Songs and Folksongs of the Hindus of Surinam*) suggests, he was more interested in documenting songs per se rather than styles of singing the canonic *Mānas*. Laxmi Tewari (2011, 75–79) briefly comments on the *Mānas* singing he heard in south Trinidad, and he includes an example in his recording from that island, *Trinidad and Tobago: Music from the North Indian Tradition* (UNESCO D8278). Meanwhile, clips of responsorial Indo-Fijian *Mānas* singing can be seen on YouTube, but I have not been able to research this tradition.

25. Platts (1884) defines *vāni* (Sanskrit) and *bānī* (Hindi) as "sound, speech, voice," with *bānī* additionally meaning "sectarian verses of mendicants . . . (used in compounds) voiced, tongued (e.g., *amrit-bānī*)." Hence, perhaps, the Guyanese compound "Ramayan-bānī." Lutgendorf did not hear his Banarsi singers use the term "bānī," but he does not doubt that it may have been current (p.c.). The use of the term in both Trinidad and Guyana strongly suggests that such would be the case. However, Lutgendorf observes that in some styles of chanting, the recurring insertion is called a "*sampūṭ*" (wrapper), with one particular verse being especially popular (1991, 69–70). Tewari, in the notes accompanying his 1991 recording of a Trinidadian jhāl Ramayan group, calls the bānī the "*sampūṭ*," although neither my Trinidadian nor Guyanese informants knew that term.

26. Chaturvedi (1989, 214) uses these terms the same way in his representation of similar lines in chowtal (as noted in chapter 3).

27. Hindustani *dīpchandī* may be regarded as a light-classical, decelerated stylization of the seven- or fourteen-beat rhythms common in Bhojpuri-region folk music. (Confusingly, as befits a term derived from folk music, in India "*dīpchandī*" is often used interchangeably with the terms *jat* and *chānchar*, and to further confound matters, all three terms may also denote a sixteen-beat tāl with identical stroke patterns.) While there is no canonic standard pattern for the corresponding Indo-Caribbean meter, the drummer often plays, on the dholak's bass drumhead, a pattern that could be schematized as:

dhīn dhīn - dhīn - dhīn - / dhīn - - - - - - ://

The two meters differ in tempo; the *dīpchandi* of a light-classical *bol banāo thumri* is typically around MM60, while that of Bhojpuri folk genres, including *Mānas* singing, is a brisk MM240, better notated as 7/8 or 14/8.

28. Both terms *daur* and *chaubola* may have come to Indo-Caribbean music from folk music theater such as *Gopichand* and *Raja Harichand*, which came to be generically called *nautanki* in twentieth-century India; see Manuel 2000a, 19–20, 29–30. The term "*daur*," however (otherwise meaning "revolving"), is also found in various musical contexts in the Muslim world, designating, for example, the faster movement, in quadratic meter, to which Arab and Turkish classical *samāi* and *peshrev*, respectively, segue Amir Khusrau (1253–1325), in his *Qirān-us Sa'dain,* also used the term to denote "rhythmic cycle" (in Sarmadee 2003, 394). Within South Asia, as Wolf (2014) has noted, the term is also variously used by drummers in Andhra Pradesh and by dhol-tasha players in Hyderabad (Sindh), with roots in Bharatpur, India. It is curious that the term died out in the classical music lexicon but persists in vernacular music discourse.

29. See page 25 in the Motilal Banarsidass edition (1990).

30. For further details about *Mānas*-singing, see Manuel 2012.

31. See Henry 1988, 155–59, for further discussion of Ālhā-singing in the Bhojpuri region.

32. See Tewari 1993, 16, and Schomer 1992, 67. I use "dandtāl" to denote the instrument as encountered in India and "dantāl" for its Caribbean counterpart.

33. Jaggernath's tune is not identical to any of those presented by Schomer (1992) and Tewari (1993), but both authors note that many tunes are used in singing the genre. It does resemble one of the tunes recorded by Henry on *Chant the Names of God: Village Music of the Bhojpuri-Speaking Area of India* (Rounder Records 5008), side 1, track 8.

34. Jaggernath can be seen singing the epic in Manuel, *Tassa Thunder*, from 6:25.

35. Raymond Smith cited an illustrative anecdote from the 1950s: "A group of Indian men were standing around talking when one of them declared, 'Me a Kshattriya; me got warrior blood,' whereupon another man gave him a blow which sent him sprawling into a ditch and taunted him with, 'Where you warrior blood now?'" (1962, 121).

Chapter 3. Chowtal and the Dantāl

1. In deference to Caribbean and Fijian conventional romanizations, I use the transliteration "chowtal" in place of the more academic "*cautāl*."

2. Extant literature regarding chowtal itself is limited, whether in reference to India or the diaspora. The most extensive and insightful discussion of the genre is Kevin Miller's dissertation chapter (2008) on Indo-Fijian chowtal, much of which is applicable to the Caribbean as well. Usharbudh Arya, in his volume on Indo-Surinamese folksong, provides a succinct description of chowtal and a few lyrics with

translations (Arya 1968, 22–23, 100–103). Stephen Slawek briefly describes and schematically notates two chowtals sung by a *kīrtan* group (the Birla Kirtan Samaj) in Banaras (Slawek 1986, 188, 263–65, 275–77), as does Helen Myers (1998, 74–78) with a Trinidadian example. Henry (2001–02, 36) devotes a paragraph to the subject in an article on Bhojpuri folk music in India, and he also recorded a few chowtals in 1972 in a Ghazipur district village northeast of Banaras in 1972. In the realm of literature in Hindi on Bhojpuri music, schematic transcriptions of chowtal in *sargam* notation are given in Mehrotra's songbook (1977, 187–89, 211–14) and in an article by Rajendra "Vanshi" Mishra (1966, 215–16). Short descriptions of the genre are also found in books by Hiralal Tiwari (1980, 83–84), Shanti Jain (1980, 31–2), and Rajkumari Mishra (2007, 186). Several surveys of Bhojpuri-region music do not mention chowtal at all, including: Chaturvedi (1989), Faruqi (1981), Henry (1988), Prasad (1987), Sinha (1971), Sisira (1954), Tewari (1974), and Upadhyaya (1954). Grierson's articles (1884, 1886) on Bhojpuri and Bihari folk music also do not mention the genre.

3. My fieldwork included two trips, of two weeks each, to India's Bhojpuri region in 2007 and 2009, attendance at an Indo-Fijian chowtal competition in California in 2008, interviews with informants in Trinidad and Suriname later that year, and ongoing engagement with Indo-Caribbeans in New York City, during which I became an ad hoc member of one of the leading Guyanese chowtal groups and participated in various performances. While my research on Indo-Caribbean chowtal has thus focused on the New York community, this population of around one hundred thousand Indo-Trinidadians and Guyanese sustains over a dozen groups and some of the most knowledgeable and skilled performers in the field.

4. See Henry 1988, 121–33, for further discussion of Bhojpuri Holi music and festivities.

5. See Manuel 2009 for further discussion of these forms.

6. I am grateful to Henry for providing me with this recording.

7. A drummer would practice greater restraint in the Indo-Caribbean local-classical context; I once heard a Trinidadian local-classical singer curtly reprimand his over-eager drummer, saying, "What you playin,' man, chowtal?"

As in *Mānas* singing in both India and the Caribbean, drummers may signal section ends by a cadential figure: x-xx-xx-x (or ONE-two-THREE-ONE-two-THREE-ONE-two-ONE), which might be accompanied by the shouted exclamation it signifies, "RA-ma CHAN-dar KI JAY!" (Hail Ramchandar!).

8. Such poets can be especially useful informants regarding folk music, as they are often at once in touch with vernacular music and, unlike many village performers, are able to speak articulately about diverse aspects of the music, including formal features like metrical schemes, rhythms, and the like. Hence, poets of *rasiyā akhāra*s were among my best guides in my earlier research on Braj folk *rasiyā*, and useful informants in my chowtal research in India included birhā poets Shyam Lal Khalifa, Laxmi Narayan Yadav, Kasi Nath (Banaras), Suraj Singh (Sitamadhi), and Lallan Guru (poet and leader of a Mirzapur *kajri akhāra*). On more than one occasion I

came to feel that I was mildly annoying such informants by my persistent questions about chowtal, which they regarded as inferior to their own specialties. Thus, Kasi Nath eventually told me, "Chowtal is nothing special."

The music of the Mirzapur *kajri akhāra*s merits detailed study, not only for its richness but also because, like *Hāthrasi rasiyā* (see Manuel 1993, 1994), it is in a state of lamentable decline. The parallels between the two genres are close.

9. I have uploaded a pdf copy of this book onto my academia.edu website.

10. As related in the introduction to this book, a typical response to my questions about chowtal, even when posed to those knowledgeable about other folk genres, was "'Chowtal'? No, you must mean *caitā*," or, "You must mean *caupāī*." Accordingly, when I brought five acquaintances from a village north of Banaras to attend chowtal sessions in Kachhwa Bazar, they subsequently said they had never heard the genre or anything much like it.

11. The chowtals of both singers (Sucharita Gupta and Santosh Srivastava) derived from an anthology by Banaras-based folklorist Hariram Dwivedi. Gupta can also be heard singing a chowtal in this fashion at www.beatsofindia.com (under "Bhojpuri").

12. See Manuel, *Tassa Thunder*, the section from 24:10 devoted to chowtal.

13. As of April 2014, the pdf file of the anthology *Chowtal Rang Bahar* on my academia.edu website has more than seven hundred hits, including dozens of downloads from such far-flung communities.

14. For example, Pandit Daulat Ram Chaube of Guyana had his booklet printed in Bombay by Venkateshvar Steam Press, printer of other chowtal anthologies known in the Caribbean. A Trinidadian named Moti Das also published a chowtal booklet.

15. Comedian and Hindi poet Sampath Mannie, conversation in 1996.

16. Letter to the *Trinidad Guardian*, April 16, 1993.

17. Quoted in the *Trinidad Guardian*, March 29, 1993.

18. See Manuel, *Tassa Thunder*, at 25:05.

19. For further discussion of subsidiary chowtal genres, see Manuel 2009.

20. Amanda Vincent (2006, chap. 5) has pithily emphasized this point in reference to cognate songs found in both Afro-Cuban and Nigerian Yoruba music.

21. See also the comments of Brenneis in relation to Indo-Fijian music (1991, 370).

22. Sharpening one end is said to enhance the sound; the loop on the other end should form a slightly incomplete circle, through which a piece of paper can barely pass. See Manuel, *Tassa Thunder*, in the section from 28:12 for coverage of the dantāl.

23. See Ramnarine 2001, 64.

24. The singers can be heard discussing the instrument in Manuel, *Tassa Thunder*, at 29:10.

25. See page 369. Tiwari's depiction shows a slightly distinct rod, looking more like a ribbed bar and lacking the hooked end; the alignment of figures and labels on the page (also showing *kartāl* and *kaṭhtāl* idiophones) is jumbled, though not unintelligibly so. Trinidadian Ashvini Raghunanan also informed me that he saw a dantāl in a village in Uttar Pradesh, near the Bihar border.

26. Other instruments have evolved from similarly quotidian implements. Thus,

the Peruvian and Cuban *cajon* (box, now also common in flamenco) are newly made versions of utilitarian predecessors, especially codfish boxes.

27. For example, while I have not found statistics detailing second-time migrants to Fiji from the Caribbean, between 1877 and 1892 only forty-five such migrants came to the Caribbean from prior indentureships in Fiji (Roopnarine 2009, 88). Since the Trinidadian indentureship program predated that in Fiji, the numbers of second-time migrants to Fiji would presumably be somewhat higher, though not exponentially so.

28. Jhaṇḍis can be seen in Manuel, *Tassa Thunder*, at 3:00.

Chapter 4. Bhojpuri Diasporic Music and the Encounter with India

1. See Niranjana 2006, chapter 5, for further discussion of the consumption of Hindi films in Trinidad.

2. Meanwhile, just as a relatively high percentage of Muslim indentured immigrants were of urban origin, their form of Islam corresponded more closely to that encountered throughout North India and had fewer specifically parochial or "folk" elements than did Bhojpuri-region Hinduism.

3. It should be acknowledged that the notion of great and little traditions has been critiqued on various grounds, although in my opinion the categorizations retain considerable utility if deployed with appropriate caveats and clarifications. There is no need, for example, to endorse Redfield's notion of the little tradition as involving "misinterpretations" of the great tradition (see Dumont and Pocock 1957), nor should the little tradition be regarded as a local variant of the great (see Wolf 2009, 9). By extension, despite the ongoing interactions between the two categories, elements in the little tradition should not necessarily be misconstrued as embryonic or derivative components of the great tradition; for example, it would be unproductive and distorting to regard a distinctive vernacular drum genre like tassa music as either a simplified derivative or a potentially embryonic form of any related entity in classical music. Further, researchers should be sensitive to the extent to which the analytic dichotomization does or does not correspond to emic concepts entertained by the relevant communities themselves. Nevertheless, with these caveats in mind, there is an obvious applicability of an analytical contrast between, on the one hand, a regional oral tradition (such as Bhojpuri folk music) unsupported by scripture, elite patronage, or extensive mass media, and on the other hand, pan-Indian cultural phenomena (such as art music or film music) that use a broad lingua franca and enjoy substantial forms of textual grounding (from treatises to fanzines) and elite, institutional, and/or corporate patronage. There is no other terminology that so conveniently encompasses these dialectic dualities of regional/panregional, oral/literate, colloquial/classical, and, in modern times, grassroots/corporate. It is in these senses that I find the taxonomy of great and little traditions to be useful and convenient, regardless of whatever unproductive baggage it may have been acquired in the past.

4. Anna Schultz discussed such distinctions in an unpublished paper, "Bollywood *Bhajans*: Style as 'Air' in an Indo-Guyanese Twice Migrant Community."

5. The Hindi term *langra* (limping) is in fact used in India to denote various irregular rhythmic patterns. See Manuel 1983 for its use in describing asymmetric ways of playing dīpchandi/*jat* in accompanying thumri.

6. A Surinamese temple group can be seen singing a khanjri gīt/sadhua bhajan in Manuel, *Tassa Thunder*, at 45:38.

7. *Kabir Bhajans and Aarti.*

8. Inexpensive booklets of Kabir verses, unlike some of the obscure nineteenth-century song-lyric anthologies hoarded by tān-singers, are easily available at Indian goods stores. Some of these booklets, in typical premodern style, preface songs with often inscrutable headings predating the twentieth-century standardization of Hindustani music. Thus, for example, the popular *Kabir Bhajan Ratnāvali* indicates verses to be sung in "Rāg Varshāti Pūrvi," "Rāg Banjāra," "Gazal Chāl Mārvāri," "Rāg Thumri," and "Bhajan Thumri." As noted elsewhere, such headings were presumably included as cues to communities who retained traditions of rendering the verses in specific tunes; once those performance traditions disappeared, or to outsiders to those traditions, the designations would be essentially meaningless, unless idiosyncratically interpreted.

9. Very little has been written about Siewnarainis either in India or in the Caribbean. Data regarding subcontinental Siewnarainis presented here are derived in part from passing references in Wilson (1846, 231–32) and Briggs (1920, 211–13).

10. The *Shabd Granthshabdāvli*, like other pre-twentieth-century songbooks, prefaces lyrics with suggestions for settings, some of which are familiar, such as *"sohar,"* *"mallār,"* and *"sārang"* and many of which are enigmatic, such as *"sirhad,"* *"krinda,"* *"chute,"* *"shooti,"* and *"bidhāpad."* As I discuss in my volume *East Indian Music in the West Indies,* "bidāpat" is a melody-type in local-classical music; final verses generally contain the word "bidāpat," which may be assumed to be a centuries-old corruption of "Vidyapathi," the fourteenth-century Maithili poet. The "bidhāpads" in the *Shabd Granthshabdāvli* also feature this insignia, despite their attribution to Shivnarayan.

11. At the numerous Mastana Bahar and other amateur performance events I have attended in Trinidad, I have consistently been impressed, as it were, by the predilection of so many vocalists to sing egregiously out of tune, and by the evident indifference of audiences to such vagaries of intonation. (Some of the better-known calypsonians, not to mention lesser contenders, exhibit the same trait.) I need to remind myself that in certain genres, such as local-classical music, standards of intonation are thoroughly professional. I suspect that the phenomenon reflects less a musical deficiency per se than a fondness for solo amateur singing in public.

12. A few minutes later, he berated the assembled listeners and competitors for their lack of creativity, brandishing a copy of my book *Cassette Culture*, which I had just given him, and shouting, to my chagrin, that it had expressed the same sentiment (which it does not).

13. By the 1980s, it was common for some Hindi films and filmsong sequences

to be shown with English subtitles, which would certainly promote not only comprehension but also their popularity. However, even in the 1990s many films were commonly shown without subtitles. As Mungal Patasar (of my own generation) told me, "We all grew up watching Hindi films without subtitles." Meanwhile, subjective impressions suggest that Bollywood music may no longer be as popular at present as it was in earlier decades.

14. The Bombay-based duo Babla and Kanchan enjoyed some success in both India and the Caribbean with their versions of Indo-Caribbean songs like "Kaisi bani."

15. Thus, for example, a booklet on dhrupad written by a BVS student repeatedly contrasted the distinctive local-classical dhrupad with the "authentic" and "true" dhrupad of India (see Manuel 2000a, 106). The distinctive local-classical dhrupad is better regarded as a bona fide member of a broader dhrupad family that would encompass Braj-region *samāj gāyan* and Vallabha *haveli sangīt* as well as concert dhrupad.

16. Meanwhile, as Narsaloo Ramaya related (1965), "If perchance visitors from India heard [local-classical singers], they were very often flabbergasted at the strange mixture that passed for classical singing."

17. See, for example, my discussions of some of these polemics in Manuel 2000a, chapter 6, and Manuel 1997/1998.

18. I confess that as an ardent lover of both genres, I consider them to be ideal and exemplary artistic "solutions," and it is not coincidental that I have devoted an earlier book to the former, the longest chapter of the present work to the latter, and a documentary video to each.

19. In Manuel, *Tassa Thunder* (at 5:30), a mixed crowd of Afro-Surinamese and East Indians can be seen dancing enthusiastically to chutney sung by Bishnuwati Kusal, who possesses the sharp, clear voice best suited to that genre.

20. For their part, the commercial mass media in Trinidad represent a reasonably diverse fare of musics, although it would be too much too expect traditional folk genres to be extensively disseminated. While the Mohammed family has been perhaps best known for its promotion of chutney and Bollywood fare, both Moean and Kamal were ardent enthusiasts and promoters of local-classical music, which they disseminated via recordings, competitions, and radio shows. The first Indian radio show, Kamal's "Indian Talent on Parade," broadcast from 1947, foregrounded local-classical music, as did the "Sunday Morning Indian Hour" from 1962. Contemporary Trinidadian radio stations (broadcast and online) offer diverse sorts of programming, although oriented more toward commercial popular music: as of 2012, Radio 90FM is Bollywood-oriented; 103FM showcases more local Indian music, especially chutney and "Indi-pop"; Sangit 106.1 offers both chutney and filmi; and Radio Jagriti is a mouthpiece of the Hindu SDMS. Among online stations, Bacchanal Radio highlights chutney-soca, Bollywood remixes, reggae, bhangra, and the like, while Masala Radio offers a similar range of "masala mixes, chutney, soca, and world beat music, with an underlying East Indian Music flavor" (according to its website). Commercial recordings, from the cassettes of the 1980s and 1990s to current CDs, range from the

usual "Local Mukesh" to chutney, chutney-soca, local and imported bhajans, and of course, Indian film music.

21. See Myers 1998, chapters 8 and 9, for fuller discussion of Trinidad weddings and their traditional songs. Also see Arya 1968.

22. Indo-Caribbean weddings can also accommodate a variety of ideologies as expressed in the sermons that pandits offer. Indeed, Indo-Caribbeans seem to have great reverence for religious speechifying, whether by a pandit or some aspiring sage, in which the content appears to be less important than the inspired verbal flow. However, the dilations of pandits are not always accepted uncritically. At one Trinidadian wedding I attended, the pandit bloviated at length about how hellfire awaited the libertine parents who had allowed their children to choose their own spouses; with such "love marriages" being the well-established norm in Trinidad, I was not surprised to see the guests around me groaning, laughing, and rolling their eyes. By contrast, the pandit at an otherwise similar Guyanese wedding devoted his sermon to extolling the importance of the love between the young couple, just as, he argued, such a romantic bond linked Rama and Sita. Such an interpretation would have to be seen as a modern and perhaps Western invention, as the Ramayan, in its various forms, generally portrays Rama as perpetually guided by duty, image, and propriety rather than sentiment. In fact, such concerns led him to banish Sita to the forest even after exerting himself to free her from the demon Ravana.

23. In Manuel, *Tassa Thunder* (at around 35:20), one of her spin-off troupes can be seen singing at a Sunday wedding, using her book. (The song is "Bāje nagāra ke dhol," on p. 78.) Rawatie Ali is another prominent Trinidadian teacher and group leader specializing in traditional women's songs.

24. A brief segment of such a competition is shown in Manuel, *Tassa Thunder*, at 18:38.

25. For a fuller discussion of the subject, see the insightful essay by Raviji Maharaj (2010).

26. Champa Devi had been preceded by Alice Jan, who, although achieving some local renown in the 1920s and 1930s, was regarded by many as a somewhat less than "respectable" personage, because or in spite of her being the mistress of a wealthy politician.

27. "Wine" is sometimes spelled "whine," but clearly derives from "wind" (one's waist), as in this 1790 Jamaican song verse quoted by Brathwaite (1971/2005, 222): "Hipsaw! My deaa! You no shake like a-me / You no wind like a-me! Go yondaa!" Some exemplary wining can be seen in Manuel, *Tassa Thunder*, at 5:50.

28. Dancer, choreographer, and scholar Satnarine Balkaransingh has categorized twelve different kinds of wining in Trindadian and Indian dancing, including the circular hip rolling of Bhojpuri women's dance, the jerky lateral Bollywood *jhatka*, and the exaggerated frontal pelvic thrusting of creole soca dancing.

Chapter 5. Tassa Drumming from India to the Caribbean and Beyond

1. The only occurrence of the word "tassa" in Zeno Obi Constance's book *Tassa, Chutney and Soca: The East Indian Contribution to the Calypso* (1991) is in the title. As mentioned in the introduction, Richard Wolf's *The Voice in the Drum* (2014) contains much information on and analysis of Muharram tassa drumming in India and Pakistan, and Christopher Ballengee's 2013 dissertation constitutes a solid study, complementary to this one, of Trinidadian tassa.

2. I thank Bradford Garvey (p.c.) for information on tassa drumming in Yemen.

3. The term *murfa'* is still used to denote such a drum in Andhra Pradesh and Yemen (Richard Wolf, p.c.).

4. I am grateful to Christopher Ballengee for unearthing these references and allowing me to cite them.

5. Video clips of these competitions can be seen on YouTube. See my 17" video documentary, *Drumming for Ganesh: Music at Pune's Ganpati Festival* (Manuel 2014), presently accessible on YouTube and Vimeo.

6. When I was trying to negotiate a session with some Banaras tassa players via the marching band office that booked them, the agent kept insisting, "You should at least also book an E-flat [clarinet] to play with them." *Tassa Thunder* (from 36:00) shows Banarsi tassa groups playing in Muharrum processions, a political rally, and a protest against careless kite flying.

7. Wolf (p.c.) opined that the playing of some of the Delhi drummers was of a professional standard. The Pune tassa bands, though impressive in size and choreography, do not feature the sort of small-group virtuosity foregrounded in Trini playing.

8. *Tassa Thunder* (Manuel) contains scenes of Ahir dancing, and demonstrations of nagāra rhythms, from 9:28. In the Braj region, the folk and folk-pop genre *rasiya* is invariably accompanied by nagāra, with harmonium and dholak.

9. See Angel 1995, 65.

10. One observer of Guyanese Muharram in 1897 commented, "The Coolies bring their Tadjhas and Tom Toms and we give them trousers and other advantages of civilization" (cited in Mohapatra n.d.). Kelvin Singh (1988) refers to tassas being played in nineteenth-century Hosay processions, but his statement appears to be a (safe) assumption rather than a documented fact (21).

11. For example, Rudy Sasenarine; and Tulsie Madan, who claims to have initiated the revival of tassa drumming in Suriname (p.c.). In that country I had occasion to hear a few other noisy youth groups.

12. For that matter, the Hindi word *kaṭ* (infinitive: *kaṭna*) is a precise cognate and homonym of English "cut" (including in its retroflex 'ṭ').

13. Speaking of marginal survivals, the Trinidadian word "dotish" appears to be an archaism from nineteenth-century British English.

14. See Mahabir 1984, 3. "Taireen" presumably derives from "tureen," perhaps as reinforced or altered by the Hindi "*tāi*," a clay frying pan. Raiaz Ali showed me the shallow taireen allegedly used by his great-grandfather. Since both clay and metal

shells are encountered in India, it may be difficult to ascertain which is of greater antiquity.

15. From Hindi, *ḍabbu*, a spoon or ladle. The deeper clay pots can be seen (and heard) in my footage of the 1993 Hosay commemoration in *Tassa Thunder*, from 39:00.

16. In North India, *ḍankā* is an archaic term for a single-headed bass drum. See Shurreef 1832, 50, also as cited in Ballengee, 77. Also compare with Platts's 1884 (1930, 548) definition of *dhunkār* or *dhankār*: "noise report, explosion, roar."

17. In Manuel, *Tassa Thunder*, from 49:45.

18. In Manuel, *Tassa Thunder*, from 3:17.

19. See Ballengee, 54–77 for further information on tassa and ḍhol construction.

20. Veteran drum maker and potter Gulcharan explained, "The plastic head came about because the goatskin became hard to get. Here we don't have plenty goats. Raising goats need plenty land, and they need a lot of grass to eat, and without grass you don't get good skin. They feedin' them the feed that chicken eat, and the skin don't come up tough. Between the skin and the flesh it has fat nowadays, and that fat never dries" (p.c.).

21. See Ballengee, chapter 4, for further discussion of the wedding events and the role of tassa therein.

22. A Trinidadian agwāni meeting, with tassa groups, can be seen in Manuel, *Tassa Thunder*, from 40:22.

23. A lively postnuptial jassle can be seen in Manuel, *Tassa Thunder*, at 41:20. At one wedding I attended, with the drummers crowded into a small space, I was not surprised when one ardent bass player inadvertently whacked the elbow of another with his heavy, ball-tipped stick; wincing in pain, the injured player retired from the fray, gave up his drum and proceeded to self-medicate with a cup of rum.

24. This problem is hardly unique to tassa competitions. In the formal competitions that came to dominate Scottish highland bagpipe performance in the 1800s, judges were deliberately chosen from upper-class aficionados rather than from the ranks of working-class pipers themselves, due to "the jealousies that are usually found to exist among those of the same profession and in the same rank of life as those competing" (in Cannon 2002, 82).

25. See Ballengee, chapter 6, for discussion of some of these popular theatrics.

26. Such theatrics are generally presented only at the finals, leaving the semi-finals devoted to pure drumming. Clips of tassa performances with dancers and fireworks can be seen (as of 2013) on various YouTube postings, such as:

http://www.youtube.com/watch?v=H78g1Rg9EuI

"Malick Rhythm Boyz (Tassa Grand Finals 2011 @Samaar Ent. Center Penal)" and:

http://www.youtube.com/watch?v=RgvpXYVyPYU&feature=related

"Tropical Power Country Boys Tassa Group"

27. One bandleader related to me that for a recent competition he had hired and trained a dance troupe for US$1000. Upon arriving at the concert venue, he discov-

ered the stage to be so small that the dancers would have thoroughly obscured his group, so, with great reservations, he dismissed them without having them perform.

28. Fine studies of Trinidadian Hosay are Frank Korom's insightful monograph *Hosay Trinidad* (2003) and eponymous documentary film (with John Bishop). A useful historical source is Kelvin Singh's *Bloodstained Tombs: The Muharram Massacre 1884* (1988).

29. See Manuel, *Tassa Thunder*, around 36:00, for scenes of Muharram in Delhi and Banaras.

30. See Wolf 2014. The kalma is rendered in various parts of the Muslim world as a quasi-musical repeated pattern (*zikr*), whether articulated verbally or instrumentally.

31. In some sites, such as Jaipur, Muharram is thoroughly dominated by Sunnis. An acquaintance from Bihar told me that in his village, which contains only two Muslim families, it is the Hindu community that performs the event, building tazias, drumming, and even chanting anti-Hindu verses.

32. Footage of St. James Hosay can be seen in Manuel, *Tassa Thunder*, from 39:00.

33. Wolf (p.c.) relates that ḍhol players in some North Indian tassa groups employ damped strokes to render the *khālī* ("empty," unstressed) segments of Hindustani tāls.

34. See Manuel 2000a, 129, for further discussion of the "tāl" cadence in local-classical music. The tāls/tihāīs in local-classical music are short and simple, generally consisting of a pattern that can be schematized as: - - x - -x - - /x. Trinidadian thumri incorporates a longer tāl/tihāī into its fixed rhythmic structure. See Manuel 2000a, 133–34.

35. Platts defines *bharti* as "filling, insertion, stuffing," but the more likely source is *barhti*, which he glosses as "increasing, advancing, [as in] *barhti cal*: accelerated motion or velocity" (1884[1930], 186, 153). Platts gives no relevant gloss of *laggi*.

36. See also Ballengee (106), to whom I am grateful for discovering this reference and allowing me to cite it.

37. Given Platts's extraordinary erudition, his characterization of the drum as "Moorish" is surprisingly quaint and imprecise, though correctly suggesting its origins in the Middle East rather than South Asia. However, the retroflex "ṭ" in ṭikora/ṭakora (contrasting with the dental "t" is Shurreef's rendering) suggests a Hindi rather than Perso-Arabic etymology. Wolf (2014, chapter 6) documents that Sindhi Manganhār drummers may refer to the tripartite tihāī cadence as "ṭiko."

38. Ballengee notes that the roll is in fact executed by bounce strokes only on the nondominant hand alternating with single strokes on the dominant hand (107). Interested readers may wish to peruse Ballengee's notations of tikora and other hands for complementary perspectives.

39. The term "na-dhi-dhin," while sounding like a fragment of Hindustani tīntāl *theka*, also denotes a "hand" played by Pune ḍhol-tasha groups, and, as documented by Wolf (2014: chapter 4) a rhythm played by a Delhi-based tassa group.

40. See Manuel, *Tassa Thunder*, at 43:35.

41. A young drummer is depicted playing tāl #2 in Manuel, *Tassa Thunder*, at 49:42.

42. Personnel listed on Lomax's tassa recordings, in Pasea Village (near St. Augustine), include Rambarran Harry Bans, Barran Datto, Ramdhan Maharaj, Bal Moonsamy, Bharat Moonsammy, Chattergoon Moonsammy, Harry (Jack) Paul, and K. B. Singh, although only four of these individuals were in the tassa group. (K. B. Singh was a classical vocalist.) Barran Datto (age around 62) identifies himself in an interview; he is presumably an older relative of another drummer named Datto, who was a leading San Juan-area tassa player of the next generation. In the interview, Barran's fellow drummers related that they played year-round, several times a month, most often at weddings, at which they might earn $35 TT. Materials for a bass drum, he added, might cost well over $100 TT. One of the drummers, in response to Lomax's question about dueling with creole drummers like "Negro Thomas," laughed and said that their group could play anything the negros played. (Accessible at earch.culturalequity.org/rc-b2/get-audio-ix.do?ix=recording&id=11120&idType=sessionId&sortBy=abc.)

43. Ballengee's informants credit the invention of this hand to Harry Latchman (132).

44. See Manuel, *Tassa Thunder*, at 43:58 and 35:12.

45. On Smithsonian Folkways, *Bamboo-Tamboo, Bongo and Belair* (Various Artists) COOK05017. The Lomax recordings can also be heard on the Smithsonian website.

46. The tassa group recorded by Lomax in 1962 played a recognizable version of hori/holi, with a somewhat artless segue to duple meter, and thence back to 7/8.

47. See Manuel, *Tassa Thunder*, at 44:00.

48. I am grateful to Wolf for sharing with me his insights and materials, gathered through his extensive and indefatigable fieldwork.

49. Wolf points out (p.c.) that an important part of Muharram in South Asia is to provide sharbat (sweet cool drinks) at stalls along the processional route, as if symbolically providing relief to the thirsting parties in the desert at Karbala.

50. As mentioned above, the Indo-Pakistani Muharram tassa drummers studied by Wolf played rhythms called "ek/do/tin/char ka mātam," in other words, "mātam of one/two/three/four [beats]." Conceivably, at some point the term "sāda mātam" might have been used to distinguish from these subvariants.

51. Such a jassle can be seen in Manuel, *Tassa Thunder*, at 41:00. The two groups, while playing in the same pulse, are deliberately out of sync with each other, as can be heard in the interlocking bass parts.

52. See Ballengee (118–23) for discussion of southern-style wedding hand.

53. See Manuel, *Tassa Thunder*, at 48:20.

54. The term "decreolization" has been used in other contexts—as in Mauritius, with its strikingly similar ethnic dynamics—to denote instances where the Indian community rejects formerly assimilated Afro-creole cultural elements or practices, self-consciously replacing them with those adopted in recent times from India (see Eriksen 2007, 174–75).

Chapter 6. Concluding Perspectives

1. Among this considerable body of literature, representative are Stewart (2007) and Khan (2004).

2. Obviously, this narrow and problematic Trinidadian understanding of "creolization" differs from the more common cosmopolitan use of the term as connoting an ideologically neutral syncretism. One might wonder why *American Anthropologist* devoted much of a single issue to an article by Munasinghe, with responses, belaboring this point and discussing whether the term should be inappropriate for broader usage (Munasinghe et al. 2006).

3. The greater cultural continuity enjoyed by Indians, as opposed to the traumatic deculturation experienced by blacks under slavery, is among the factors that problematize the standard characterization of Indians as subordinate and blacks as dominant in Trinidad. Indians have been and continue to be discriminated against in various ways, but they currently wield as much economic and political power as Afro-creoles, and within their own communities they always maintained a strong sense of ethnic identity and pride.

4. See Ballengee (2013, 227–40) for further discussion of the movement to enshrine tassa as a national instrument.

Glossary

Hindi and Urdu terms are presented here in the forms used in the text, followed, where appropriate, by standard academic transliterations in parentheses. In the latter system, *d* and *t* are dental, unaspirated plosives, while *ḍ* and *ṭ* are retroflex, close to their English equivalents. Short *a* is like the vowel in "but"; *pad* thus rhymes with "bud," not with English "pad."

ādhā: Half; in chowtal and Ramayan-singing, the practice of replacing the first half of a verse line with the second half (which is then repeated).

agwānī: In a Hindu wedding, the occasion when the groom's procession (the barāt) and the bride's family approach each other in front of the bride's home.

Ahīr: A North Indian agricultural caste traditionally associated with cowherding; in modern times, more often referred to as Yādav.

ahīrva nāch (ahirva kā nāch): A traditional, energetic dance style performed by Ahīr men at festivities, typically accompanied by nagāra drumming.

ālhā: A narrative epic ballad, sung in the Gangetic plains region, relating the martial exploits of medieval Rajput clans.

ālhet: A singer of Ālhā.

antara: In North Indian music, the second line or couplet of a musical composition, which generally ascends to a higher register before returning to the sthāī, or first line.

ārtī: A ceremony for a Hindu deity, typically involving chanting of a prayer while a devotee moves an adorned brass plate in a clockwise fashion before the god's image.

Avadhi (Awadhi): A member of the Hindi group of languages, spoken in central Uttar Pradesh (Awadh, Oudh); the language in which Tulsidas's *Rāmcharitmānas* was composed.

bānī: Sound, speech, voice; in Indo-Caribbean Ramayan-singing, a line or two of inserted nonscriptural text, with melodic setting, which introduces and punctuates verse passages; elsewhere called "sampūṭ."

bārāt (barāt): The groom's wedding party, which proceeds to the bride's house on the day of the marriage.

barti (barhtī, baḍhtī): Increase, augmentation; in the Caribbean, the accelerated, rhythmically dense portion of a song during which the *ṭek* or previously sung verses are usually reiterated, and the drummer plays fast, virtuoso patterns (syn., *daur, chaltī*, and in North India, *laggī*).

bhajan: Hindu devotional song (roughly synonymous with *kīrtan*), implicitly in generic, largely precomposed sthāī-antara form, as opposed to distinctive genres like chowtal or thumri.

bhakti: Hindu devotion, especially as experienced in an immediate, personal manner transcending caste and ritual, and often involving song.

Bhojpuri: A member of the Hindi language group spoken in eastern Uttar Pradesh and Bihar; formerly referred to in India as Bihārī.

birhā: Separation; a Bhojpuri verse form, traditionally and in the Caribbean sung to a simple stock tune; in modern India, an extended narrative sung to a medley of tunes from diverse sources.

chaubola: In nauṭanki theater, the second section of the dohā-chaubola-daur format in which verses are rendered; in the discourse of knowledgeable Indo-Caribbean dholak players, a common quadratic meter resembling North Indian kaharva; a tassa hand or composite rhythm.

chaupāī: A verse of four lines (or *pads*).

chob: A drumstick, especially as used to play tassa.

chowtal (ćautāl): A Bhojpuri-region antiphonal folksong genre sung during Holi/Phagwa season; the collective term for songs rendered in that format, including chowtal itself and such subgenres as jhūmar, lej, jati, and dhamār; in Hindustani music, a fourteen-beat meter used in dhrupad.

cutter: The lead tassa drum.

ḍabbū: A large spoon; the clay pot traditionally used as a shell for a tassa drum.

dangal: An assembly, or arena for a competition (as in wrestling or music).

ḍankā: The heavy, ball-tipped stick used by players of the ḍhol or bass in the tassa ensemble.

ḍantāl, ḍanḍtāl (Trinidad: dhantal): An idiophone consisting of a vertically held metal rod, about a yard long, struck with a U-shaped clapper or *tālī* (from *ḍanḍ*: stick, rod; and *tāl*: rhythm).

daur: Lit., revolving; in nauṭanki theater, the third section of the dohā-chaubola-daur format of rendering verses; in Indo-Caribbean music, synonym of bartī.

Devnagari: The script used in Hindi, Sanskrit, Marathi, and certain other North Indian languages.

dhol (ḍhol): A large, cylindrical double-headed drum.

dholak (ḍholak): A medium-sized double-headed drum, played with the hands, common in vernacular music in North India and the Indic Caribbean.

dīpchandī: In North Indian light-classical music (especially thumri), a tāl or meter of fourteen or sixteen beats.

dohā: A Hindi couplet; a prosodic meter; a couplet sung in free rhythm preceding a song, as in the *dohā-chaubolā-daur* format of nautanki theater.

dougla (doghlā): Hybrid, mongrel; in the West Indies, someone of mixed racial ancestry (typically, East Indian and Afro-Caribbean).

foulay, fulé, fuller: The accompanying tassa drum(s) in a tassa ensemble; a medium-pitched bamboo idiophone in the Trinidadian tamboo-bamboo ensemble; Manding: flute; Kikongo: hammer; Bamana: second.

gaj: A yard; a metal rod used as a yard measure.

gālī: Abuse; a women's wedding song abusing the groom and his family.

hāth: Hand; in Bhojpuri-region nagara and tassa drumming, a composite meter.

jhāl: A pair of cymbals (larger than the manjīra chime), played by chowtal and Ramayan singers, and, in a larger form, as part of a tassa ensemble.

jhanḍi: Flag; a triangular flag erected on a bamboo pole in front of a Sanatanist Hindu home in the Bhojpuri diaspora.

jhānjh: The medium-sized cymbal pair used in the tassa ensemble (now more commonly called jhāl).

jhīk, jhīkā: An idiophone with metal jingles on a wooden frame; a metal rod (such as an elephant prod) struck idiophonically with another piece of metal.

jhūmar: A North Indian folksong genre, existing in diverse regional forms.

jogirā: A sub-genre of chowtal singing in which a soloist improvises a short verse, which segues to an antiphonally rendered refrain.

Kabīr, kabīr. The poet Kabir Das; poetry, as in the phrase sung in jogirā: "Sun lo meri kabīr" (Listen to my verse); Platts (1930, 810): a kind of indecent song.

kaharva: The common quadratic meter used in North Indian folk and light-classical music.

kalinda (calinda, calenda, and the like): The name for a variety of diverse Afro-Caribbean song and dance forms; in Trinidad: a song, sung responsorially in French creole, typically accompanying stick fighting; a tassa hand.

kartāl, khartāl: An idiophone consisting of a pair of metal or wooden clappers held in one hand.

kata, katá: A drum used in Trinidad Orisha (Shango) worship; a drum used in Haitian voodoo music; Fon: a kind of drum.

khaṅjri: A small, round frame drum, like a tambourine without jingles, typically used to accompany *sadhua* (sadhu-style) bhajans.

khari birhā: Lit., "standing" birhā; the traditional, musically plain form of birhā using a simple stock melody.

khemta: A tāl or meter (roughly in 6/8) in North India and Indo-Caribbean folk music; a corresponding tassa hand.

koine: A lingua franca evolving from the admixture of related languages or dialects (versus a creole, involving unrelated languages).

lāchārī: Helplessness, forlornness; a folksong genre in the Bhojpuri region.

lakrī: Wood; in Bhojpuri-region nagāra playing, the generic term for a composite meter (compare to *hāth*, *jāti*, *dhun*, and the like).

launḍā: A boy; in Bhojpuri and Indo-Caribbean culture, a transvestite dancer.

lāwā, lāvā: Parched rice; a ritual involving parched rice (cooked the previous evening) in a Bhojpuri and Indo-Caribbean Hindu wedding; a tassa hand associated with this ritual.

lej: Rope; a subgenre of chowtal singing, with a distinctive prosodic meter and melody.

mahānt: An officiant or holy man, as in the Kabir-panth community

Mānas: Abbreviated term for the *Rāmcharitmānas* of Tulsidas.

manjīrā: A pair of small cymbals.

mārfat: Knowledge, especially of a spiritual nature.

maṭkor, maṭikor, matticore: An "earth-digging" ritual performed by Bhojpuri-region and Indo-Caribbean Hindu women a few days before a wedding.

nagāra (naqqāra): A kettledrum pair, played throughout much of North India.

nauṭankī: A vernacular Hindi-Urdu drama about the princess Nautanki; generic term for similar North Indian dramas (*Gopichand*, *Raja Harishchandra,* and so on).

pad: A line of verse.

panth: Sect, religious order, spiritual path (for example, the Kabir panth).

parang: A Venezuelan-derived folksong genre of Trinidad sung during Christmas season (from Spanish, *parranda*).

phagwa (phāg, fāg, fāgun): A month in the Hindu calendar; the vernal festival (syn. Holī) associated with that month.

pichkārī: A syringe-like squirt gun traditionally used to spray colored water during Phagwā/Holī; in Trinidad: a kind of English-language topical song promoted since the 1980s.

prattlin': In the discourse of some tassa drummers: fast triplets.

pūrab: Eastern, implicitly, the Bhojpuri region of North India.

qawwāli: An Indo-Muslim song genre, usually with devotional lyrics in Urdu.

rāg: In Hindustani music, a melodic mode; in the Caribbean and in vernacular Indian discourse, a melody or type of melody.

Rāmcharitmānas: The Avadhi-language version of the Ramayana penned by Goswami Tulsidas.

Ramlila: A vernacular theater form, with music and dance, presenting the story of the Ramayan over the course of several (usually nine) evenings.

rīti: Procedure; the rhetorically oriented, amatory style of Hindi (especially Brajbhāsha) poetry dominant in the eighteenth and nineteenth centuries, and in Hindustani song forms such as thumri and khyal.

sadā-ānand: Lit., everlasting joy: a song sung by Indo-Caribbean chowtal groups.

sādhu: A Hindu mendicant.

Sanātan Dharm: Lit., the eternal law; an institutionalized form of Hinduism constituting a mainstream in Indo-Caribbean and much of North Indian culture.

satsang: Lit., associating with the good; in Indo-Caribbean culture, a gathering of Hindus, typically at a temple, involving song and worship.

sohar: A song celebrating the birth of a child, especially a boy.

sthāī (sthāyī): The first line, and refrain, of a song in Hindustani music (for example, khyāl and thumri).

sumiran: Remembering; an opening invocatory verse preceding chowtal or Ramayan song sessions.

tāl: In Hindustani music, a meter; in Indo-Caribbean tassa drumming and local classical music, a rhythmic cadence.

ṭappū: A large, circular-frame drum played in South India, and in South Indian-derived ceremonies in the Caribbean.

tāzia: An imaginative replica of the shrine of the Shi'ite martyrs Hussein and Hassan that is borne in a procession during the Muharram (Trinidad: Hosay) commemoration.

ṭek: The first line of a song, which also serves as a refrain (roughly synonymous with *sthāī*).

theka: In Hindustani music, a basic drum pattern that embodies the structural features of a given tāl or meter.

thumri: A genre of North Indian light-classical music, emphasizing textual-melodic elaboration of a romantic verse.

tihāī: In Hindustani music, a rhythmic cadence consisting of a pattern repeated three times, typically ending on the *sam* or first beat of a tāl.

tikora (ṭīkorā): In Trinidad, a tassa hand.

tillana: In South Indian and certain North Indian music contexts, a genre featuring nonlexical and choreographic syllables.

ulārā (ullārā): In chowtal, a verse section sung in fast quadratic meter that follows the chowtal proper (from *ulārnā*, to overturn).

Yadav: Modern term for Ahīr, a North Indian caste of farmers and cowherds.

References

Abrahams, Roger, and John Szwed. 1983. *After Africa: Extracts from British Travel Accounts and Journals of the Seventeenth, Eighteenth, and Nineteenth Centuries Concerning the Slaves, their Manners, and Customs in the British West Indies.* New Haven, Conn.: Yale University Press.

Angel, W. H. (1921) 1995. *A Return to the Middle Passage: The Clipper Ship "Sheila."* Edited by Kenneth Ramchand and Brinsley Samaroo. Port of Spain: Caribbean Information Systems.

Arya, Usharbudh. 1968. *Ritual Songs and Folksongs of the Hindus of Surinam.* London: Brill.

Babiracki, Carol. 1991. "Musical and Cultural Interaction in Tribal India: The Karam Repertory of the Mundas of Chotanagpur." PhD diss., University of Illinois at Urbana-Champaign.

Ballengee, Christopher. 2013. "From Indian to Indo-Creole: Tassa Drumming, Creolization, and Caribbean Nationalism in Trinidad and Tobago." PhD diss., University of Florida.

Bissoondialsingh, Tara. 1973. *Dhrupad Singing in Trinidad.* Trinidad: Bharatiya Vidya Sansthan.

Bohlman, Philip. 1988. *The Study of Folk Music in the Modern World.* Bloomington: Indiana University Press.

Brathwaite, Kamau. (1971) 2005. *The Development of Creole Society in Jamaica, 1770–1820.* Kingston: Randle.

Brenneis, Donald. 1991. "Aesthetics, Performance, and the Enactment of Tradition in a Fiji Indian Community." In *Gender, Genre, and Power in South Asian Expressive Traditions*, edited by Arjun Appadurai, Frank Korom, and Margaret Mills, 362–78. Philadelphia: University of Pennsylvania Press.

Briggs, G. W. 1920. *The Chamars.* Delhi: Low Price.

Cannon, Roderick. 2002. *The Highland Bagpipe and Its Music*. 2nd ed. Edinburgh: John Donald.

Chaturvedi, Narmadeswar, ed. 1989. *Bhojpurī Lok Gīt* (Bhojpuri Folk Song). Lucknow: Uttar Pradesh Sangeet Natak Akademi.

Clifford, James. 1994. "Diasporas." *Cultural Anthropology* 9, no. 3: 302–38. Reprinted in *Routes: Travel and Translation in the Late Twentieth Century*, by James Clifford, 244–78. Cambridge, Mass.: Harvard University Press, 1997.

Cohen, R. 1997. *Global Diaspora*. London: University College London Press.

Constance, Zeno Obi. 1991. *Tassa, Chutney and Soca: The East Indian Contribution to the Calypso*. Trinidad: self-published.

Dumont, L., and D. Pocock. 1957. "Village Studies." *Contributions to Indian Sociology* 1:23–41.

Eriksen, Thomas H. 2007. "Creolization in Anthropological Theory and in Mauritius." In *Creolization: History, Ethnography, Theory*, edited by Charles Stewart, 153–77. Walnut Creek, Calif.: Left Coast.

Faruqi, Ali Azhar. 1981. *Uttar Pradesh ke Lok Gīt* (Folk Songs of Uttar Pradesh). New Delhi: Bureau for Promotion of Urdu.

Fazl, Abul. 1927. *Ain-i-Akbari* (The A-in-I Akbari). Vol. I. Translated by H. Blochmann. Delhi: Low Price Publications.

Froude, James. 1888. *The English in the West Indies; or, The Bow of Ulysses*. London: Longmans, Green.

Gerstin, Julian. 2004. "Tangled Roots: Kalenda and Other Neo-African Dances in the Circum-Caribbean." *New West Indian Guide* 78, no. 1–2: 5–41.

Gilroy, Paul. 1993. *The Black Atlantic*. Cambridge, Mass.: Harvard University Press.

Glissant, Edouard. 1989. *Le Discours Antillais*. Paris: Éditions du Seuil.

Grierson, George. 1884. "Some Bihari Folk-Songs." *Journal of the Royal Asiatic Society* 16:196–246.

———. 1886. "Some Bhojpuri Folk-Songs." *Journal of the Royal Asiatic Society* 18: 207–67.

Hannerz, Ulf. 1987. "The World in Creolisation." *Africa* 57, no. 4: 546–59.

Henry, Edward O. 1988. *Chant the Names of God: Music and Culture in Bhojpuri-Speaking India*. San Diego, Calif.: San Diego State University Press.

———. 2000. "Folk Song Genres and Their Melodies in India: Music Use and Genre Process." *Asian Music* 21, no. 2: 71–106.

———. 2001–2. "Melodic Structure of the Kharī Birhā of North India: A Simple Mode." *Asian Music* 33, no. 1: 105–24.

———. 2002. "The Rationalization of Intensity in Indian Music." *Ethnomusicology* 46, no. 1: 33–56.

Hill, Donald. 1993. *Calypso Calaloo: Early Carnival Music in Trinidad*. Gainesville: University of Florida Press.

Holass-Beepath, Rukminee. 2002. *Vivaaha Geet: 108 (Appropriate) Traditional Hindu Wedding Songs*. Trinidad: self-published.

Jain, Ravindra. 1988. "Overseas Indian in Malaysia and the Caribbean: A Comparative Overview." *Immigrants and Minorities* 7:123–43.

Jain, Shanti. 1980. *Chaiti*. Lucknow: Uttar Pradesh Sangeet Natak Akademi.

Kangal, Stephen. 2003. "Declaring Tassa a National Instrument." *Trinidad and Tobago News*, October 2.

Kartomi, Margaret. 1981. "The Processes and Results of Musical Culture Contact: A Discussion of Terminology and Concepts." *Ethnomusicology* 25, no. 2: 227–50.

Khan, Aisha. 2004. "Syncretic Creoles, the Indo-Caribbean, and Culture's In-between." *Radical History Review* 89:165–84.

Klass, Morton. 1961. *East Indians in Trinidad: A Study in Cultural Persistence.* Prospect Heights, Ill.: Waveland.

Korom, Frank. 1994. "The Transformation of Language to Rhythm: The Hosay Drum of Trinidad." *World of Music* 36, no. 3: 68–86.

———. 2003. *Hosay Trinidad: Muharram Performances in an Indo-Caribbean Diaspora.* Philadelphia: University of Pennsylvania Press.

La Guerre, John, ed. 1985. *Calcutta to Caroni: The East Indians of Trinidad.* Port of Spain: Longman Caribbean.

Laurence, K. O. 1994. *A Question of Labour: Indentured Immigration into Trinidad and British Guiana 1875–1917.* London: Currey.

Lutgendorf, Philip. 1991. *The Life of a Text: Performing the Rāmcaritmānas of Tulsidas.* Berkeley: University of California Press.

Mahabir, Noor Kumar. 1984. "The Influence of Tassa on the Making of the Steelband: The East Indian Contribution to Trinidad Carnival." Carapichaima, Trinidad and Tobago: The Indian Review Committee.

Maharaj, Ravindra Nath "Raviji." 2010. "A Narrative on the Framework of the Presence, Change, and Continuity of Indian Dance in Trinidad." In *Making Caribbean Dance: Continuity and Creativity in Island Cultures,* edited by Susanna Sloat, 321–36. Gainesville: University Press of Florida.

Manuel, Peter. 1983. "The Concept of *Tala* in Semi-Classical Music." *National Centre for the Performing Arts: Quarterly Journal* (Bombay) 12, no. 4: 7–14.

———. 1988. *Popular Musics of the Non-Western World: An Introductory Survey.* New York: Oxford University Press.

———. 1993. *Cassette Culture: Popular Music and Technology in North India.* Chicago: University of Chicago Press.

———. 1994. "Syncretism and Adaptation in Rasiya, a Braj Folksong Genre." *Journal of Vaishnavite Studies* 1:33–60.

———. 1997/1998. "Music, Identity, and Images of India in the Indo-Caribbean Diaspora." *Asian Music* 29, no. 1: 17–36.

———. 1998. "Chutney and Indo-Trinidadian Cultural Identity." *Popular Music* 17, no. 1: 21–42.

———. 2000a. *East Indian Music in the West Indies: Tan-Singing, Chutney, and the Making of Indo-Caribbean Culture.* Philadelphia: Temple University Press.

———. 2000b. *Tan-Singing of Trinidad and Guyana: Indo-Caribbean "Local-Classical Music."* Documentary video.

———. 2000c. "Ethnic Identity, National Identity, and Music in Indo-Caribbean Culture." In *Music and the Racial Imagination*, edited by Philip Bohlman and Ronald Radano, 318–45. Chicago: University of Chicago Press.

———. 2009. "Transnational Chowtal: Bhojpuri Folksong from North India to the Caribbean, Fiji, and Beyond." *Asian Music* 40, no. 2: 1–32.

———. 2012. "The Trajectories of Transplants: Singing Alhā, Birhā, and the Rāmāyan in the Indic Caribbean." *Asian Music* 43, no. 2: 115–54.

———. 2014. *Drumming for Ganesh: Music at Pune's Ganpati Festival.* Documentary video.

Marcus, Scott. 1989. "The Rise of a Folk Music Genre: Birha." In *Culture and Power in Banaras: Community, Performance, and Environment 1800–1980*, edited by Cynthia Frietag, 93–113. Berkeley: University of California Press.

Marriott, McKim. 1955. "Little Communities in an Indigenous Civilization." In *Village India: Studies in the Little Community*, edited by McKim Marriott, 171–222. Chicago: University of Chicago Press.

Martin, Robert Montgomery. 1838. *The History, Antiquities, Topography, and Statistics of Eastern India.* Vol. 3. London: W. H. Allen.

Marx, Karl. 1859. Introduction to *A Contribution to the Critique of Political Economy*. Excerpted in "Marx and Engels: A Reader in Marxist Aesthetics—Selected Texts; Art and Society. Marx: The Immanence of Artistic Development, I," in *Marxism and Art: Essays Classic and Contemporary*, edited by Maynard Solomon, 61–62. Detroit: Wayne State University Press, 1979.

Mehrotra, Narender Mohan. 1977. *Unchī Atarya Rāg Bhari* (The Lofty and Colorful Attic). Lucknow: Sangeet Natak Akademi.

Miller, Kevin. 2008. "A Community of Sentiment: Indo-Fijian Music and Identity Discourse in Fiji and Its Diaspora." PhD diss., University of California, Los Angeles.

Mintz, Sidney. 1996. "Enduring Substances, Trying Theories: The Caribbean Region as *Oikoumene*." *Journal of the Royal Anthropological Institute* 2, no. 2: 289–311.

Mishra, Rajendra "Vanshi." 1966. "Purvi-Uttarpradeshiya Lok Gīt" (Folk Music of Eastern Uttar Pradesh). In *Lok Sangīt Ank* (Folk Music Issue) (January). Edited by Lakshminarayan Garg, 212–26. Hathras: Sangit Karyalaya.

Mishra, Rajkumari. 2007. *Bhojpuri Mangal Gīt* (Bhojpuri Music of Auspicious Occasions). Varanasi: Sevak Prakashan.

Mohammed, Shamoon. 1982. *Mastana Bahar and Indian Culture in Trinidad and Tobago.* Trinidad: self-published.

Mohapatra, Prabhu. n.d. "The Politics of Representation in the Indian Labour Diaspora: West Indies, 1880–1920. Available at http://www.indialabourarchives.org/publications/prabhu2.htm (accessed February 17, 2014).

Moore, Brian. 1995. *Cultural Power, Resistance and Pluralism: Colonial Guyana 1838–1900.* Barbados: University of the West Indies Press.

Munasinghe, Viranjani. 2001. *Callaloo or Tossed Salad? East Indians and the Cultural Politics of Identity in Trinidad*. Ithaca, N.Y.: Cornell University Press.

———. 2006. "Theorizing World Culture through the New World: East Indians and Creolization." *American Ethnologist* 33, no. 4: 549–62, with responses by Ulf Hannerz (563–65), Aisha Khan (566–70), John Tomlinson (571–72), Deborah Thomas (573–75), Vicente Diaz (576–78), Daniel Segal (579–81), Verena Stolcke (582–84), and Pauline Turner Strong (585–87).

Myers, Helen. 1998. *Music of Hindu Trinidad: Songs from the India Diaspora*. Chicago: University of Chicago Press.

Naipaul, V. S. 1976. *The Overcrowded Barracoon and Other Stories*. New York: Penguin.

———. 1977. *India: A Wounded Civilization*. New York: Knopf.

Nettl, Bruno. 1978. "Some Aspects of the History of World Music in the Twentieth Century: Questions, Problems, and Concepts." *Ethnomusicology* 22, no. 1: 123–36.

———. 1985. *The Western Impact on World Music: Change, Adaptation, and Survival*. London: Schirmer.

Niranjana, Tejaswini. 2006. *Mobilizing India: Women, Music, and Migration between India and Trinidad*. Chapel Hill: Duke University Press.

Ong, Walter. 1982. *Orality and Literacy*. New York: Methuen.

Patasar, Sharda. "The Evolution of Indian Musical Forms in Trinidad from 1845 to the Present." Caribbean Studies thesis, University of the West Indies, St. Augustine, Trinidad.

Platts, John. (1884, 1930) 1960. *A Dictionary of Urdu, Classical Hindu, and English*. London: Oxford University Press.

Powers, Harold. 1980. "India." In *The New Grove Dictionary of Music and Musicians*, edited by Stanley Sadie. London: MacMillan.

Praimsingh, Ajeet. 2004. *Praimsingh Presents Biraha Singing Trinidad Style*. CD. Trinidad.

Prasad, Onkar. 1987. *Folk Music and Folk Dances of Banaras*. Calcutta: Anthropological Survey of India.

Puri, Shalini. 1999. "Canonized Hybridities, Resistant Hybridities: Chutney Soca, Carnival, and the Politics of Nationalism." In *Caribbean Romances: The Politics of Regional Representation*, edited by Belinda Edmondson, 12–38. Charlottesville: University Press of Virginia.

Ramaya, Narsaloo. 1965. "Indian Music in Trinidad." Manuscript (held by the author).

———. 1996. "Indian Music and the Muslim Influence." Manuscript (held by the author).

Ramkhelawan, Kries. n.d. *Dodo Popo: Hot Caribbean Dance Tracks*. CD. Paramaribo, Suriname.

Ramnarine, Tina. 2001. *Creating Their Own Space: The Development of an Indian-Caribbean Musical Tradition*. Kingston, Jamaica: University of the West Indies Press.

Roopnarine, Lomarsh. 2009. "The Repatriation, Readjustment, and Second-Term

Migration of Ex-Indentured Indian Laborers from British Guiana and Trinidad to India, 1838–1955." *New West Indian Guide* 83, nos. 1 and 2: 71–97.

Safran, William. 1991. "Diasporas in Modern Societies: Myths of Homeland and Return." *Diaspora* 1, no. 1: 83–99.

Sarmadee, Shahab. 2003. *Nur Ratnakar* (Ocean of Light). Vol. 1. Edited by Prem Lata Sharma and Francoise "Nalini" Delvoye. Calcutta: ITC Sangeet Research Academy.

Sasenarine, Ramnarine "Rudy," compiler. 2009. *Chowtal Rang Bahar: A Treasury of Chowtal Songs from India and the Caribbean.* Edited by Peter Manuel. Queens, N.Y.: Rajkumari Centre.

Schomer, Karine. 1990. "The 'Ālhā' Epic in Contemporary Performance." *World of Music* 32, no. 2: 58–80.

———. 1992. "The Audience as Patron: Dramatization and Texture of a Hindi Oral Epic Performance." In *Arts Patronage in India: Methods, Motives and Markets*, edited by Joan Erdman, 47–88. Delhi: Manohar.

Schultz, Anna. n.d. "Bollywood *Bhajans*: Style as 'Air' in an Indo-Guyanese Twice Migrant Community." Manuscript (held by the author).

Sharar, Abdul Halim. 1975. *Lucknow: The Last Phase of an Oriental Culture.* Translated and edited by E. S. Harcourt and Fakhir Husain. London: Elek.

Shrikrishandas, Khemraj. 1985. *Holī Cautāl Sangrah* (Anthology of Holi Cautāl Songs). Bombay: Shrivenkateshvar Steam Press.

Shri Sadholalji. (1977) 1988. *Cautāl Phāgsangrah.* Bombay: Khemraj Shrikrishandas Bombay Prakashan.

Shurreef, Jaffur. 1832. *Qanoon-e-Islam; or, the Customs of the Moosulmans of India.* Translated by G. A. Herklots. London: Parbury, Allen.

Singer, Milton. 1972. *When a Great Tradition Modernizes.* New York: Praeger.

Singh, Gora. 1994. "The Forgotten Indian—The Performing Arts and East Indian Artists of Guyana: Tradition, Creativity, and Development." In *The East Indian Odyssey: Dilemmas of a Migrant People*, edited by Mahine Gosain, 225–38. New York: self-published.

Singh, Kelvin. 1988. *Bloodstained Tombs: The Muharram Massacre 1884.* Warwick: Warwick University Caribbean Studies.

Sinha, D. M. 1971. *Folk Songs and Folk Music of Uttar Pradesh.* Delhi: Census of India.

Sisira, Karmendu. 1954. *Bhojpurī Holī Gīt* (Bhojpuri Holi Songs). Patna: Bhojpuri Academy.

Slawek, Stephen. 1986. "Kīrtan: A Study of the Sonic Manifestations of the Divine in the Popular Hindu Culture of Banaras." PhD diss., University of Illinois at Urbana-Champaign.

Slobin, Mark. 1992. "Micromusics of the West: A Comparative Approach," *Ethnomusicology* 36, no. 1: 1–87.

Smith, M. G. 1965. *The Plural Society in the British West Indies.* Berkeley: University of California Press.

Smith, Raymond. 1962. *British Guiana.* Westport, Conn.: Greenwood.

Stewart, Charles, ed. 2007. *Creolization: History, Ethnography, Theory*. Walnut Creek, Calif.: Left Coast.

Tewari, Laxmi Ganesh. 1974. "Folk Music of India: Uttar Pradesh." PhD diss., Wesleyan University, Middletown, Conn.

———. 1991. *Folk Music of Uttar Pradesh*. CD. Berlin: UNESCO.

———. 1993. *Alhākhānd ki Parampara* (The Alhākhānd Tradition). Lucknow: Uttar Pradesh Sangeet Natak Akademi.

———. 1994. *Folk Songs of Trinidad Indians*. Self-published.

———. 2011. *Music of the Indian Diaspora in Trinidad*. Coconut Creek, Fla.: Caribbean Studies.

Tiwari, Hiralal. 1980. *Gangaghāti ke Gīt* (Songs of the Ganges Valley). Varanasi: Vishvavidhyalaya Prakash.

Tulsidas, Goswami. 1990. *Tulasidasa's Shri Ramacharitamanas* (Lake of the Deeds of Rama). Edited and translated by R. C. Prasad. Delhi: Motilal Banarsidass.

Upadhyaya, Krishnadeva. 1954. *Bhojpurī Lok-Sangīt* (Bhojpuri Folk Music). Vols. 1 and 2. Varanasi: Bharatiya Lok-sanskriti Shodh-Sansthan.

Vatuk, Ved. 1979. *Studies in Indian Folk Traditions*. Delhi: Manohar.

Vertovec, Steven. 1992. *Hindu Trinidad: Religion, Ethnicity and Socio-Economic Change*. London: MacMillan/Warwick: University of Warwick.

Vincent, Amanda. 2006. "Batá Conversations: Guardianship and Entitlement Narratives about the Batá in Nigeria and Cuba." PhD diss., School of Oriental and African Studies, London.

Williams, Eric. 1982. *History of the People of Trinidad and Tobago*. Reprint. London: Deutsch.

Wilson, H. H. 1846. *Sketch of the Religious Sects of the Hindus*. Calcutta: Bishop's College Press.

Winer, Lise. 2009. *Dictionary of the English/Creole of Trinidad and Tobago*. Montreal/Kingston: McGill-Queens University Press.

Wolf, Richard. 2000. "Embodiment and Ambivalence: Emotion in South Asian Muharram Drumming." *Yearbook for Traditional Music*, 81–115.

———, ed. 2009. *Theorizing the Local: Music, Practice, and Experience in South Asian and Beyond*. New York: Oxford University Press.

———. 2014. *The Voice in the Drum: Music, Language and Emotion in Islamicate South and West Asia*. Urbana: University of Illinois Press.

Wood, Donald. 1968. *Trinidad in Transition*. London: Oxford University Press.

Index

Peter Manuel is a professor of ethnomusicology at John Jay College and the Graduate Center of the City University of New York. His several books include *Popular Musics of the Non-Western World: An Introductory Survey* and *Caribbean Currents: Caribbean Music from Rumba to Reggae.*

The University of Illinois Press
is a founding member of the
Association of American University Presses.

Composed in 10.5/13 Times New Roman
with Mezz display
at the University of Illinois Press
Manufactured by Sheridan Books, Inc.

University of Illinois Press
1325 South Oak Street
Champaign, IL 61820-6903
www.press.uillinois.edu

D1715250

Tales, Tunes, and Tassa Drums

Retention and Invention in Indo-Caribbean Music

Peter Manuel

University of Illinois Press
Urbana, Chicago, and Springfield

Library of Congress Cataloging-in-Publication Data
Manuel, Peter, 1952–
Tales, tunes, and tassa drums: retention and invention
in Indo-Caribbean music / Peter Manuel.
pages   cm
Includes bibliographical references and index.
ISBN 978-0-252-03881-5 (hardback)
ISBN 978-0-252-09677-8 (ebook)
1. Bhojpuri (Indic people)—Caribbean area—
Music—History and criticism. 2. Folk music—
Caribbean Area—History and criticism.
I. Title.
ML3565.M373   2015
781.62'91454072983—dc23   2014016323

In fond memory of
Rudy Sasenarine
1967–2012

Contents

Preface

In 2000 I completed what turned out to be for me an initial phase of research in Indo-Caribbean music, having generated a book, a documentary video, and several articles, most dealing with the idiosyncratic genre of "local-classical music" and chutney, which had turned into a pop phenomenon. I had noted that genres like chowtal, a springtime group folksong, and tassa, a Trinidadian drum style, clearly merited serious study, whether by myself or someone else, but my own research interests meandered northward, as they had before, to the Spanish Caribbean. In early spring 2007, however, I found myself in India, concluding a research trip on Sufi music. Visiting Banaras, the urban hub of the Bhojpuri region whence most Indo-Caribbean immigrants had come, I decided to look for local chowtal groups, assuming that since such ensembles abounded in the Caribbean and Fijian diasporas, I would have no difficulty locating them in their ancestral homeland. However, I was at once surprised, frustrated, and intrigued to find that the genres were utterly unknown to most of my informants. Even specialists in local folk music responded to my inquiries with what became a refrain, "Chowtal?—There is no such thing; no, you must mean *chaupāi*," or "You must mean *chaitā*," or "You must mean *chaupadi*." Actually, however, I did mean "chowtal," and with some perseverance and luck I eventually found some groups in the region whose style closely resembled that of the Guyanese group with whom I occasionally sang in New York. Returning home to New York, I immersed myself in the local Guyanese and Trinidadian chowtal scenes, and as my interest extended to the thriving local tassa scene, I found myself exploring a vast stratum of Indo-Caribbean music that was quite new to me and conspicuously in need of documentation.

For its part, Trinidadian tassa drumming turned out to be a thriving music idiom of considerable richness and variety, and, as I discovered, with its own complex relationship with its North Indian counterpart. Unlike chowtal, tassa was easy to find in the Banaras area, but rather than representing a vital parallel tradition, the Banaras-region drumming I found was simple, crude, and amateurish—nothing like the virtuosic and exciting Trinidadian style, with its formalized composite meters and cadences, its balance of tradition and innovation, and its lively performance scene of competitions and weddings. Obviously, in the tassa and chowtal realms there was more going on than the various predictable processes of retention, decline, or creolization. As one thing led to another, my interests at once widened in scope and congealed in thematic focus, and subsequent return trips to Trinidad, Suriname, and Bhojpuri India provided the rest of the data that generated this book.

In focusing on this more traditional layer of Indo-Caribbean music culture, I am aware that I could be regarded as nostalgically fetishizing retentions, as Morton Klass had been accused of doing in his 1961 study of an Indo-Trinidadian village. Certainly, in shunning contemporary hit-parade ephemera like reggae-chutney fusions I was guilty of turning my back on the phenomena of pop hybridity and secondary-diaspora transnationalism that so excites modern cultural-studies devotees. And yet the reasons for studying traditional and neotraditional Indo-Caribbean musics are compelling. As genres, chowtal, tassa, birha, and antiphonal Ramayan singing either had been or remained prodigiously cherished and important components of Indo-Caribbean culture, and are of such richness and broad popularity that they cried out for analytical study. Particularly enigmatic, intriguing, and unexplored are their historical relationships to counterparts in Bhojpuri India. What elements had been brought from India to the Caribbean? What, or where, were their precise sources? What was created anew in the Caribbean? Why had some genres flourished and others declined? What explained the various similarities to or differences from contemporary North Indian counterparts? How had their meanings changed? And above all, what were the sociomusical dynamics that conditioned their trajectories?

Such issues, I believe, far from being of purely antiquarian interest, are—or should be—central to the burgeoning field of diaspora studies, however much contemporary diaspora scholars remain enthralled by postmodern transnationalism. Further, in multiethnic Guyana, Suriname, and especially Trinidad, questions about the origins of musical entities are often hotly debated, especially as they are invoked in polemics about the status of Indo-Caribbeans in national polities or the place of certain music forms in local culture. Hence, in different Trinidadian discursive contexts, one finds various arguments made, generally

without adequate substantiation, about the origins of various musical entities. In some cases, attempts are made to legitimize a genre or practice by asserting its antiquity and its direct derivation from India. In other contexts, Trinidadians may assert, however dubiously, the local invention of entities like the dantāl idiophone, or even tassa drumming. Such theories may be advanced in order to match the local creole creation of the steel drum and to counter the accusation that Indo-Trinidadians remain wedded to Old World tradition and are thus somehow less Trinidadian than their Afro-Caribbean compatriots. Indeed, some of my own findings have already on occasion been invoked, appropriately or not, by polemicists.

As a North American academic and an outsider to Caribbean ethnic negotiations, my own interest in the dynamics of musical retention and invention has been primarily academic, but I am happy to be able to contribute in my own pedantic way to the enhanced appreciation and understanding of Indo-Caribbean music culture in its diverse forms. If, for example, chowtal is recognized as being largely a retention in terms of style, the fact that it is thriving in the diaspora while declining in India should make its survival a matter of pride and import for Indo-Caribbeans. Meanwhile, the importance of Trinidadian tassa drumming derives, by contrast, from its very uniqueness as an art form that, while originating in North Indian tradition, has evolved into a distinctly and dynamically local entity. A dispassionate historical understanding of these genres may, I believe, inform and enhance a passionate appreciation of them, whether on the part of Indo-Caribbeans or others.

Any study hoping to trace Indo-Caribbean folk music elements to Bhojpuri-region sources, or even to relate such elements to modern North Indian counterparts, is doomed to being provisional and tentative. First, there is no doubt that many aspects of Bhojpuri diasporic music culture, including, for example, specific songs and tunes, derive from entities that have changed unrecognizably or disappeared in North India since the indenture period and hence will not be unearthed by even the most assiduous researcher. Moreover, it is entirely likely that many such diasporic entities derive from Bhojpuri-region sources that were not generalized or widespread but were peculiar to a specific region or perhaps even one village. The Bhojpuri region, however, is vast, and documentation of its folk music remains woefully uneven and incomplete, despite the earnest studies of several researchers, both Western and Indian. Many areas, particularly in Bihar, are unsafe for travel, not to mention for extended ethnomusicological fieldwork, infested as they are with Maoist rebels, criminal gangs, or landlords' paramilitary thugs. The music of such regions thus remains poorly documented. Moreover, even the researcher-friendly areas like the Banaras region remain understudied. Scholars such as Edward O. Henry and Hiralal Tiwari have pub-

lished excellent and wide-ranging surveys of that region's music, but even these cannot hope to be comprehensive, and many significant and rich genres of that region, from Mirzapuri kajri to chowtal, remain essentially unstudied.

A thorough attempt to relate Bhojpuri diasporic music to its ancestral roots and counterparts should properly and ideally be undertaken by a scholar who has spent several years traversing Bihar and eastern Uttar Pradesh, documenting the full breadth of its folk music traditions. Unfortunately, whether any scholar can claim to have such experience and expertise, I cannot, nor can I credibly present myself as an authority on Bhojpuri-region music. Although I have visited the Banaras area several times since 1970, my original specialization was North Indian classical music. Around 1990, in the course of writing my book *Cassette Culture: Popular Music and Technology in North India*, I conducted a few weeks of research on folk-pop hybrids in the region; finally, in recent years I was able to spend several weeks there, in two trips, focusing on genres relevant to the current volume. My competence in Urdu and passable command of Hindi enabled me to converse comfortably with locals there, as in Suriname, and where needed I sought assistance in translating Bhojpuri song texts. Needless to say, I have not hesitated to pester scholars like Henry or to seek the counsel of Indian experts in the course of my research. For its part, researching tassa drumming has presented its own obstacles, as Indian tassa, far from being unique to the Bhojpuri region, is played throughout North India and remains inadequately documented, with the exception of my own fieldwork and some specialized but significant studies by Richard Wolf. Thus, any attempt to relate Bhojpuri diasporic music to North Indian roots or counterparts must remain in many respects tentative and incomplete, given the unsatisfactory documentation of Bhojpuri music, past and present, and the possibility of origins in other regions. The treatment of tassa music in this volume is also far from exhaustive; Trinidadian tassa drumming is an art form of such complexity, richness, and even national visibility that it merits being the subject of a full book rather than the extended chapter provided in this volume.

Such problems and limitations notwithstanding, I would not have written this book were I not convinced that it constitutes a contribution to the studies of Indo-Caribbean and South Asian music, as well as to diaspora theory in general. What I have attempted to illuminate is, first, an entire stratum of neotraditional Indo-Caribbean music-making that has hitherto entirely escaped scholarly attention. Second, I have attempted to trace and reconstruct the development of these genres and entities in relation to Bhojpuri-region sources and counterparts in the hopes that we can then speak with some specificity and rigor about their histories in the Caribbean. Third, I explore the complex and in some ways competitive relation between these transplanted Bhojpuri-derived musics

in the Caribbean and the mainstream North Indian musics that increasingly influenced the region since the 1940s. Fourth, I suggest some ways in which these histories and formal developments reflect aspects of broader diasporic dynamics, most specifically about the Indo-Caribbean experience, but with implications for other diasporas as well. A recurrent theme emerging from these investigatory pursuits is that Indo-Caribbean Bhojpuri music culture, even in its traditional and neotraditional forms, is neither a cross-section nor a miniature version of North Indian Bhojpuri culture; it is, rather, a distinctive entity, some of whose elements are in fact more vital than their South Asian counterparts and sources. Finally, I suggest that an understanding of neotraditional musics such as tassa obliges scholars to reconsider some of the approaches taken to frame Indo-Caribbean culture in relation to the creole and, more specifically, Afro-creole West Indian culture that has traditionally been understood as a local "mainstream." While some scholars, noting how this configuration discriminates against Indo-Caribbeans, have argued that Indo-Caribbean culture should be included within this creole norm, I contend that some of the most dynamic and important aspects of local culture—such as tassa—are uniquely Indo-Trinidadian in a way that owes little to creole borrowings.

My interest in this volume is largely confined to those aspects of traditional and neotraditional Indo-Caribbean music culture that derive from the legacy of the Bhojpuri (and neighboring Awadhi) region, the source not only of more than two-thirds of the immigrants but also of what became something of a mainstream in local Indian culture. My focus thus excludes the legacy of the relatively small but not insignificant percentage of immigrants who came from South India, arriving primarily before 1860. The so-called "Madrasis," like their North Indian counterparts, have energetically maintained many aspects of their traditional culture, including drumming and song traditions related to worship of the goddess Mariamman. These traditions are sorely in need of scholarly study, but such research should properly be undertaken by someone who, unlike myself, is familiar with Tamil language and folk culture.[1] Similarly, pop chutney and other contemporary faddish hybrids are given only passing reference in this volume, partly because I have discussed chutney at some length in my earlier book (Manuel 2000a). For the same reason, and because it derives only in part from an identifiable Bhojpuri legacy, local-classical music is covered only tangentially in this book; readers interested in this subject are referred to my prior book and documentary video on the same topic. Further, although women's songs (such as wedding and childbirth songs) are an important part of the Indo-Caribbean Bhojpuri legacy, this book treats them only in passing, to some extent because of their extant coverage in Helen Myers's *Music of Hindu Trinidad* (1998).

The first chapter of this book provides background data on Indo-Caribbean history and situates that culture's development in the context of diasporic studies as a whole. It provides an overview of North Indian Bhojpuri music culture and of Indo-Caribbean music culture, with reference to traditional Bhojpuri aspects, creolized entities like chutney-soca, and the ramifications of exposure to North Indian "great tradition" musics—both pop and classical—since the 1940s. Chapter 2 looks at three oral-tradition, text-driven genres—birha, the Ālhā epic, and antiphonal Ramayan singing—suggesting how their functions, inherent features, and relation to print culture have conditioned their trajectories in the Caribbean context. Chapter 3 explores two distinct entities—chowtal, and the dantāl metallophone—that have spread more in the Caribbean and Fijian diasporas than in the ancestral Bhojpuri region itself; hypotheses are advanced as to the enigmatic vitality of these entities vis-à-vis in North India. Chapter 4 is devoted to the more general topic of the Indo-Caribbean Bhojpuri legacy's confrontation with music flowing from North India itself in the postindenture period, in the form of mass-mediated film music and other pop, including panregional Hindi devotional songs. Of particular relevance is the influence of these imported sounds on wedding songs, Kabir-panthi music, and Ramayan singing. Chapter 5 discusses tassa drumming in its relation to North Indian counterparts and with regard to its present forms, styles, and social contexts. Formal analyses are presented both as timely documentation of this impressive and understudied art form and in order to advance arguments about its evolution and the nature of its incorporation of creole elements. In the concluding chapter I suggest some hypotheses and conclusions about Bhojpuri diasporic dynamics, broader implications for diaspora studies in general, the relation of music genres like tassa to Afro-creole culture, and the implications of this relationship for our understanding of the phenomenon of Caribbean creolization.

Longer versions of chapters 2 and 3 were published in the journal *Asian Music*, under the respective titles "Transnational Chowtal: Bhojpuri Folksong from North India to the Caribbean, Fiji, and Beyond" and "The Trajectories of Transplants: Singing Ālhā, Birhā, and the Ramayan in the Indic Caribbean" (issues 40/2 and 43/2, respectively).

In 2010 I completed a video documentary titled *Tassa Thunder: Folk Music from India to the Caribbean*. This film covers, in its way, much of the same material as this volume, which constitutes to some extent a more thorough literary sequel. At several points in the text I refer to relevant scenes in this film, which can currently be viewed online at https://vimeo.com/89400663 and at https://www.youtube.com/watch?v=jLu0dXWslcg.

Sources and Methodologies

Caribbean Bhojpuri folk music has been the subject of a handful of significant studies. Prominent among these is Usharbudh Arya's *Ritual Songs and Folk-songs of the Hindus of Surinam* (1968), written by an Indian folklorist well familiar with North Indian Bhojpuri culture. His book offers an informative and concise (at thirty-seven pages) introduction, followed by a hundred song texts and their translations. In a similar vein are the more recent publications *Music of the Indian Diaspora in Trinidad* (2011) and an earlier self-published song-text anthology, *Folk Songs of Trinidad Indians* (1994), by Laxmi Tewari, who is well qualified to document Bhojpuri diasporic music. Tewari has also produced fine CDs of Indo-Caribbean and North Indian traditional music. A different sort of work is Helen Myers's *Music of Hindu Trinidad* (1998), which offers some useful data amid a rather subjective and idiosyncratic account of the fieldwork experience. Myers, like myself in the present volume, is keenly interested in tracing musical entities back to their Bhojpuri-region roots, to which end she conducted an impressive amount of fieldwork in this most challenging of sites. However, her interest and expertise are mainly in the realm of women's folksongs, whereas the orientation of the present volume is more toward formal musical elements, male-dominated genres like tassa drumming, and the general diasporic dynamics that have conditioned musical continuity and change. Other aspects of Indo-Caribbean music culture were documented in my earlier volume *East Indian Music in the West Indies: Tan-singing, Chutney, and the Making of Indo-Caribbean Culture* (2000). It is testimony not to the inadequacy of these extant works but to the richness of Bhojpuri diasporic music culture that the genres focused on in the present work—especially birha, chowtal, Ramayan singing, and tassa—have hitherto remained largely undocumented. However, as the present volume was being completed, ethnomusicologist Christopher Ballengee finished an informative dissertation on Trinidadian tassa drumming (2013), which refers several times to an early draft of my own book I had shared with him, paralleling and complementing the present volume.

Equally important to this study has been the extant literature on Bhojpuri folk music in India. After George Grierson's illuminating articles of the 1880s, nearly a century would elapse before further notable publications would emerge on this subject, especially in the form of Edward Henry's *Chant the Names of God: Music and Culture in Bhojpuri-Speaking India* (1988), Hiralal Tiwari's *Gangaghāti ke Gīt* (Songs of the Ganges Valley, 1980), and Onkar Prasad's *Folk Music and Folk Dances of Banaras* (1987). Also useful and relevant has been Kevin Miller's dissertation, "A Community of Sentiment: Indo-Fijian

Music and Identity Discourse in Fiji and Its Diaspora" (2008), especially for its coverage of a chowtal scene remarkably similar to that of the Caribbean.

Meanwhile, recent decades have seen the emergence of an impressive and ever-growing body of anthropological and historical literature on Indo-Caribbean society, whether written by West Indians like Noor Kumar Mahabir or Euro-Americans like Steven Vertovec. A few works within this corpus engage, whether directly or in passing, with vernacular Bhojpuri-derived culture, but there has been little sustained attempt to trace or relate these folkways to North Indian sources—a task that would require multisite research and command of Hindi. As a result, for example, an entity like the once-widespread Siewnaraini sect is disappearing in the Caribbean without ever having been properly documented, either there or in Bhojpuri India itself. Such lacunae impoverish our understanding of Indo-Caribbean cultural history and of the processes of persistence, rearticulation, innovation, and creolization that have animated it.

Most of the data presented in this book derives from several field trips to Trinidad, Suriname, and North India from 2007 to 2010, and from ongoing engagement with Indo-Caribbean musicians in the New York area. Much of the research I conducted in the 1990s in these sites, although oriented toward different subjects, also proved useful to the present study, as did my numerous prior research trips to North India since 1970, exceeding five years' worth of residence. Although my research has comprised more observation and interviews than participation, I have regularly lent my unpolished tenor voice to Guyanese chowtal and Ramayan groups in the New York area and have even had occasion to perform the odd Trinidad-style local-classical thumri onstage, both vocally and on sitar. Much as I relish tassa drumming, I have not endeavored to learn the instrument (and have spared my ears and back considerable stress in doing so).

Acknowledgments

It perhaps goes without saying that most of the research for this volume was conducted not on the Internet, nor in musty archives, but in interaction with knowledgeable musicians. Given my special interest in traditional musics, both in India and the Caribbean, many of my informants were elderly retirees who could often be found relaxing in their homes with nothing particularly better to do than chat with the visiting ethnomusicologist who turned up unannounced. In other instances I may have distinguished myself as a minor pest on the music scene, pushing the limits of my informants' patience with tedious and difficult questions.

While I am naturally grateful to all the various informants cited in this volume, several individuals merit special mention. Kevin Miller generously shared his Indo-Fijian materials with me. Edward O. Henry provided astute comments on manuscripts of two chapters and kindly sent me copies of his Ghazipur chowtal recordings. Rupert Snell assisted me with scansion and translation of chowtal texts. Pandit Ravendra Maraj became my generous host when I visited Sacramento in 2008 to attend a Fijian chowtal festival. Indologist Narender Mohkamsingh was my indispensable guide and host during my Suriname visit that year. In Trinidad, Mukesh (Dev) Ragoo and his wife Donna Ramsumair were marvelously congenial and welcoming guides to the tassa world, while other artists, including Lenny Kumar, Laki Bhagan, Sunil Mathura, and Raiaz Ali, provided invaluable insights and information. In New York, I learned much from tassa drummers Amidh Mohammad, Sayyid Mohammad, Ryan Ali, and especially Jason Nandoo, who possesses an unusually keen analytical disposition. Thanks are also due to the Mahatma Gandhi Satsang Society of Queens, New York, for accepting me into their midst in the 2007 and 2008 Phagwa seasons. Pritha Singh, of the Rajkumari Centre in New York, has been an inspiring figure for much of my work, and it has been my pleasure to be able to collaborate in some of the Rajkumari Centre's activities. Of particular use and inspiration in writing this book has been the research of Richard Wolf and Frank Korom. Both these fine scholars also provided invaluable commentary on the manuscript of this book, and Wolf generously shared relevant footage of South Asian tassa drummers with me. Fellow tassa enthusiast Christopher Ballengee shared with me his aforementioned dissertation and allowed me to reference the valuable historical documents he unearthed.

Special mention must be made of an extraordinary individual, Rudy (Ramnarine) Sasenarine, a drummer, singer, and "organic intellectual" who was my mentor in Indo-Guyanese music for nearly twenty years. When I first met Rudy in the early 1990s, at age 26 he had already cultivated the sort of musical erudition that is otherwise more characteristic of revered octogenarian "stalwarts." A virtuoso dholak player, he also founded and led two chowtal and Ramayan groups in Queens, New York, and had acquired a virtually encyclopedic knowledge of Guyanese and Trinidadian local-classical music, Madrasi Mariamman drumming, and local Bhojpuri folksongs. Over the years, we collaborated on various projects, including the compilation and publication of an anthology of chowtal songs (Sasenarine 2009), and I was one of the many who was cherished his generosity, friendship, and humor. His untimely and unanticipated death, by heart attack in 2012 at age 43, was a deep shock to all who knew him and a tragic and irreplaceable cultural loss to the Indo-

Guyanese community. I conceive of this book, which owes so much to his input, as my own sort of humble tribute to him.

Terminology and Transliteration

Writing about West Indian ethnicities involves making various terminological and orthographic decisions that can involve matters not only of convenience, consistency, and academic rigor, but also of politics, often obliging the author to choose between diverse, unsatisfactory options. Trinidadians and Guyanese typically designate their nations' primary ethnicities as "Indian" or "East Indian," and "African." However, for the purposes of a book concerned with relations between the Caribbean and the Old Worlds of India and Africa, such terminology can be inherently misleading, and hence I generally opt for more precise, if long-winded, terms like "Indo-Caribbean" and "Afro-Caribbean," which are also in common use among West Indian academics and journalists. The term "creole," although laden with problematic implications discussed below, is generally used in this book in accordance with its customary West Indian connotation of the English-speaking traditional cultural "mainstream" associated with Afro-Caribbeans. The country of Trinidad and Tobago shall be referred to here as Trinidad.

In transliterating Hindi terms I have chosen a hybrid between Indological academese and colloquial West Indian renderings. On the one hand, I shun the pedantic, if logical, renderings of the phonemes *ch* and *sh* as *c* and *ś*, by which common words like "chamar" and "shakti" become *camār* and *śakti* in arrogant disdain not only for standard West Indian spellings of these words but also for conventional lay South Asian romanizations. (However, the most widely used recension of the Tulsi Ramayan does use "c" to indicate English "ch.") Conversely, however, I do not follow such West Indianisms as the random and phonetically incorrect insertion (even by scholars and pseudoscholars) of the letter "h" in various Hindi words, as some sort of icon of Indianness, as in "dhantal" and "mathkor." My practice in this book is to use a reasonably accurate shorthand approximation, on occasion providing alternate or more precise transliterations in parentheses upon first usage—for example, "matkor" (matticore). Since most Indo-Trinidadians and Guyanese, including those who are able to read or speak some Hindi, do not observe the crucial Hindi distinctions between retroflex and dental *t* and *d*, the underdots that should distinguish the former phonemes do not correspond to vernacular pronunciation. To clarify pronunciation, I do add macrons in such common musical terms as "tāl" and "jhāl." The appendix includes a glossary wherein I provide definitions and standard academic transliterations for Hindi-Urdu terms.

Introduction

Global Perspectives on the Indo-Caribbean Bhojpuri Diaspora and Its Music

Indo-Trinidadian author V. S. Naipaul once wrote that he grew up conceiving of his South Asian heritage as "a trapdoor into a bottomless past" (1977, xi). On my first evening in a North Indian farm town in the Bhojpuri region, whence most Indo-Caribbeans had emigrated in the nineteenth century, I felt as if I had passed through that trapdoor and reached some shadowy netherworld where the ancestral sources of Indo-Caribbean music culture were all around me. As a local acquaintance and I walked through the town, Kachhwa Bazaar, to find an elderly singer I had met the day before, music seemed to be happening everywhere, resounding from pockets of light and activity in the otherwise dark alleys. On one side a few teenage boys were clustered in a cramped Hanuman temple, honoring the monkey-god's weekly worship day by singing a ragged, Caribbean-sounding devotional bhajan to the accompaniment of a dholak barrel drum. Through a doorway down another lane I could see some women huddled around a lantern, singing a vernal Phagwa-season song to what struck me as a typical Trinidadian chutney tune. It being wedding season, twice we were obliged to flatten ourselves against doorways to make way for raucous marriage processions in which a poker-faced groom on horseback was surrounded by young men laughing and energetically gyrating to the thunderous drumming of tassa ensembles nearly identical to those that enliven Hindu weddings in Trinidad. Eventually reaching the old singer's patio, we found him asleep on a cot, but, happy to be roused, he was soon fingering a dilapidated harmonium and singing for me what he called a thumri—a light-classical form extant in very different styles in Trinidad and North India. A classical musician from nearby Banaras would have scoffed at his skeletal and rustic thumri, but I could

easily hear in his quavering voice the same tunes that pervade the thumris of Trinidadian local-classical music. Eventually we proceeded to a slightly larger Hanuman temple, where a dozen or so men were engaged in another song session. Hearing of my interest in chowtal, a Phagwa-season group folksong, they proceeded to sing a few chowtals essentially interchangeable with those I would be singing the following week with the Indo-Guyanese group I had joined in New York City. For me the entire experience was somewhat surreal, and I felt as if I had been transported back a century, or that I was hearing the Caribbean songs I knew being performed in a parallel universe that was at once strange and yet eerily familiar.

The following summer I was witness to another cultural encounter involving chowtal, in which I helped a New York Indo-Guyanese cultural organization bring four Indo-Fijian chowtal singers from California for a performance. Without any rehearsal, some New York Guyanese singers and I joined the Fijians on stage to fill out the chorus for their chowtal rendition, which differed only slightly from the familiar Guyanese style.

These cultural encounters illustrated some of the prodigious degree of continuity between Indo-Fijian music, Indo-Caribbean music, and the North Indian Bhojpuri folk music culture from which the two diasporic traditions had emerged a century earlier. The compatibilities are all the more remarkable in view of the almost complete lack of cultural contact between the three societies since the traffic of indentured workers ceased in 1917. What was in evidence was the extraordinary resilience of this stratum of Bhojpuri folk music, which had persisted not only over the several generations since 1917, and through all the sociocultural changes in each site during this period, but also over the vast distances that separated the three from each other. Not even the vicissitudes of the secondary diasporas—of Fijians to California and Indo-Caribbeans to New York—had attenuated the vigor of chowtal or generated stylistic developments that could prevent members of one community from joining the other in song.

In the more than ninety years that have elapsed since contacts between Bhojpuri India and the diasporic communities ceased, much has changed in their respective music cultures. Entire genres, not to mention songs, have died out, and new ones have arisen to take their places, whether under the influence of new technologies, new demographic contacts, or new socioeconomic conditions in general. Even within the realm of neotraditional musics, one could see significant changes and differences, including some that had nothing to do with the sorts of decline, deculturation, and creolization that one could expect (and indeed document) in scattered diasporas isolated from the ancestral homeland. The tassa drummers I saw in Kachhwa Bazaar, like those with whom I worked on my next trip to the region, seemed to play only a limited set of

simple rhythms and did not appear to regard their playing as constituting more than a festive processional noise, like the artless brass bands they sometimes accompanied. In Trinidad, by contrast, tassa drumming had evolved into a sophisticated and rich art form, vigorously cultivated by Indian musicians of all generations and animated by a lively sense of connoisseurship, competition, and cultural pride. I could see that to arrange an encounter between Bhojpuri-region tassa drummers and Trinidadian counterparts would probably be pointless and awkward, with the North Indians quite unable to join the "Trini" drummers in their elaborate metrical modulations and virtuoso pyrotechnics. If the compatibilities between the three communities' chowtals demonstrated an extraordinary degree of stylistic retention, the disparate tassa traditions showed how a diasporic community could take a North Indian transplant and avidly elaborate and develop it.

The Bhojpuri musical inheritance in Indo-Caribbean culture, indeed, encompasses a wide range of genres representing different sorts of trajectories. Some Bhojpuri music genres do not appear to have taken root in the Caribbean at all. Others survived being transplanted but subsequently disappeared or declined, especially as Bhojpuri Hindi ceased to be a living language in Guyana and Trinidad. Still other genres persisted intact, in some cases constituting marginal survivals of forms that had changed or died out in India itself. And a few, like tassa, underwent dramatic evolution and refinement. These processes and trajectories themselves were conditioned by the distinctive features of the diasporic setting and the way that setting has interacted with features inherent to the music genres themselves. Some of these features are naturally specific to a given diasporic locale, but continuities between Fiji and the Caribbean illustrate not only the resilience of the Bhojpuri ancestry but also ways in which Bhojpuri diasporic cultures, however scattered and isolated, came to share features distinct from those of the North Indian homeland. Collectively, the various trajectories and the form of Bhojpuri diasporic music in general must be attributed primarily not to inherent features of particular genres or to the activities of particular artists but rather to intricate dynamics of diaspora culture—in this case, Bhojpuri Caribbean diasporic culture. It is this set of dynamics that this book ultimately seeks to explore.

The Indo-Caribbean Experience

The history of East Indians in the Caribbean is an impressive and inspiring saga, in which isolated communities of largely illiterate, provincial, and harshly exploited subalterns evolved over the course of roughly a century into an economically, politically, and culturally dynamic West Indian population. By now

this story has been narrated in so many publications that there is little need to do more than outline it in these pages. After the cessation of slave importation in the British West Indies in 1804, sugarcane planters in Trinidad, British Guiana, and Jamaica became concerned about replenishing their labor force, and with Emancipation in 1834–38 and the abandonment of the plantations by freed slaves, the planters' clamor for cheap labor became insistent. (As for Englishmen doing the work themselves, one of them wrote, "It goes without argument that it is impossible for white men to work in the open in such terrific heat as obtains in this climate" [in Angel (1921) 1995, 104].) Hence the colonial administration commenced programs of indentured labor, whereby guest workers would toil for minimal wages under contract, typically for five years, at which point, depending on various factors, they could return to their homelands, renew their contracts, or start new lives on their own in the West Indies. Thousands of workers were brought from China, Madeira, and even West Africa (primarily Yorubas), but they proved unwilling either to come in large numbers or to commit themselves to extended plantation labor. Recruitment of workers from the sister British colony of India proved to be the solution to the planters' needs. Indian farmers, while historically impoverished, had unprecedented incentives to seek their fortunes abroad. As British rule, direct or indirect, spread through India in the 1800s, ruinous taxation, dismantling of traditional land-tenure conventions, and evisceration of local handicraft industries generated widespread famines and unprecedented poverty. Indentureship, especially as glorified by deceitful recruiting agents, appealed to many young men who could otherwise foresee nothing in their lives but deprivation and toil on increasingly exhausted and infertile land. As one immigrant to British Guiana said (as related to me by his grandson), "They tricked me into coming here, but I would never go back to India." It may also be surmised that the ranks of the indentured included a disproportionate number of especially adventurous and enterprising individuals (as well as assorted fugitives and misfits) whose energetic dispositions may have contributed to the character of the expatriate community in general.

Between 1845 and 1917, some 144,000 Indians came to Trinidad, around 239,000 to British Guiana, and lesser but not insubstantial numbers to Jamaica, Martinique, Guadeloupe, and elsewhere. From 1873 Dutch planters in Suriname contracted another 34,000 to come to that colony. Although roughly a fifth of these workers returned to India, the rest opted to remain, founding communities whose numbers grew in both relative and absolute terms. Their descendants now constitute a majority of the population in Guyana, and the largest ethnic groups in Trinidad and Suriname (at about 43 and 35 percent, respectively). Meanwhile, between 1879 and 1916, 62,000 Indians migrated to

the Fiji Islands, another British colony in the remote Pacific; their descendants now number over 300,000. Since the 1970s a substantial secondary diaspora has taken place, as Indo-Caribbeans have migrated en masse to New York, Toronto, the Netherlands, and elsewhere; the New York community is estimated to exceed half a million. Emigrant Indo-Guyanese now outnumber their counterparts in Guyana. For their part, roughly half the Indo-Fijian population has emigrated to Australia, New Zealand, and the west coasts of the United States and Canada.

The indentured migrants were to some extent diverse, coming from different regions of India with mutually unintelligible languages and representing a certain spectrum of castes and occupational backgrounds. In other respects, however, they exhibited a considerable degree of cohesion. Most were young men of peasant stock. Around 85 percent came from the Bhojpuri-speaking (pūrab or "eastern") region of modern-day Bihar and eastern Uttar Pradesh, or from the adjacent Avadhi-speaking area of central Uttar Pradesh. Like North Indians as a whole, around four-fifths were Hindu, and most of the rest Muslim. Most would have been illiterate, though their ranks also comprised some educated individuals, including numbers of Brahmins literate in Sanskrit as well as Hindi, who were able to establish themselves as pandits (Hindu priests) in the Caribbean.

The typical indentureship contract obliged the laborer to work for five years at a given plantation, for a modest wage, after which he or she could return to India (generally at the worker's expense), enroll in another contract, or start a new life, typically as a cultivator. Colonial administrations enacted various policies designed to bind workers to the plantations and frustrate their attempts to acquire land independently. Nevertheless, over the decades considerable numbers of immigrants, having completed their initial indentureships, managed through diligence, persistence, and social networking to rent or buy land and establish themselves as independent cultivators and, in many cases, merchants. Cohesive East Indian communities grew apace, and the increasing arrivals of women and the births of daughters gradually mitigated gender imbalances and enabled the establishment of families and the kinship networks so important in Indian society.

The conditions of indentured labor were harsh and in many ways akin to slavery. Many laborers were housed in the squalid barracks of former slaves. Work requirements were onerous, malingering was harshly punished, and malnutrition and infectious parasites were rampant. Workers were generally not allowed to leave the plantations for any reason. Many planters contrived to cheat their laborers out of their meager remunerations. Even after indentureship ended in 1917, a large percentage of Indians lived in absolute indigence, many

as homeless street dwellers whose visible plight shocked foreign visitors to Port of Spain. In general, Indians were despised by society as a whole. Whites saw them as coolie heathens who fought and drank excessively, abused their womenfolk, and clung stubbornly to their backward ways and pagan religions. Their music was dismissed as "lugubrious and depressing" (La Guerre 1985, 37). For their part, most Afro-Caribbeans, long since Christianized and largely alienated from their ancestral African cultures, shared these colonial prejudices, while further resenting the Indians as scabs who had been imported to undercut wages and who performed the menial field labor the blacks had left behind. Indian marriages were not legally recognized until 1946. Colonial governments took little interest in educating Indians, such that well into the twentieth century, the only accessible schools were run by Christian missionaries. Indians wary of proselytization tended to keep their children away from such schools during the colonial period, and in any case they saw little advantage to education in a situation where jobs in civil service, teaching, and other professions were dominated by Creoles, who enjoyed a head start in education. Hence, as late as 1950 roughly half the Indo-Trinidadian population was illiterate. Facing hostility and discrimination, Indians tended to cluster in their own rural settlements, avoiding contact with Creoles and affording a configuration described by historians as a "plural society" whose constituent communities coexisted without mixing, like oil and water (Smith 1965).

Despite the harshness of indentureship and its affinities to slavery, the differences between the two institutions were significant and allowed Indo-Caribbean communities to make slow but steady economic progress while retaining incomparably more cultural continuity than was possible for Afro-Caribbeans. Although kinship networks had to start from scratch in the new setting, the institution of the family appears to have remained considerably stronger than among black West Indians and provided a secure basis for social stability and gradual economic achievement. Despite the Indians' legendary fondness for rum, their traditions of thrift, hard work, and family solidarity, in addition to agricultural expertise, enabled increasing numbers to acquire and expand landholdings until they came to dominate agriculture in Trinidad, Guyana, and Suriname. These same cultural characteristics have often been contrasted with those attributed to Creoles, especially their alleged tendency to value individualism, consumption, and ephemeral pleasures over kinship obligations, hard work, and investment. While the accuracy of such stereotypes could be endlessly debated, by the 1950s many Indians were moving out of their formerly insular villages and expanding dramatically into commerce, the professions, and politics. Meanwhile, due to high birth rates, Indians have come to outnumber blacks in all three countries. The subsequently increased contacts with Creoles

Tales, Tunes, and Tassa Drums